Undead
in the
Federal Courts

edited by
JOSHUA WARREN

DEDICATION

To the memory of the dead

and the living remains

ACKNOWLEDGMENT

This book would not be possible without the continuing support of my family and all our wonderful dogs.

EDITOR'S NOTE

The following are nearly full federal court opinions with minimal editing. Where excerpts have been removed the symbol #***# has been added. All other marks are from the original opinion text. As best as possible, footnotes retain their numbering but original page numbers have been removed. In each case the phrase "undead" has been bolded and made larger for easier visibility.

FOREWARD

The idea of studying law by searching for a single term would usually be considered poor legal research. While "undead" is a word this raw search view of law will not yield any kind of complete picture of law related to the undead. The law deals with abstract concepts of responsibilities and liabilities, causation and consideration. Learning the law for a type of object requires more than merely the history of the legal interactions regarding a single word for that object.

Nevertheless because of computer search technology it is now relatively easy to search for words and read the case opinions. This can be both entertaining and informative for those with an interest in law and/or the undead. These real case decisions should be read primarily for entertainment but also to increase the readers' vocabulary of legal procedure and to increase general understanding of American jurisprudence.

INTRODUCTION TO STRUCTURE
of the U.S. FEDERAL COURTS

U.S. SUPREME COURT

U.S. COURT OF APPEALS
12 Circuit Courts of Appeals
1 U.S. Court of Appeals for the Federal Circuit

U.S. DISTRICT COURTS
94 Judicial Districts
U.S Bankruptcy Courts

U.S. COURT OF INTERNATIONAL TRADE
U.S. COURT OF FEDERAL CLAIMS

OTHER FEDERAL COURTS
Military Courts (Trial and Appellate)
Court of Veteran's Appeals
U.S. Tax Court
Federal administrative agencies and boards

for much more information about the structure and jurisdiction of the
US Courts see their website at UScourts.gov
http://www.uscourts.gov/EducationalResources/FederalCourtBasics.aspx

INTRODUCTION TO READING COURT OPINIONS FOR FUN
(and learning)

THE ONLY RULE is PATIENCE

If you are reading this then, you already know how to read. Go somewhere with appropriate lighting and a comfortable chair and read patiently. Mark unusual words and move on, and later use a legal dictionary and internet search engines to amplify your understanding. With patience you will learn to read more.

As you begin to read a case, notice the year and notice what branch of the federal court is writing the opinion. Identify the parties, what they are seeking, what prior legal actions have occurred. Or just jump right to any paragraph you want and start reading.

This book is designed to read cases. There is no over-reaching legal thesis and the cases are not individually summarized. These real cases are simply arranged with hopes of sparking interest in reading law. The goal is merely to enjoy the reading.

Reading law will improve your ability to read law.

As you read you may consider yourself as a law clerk and try to summarize the arguments and holdings of each opinion. This is good practice and any attempt to write (and re-write) a case summary will promote your thinking. But if you prefer, just sit under a tree and enjoy the writings of the U.S. Federal Courts.

These are all serious legal texts each with a serious legal purpose but they are also appreciable as the high art of American legal civilization. This collection is gathered with the hope of finding entertainment in these works of jurisprudential art.

INTRODUCTION TO
UNDEAD
IN THE FEDERAL COURTS

This book includes case opinions from cases the U.S. Federal Courts that include the word "undead". There are only nine cases, one duplicates in appeal and one more uses the adjective "undeadly".

The first "undead" use in Federal Court opinion is in 1993. Contrast, the first "walking dead" was in 1962 and the first "zombis" in 1942, "zombi" 1949, "zombies" 1956, "zombie" 1957. First "vampire" 1902, first "ghoul" 1974 and first "ghost" 1855. So 1993 is a rather recent first appearance for "undead" in Federal judicial writings.

In 1993, TSR, Inc. v. Mayfair Games, Inc. is a case about the game "Dungeons & Dragons". Prior to this case TSR had already sued Mayfair over its Role Aids game supplements and they had settled by contractual agreement. But here a Mayfair game supplement called "Undead" was reviewed in Dragon Magazine and the reviewer "made the decision to describe that game supplement, "Undead" as an "AD&D game campaign supplement" and Mayfair quoted that review even that it had agreed not to make those claims. TSR sued for violation of the prior agreement and the Court agreed that the agreement against these advertising claims included using quotations of others making those claims - summary judgment for TSR. This is about puppet speakers, which is oddly related to the idea of an undead mindless creature controlled by other monsters.

Next in, Hogan v. DC Comics, 48 F. Supp. 2d 298, decided January 25, 1999, the Court describes the characters of Nicholas Guant: "This litigation arises out of two works each centered around a half-human, half-vampire character named Nicholas Gaunt." Hogan sued DC comics for infringement of his unpublished work. Hogan's work is called "Matchsticks" and the DC Comic is called "Dhampire: Stillborn." The Court says: "'gaunt' connotes thinness and pallor, qualities associated with the 'undead.'" Finding sufficient differences the Court grants DC comics motion for summary judgment. So the court finds as a matter of law that undead are associated to thinness and pallor.

Third, in American Amusement Mach. Ass'n v. Cottey, 115 F. Supp. 2d 943, decided October 11, 2000, the Court upheld Indianapolis General Ordinance 72-2000 which prohibits amusement machines harmful to children (video games). The plaintiffs sought a preliminary injunction to prevent enforcement but the court denied, finding that they were unlikely to prevail on the argument that the ordinance was unconstitutionally vague. In its analysis, the Court describes some violent video games including "The House of the Dead 2":

> The "plot" in "The House of the Dead 2" is that a town has been over-run by zombie-like characters who have killed many of the town's inhabitants. The player adopts the persona of "James," who is responding to the emergency. The zombies are "undead" human figures who are already substantially decayed and disfigured when James encounters them. The zombies attack James. James responds by shooting them. When shot, the undead die again in dramatic fashion. In some cases, the chest cavity explodes in a shower of blood, ribs, and gore, while in other cases the target is decapitated. The court observed at least one character whose entire upper torso appeared to have been severed from the lower half of the figure. 5

> Footnote 5: "The House of the Dead 2" displays a "Parental Advisory Warning" which informs the viewer: "This Game is Classified/Life-Like Violence/Strong." The rating is the product of a voluntary industry program. See Exs. P-68, P-69 (describing the rating system).

Subsequently, this case was reversed and remanded by the Seventh Circuit, 244 F.3d 572 (2001), rehearing was denied and writ of certiori denied by Supreme Court, 122 S. Ct. 462 (2001). The case can now stand for principle that video games are treated as speech. The Seventh Circuit Court also noted that some of the themes might be considered feminist, and cites strong women defeating men in "Ultimate Mortal Kombat 3" and might be possibly considered of beneficial value to perspective on women. The Court also highlights the violence in great literature like "the Odyssey" and the monsters "Frankenstein" and "Dracula" and Grimm's fairy tales, and says:

> Maybe video games are different. They are, after all, interactive. But this point is superficial, in fact erroneous. All literature (here broadly defined to include movies, television, and the other photographic media, and popular as well as highbrow literature) is interactive; the better it is, the more interactive. Literature when it is successful draws the reader into the story, makes him identify with the characters, invites him to judge them and quarrel with them, to experience their joys and sufferings as the reader's own. Protests from readers caused Dickens to revise Great Expectations to give it a happy ending, and tourists visit sites in Dublin and its environs in which the fictitious events of Ulysses are imagined to have occurred. The cult of Sherlock Holmes is well known. Most of the video games in the record of this case, games that the City believes violate its ordinances, are stories. Take once again "The House of the Dead." The player is armed with a gun–most fortunately, because he is being assailed by a seemingly unending succession of hideous axe-wielding zombies, the living dead conjured back to life by voodoo. The zombies have already knocked down and wounded several people, who are pleading pitiably for help; and one of the player's duties is to protect those unfortunates from renewed assaults by the zombies. His main task, however, is self-defense. Zombies are supernatural beings, therefore difficult to kill. Repeated shots are necessary to stop them as they rush headlong toward the player. He must not only be alert to the appearance of zombies from any quarter; he must be assiduous about reloading his gun periodically, lest he be overwhelmed by the rush of the zombies when his gun is empty.

> Self-defense, protection of others, dread of the "undead," fighting against overwhelming odds–these are all age-old themes of literature, and ones particularly appealing to the young. "The House of the Dead" is not distinguished

literature. Neither, perhaps, is "The Night of the Living Dead," George A. Romero's famous zombie movie that was doubtless the inspiration for "The House of the Dead." Some games, such as "Dungeons and Dragons," have achieved cult status; although it seems unlikely, some of these games, perhaps including some that are as violent as those in the record, will become cultural icons. We are in the world of kids' popular culture. But it is not lightly to be suppressed.

In Ruiz v. Cockrell, 2:00-CV-0296 , 2003 U.S. Dist. LEXIS 14978, the Court decided August 29, 2003, to deny petition for Habeas Corpus. Ruiz alleged ineffective assistance of appellate counsel because his attorney failed "to charge undeadly conduct". Now, "undeadly" is not technically a word, but that's the beauty of habeas petitions. I'm not really sure what he meant, or if the court even knows, but either way the court found the neologistic allegation "without merit". Ruiz is serving a 50 year sentence for "felony offense of aggravated assault, enhanced with prior felonies" so you can't blame him for trying whatever habeas options he could raise.

Moore v. Tangipahoa Parish Sch. Bd., 2008 U.S. Dist. LEXIS 35238, decided April 30, 2008, is a fascinating case that is part of a 43 year history of court intervention aimed at desegregation of the Tangipahoa School System and to fix the "vestiges of de jure school segregation". This decision is narrowly focused on one person's job and this court orders that the School Board hire "Mr. Alden Foster as head coach of the Amite High School football team". The case uses "undead" in a citation to a law review article by Brian J. Sutherland with the title "Killing Jim Crow and the Undead Nondelegation Doctrine with Privately Enforceable Federal Regulations" 29 Seattle Univ. L. R. 917 (2006). This case is the in 2008, a court intervening so closely in school politics as to mandate the choice of football coach. Foster became the first black head coach of this high school's football team. The use of the word "undead" is only in the title of a footnotes article but this exercise of judicial power could also be read as a suggestion that the civil rights era was not dead.

Similarly the next few cases are also only mere citation to law review articles with "undead" in those article titles. In re Davis, 2010 U.S.

Dist. LEXIS 87340, decided August 24, 2010, is the denial of habeas petition for Troy Davis. The court decided that he failed to prove his innocence in a way that would make it unconstitutional to execute him. The New York Times strongly disagreed in an editorial before his execution and the execution was a highlighted rallying point for early Occupy Wall Street protesters. The court opinion cites to Harlan Grant Cohen, "Undead" Wartime Cases: Stare Decisis and the Lessons of History, 84 Tul. L. Rev. 957 (2010). In which Grant writes:

> World War II cases [like Quirin, Eisentrager, Yamashita, and Hirota] might best be thought of as "undead." They no longer seem to be live precedents, the passage of time and reflection having sapped them of their vigor, but they are not quite dead either, no later decision inflicting the final fatal blow.

> Instead, they refuse to be forgotten, lurching back into the frame. The dilemma posed by the rival histories of these cases thus resembles the one faced by the hero of a zombie movie: whether to put these decisions out of their misery once and for all or to try to save them and give them back their former lives.

The next two cases in this book collection, United States v. Sturm, 426 Fed. Appx. 582, (decided April 4, 2011, about child pornography and the transport of digital files) and Pearson v. Fairlakes Vill. Condo. Assoc., 2012 U.S. Dist. LEXIS 35306, (decided March 13, 2012, about liquidation proceedings in Puerto Rico), both cite t an article by Jeff Todd, "Undead Precedent: The Curse of a Holding 'Limited To Its Facts'", 40 Tex. Tech L. Rev. 67 (2007). Todd's article uses undead in a similar way as the Cohen quote from the Davis case. The Todd article predates the Cohen article and both elude to aberrant case precedent and their questionable application in state decisis. Todd makes an analogy that the case decisions that have been limited to specific facts are like Count Dracula in that he "defies God's law and is given eternal existence, not as a blessing but as a curse." Both of these law review articles are using the word "undead" to refer to old cases that are not technically overruled but are practically so. These judges seem less inclined to revive these precedents in the way that desegregation intervention stirred from its perceived grave in Tangipahoa Parish.

A recent "undead" reference in U.S. Federal Courts, May 31, 2012, in Kaufhold v. Caiafa, 2012 U.S. Dist. LEXIS 75215, involving the former band members of the group The Misfits:

> Plaintiffs Robert C. Kaufhold and Joseph Aurthur McGuckin were the guitarist and drummer of the iconic punk rock band, the Misfits. Plaintiffs filed this action against the band's bassist, Gerald Caiafa, and his music label, Cyclopian Music, Inc. ("Cyclopian") (collectively "Defendants"), alleging that Defendants improperly asserted exclusive ownership rights over the Misfits trademarks.
> ...
> The Misfits was a punk rock band formed in 1977. The band is known for pioneering and defining the musical genre of "horror punk," combining the themes, imagery, and narrative of horror fiction with punk rock music.
> ...
> From 1988 through 1992, Kaufhold sold the Misfits Live '79 record (which prominently features the Misfits trademark) at shows for his band the Undead. Kaufhold continues to sell the Misfits Live '79 album to this day from his website.

The Court found continued use of the mark and thus ruled against the drummer's improperly filed trademarks. Though the Misfits had not performed for years, their rights in the intellectual property were not dead yet.

The final case in this book is the response to a pro se petition filled with non cognizable claims, bizarre words and basically nonsense. Bair v. AG, 116 Fed. Cl. 699 (decided June 13, 2014), is a good reminder that just because a word appears in the writing of the judiciary, doesn't mean it's necessarily valuable. The courts have to deal with many strange claims, when individuals appear before a court without an attorney, the court tries its best to understand the claims as best it can before dismissing them. Clearly delineating nonsense helps set limits for the application of legal reason.

So, what does "undead" mean in the courts? Many of the cases are related to intellectual property: Dungeons & Dragons, DC Comics, House of the Dead 2, Kaufhold's band. There does seem to be a racial thread in the Troy Davis and Tangipahoa Schools cases. Then there's criminal connections with the habeas for ineffective counsel, and the interstate transport of digital child pornography, and a liquidation in Puerto Rico. This set of opinions is too few to be confident in any larger patterns, but they do present a character of the undead that can be somewhat inspiring.

In civil rights and punk rock, we are both dead and not dead yet. Still it's a question of how much to tell the children. Can they play these games? Can the government ban them or are they just regular fictions? What are the limits of free speech? Governments can regulate the distribution of child pornography (to destroy the market and reduce the danger to children) but can't regulate the violent video games that they believe endanger the child audience directly? What are the limits of civil rights? Federal Courts are making hiring decisions in local schools, football even, but wouldn't stop the questionable execution of Troy Davis. Arguably Louisiana high school football may be more sacrosanct than a single human life, and so it's extremely hard to understand the amorphous limits of federal intervention, but it's not dead.

Like the cases in this book that are actual responses to pro se nonsense, this book collection, like all the books in this series, is a somewhat absurdist tour de nonsense. It is real case opinions, all with the word "undead" and it is worth trying to read legal opinions and investigating any ideas you find interesting in further research. Remember, each case presented herein is just one writing in a sometimes long narrative of case history. Dig further (use Google). Dead text, is more alive than you might think. Don't take my word for it, read them yourself.

CHRONOLOGICAL
TABLE OF CASES

6. PAGE 175
Moore v. Tangipahoa Parish Sch. Bd.,
2008 U.S. Dist. LEXIS 35238 (E.D.La., April 30, 2008), Stay granted by Moore v. Tangipahoa Parish Sch. Bd., 2013 U.S. App. LEXIS 877 (5th Cir. La., Jan. 14, 2013)

see also Brian J. Sutherland, Killing Jim Crow and the Undead Nondelegation Doctrine with Privately Enforceable Federal Regulations, 29 Seattle Univ. L. R. 917

7. PAGE 192
In re Davis,
2010 U.S. Dist. LEXIS 87340 (S.D. Ga., Aug. 24, 2010)

see Harlan Grant Cohen, "Undead" Wartime Cases: Stare Decisis and the Lessons of History, 84 Tul. L. Rev. 957 (2010)

8. PAGE 304
United States v. Sturm,
426 Fed. Appx. 582 (10th Cir., April 4, 2011). On rehearing at, En banc, Remanded by United States v. Sturm, 2012 U.S. App. LEXIS 4755 (10th Cir. Colo., Feb. 24, 2012)

see also Jeff Todd, Undead Precedent: The Curse of a Holding "Limited To Its Facts", 40 Tex. Tech L. Rev. 67, 75 (2007)

UNDEAD IN THE FEDERAL COURTS

TSR, INC., Plaintiff,
v.
MAYFAIR GAMES, INC., a corporation and DARWIN P. BROMLEY, individually and as President of Mayfair Games, Inc., Defendants.

No. 91 C 0417
UNITED STATES DISTRICT COURT FOR THE NORTHERN DISTRICT OF ILLINOIS, EASTERN DIVISION

1993 U.S. Dist. LEXIS 3355

March 15, 1993, Decided
March 17, 1993, Docketed

JUDGE MILTON I. SHADUR

MEMORANDUM OPINION AND ORDER

TSR, Inc. ("TSR") has sued Mayfair Games, Inc. ("Mayfair") and its President Darwin Bromley ("Bromley"), seeking injunctive relief, damages and contract rescission on the basis of several claims: (1) copyright infringement, (2) trademark infringement, false designation and misappropriation, (3) unfair competition and (4) breach of contract, all arising from Mayfair's use on its products of TSR's "Advanced Dungeons and Dragons" trademark. TSR currently moves for summary judgment on the Fourth Count of its Amended Complaint, which asserts that Mayfair breached a 1984 Settlement Agreement (the "Agreement") between the parties. [1] Mayfair responds by asking for summary dismissal of that breach of contract claim. For the reasons stated in this memorandum opinion and order, each motion is granted in part and denied in part.

> 1 According to TSR's Mem. 1 n.1, its success on that claim "would subsume the relief it seeks for trademark infringement." And because Mayfair is not now distributing the book that gave rise to TSR's copyright infringement claim, "the crux of the current dispute would be decided" *(id.)*.

Fed. R. Civ. P. ("Rule") 56 Standards

Rule 56 principles impose on the movant the burden of establishing the lack of a genuine issue of material fact (*Celotex Corp. v. Catrett,* 477 U.S. 317, 322-23 (1986)). For that purpose this Court is "not required to draw every conceivable inference from the record--only those inferences that are reasonable"--in the light most favorable to the nonmovant (*Bank Leumi Le-Israel, B.M. v. Lee,* 928 F.2d 232, 236 (7th Cir. 1991)). Where as here cross-motions are involved, that principle thus demands a dual perspective--one that this Court has described as Janus-like--that sometimes calls for the denial of both motions.

This District Court's General Rule ("GR") 12(m) and 12(n) require factual statements in support of and in opposition to Rule 56 motions, and both sides have tendered such statements. TSR's statement in support of its motion is cited "P. 12(m)," while Mayfair's responsive statement is cited "D. 12(n)." Mayfair's statement of additional facts in support of its crossmotion is cited "D. 12(m)," and TSR's responsive statement is cited "P. 12(n)." [2] Where one party's assertion within its GR 12(m) statement is admitted by the other party, that will be indicated here by omitting "12(m)" and "12(n)," so that the citation will simply read "P-D P --" or "D-P P --" (the first-listed party being the one whose Rule 12(m) statement has been admitted).

> 2 Because Mayfair's Statement of Additional Facts was appended to its GR 12(m) statement, the D. 12(m) and P. 12(n) numbering began where the P. 12(m) and D. 12(n) numbering left off.

Facts

TSR owns trademarks for the "Advanced Dungeons and Dragons" ("AD&D") [3] and "Dungeons and Dragons" ("D&D") role-playing game systems, [4] which were created by TSR co-founder E. Gary Gygax ("Gygax") (P. 12(m) P 8). [5] Such a role-playing game is a system of interactive story telling using maps, dice and an extensive set of rules (P-D P 7). "One participant acts as a referee narrating the adventure, describing problems and controlling the actions of supporting characters and events. The remaining players play out their roles in accordance with the rules." (P-D P 10). TSR places the AD&D trademarks on rules and accessories, as well as on adventure modules and supplements (P-D P 21).

3 Trademarks involved include "Advanced Dungeons and Dragons," "AD&D," "Dungeons and Dragons" and "D&D." For brevity's sake, this opinion refers to each set of trademarks by employing only the abbreviated version. But where either set of initials is used in the singular, it will stand for the full-length mark ("Dungeons and Dragons" or "Advance Dungeons and Dragons") unless otherwise specified.

4 Mayfair's responsive statements have devoted a substantial amount of rhetoric to disputing the characterization of Advanced Dungeons and Dragons and Dungeons and Dragons as "games," contending in part that TSR does not "own" either of them (see D. 12(n) PP 7-10, 12, 14, 15, 17, 23). For those propositions Mayfair cites to Bromley's Aff. P 3:

> A role-playing game is quantified, interactive storytelling, in accordance with a series of rules and algorithms which define how the players interact with one another and the game master. A role-playing game is intangible, does not have a brand or trademark and is not itself sold or owned. Books and reference information may be used but are not essential for a role-playing game.

Interestingly, Mayfair does not dispute TSR's contention that Mayfair "produces its own role-playing games" (P-D P 22). Moreover, Mayfair is not consistent in its own semantic insistence. It states at D. Mem. 10 that "Advanced Dungeons and Dragons is different from other role-playing games because it is based on different rules." As TSR has pointed out, the only function of Mayfair's contentions seems to be an end run around the Agreement's ban on its contesting the validity of the AD&D trademarks.

5 David Arneson ("Arneson") was co-creator of Dungeons and Dragons.

In 1982 Mayfair began to produce and market adventure and reference books under the trademark "Role Aids" for use in playing AD&D (D. Mem. 10, P-D P 22). TSR complained to Mayfair that Mayfair was making improper and infringing use of the AD&D trademark, and the parties signed the Agreement on September 28, 1984 to govern Mayfair's future use of TSR's trademarks (P-D P 28).

Under the Agreement Mayfair acknowledged TSR's ownership of the D&D and AD&D trademarks and agreed not to contest their validity (P. Ex. 1 § III, P-D P 29). Mayfair also agreed to use the AD&D trademarks solely in connection with Role Aids modules, advertising and promotional materials. TSR's trademark was to appear once on an advertisement, catalog, flyer or press release, and only within a specific emblem form [6] in which Mayfair would state that the Role Aids product involved is for use with the AD&D role-playing game and that AD&D is a registered trademark of TSR, and would disclaim TSR's approval of that specific use of TSR's trademark by Mayfair (P. Ex. 1 § I and Ex. B, P-D PP 30-32). Mayfair's own symbol was required to appear on the same page. Mayfair also agreed (2) to phase out all noncomplying packaging, (2) not to use TSR's trademark in any other manner and (3) not to include statements on Role Aids modules carrying the AD&D trademark that such modules were suitable for use with other role-playing games (P. Ex. 1 §§ IV-V and Ex. B, P-D P 36). If materials violating the Agreement were distributed, Mayfair was required to make good faith efforts to recover such materials and to withdraw and withhold offending materials from distribution (P. Ex. 1 § VI, P-D 12(n) P 38). Despite the foregoing prohibitions, Mayfair was not prohibited from acquiring from the creators of Dungeons and Dragons, Arneson and Gygax, any of their rights to use the D&D trademark (P. Ex. 1 § V, D-P P 121).

6 Although the Agreement characterized that form as an "oval," its physical depiction in P. Ex. 1 Ex. B is that of an oblong cartouche drawn to appear three-dimensional. It seems that the parties are better developers of games than they are lexicographers. This opinion will use "cartouche" rather than "oval" to refer to the emblem.

Unsatisfied with Mayfair's performance, on January 22, 1991 TSR filed its initial Complaint against Mayfair advancing the four claims described at the outset of this opinion. After discovery TSR filed an Amended Complaint on December 19, 1991. Only the Fourth Count is at issue on the current cross-motions, which dispute whether various Mayfair products violate the terms of the Agreement (P. 12(m) PP 40-106).

Breach of the Agreement

TSR's allegations of breach of the Agreement by various Mayfair products fall into three categories: (1) packaging and promotional materials for the "City State of the Invincible Overlord" product, (2)

"Role Aids" promotional materials and (3) advertising materials for the "Freedom of Choice" campaign. This opinion addresses each in turn.

City State of the Invincible Overlord

In July 1987 Mayfair acquired the rights in, and began to produce and market, a new role-playing game called "City-State of the Invincible Overlord" (the "Invincible Overlord" game) (P-D P 41). On July 9 Mayfair and Gygax entered into a written agreement under which the Invincible Overlord box cover would state that it came "With an introduction by E. Gary Gygax, creator of Advanced Dungeons & Dragons" ("Gygax statement") (D-P P 122). TSR's trademark was not placed within the cartouche as specified in the Agreement, and no disclaimer of TSR's approval of the use of the AD&D trademark was visible (P-D P 44). Mayfair used the Gygax statement in the text of a flyer promoting Invincible Overlord, and it used the AD&D trademark again at the bottom of the flyer to identify AD&D as a registered trademark of TSR (P-D P 47). Mayfair also used the AD&D trademark in various promotional materials that depicted the Invincible Overlord box cover or described Invincible Overlord as compatible with AD&D, without an accompanying disclaimer of TSR's approval of the use of its trademark (P-D PP 50, 52, 54, 56). [7]

> 7 Mayfair's 1990 Trade Catalog did contain a footnote marker after the AD&D trademark. Ten pages later "in small print at the bottom of the page" was a disclaimer of TSR's approval of Mayfair's use of its trademark (P-D P 50). TSR also points out, without alleging violation of the Agreement, that both the 1990 Mayfair catalog and the Mayfair customer reply card (P. Ex. 16) identified Invincible Overlord as adaptable for use with any fantasy role-playing system (P. 12(m) PP 50, 56). Although Agreement Ex. B P 6 prohibited Role Aids modules that utilized the trademark statement from also including statements that such modules are suitable for use with other role-playing games, TSR has not attempted to argue that use of the AD&D trademark on a non-Role Aids product is governed by a similar restriction.

TSR asserts that all uses of the AD&D trademark in connection with the Invincible Overlord game violate the Agreement. Mayfair admits that the use of the AD&D trademark in the 1990 Mayfair Trade

Catalog violated the Agreement (D. 12(n) P 51), but it denies that the other uses violate the Agreement (D. 12(n) PP 46, 48, 53, 55).

A. Gygax Statement

Mayfair's use of the AD&D trademark within the Gygax statement in conjunction with Invincible Overlord and related advertisements contravenes the plain language of the Agreement, which states in part (P. Ex. 1 P I):

> Mayfair agrees that except as otherwise provided herein, any use of TSR's Advanced Dungeons & Dragons trademark shall be limited to use within a specified Trademark Statement, solely in connection with "Role Aids" modules, and advertising and promotional materials therefor, and strictly in compliance with the Trademark Use Requirements as set forth in Exhibit B attached hereto and incorporated herein by reference.

Invincible Overlord is not of course a Role Aids product. Even though the Agreement later went on (P. Ex. 1 P V) to carve out a total exception for rights acquired from Gygax, that exception was limited to rights in the D&D trademark, and the AD&D trademark did not appear in the oval emblem form. Mayfair's Mem. 5 argues that it used the Gygax statement based on his representation that under his confidential termination of employment agreement with TSR he had the right to allow Mayfair to use the statement. However, Mayfair's belief in that respect could not of course justify a patent breach of the Agreement's limitations. [8]

---

[8] One issue that TSR has steered clear of is how, given the standards of trademark law as to likelihood of confusion and confusing similarity, it could create an unlimited exception to the Agreement's restrictions on Mayfair to allow Mayfair to deal with Gygax for use of the *D&D* trademarks, and yet cavil at Mayfair's acquisition of rights that Gygax apparently had in the *AD&D* trademarks. Before TSR will be heard to make anything out of that aspect of Mayfair's claimed breaches (an issue deferred by the summary judgment context of this opinion), it has some more explaining to do.

But Mayfair also contends that TSR's acceptance of several ads for Invincible Overlord that showed the Gygax statement operate as a waiver of TSR's claim of a material breach (D. Mem. 10). TSR's own *Dragon Magazine* published three Mayfair ads for Invincible Overlord in March 1988, April 1989 and February 1990 (D-P P 124). TSR claims that portions of the ads with the Gygax statement were not visible in the ads (P. 12(n) P 124). While TSR admits that a lawyer reviews "certain advertisements" for possible misuse of trademarks, TSR's attorney was employed only for "some portions of the pertinent time period" (P. 12(n) P 123).

Under Wisconsin law waiver requires proof of (1) a right possessed by the waiving party, (2) knowledge of the right by the waiving party and (3) an intentional and voluntary waiver *(Shannon v. Shannon*, 145 Wis. 2d 763, 429 N.W.2d 525, 530 (Wis. App. 1988)). Intent to waive a known right may be inferred from the conduct of the parties *(Christensen v. Equity Coop. Livestock Sale Ass'n*, 134 Wis. 2d 300, 396 N.W.2d 762, 763 (Wis. 1986)).

Under a view of the facts in the light most favorable to Mayfair, TSR's knowing acceptance of the Invincible Overlord advertisements, which displayed a picture of the Invincible Overlord box cover with the Gygax statement, could be construed as a waiver of the materiality of any breach by Mayfair's packaging and advertising. Mayfair used the Gygax statement on the Invincible Overlord box cover (P. Ex. 12) and in the Invincible Overlord flyer (P. Ex. 13), the Invincible Overlord product description sheet (P. Ex. 14), the Mayfair reply card (P. Ex. 16) and the 1990 Mayfair trade catalog (P. Ex. 17). To the extent that TSR's motion for summary judgment charges Mayfair with breach of the Agreement by its use of the Gygax statement in Invincible Overlord advertising and packaging, the motion is therefore denied.

On the other side of the coin, Mayfair's motion for summary dismissal of that same charge on grounds of waiver by acceptance must be denied as well. By definition TSR could not waive any objection to use of the Gygax statement if it did not know or should not have known of that use *(Shannon*, 429 N.W.2d at 530). Although the visibility of the Gygax statement varies within the ads, in all three of the ads the box cover print is greatly reduced, so that the statement is not as readily noticed as it would be on the full-sized box cover. TSR also asserts that "the legal department at TSR had an attorney employee for only some portions of the pertinent time period" (P. 12(n) P 123). But the statement that TSR cites for that statement (Moore Dep. 18-20) does not really support its proposition. [9] Nevertheless it remains possible that the TSR attorney reviewers, if any, may not have noticed the Gygax statement in the Invincible Overlord ads. [10]

9 Moore testified that the legal department reviewed ads before placement for misuse of TSR's trademarks (Moore Dep. 18-19). Moore also testified that when he took the editorship of *Dragon Magazine* in 1986, policies for review of ads may have been "in flux" and he was "not sure at what point they settled out" *(id.* at 19).

10 What has just been said in the text truly gives TSR the benefit of the most favorable reasonable inferences. Even though waiver law speaks of a party's knowledge, the concept would seem to extend to charged knowledge as well--to prevent a party from playing ostrich. Indeed, *Shannon,* 429 N.W.2d at 530 speaks of what the party knew or should have known. Thus final resolution of the issue will require examination of whether TSR should have known of the Invincible Overlord ads' contents, given its keen awareness of the importance of its trademark rights and of the nature of the role-playing game industry.

Mayfair's Mem. 10 also contends that TSR's failure to object to the use of the AD&D trademark before filing the motion for summary judgment operates as a waiver on delay grounds. Although Mayfair has not labeled (nor argued) the contention in this fashion, this Court views the argument--waiver due to the passage of time--as one for the application of laches. Wisconsin law requires four elements for laches to apply: (1) unreasonable delay, (2) knowledge of the basis of the claim and failure to act on the part of the plaintiff, (3) lack of knowledge on the part of the party asserting the defense that the other party would assert the right on which he bases his suit and (4) prejudice to the party asserting the defense in the event the action is maintained *(Jensen v. Janesville Sand & Gravel Co.,* 141 Wis. 2d 521, 415 N.W.2d 559, 562 (Wis. App. 1987)).

Again on a po-Mayfair look at the facts, TSR knew of the Invincible Overlord ad by March 1988 but did not raise any objection until it filed its summary judgment motion on June 17, 1992. [11] That four-year lapse before objection may well be unreasonable (see *Money Store v. Harriscorp Finance, Inc.,* 689 F.2d 666, 674 (7th Cir. 1982), upholding the district court's determination that a 22-month delay was unreasonable). [12] Such an unreasonable delay in trademark actions precludes recovery of damages or wrongfully derived profits during the period before suit was filed *(James Burrough Ltd. v. Sign of the Beefeater, Inc,* 572 F.2d 574, 578 (7th Cir. 1978)). Although injunctive relief and damages and profits for the period after the filing of suit may not be precluded *(id.,* citing *McLean v. Fleming,* 96 U.S. 245 (1877)), Mayfair has said it ceased distribution of Invincible Overlord in June 1992 (Bromley Aff. P 12). If so, and if Mayfair can make the appropriate showing of prejudice due to TSR's delay, the laches defense would in effect be a complete bar to relief on the issue of breach by the Invincible Overlord product.

11 Neither TSR's original Complaint nor its Amended Complaint had mentioned Invincible Overlord.

12 Although the analogous statute of limitations for breach of contract has yet to run in this case, Wisconsin law allows application of a laches defense within the limitations period *(Schafer v. Wegner,* 78 Wis. 2d 127, 254 N.W.2d 193, 196-97 (Wis. 1977)).

To take the opposite view as was done with Mayfair's estoppel defense, the defense of laches requires knowledge (or at least constructive knowledge) on TSR's part. Because this opinion must assume lack of knowledge by TSR in considering Mayfair's motion to dismiss, [13] laches cannot now provide grounds to grant Mayfair's motion.

13 But see n.10.

B. *Compatibility with AD&D*

TSR also alleges breach of the Agreement by two Invincible Overlord materials that state that the series is compatible with AD&D. Mayfair has admitted that the Mayfair 1990 trade catalog, which stated that "The Invincible Overlord series is compatible with the Advanced Dungeons & Dragons role-playing game" (with the only disclaimer statement being placed in a footnote ten pages later) violated the Agreement. Because Mayfair has also made no defense of waiver as to that catalog (see D. Mem. 10), TSR's motion for summary judgment is granted to the extent that it is based on breach of the Agreement by the 1990 Mayfair trade catalog.

TSR has also alleged violation by writers' guidelines that Mayfair distributed to authors and potential authors of its publications. Those guidelines stated that "The Overlord and Role Aids product lines are designed for use with TSR's Advanced Dungeons & Dragons" system" (P. 12(m) P 53, P. Ex. 11)). Mayfair denies violation, but without any attempt at providing an explanation or evidence (D. 12(n) P 53). Accordingly breach of the Agreement by the writers' guidelines is deemed admitted, and summary judgment is granted to that extent as well.

Role Aids Promotional Materials

In 1988 or 1989 Mayfair began a marketing drive for the Role Aids product line, and in 1990 it introduced the new Role Aids modules "Witches," "Psionics" and "Lizardmen" (P-D P 57). TSR claims that the advertising materials for the Role Aids products (reply cards, trade and consumer catalogs, posters, flyers, slick sheets, press releases, product description sheets and Mayfair Games News letters) violated the terms of the Agreement (P. 12(m) PP 57-93).

A. Violations Admitted by Mayfair

Mayfair acknowledges many of TSR's assertions. It admits that its reply card (P. Ex. 16, D. 12(n) P 59), its 1990 summer catalog (P. Ex. 18, D. 12(n) P 63), a flyer for the "Witches" module (P. Ex. 21, D. 12(n) P 65), the Role Aids slick sheets (P. Ex. 22, D. 12(n) P 68), an advertisement for "Psionics" (P. Ex. 20, D. 12(n) P 70), its 1990 and 1991 trade catalogs (P. Exs. 17, 19, D. 12(n) PP 72, 74), the July 1990 and June 1992 Mayfair Games News letters (P. Exs. 25, 27, D. 12(n) PP 79, 81) and several Role Aids product description sheets (P. Ex. 28-1 to -4, and -6 to - 15, D. 12(n) PP 84, 86, 88) all violated the Agreement. Mayfair also admits that the "People, Places & Things" sourcebook and "Demons" module product description sheets violate the Agreement (p. Exs. 29-1 and -2, D. 12(n) PP 99, 100).

Mayfair makes three arguments as to those admitted violations by the Role Aids promotional materials: (1) TSR has waived its right to object because Mayfair gave TSR copies of the Role Aids promotional materials violating the Agreement at game conventions between 1988 and 1991, but TSR did not alert Mayfair to the violations until the Amended Complaint was filed in December 1991, (2) the breaches were not material and (3) the violations caused no injury to TSR. Those arguments are addressed in turn.

1. *Waiver*

As already indicated, Mayfair says that it provided TSR representatives with copies of the Role Aids promotional materials from 1988 to 1991 (D. Mem. 11; Bromley Aff. P 19). Because TSR assertedly did not notify Mayfair of the violations until the December 1991 filing of the Amended Complaint, Mayfair urges that TSR has waived its right to object to the violations (D. Mem. 11). Again this will be treated as an argument for the application of laches.

TSR admits that "Darwin Bromley and perhaps other representatives of Mayfair have passed out some catalogs and promotional materials to some representatives of TSR for general promotional purposes" (P. 12(n) P 135). However, TSR Mem. 6 argues that it did not knowingly relinquish its right to object to the Role Aids promotional materials. TSR asserts that the promotional materials were distributed primarily during 1990 through 1992, that TSR filed its initial Complaint here on January 22, 1991 and that many Mayfair documents were not produced until Bromley's deposition was taken on October 1 and 2, 1991, after which TSR filed its Amended Complaint expanding the Fourth Count on December 16, 1991 (P. R. Mem. 5, Bromley Dep. 81).

Only one of the materials that Mayfair acknowledges as violations is dated in 1988, with the rest dated in 1990, 1991 or 1992. [14] Measured back from the filing of the Amended Complaint, the earliest of the undated 1990 materials could not have been as much as 24 months old before TSR lodged its objections. Case law in this circuit has noted "that two years has rarely, if ever, been held to be a delay of sufficient length to establish laches" (*Piper Aircraft Corp. v. Wag-Aero, Inc.,* 741 F.2d 925, 933 (7th Cir. 1984)). Even if TSR knew of each offending Mayfair item at the time of issue (an unlikely situation, and certainly not established on the current record), Mayfair would have a potential laches defense only as to a single product description sheet dated in 1988. And TSR's failure to object to a single isolated item cannot form the basis for a laches defense.

14 TSR could not have known of many of the Role Aids items until 1990 at the earliest. That was the year in which Mayfair introduced the Witches, Psionics and Lizardmen modules. Those promotional materials would include an advertisement for "Psionics" (P. Ex. 20, D. 12(n) P 70) a flyer for the Witches module (P. Ex. 21, D. 12(n) P 65), a product description sheet for Witches (P. Ex. 28-1), the 1990 summer catalog (P. Ex. 18, D. 12(n) P 63), the 1990 and 1991 trade catalogs (P. Exs. 17, 19, D. 12(n) PP 72, 74), and the July 1990 and June 1992 Mayfair Games News letters (P. Exs. 25, 27, D. 12(n) PP 79, 81). In addition, the product description sheets for People, Places and Things and Demons (P. Ex. 29-1 and -2) were for products to be introduced in 1992 (P-D P 98). One product description sheet (P. Ex. 28-2) is dated in 1988, while the rest are dated from 1983 to 1986 (P. Exs. 28-5 to 28-15). Some materials are undated: Mayfair's reply card (P. Ex. 16), Role Aids slick sheets (P. Ex. 22) and two Role Aids product description sheets (P. Exs. 28-3 and -4).

Thus Mayfair's motion to dismiss the breach of contract claim on the basis of laches must be denied. TSR's statement that it had only limited knowledge of the offending materials before filing its December 1991 Amended Complaint is enough to negate the required element of knowledge of facts sufficient to raise a claim for breach. In fact, Mayfair may have contributed to TSR's delay by its own delays in responding to discovery requests.

2. Lack of Materiality

Mayfair Mem. 11 advances a lack of materiality defense in one nonstop sentence:

> The promotional materials showed that they were from Mayfair and the *Role Aids* modules themselves, without exception, contained the Trademark Statement in strict compliance with the Settlement Agreement on their front covers so as to put the consumer clearly on notice as to the disclaimer sentences which, in fact, have little impact on the consumer and are not even read by the typical consumer who, in making a purchase decision, does not care which particular company produced the role-playing product.

That argument might have had force in the absence of the Agreement--but once the parties had entered into the Agreement, such a contention comes too late.

Agreement Ex. B P 5 requires, not only as to the Role Aids modules but also as to all promotional materials except for sales training literature, correspondence and press releases, that Mayfair use the AD&D trademark only in the form of the cartouche with the disclaimer statement. In the Agreement itself Mayfair "acknowledged that its failure to remedy [a] violation in accordance with the foregoing may result in immediate and irreparable damage to TSR" (P. Ex. 1 P VI). Mayfair has admitted that it has disseminated materials using the AD&D trademark outside of the cartouche form and without the disclaimer statement, but also says that it has not attempted to recover the violating Role Aids advertising and marketing materials.

In short, this branch of Mayfair's argument would effectively render the Agreement a nullity by making a violation of its key terms nonactionable. That contention too is rejected.

3. Lack of Injury

Mayfair finally contends that even if it violated the Agreement, its actions caused no injury to TSR. *Walgreen Co. v. Sara Creek Property Co.*, 775 F. Supp. 1192, 1195 (E.D. Wis. 1991) teaches that Wisconsin follows universal doctrine in that respect:

> Under Wisconsin law, a plaintiff claiming breach of contract has the burden of proving by a preponderance of the evidence that . . . the defendant's breach is material and results or will result in injury.

Mayfair says that its use of TSR's trademarks caused no customer confusion. To that end it presents the deposition of Stephen Winter, AD&D product group leader and game editor at TSR, in which he testified that he was aware of no customer confusion of Mayfair for TSR products since the Agreement (Winter Dep. 43) and that consumers do not refer to "Advanced Dungeons and Dragons" as a generic designation for role-playing game systems (*id.* at 37-38). [15] Moreover, Mayfair Mem. 12-13 states, the Trademark Statement was on the cover of every Role Aids module, the Role Aids logo was more prominent on the front cover than the AD&D logo and every Role Aids module and piece of promotional material indicated that it came from Mayfair. On the other hand, TSR says that confusion is "inevitable," and it represents (though not in evidentiary form) that retailers in London had "intermixed" TSR and Mayfair products (P. R. Mem. 9 & n. 3).

> 15 Winter was, however, aware of media use of the trademark "Dungeons and Dragons" to describe role-playing games generically. Winter also testified that most customers would not read the disclaimer language, and that at least some consumers might think that a Role Aids product was licensed by TSR (Winter Dep. 50-51).

For aught that appears, this may indeed be a case of minimal damage to TSR. So far as the ultimate consumer is concerned, Mayfair's compliance with the Agreement on all Role Aids modules negates any potential damage--for having bargained for the precise form of disclaimer that it wanted, TSR will not be heard to say that it has been hurt when that disclaimer has been adhered to. As for the sales market in which TSR and Mayfair compete, whether wholesalers or retailers, there has been no showing of lost sales or damage to the value of TSR's trademarks because of Mayfair's violations of the Agreement in promotional materials. That subject remains for future determination. [16] And as stated later, the record here does not support TSR's claim for rescission of the Agreement.

> 16 This is not said to be critical. This Court earlier entered an order bifurcating liability from damages.

Accordingly the appropriate action at this point is simply to declare the existence of the breaches that have been admitted by Mayfair. To that extent TSR is entitled to a judgment as a matter of law, with the decision as to the extent of any damages remedy to await further proceedings.

B. *Violations Denied by Mayfair*

1. *Demons*

TSR contends and Mayfair denies that the cover of its new "Demons" module violates the Agreement (P-D P 108). [17] According to TSR, Mayfair has failed to comply with the contractual requirement that the Mayfair trademark be visually more prominent than the AD&D trademark--a requirement buttressed by express standards. TSR's Supp. Mem. 2 argues that in violation of those standards the Role Aids logo is "almost invisible" in the upper corner of Demons, in gold lettering on a red background. Mayfair admits that "the degree of contrast of the Role Aids logo on Mayfair's Demons product cover. is substantially less than it was on the final proof submitted by the printer and approved by Mayfair" (Bromley Aff. P 37). Even so, Mayfair urges that the Role Aids logo is nonetheless visible, that the second page of Demons makes clear that it is a Mayfair product and that "future production runs of Demons will have the Role Aids logo in white on a red background" (D. 12(m) P 149, Bromley Aff. P 37, D. Ex. 7).

17 TSR first saw the newly-developed Demons product at a trade show in late August 1992, after its summary judgment motion had been filed and briefing was under way (P-D P 107). TSR then obtained leave to file a supplemental memorandum in support of its motion, in which it addressed the latest of Mayfair's claimed violations of the Agreement.

There is no ambiguity in the Agreement, which requires that "the ROLE AIDS trademark [be] on a color background with no less contrast than the contrast of the ADVANCED DUNGEONS & DRAGONS trademark to its background" (P. Ex. 1 P I and Ex. B P 1). Although the Role Aids logo was not visible at all in the photocopy of the Demons cover originally submitted to this Court, it is certainly legible on the Demons module itself. But the Role Aids logo is a dull gold printed on a red background, while the AD&D logo is in white on a red background. Mayfair's printer woes and future intentions notwithstanding, the cover of the present Demons module clearly does not comply with the terms of the Agreement. It too constitutes a contractual breach.

2. Quote from Dragon Magazine Review

TSR also asserts that Mayfair's 1990 and 1991 trade catalogs and the **Undead** product description sheet (P. Ex. 17 at 25, P. Ex. 19 at 11, P. Ex. 28-5) violate the Agreement by using this quote from a review of **Undead** in *Dragon Magazine* (P-D P 75):

This is a quality AD&D game campaign supplement. The setting is imaginative and fantastic; the dead guys are grim and menacing; there are plenty of neat new magic and monsters. [18]

Mayfair denies that its use of the AD&D trademark in the context of quoting from *Dragon Magazine* amounts to a violation of the Agreement (D. 12(n) P 76).

> 18 [Footnote by this Court] It may also be noted that the AD&D trademark in the *Dragon Magazine* quote in Mayfair's 1991 catalog is over twice as large as the print of the rest of the words in the sentence, and is also the largest descriptive print on the page except for the lettering on the photographs of the Role Aids modules.

Agreement P V provides in part:

> Except for use of TSR's Advanced Dungeons & Dragons trademark in accordance with this Agreement, Mayfair hereby agrees to cease and desist throughout the world from use of TSR's Advanced Dungeons & Dragons trademark or any mark confusingly similar thereto, in connection with any products or advertising or any other materials.

If the quoted review had originated with Mayfair, there could be no disputing that it violated that restriction. Mayfair would have it that the answer should be different because the reviewer and not Mayfair made the decision to describe **Undead** as an "AD&D game campaign supplement" (D. 12(n) P 76, Bromley Aff. P 36). But no use by others of the AD&D trademark in connection with Role Aids products can clear the way for Mayfair to do the same. After all, Mayfair has curtailed its own use of the AD&D trademark in the Agreement. It may not avoid those restrictions by copying the usage of someone who was not so inhibited, the *Dragon Magazine* reviewer.

Once again Mayfair points out that TSR did not complain to Mayfair until it filed the present motion. Mayfair had included the *Dragon Magazine* quote in its 1990 and 1991 catalogs, several years after issuing the product description sheet on October 20, 1986. Though Mayfair has not contended that it supplied TSR with a copy of that earlier document, it says that it gave TSR copies of the Mayfair Games catalog at trade conventions (D 12(m) P 135). But as already stated, even if TSR became aware of the violation in the 1990 catalog, [19] its failure to object before it filed the Amended Complaint in December 1991 is not so unreasonable as to bar its current claim. [20]

19 TSR's partial denial in its P. 12(n) P 135 is really ambiguous. That type of deliberate ambiguity will be construed against it, but it turns out to make no difference.

20 Mayfair contends that TSR did not complain of Mayfair's use of the *Dragon Magazine* statement until the current motion for partial summary judgment was filed in June 1992 (D. 12(m) P 143). Although TSR denies that (P. 12(n) P 143), its citation to Williams Dep. 40-41 really does not support that position. That makes no difference, however, given the allegation in Amended Complaint P 57:

> Mayfair has breached the Limited Use terms of the Settlement Agreement by its use of the TSR Trademarks in . . . connection with certain of the Role Aids publications and related materials.

Under the Rules' notice pleading regime, that is enough--TSR was not required to plead its evidence. And Mayfair's use of the quote from *Dragon Magazine* in describing **Undead**, a Role Aids product, surely comes within the scope of the pleading's allegation.

3. *"Suitable for Use with Any Fantasy Campaign"*

According to TSR, the To Hell & Back Again product description sheet (P. Ex. 29-3) also violates the Agreement because it says that the product "has numerous locations that can be worked into any fantasy campaign" (P. 12(m) P 100). Mayfair disputes that, because the relevant provision of the Agreement prevents Mayfair only from describing Role Aids as "suitable for other role-playing games" (P. Ex. 1 P I and Ex. B P 6). For that purpose "role-playing game" is defined as *(id.):*

> a structured form of social entertainment comprising a quantified interactive story telling game that allows the participants, within their imagination, and subject to the limitations of the game's rules, to adventure forward, attempting to satisfy their personal ambitions or fantasies through the use of the characteristics, perceptions and abilities of an imaginery [sic] character or person.

Mayfair Mem. 6-7 urges a difference between a role-playing game and a fantasy campaign (D. 12(n) P 101, Bromley Aff. P 18, Winter Dep. 82, Santana Aff. P 4). According to Mayfair Mem. 6, "there are multiple fantasy campaigns in Advanced Dungeons and Dragons." Winter Dep. 82 describes a fantasy campaign as "the series of adventures that's being conducted by a particular game referee or with a particular group of players with a rotating referee's position."

Although TSR seeks to deny Mayfair's assertion that the use of the term "fantasy campaign" does not violate the Agreement (P. 12(m) P 130), it does admit that "[a] fantasy campaign is different from a fantasy role-playing game" (P. 12(m) P 131). It really has advanced neither argument nor evidence to counter Mayfair's position that the use of the term "fantasy campaign" is a nonviolation.

TSR's Mem. 29-31 explains that its purpose in preventing Mayfair from stating that Role Aids were suitable for use with other role-playing games as well as AD&D was to protect TSR's trademark from becoming generic. Sounding another variation on the same theme, TSR's R. Mem. 9 asserts that "Mayfair's advertising campaign promoting ROLE AIDS modules as suitable 'for any fantasy role-playing game on the market' harms the reputation and goodwill of the ADVANCED DUNGEONS & DRAGONS mark as representing a unique brand of products."

That is really nonsense. As Mayfair's Mem. 11 asks rhetorically:

> If the producer of Gatorade claims its drink is great for football players and also claims it is great for participants in any high-energy sport, is it reasonable to argue that football is at risk of becoming generic for high-energy sports as a result thereof?

Indeed, the restriction that TSR incorrectly contends was violated in the respect now under discussion [21] is the one aspect of the Agreement that appears to find no legitimate justification in TSR's trademark rights. It seems to be purely anticompetitive and hence likely unenforceable as an unlawful extension of the trademarks.

21 As indicated earlier, that contention is incorrect as a matter of contract construction: TSR has acknowledged that "fantasy campaign" is different from "fantasy role-playing game," so that a prohibition framed in terms of the latter is not violated by a statement that speaks in terms of the former.

For present purposes, though, that issue need not be decided. It is enough to find (as this Court has) that TSR loses as a matter of contract. Mayfair is entitled to dismissal of the claim that the Agreement was breached by the To Hell and Back Again product description sheet.

C. Freedom of Choice Campaign

In late 1991 Mayfair began the "Freedom of Choice" advertising campaign (D. 12(m), P. 12(n) P 127). Mayfair has admitted that its Freedom of Choice Poster that stated Role Aids products "were for use with any role-playing game" violated the terms of the Agreement (P. Ex. 31, D. 12(n) P 96). But its Mem. 6 says that once it realized that in April 1992, it promptly terminated the use of promotional materials having the noncomplying language (Santana Aff. P 4).

Mayfair presents no evidence that it then attempted to recall the Freedom of Choice materials, but its Mem. 7 states that such attempts are futile (Bromley Aff. P 34, Santana Aff. P 6). TSR denies that Mayfair made good faith efforts to retrieve noncomplying materials (P. 12(n) PP 130, 150), pointing out that Bromley based his conclusion of the futility of recall attempts merely on the attempted recall of one shipment of Psionics (Bromley Aff. P 34). In fact, Mayfair's Jennifer Santana testified that Mayfair made no attempts at recall of the Freedom of Choice materials (Santana Aff. P 6). It does not necessarily follow from the futility of Mayfair's attempts to recall the Psionics modules that had been sent to stores that Mayfair would have been equally unsuccessful in recalling advertising materials. After all, stores may be willing to comply with a request to refrain from posting an advertisement or to replace the advertisement with another, but may be reluctant to send back what they believe will be a popular product.

Mayfair's Mem. 10 also contends that its acknowledged breach of the Agreement by the Freedom of Choice campaign literature is not material because "the trade was correctly describing Role Aids as being usable in any fantasy role-playing game for a long time prior thereto" (D. 12(m) P 128). TSR denies that, but its denial hardly seems in good faith in light of TSR's own Ex. 33, a collection of catalog pages listing Mayfair Role Aids products. Capital City's *Game Buyer's Monthly* for July 1990 and its March 1991 releases describe Mayfair's "Witches" and "Lizardmen" modules as suitable for "any fantasy roleplaying adventure or campaign" and "for use with any fantasy RPG" (P. Exs. 33-1 and -2); Capital City's "The Premium Specialty Collection" May, October and December 1990 issues describe Role Aids products as "generic" (P. Exs. 33-19, -20, -21); Wargames West's 1991 Spring catalog states that Role Aids modules "can be used with any fantasy role-playing system, especially TSR's Dungeons & Dragons and AD&D systems" (P. Ex. 33-25). Several of the pages in P. Ex. 33 list Role Aids modules under the category "Generic Fantasy Source Books and Modules" (P. Exs. 33-3 through 33-13, 33-22 and 33-23) and describe Lizardmen and Psionics as "universal," "for use with any RPG" or "designed to adapt to any fantasy roleplaying game system" (P. Ex. 33-14 through 33-16, 33-24), but no date of publication is shown on those exhibits.

Mayfair has presented Bromley's affidavit testimony that the only catalogs in P. Ex. 33 that did not precede the Freedom of Choice campaign are P. Ex. 33-17 and 33-18 (Bromley Aff. P 14). Although the last page of Exhibit 33 (left unnumbered by TSR) from the 1991-92 Winter/Spring Wargames West Catalog may have come out after the Freedom of Choice campaign, TSR has made no effort to provide the date of those materials. However, given the substantial number of dated exhibits that describe Role Aids modules generically, the undated exhibits provide only cumulative information.

To be sure, the fact that others describe Role Aids in a manner that Mayfair agreed not to use does not release Mayfair from its promise. But as has already been indicated in the discussion about the To Hell & Back Again product description sheet, there is more than a serious question whether that promise is valid and enforceable. Indeed, the usages by others that comprise the various subparts of P. Ex. 33 graphically illustrate the total lack of connection between a statement that *Role Aids* has multiple uses and any conclusion that one of those uses--that in conjunction with AD&D--somehow renders *AD&D* generic.

Again this Court would be strongly inclined to consider invalidating that component of the Agreement. But once again it is unnecessary to take that step, for at worst this claimed violation of the Agreement is both de minimis and in the past. It has potential relevance only on the issue of the relief to which TSR may be entitled.

Remedies

This opinion has earlier referred to the bifurcation of issues that has deferred the question of damages sustained by TSR as the result of Mayfair's several violations of the Agreement. Consequently all that now remains for consideration is whether TSR's prayer for rescission of the Agreement should be granted or denied.

Not surprisingly, Wisconsin law adheres to universal equitable principles in defining the conditions that entitle a party to rescission of a contract for its breach. Any party who would rescind a contract must do so within a reasonable time following its discovery of the breach (*Thompson v. Village of Hales Corners,* 115 Wis. 2d 289, 340 N.W.2d 704, 718 (Wis. 1983) (six-month delay in asserting rights bars rescission)). Rescission is not the appropriate remedy for every breach of contract--rather "the nonperformance must be substantial and the breach so serious as to destroy the essential objects of the contract" (*Seidling v. Unichem, Inc.,* 52 Wis. 2d 552, 191 N.W.2d 205, 207 (Wis. 1971)). And rescission must "restore the parties to the position they would have occupied if no contract had ever been made between them": Each party must return to the other all benefits received under the contract *(id.* at 208; *First Nat'l Bank & Trust Co. v. Notte,* 97 Wis. 2d 207, 293 N.W.2d 530, 539 (Wis. 1980)).

Merely to state those basic principles is to demonstrate why rescission is inappropriate here. Whether or not TSR acted with sufficient promptness after it learned of Mayfair's breaches, [22] the parties' many years of performance under the contract obviously render its unwinding far more difficult and less appropriate (a point elaborated on in a moment). Next, it can hardly be said that the breaches identified here have "destroyed the essence of the contract"--it will be remembered that the presentation of Mayfair's Role Aids products to the ultimate consumer has *always* (with one minor and inadvertent exception) adhered to the standards that TSR itself established to assure that Mayfair would not poach on its preserves (a point also elaborated on in a moment or two).

[22] There is understandably a very different and much shorter yardstick for rescission purposes than for the application of laches. Laches actually defeats any claim of the aggrieved party, while the denial of the rescission remedy still preserves for that party the benefit of being made whole through the recovery of damages. In this case it would seem that TSR has

failed to meet the timetable defined in *Thompson* as a precondition to rescission, but whether or not that is so, TSR fails on the other grounds discussed here.

Perhaps most importantly, there is no way in which the parties can 'effectively be restored to the status quo ante contract--no way in which the omelet can be unscrambled and put back into the egg. It is truly an impossibility, given the time span from 1984 to the present during which the parties have functioned under their contract, to "restore the parties to the position they would have occupied if no contract had been made between them." In terms of the restoration of benefits, just how can TSR repay whatever benefit it has derived from the ongoing Role Aids advertising of AD&D as the only role-playing game expressly mentioned on Mayfair's products, or it has derived from the continued reinforcement of the AD&D trademarks over the intervening years without any attack by Mayfair?

In sum, this case does not at all call for TSR to obtain the equitable benefit of contract rescission, beyond whatever damages (not yet established) that it is able to demonstrate flowing from the breaches shown here. For over eight years it has derived the principal benefits that it bargained for in the Agreement:

1. To the consuming public, Mayfair has meticulously observed the requirements marked out by TSR--standards that make plain its nonsponsorship of Mayfair's competing Role Aids modules, while at the same time keeping the AD&D name before the consumers, with TSR identified as its source. [23]

2. TSR's trademarks have remained without challenge from Mayfair, promoting the continued entrenchment of D&D and AD&D as fixtures in the consuming public's minds.

[23] Although Demons has been a single exception to Mayfair's strict adherence to the Agreement's specifications for Role Aids modules, there is no reason to discredit Mayfair's explanation that the contrast between the Role Aids name and its background in the final product turned out to be less than the original printers' proofs had shown. It will be remembered that the Demons product came onto the market over 18 months after this lawsuit was brought, and after TSR had already launched its current motion. What incentive would Mayfair have, after eight years of living by

the Agreement's standards in designing all of its other product modules, to depart from that practice deliberately in the face of this litigation and a Rule 56 motion?

As against that, TSR has shown a number of contract breaches by Mayfair--but not such as to demand rescission. In some instances Mayfair has cured the problems on its own, or (as in the Demons situation) has promptly stated its intention to correct the inadvertent error. In one instance it terminated the employee responsible for misreading the Agreement's directives. And there is no reason to believe that it will not promptly correct the remaining breaches that have been found here.

Moreover, this opinion has twice commented on the apparent overreaching by TSR in one part of the Agreement: prohibiting Mayfair's truthful advertising of the fact that Role Aids products may be utilized by members of the consuming public in conjunction with rival role-playing games as well as with AD&D. That restraint inhibits not only Mayfair's market among consumers who have purchased (or might intend to purchase) role-playing games from TSR's competitors but (not incidentally) also tends to lessen the demand for those competitive games among purchasers of Mayfair's Role Aids products. And again those anti-competitive measures appear to find no rational support in TSR's legitimate goals for protecting the integrity of its own trademarks. [24]

24 If anything, it would seem that measures that would thus tend to promote AD&D's market domination would make it more likely, rather than less likely, that AD&D might become a generic term among consumers. It is only necessary to recall such examples as Eastman's fight to prevent "Kodak" from entering the public domain, or Bayer's like fight as to "Aspirin" or GE's comparable fight as to "Frigidaire."

Whether or not those considerations invalidate that particular restraint of trade has not been decided here, because it need not be. But those considerations do tend to place in sharper focus the effect of a rescission of the Agreement here. Because of AD&D's prominence in the marketplace, any revocation of Mayfair's permission to refer to AD&D with appropriate disclaimers could bid fair to destroy Role Aids as a competitor for the marketplace with TSR's own products intended for use in that role-playing game. [25] What is reflected in the total record here simply does not support this

Court's throwing its weight into the competitive scales in that fashion, when TSR has a fully adequate remedy in the form of its recouping any damages that it can prove *and* its obtaining an injunction compelling Mayfair's correction of past violations and preventing new violations. [26]

25 Absent Mayfair's joinder in AD&D's prayer for rescission, it is assumed here that Mayfair is willing to continue to live with the specific ground rules set out in the Agreement, rather than having both parties relegated to the principles of law (such as fair use) that would apply in the absence of contract.

26 It should be emphasized that this point is only an added fillip that demonstrates the soundness of denying TSR this specific equitable relief-- one to which it has not shown its entitlement based on the equitable principles that uniformly govern the availability of the rescission remedy.

Conclusion

TSR's motion is granted to the extent that this Court finds the following materials to have violated the Agreement: the 1990 Mayfair Trade Catalog with the Invincible Overlord compatibility statement, the Invincible Overlord writers' guidelines, all the challenged Role Aids materials except for the To Hell & Back Again product description sheet and the Freedom of Choice materials. TSR's motion is denied as to Mayfair's use of the Gygax statement on the Invincible Overlord materials. Mayfair's motion is also denied as to that use of the Gygax statement, while its motion is granted as to the To Hell & Back Again product description sheet. As to remedies for the adjudicated violations, TSR's prayer for rescission of the Agreement is denied, and the scope of appropriate relief is deferred pending further submissions by the parties.

Milton I. Shadur

Senior United States District Judge

Date: March 15, 1993

FRANCIS HOGAN and DANIEL MASUCCI, Plaintiffs,

- v -

DC COMICS, WARNER COMMUNICATIONS, INC., TIME WARNER ENTERTAINMENT CO., L.P., NANCY COLLINS, and PAUL LEE, Defendants.

98 Civ. 1164 (SAS)
UNITED STATES DISTRICT COURT FOR THE SOUTHERN DISTRICT OF NEW YORK

48 F. Supp. 2d 298
1999 U.S. Dist. LEXIS 601

January 25, 1999, Decided
January 26, 1999, Filed

U.S. DISTRICT JUDGE SHIRA A. SCHEINDLIN

Plaintiffs Francis Hogan ("Hogan") and Daniel Masucci bring this action against defendants DC Comics, Warner Communications, Inc., Time Warner Entertainment Co., L.P., Nancy Collins ("Collins") and Paul Lee ("Lee") claiming that defendants infringed plaintiffs' copyright in an unpublished comic book entitled *Matchsticks* through defendants' painted graphic novel *Dhampire: Stillborn*. Plaintiffs also claim that defendants misappropriated their idea for a comic book centered around the struggles of a half-human, half-vampire character. Presently before this Court is defendants' motion to dismiss pursuant to Rule 56 of the Federal Rules of Civil Procedure.

I. Summary Judgment Standard

A motion for summary judgment may be granted only if "the pleadings, depositions, answers to interrogatories, and admissions on file, together with the affidavits, if any, show that there is no genuine issue as to any material fact and that the moving party is entitled to judgment as a matter of law." Fed.R.Civ.P. 56(c); *see also Anderson v. Liberty Lobby, Inc.*, 477 U.S. 242, 247-50, 91 L. Ed. 2d 202, 106 S. Ct. 2505 (1986). The moving party has the burden of identifying evidence that demonstrates the absence of a genuine issue of material fact. *See Celotex Corp. v. Catrett*, 477 U.S. 317, 323, 91 L. Ed. 2d 265,

106 S. Ct. 2548 (1986); *Schwapp v. Town of Avon*, 118 F.3d 106, 110 (2d Cir. 1997). Once this burden has been met, the non-moving party must come forward with evidence that is more than "mere speculation and conjecture," *Western World Ins. Co. v. Stack Oil, Inc.*, 922 F.2d 118, 121 (2d Cir. 1990), but "would be sufficient to support a jury verdict in its favor." *Goenaga v. March of Dimes Defects Foundation*, 51 F.3d 14, 18 (1995).

In determining whether summary judgment should be granted, the court resolves all ambiguities and draws all reasonable inferences against the moving party. *See D'Amico v. City of New York*, 132 F.3d 145, 148 (2d Cir. 1998), *cert. denied*, 141 L. Ed. 2d 151, 118 S. Ct. 2075 (1998). The moving party, however, is not required to affirmatively disprove unsupported assertions made by the non-movant, *see Celotex*, 477 U.S. at 323, and if the evidence presented by the non-movant is "merely colorable, or is not significantly probative, summary judgment may be granted." *Scotto v. Almenas*, 143 F.3d 105 (2d Cir. 1998) (quoting *Liberty Lobby*, 477 U.S. at 249-250). The court must also examine "the substantive law applicable to the underlying litigation since that law dictates which facts are material." *Consarc Corp. v. Marine Midland Bank, N.A.*, 996 F.2d 568, 572 (2d Cir. 1993) (citing *Anderson*, 477 U.S. at 248).

II. Background

This litigation arises out of two works each centered around a half-human, half-vampire character named Nicholas Gaunt. In defense of plaintiffs' copyright claim, defendants assert that plaintiffs' and defendants' works are not substantially similar in their copyrightable aspects as a matter of law. Because " a determination of substantial similarity requires a detailed examination of the works themselves," *Williams v. Crichton*, 84 F.3d 581, 583 (2d Cir. 1996), I have examined both works. A description of the plaintiffs' work -- a comic book -- and defendants' work -- a "painted novel," which resembles a glossy upscale comic book -- follow.

A. The Works

1. *Matchsticks*

Plaintiffs' work, *Matchsticks*, consists of three episodes of a dark, Gothic, violent comic book monthly series that revolves around a half-vampire, half-human character named Nicholas Gaunt. According to plaintiffs, the work depicts Gaunt's struggle to discover the truth about his past, particularly to uncover the identity of his father, and his internal conflict between the forces of good and evil that arise out of his dual nature.

Gaunt's struggle is not revealed through dialogue or internal monologue so much as through occasional flashbacks and violent confrontations that he experiences with other vampires. The work also features three rival groups of vampire or monster characters: a group patterned after the Catholic Church (the "Inquisition Group"), the "Thuggies," and a group of vampires or monsters led by a vampire named Fenris. The action in the work jumps quickly among Gaunt and these three groups, with each having their own story line. At times, it is difficult to follow the action, as different characters are introduced without explanation and the work switches from one story to the next. According to plaintiff, this effect was intentional; he wanted to "hint at" but not completely reveal the story. *See* Deposition of Francis Hogan ("Hogan Dep."), Exhibit A to Declaration of Philip J. Iovieno, plaintiffs' counsel ("Iovieno Decl."), at 73.

The work is set in the future, in the year 2017. *Matchsticks* begins with an image of Maxwell Niphe, the leader of the Thuggies and an imposing character with long white hair, dark eyes and long black robes who has been around for thousands of years, and who cryptically states the "the game is about to start" but that "one piece is not yet on board." The work then switches to Hong Kong, where Gaunt has just completed training in the martial arts. As a box of text states that "something is very very wrong," Gaunt receives a letter stating that "the wolf will devour the son." The letter also encloses a key to a room at the No-Tell Motel in Los Angeles; the key has been drawn over the "u" in sun, obscuring whether the word is "sun" or "son." The next few images are of a character named Ma Fat, who informs another character named Maggie Darden over the telephone that Gaunt is "on his way."

The comic book then skips to the Los Angeles Airport, where a female vampire named Kat, who is later revealed to be allied with

Fenris, waits for Gaunt. Kat, armed with supernatural ability, travels to the No-Tell Motel with the intention of fulfilling her command to slaughter Gaunt, while on the way briefly stopping to kill her taxi driver in a gruesome, violent manner. Gaunt, able to anticipate Kat's moves because of his own supernatural senses, kills her before she is able to complete her mission. Before she dies, Gaunt asks Kat who sent her; she responds "don't . . . you . . . know" and looks into his eyes, which are shown in extreme close-up.

Gaunt then experiences a flashback to the day from his childhood on which his mother and uncle were killed and he was found by a detective named Stanz, who took him in and raised him. Gaunt flashes back to a room in which blood is pooled on the floor and splattered on the walls, and in which someone has written, also apparently in blood, that "the wolf will devour the sun." Again, it is not clear whether "sun" has been spelled with a "u" or an "o." Gaunt is then shown leaving Los Angeles.

The work next shifts to a few frames of characters who are members of the Inquisition Group and inhabit St. Patrick's Cathedral in New York City. The group is led by a character wearing a cardinal's hat (the "Cardinal"), who is assisted by Inquisitor Hargroves, an angular, boney character with a tattoo of a question mark on his forehead. Hargroves informs the Cardinal that they have intercepted messages from the Thuggies.

Next, Gaunt is shown returning to his hometown of Albany, New York. The "Asgard Estate," home of Fenris and his vampires, is also in Albany. Fenris is then visited by a character named Zodiac, who sports sunglasses, a leather jacket and what appear to be dreadlocks. Fenris, told by Zodiac that he is delivering bad news, punches Zodiac and grabs him by the neck, at which point Zodiac reveals that Kat has been killed. Fenris expresses no remorse upon hearing this news and informs Zodiac that he had intended to kill her and Zodiac.

Matchsticks then moves back to the Inquisition Group and a character named Brother Flux, who appears to have technological apparatus incorporated into his body and is attempting to enter cyberspace. The story then focuses on Maxwell Niphe, the leader of the Thuggie vampire group. Niphe states that he is "Sudeah of my people: judge, jury, and executioner. I carry out my duty in a society of monsters, vampires, werewolves, ghouls, call them what you like." Niphe

48

instructs Maggie, a female Thuggie who was once human, to go to Albany because a "hunter" is going there.

The story returns to Albany, where Gaunt reunites with Stanz. It then moves back to St. Patrick's Cathedral, where the Cardinal, after being informed by Hargroves that he has received a report of Thuggie activity in the Albany area, decides to send a Swiss Guard platoon into the region. These members of the platoon, led by Joan Ark, wear high-tech armor, giving them a robotic appearance, and appear to have returned from a mission in Bosnia. In the background, a scantily clad female character wearing a nun's habit with the word "mercy" inscribed on the front is shown engaging in some form of ritualistic torture on an altar boy.

Meanwhile, back in Albany, Gaunt and Stanz visit a local bar. A character with a cross inscribed on the back of his head, who appears to be Zodiac, attempts to kill Gaunt but is shot by Stanz, who tells Gaunt to escape to Stanz's house in the country. On his way to the house, Gaunt is again attacked by Zodiac. Stanz again appears and shoots Zodiac before he kills Gaunt. Gaunt is then shown standing over what may be a severed head with a sword in his hand, and a box of text states that "now he is one of us." According to plaintiffs, Gaunt has just taken a step toward becoming a full-fledged vampire.

As a police car pulls up to Stanz and Gaunt, Stanz tells Gaunt that he'll take care of the situation and orders him to leave. Shortly thereafter, Stanz is captured and killed by police officers, who are really disguised agents of the Inquisition Group.

Meanwhile, Fenris is informed that Zodiac was killed when he "engaged Gaunt in a public display of fighting." He is also told that Maggie of the Thuggies seeks an audience with him. Fenris orders his monsters Sharkey and Angel to bring Gaunt to him.

Next, Gaunt is shown driving up to Stanz's house, the place where he was raised after the murder of his mother and uncle and to which he had not returned in ten years. Gaunt experiences a memory or a flashback to when he was a child in Stanz's house, raised with a young girl, perhaps a sister, called Elise. Gaunt then discovers Stanz's severed head in a paper bag, which had been placed on a table in the house. Gaunt, experiencing remorse over having caused Stanz's death, is then set upon by members of the Inquisition Group, though Gaunt successfully manages to escape.

Meanwhile, as Maggie Darden waits in Fenris' cellar, a watch that is pinned to her chest starts to ring, an event which inexplicably causes her to call Maxwell Niphe. Upon learning that the watch had been activated, Niphe informs Maggie that he is coming to Albany personally.

The story then returns to Gaunt, who is resting in an Albany motel. Gaunt is awakened by a telephone caller, who instructs him that "if you seek the wolf, come to Quail and Clinton." Gaunt goes to that location, where he is captured and sedated by Angel and Sharkey. They bring Gaunt to Fenris, attaching him to an X-shaped cross. Fenris says to Gaunt "welcome to the family son." Gaunt, apparently still unaware of his relationship to Fenris, accuses Fenris of killing his mother and uncle. Fenris, at first becomes enraged at Gaunt, then turns more subdued, calling Gaunt "son," and telling him that he loves him. Fenris explains, "I was once as you are now, human. I was killed Nicholas . . . I rose, resurrected, as something more than human and yet something less than a man, darker. Your mother loved me. She took me back." Gaunt says nothing, but is depicted with a look of wide-eyed shock on his face.

Fenris then offers Gaunt immortality, apparently attempting to convince Gaunt to become a vampire. Fenris is then called away to attend to some unexplained business concerning a "vial." While Fenris is away, Gaunt overpowers and kills Angel. Fenris returns and is attacked by Gaunt. The two engage in a fierce struggle, demonstrating their martial arts skills and supernatural abilities. Gaunt, vowing never to join Fenris, finally kills him with a sword, yelling "For my mother . . . For my Uncle . . . For Me!", apparently feeling some retribution for Fenris' murder of his mother and uncle. Boxes of text then state, "The wolf is slain . . . and releases the son."

Gaunt has barely recovered from his struggle with Fenris when Maxwell Niphe appears. Gaunt attacks Niphe but is overpowered. Niphe then offers Gaunt a proposal: die at the hands of "Asgard's Monsters" or become a Thuggee, with the option of hunting renegade vampires if he still feels the urge to die. At this point it is unclear which route Gaunt has decided to follow.

The work ends with the introduction of a new character, Adolp Krupper, who is holding a vial--an image that recurs periodically throughout the story--and plotting revenge. The last few pages present images of Hargroves, Maggie Darden, Adolp Krupper and Gaunt.

2. *Dhampire: Stillborn*

Dhampire: Stillborn is the story of a troubled half-human, half-vampire young adult who searches to uncover the truth about his heritage and eventually chooses to become a full-fledged vampire. Like in *Matchsticks*, the main character's name is Nicholas Gaunt. Gaunt is depicted as a young, white male, with pale skin and short, dark, unkempt hair that falls in strands down the sides of his face. He is skinny, with little muscle tone, and has an elaborate tattoo of a cross on his left arm.

The story in *Dhampire*, which takes place in the present day, follows one story, which proceeds in a linear fashion interspersed with frequent flashbacks to Gaunt's childhood. The art work is depicted in a realistic style. The characters all appear human, with normal features and proportions and present-day clothing. When certain of the characters become vampires, they acquire fangs and pointed ears.

The story begins with close-up images of a razor blade, a wrist dripping blood and a pool of blood. It then switches to a scene of Gaunt in a bathroom attempting, for the third time, to commit suicide by slashing his wrists. Gaunt, trying to figure out why he is so troubled, recalls the story of his birth: born to a middle-aged widow, Gaunt was originally believed to have been stillborn, until an orderly taking him down to the morgue discovered that he was, in fact, alive. Gaunt is committed to a psychiatric ward, where he is assigned to Dr. Merrick.

Dr. Merrick, attempting to uncover the source of Gaunt's self-destructive behavior, reviews Gaunt's case file and the history of his early childhood. Dr. Merrick reveals that Gaunt suffered a seizure at three years old, after which he showed behavioral problems, including the killing and preservation of small animals. He also had a history of suicide attempts and of fighting with schoolmates, culminating in an episode in which he bit a fellow student on the neck and was expelled.

Suspecting that some early trauma caused Gaunt's emotional problems, Dr. Merrick convinces him to undergo hypnosis to release his repressed memories. Dr. Merrick tells Gaunt to picture himself in a long corridor full of doors behind which are events from his past. Looking through a small door, Gaunt sees his grandmother protecting him from his verbally abusive mother and his much older sister Natalie, who, he recalls, used to leave the family for long stretches of time. Looking through another door, Gaunt remembers an episode when he was three years old and Natalie appeared in his bedroom window as a vampire, with pale skin, fangs, pointed ears and long black hair streaming in the wind, and attempted to take him away. Gaunt is saved by his grandmother, who scares Natalie away with a cross, tells young Gaunt that he's just had a bad dream and then drops dead on top of him.

Upon awakening from hypnosis, Gaunt, who had believed himself to be an only child, is shocked to hear from Dr. Merrick that he has a sister, but is convinced when Dr. Merrick presents him with Natalie's birth certificate. Equating Gaunt's heightened interest in finding out his family's secrets with increased psychological health, Dr. Merrick releases Gaunt from the hospital.

Gaunt immediately travels home to his mother's house in Philadelphia and confronts her with his newly discovered family secrets. Gaunt's mother reveals that Natalie was, in fact, not his sister but his mother, and that Natalie left Gaunt with her -- his grandmother -- when he was just an infant. She also tells Gaunt that Natalie has been dead for twenty years. Asked about the identity of Gaunt's father, his "grandmother" says she does not know, but that Natalie frequently mentioned a gangster named "Izzy."

Confused by all of this new information, Gaunt visits a local strip club, where he catches the eye of a scantily clad stripper named Tanith, who is wearing a black leather bustier and gloves and a long blond wig. Tanith, newly dressed and now sporting a brunette close-cropped haircut, approaches Gaunt and later goes back to his hotel room to engage in sexual relations, an event which causes Gaunt to believe that his luck is finally changing for the better. During their post-coital conversation, Gaunt reveals his family secrets and Tanith offers to drive him to Bethlehem, Pennsylvania, the town in which he was born, in order to search for his father.

In Bethlehem, Gaunt searches out "Izzy," whose real name is the Iscariot, but discovers that Izzy is African-American and, therefore, obviously not his biological father. Upon Tanith's suggestion, the two decide to visit the graveyard where Natalie is buried. After a small spat and a brief separation, Gaunt discovers Tanith lying on the ground with a gaping bloody wound in her neck and looks up to find Natalie perched on top of her own tombstone, blood flowing from her mouth. Natalie then recounts for Gaunt the story of her life: kicked out the house by her father, Natalie traveled to New York City and became a prostitute. One night, having inadvertently given her services to a vice cop, Natalie was rescued by the Iscariot, who then took her in as a stripper at his club.

Natalie became the Iscariot's lover, but was kicked out when he discovered that she was pregnant (apparently the living dead despise pregnant women and children since they are reminders of vampires' unnatural state). Natalie returned to Bethlehem to give birth to Gaunt, but returned shortly thereafter to the Iscariot, who decided that she was ready for the "final kiss" and to be reborn as his bride.

Natalie informs Gaunt that his biological father is most likely the vice cop but that while pregnant, Natalie was bitten by the Iscariot, exposing Gaunt in utero to vampire venom. This exposure caused Gaunt to be born a "dhampire," a "half-human, half-vampire hybrid." According to Natalie, most dhampires are stillborn, and those that survive are possessed of dark appetites and moods, morbid interests and a relentless hunger that drives them to acts of "cannibalistic murder." Alarmed at the news of his unfortunate lineage, Gaunt flees back to his motel room.

Later, Tanith, reborn as a vampire, visits Gaunt and attempts to give him eternal life through her bite. Natalie arrives, however, and informs Gaunt that since he was born a dhampire, in order to become a full vampire he must make the decision to "damn [himself] by committing crimes so hideous that [he] is branded with the mark of Cain." Upon his violent death, he will arise on the third night as one of the **undead**.

At the next scene, three months later, it is apparent that Gaunt has chosen to become a vampire. He has slaughtered at least five people, hanging them upside down from the ceiling with their blood draining into buckets below, repeating the images from the work's opening page. Gaunt dips his fingers in the blood and marks a red X over his heart. In a scene that Gaunt has set up, he is ambushed by police officers and then shot to death with a bullet through the X; his last word spoken is "father."

In the next and last scene, set in the graveyard, Natalie and Tanith call out to Gaunt, who rises from the earth. Natalie asks Gaunt if he is ready to meet his "sire." The last image of the work is a full-page drawing of Gaunt, now with pointed ears, fangs, and catlike pupils, responding "Ready? I was ready all my life."

B. Hogan's Contact with Defendant

Plaintiffs created *Matchsticks* pursuant to an agreement with comic book publisher Neotek Iconography. *See* Hogan Dep., at 78-80, 111. In August 1994, however, after Neotek informed plaintiffs that it was going to pay them a royalty based on sales rather than the originally agreed upon page rate, plaintiffs elected to find another publisher. *See id.* at 119, 139.

In August or September of 1994, Hogan made an unsolicited cold-call to DC Comics and was put in touch with Axel Alonso ("Alonso"), an assistant editor. *See id.* at 142-44. Hogan called to inquire about getting work as an "inker" for DC Comics and to determine whether the company had any interest in publishing *Matchsticks. See id.* at 144-45. Alonso and Hogan first discussed Hogan's experience with inking and DC Comics' methods for recruiting inkers, and Alonso offered to send Hogan some samples to ink to see if his style was compatible with DC Comics' other artists. *See id.* at 144-46. [1]

> 1 Alonso asserts that he has no recollection of speaking with Hogan or of ever reviewing *Matchsticks* prior to the filing of this lawsuit. *See* Declaration of Axel Alonso in Support of Defendants' Motion for Summary Judgment, dated September 24, 1998 ("Alonso Decl."), at P 5. For purposes of this motion, I assume that the interactions between Alonso and Hogan proceeded just as Hogan remembers it.

Hogan then attempted to sell *Matchsticks* to Alonso, telling him that it involved a story about vampires and the supernatural, and a character who has lost his memory of his past. *See id.* at 147. Hogan then asked

Alonso whether DC Comics would look at *Matchsticks* if he sent it over and treat it as a "professional submission"; according to Hogan, he "made it clear that [he was] submitting it for the purpose of selling it." *Id.* at 147-48. Alonso answered affirmatively and inquired further about the work. *Id.* at 148. Hogan again asked Alonso if he was sure that he wanted Hogan to send him the work, and Alonso again responded positively. *Id.*

According to Hogan, he explained to Alonso that he had completed a draft for issues one through three of the series, but that he had ideas for additional stories for issues four through nine. *See id.* at 154. He explained that Gaunt would become a member of the Thuggie vampire group and commit more and more "heinous acts," with the "cliffhanger" of the story involving whether Gaunt would give in to his humanity or the monster inside of him. *See id.* Hogan also told Alonso about a subplot involving a "vial," over which Gaunt, a character named Adolph Krupper, the Thuggies, the "Inquisition" and "Sporn Tech" would struggle for control. *See id.* at 154-56. In addition, Hogan told Alonso how the relationship between Gaunt and Maggie Darden would "blossom into a doomed romance." *Id.* at 158.

Soon after this conversation, Hogan submitted a draft of the first three issues of *Matchsticks*. *See id.* at 166-67. Approximately one week later, Hogan placed a second call to Alonso to get DC Comics' impression of the comic book. *See id.* at 178. Alonso told Hogan that they had received the package and had reviewed it, but that it was not what they were looking for at that time. *See id.* Hogan received a package from Alonso some time thereafter containing a rejection letter for *Matchsticks* and some sample pages for Hogan to ink and return to DC Comics for evaluation. *See id.* at 179-80. Approximately one month later, Hogan sent the inking work back to DC Comics and also included another copy of issues one through three of *Matchsticks*, some covers, some advertising art, and a promotional matchbook-cover design, hoping that DC Comics would reconsider publishing the work. *See id.* at 182-184, 187.

C. Creation of *Dhampire: Stillborn*

Dhampire was created by Nancy Collins, a freelance writer and author of ten published novels and forty published short stories, including five novels featuring vampires, and free-lance artist Paul Lee. *See*

Declaration of Nancy A. Collins in Support of Defendants' Motion for Summary Judgment, dated September 23, 1998 ("Collins Decl."), at P 2; Declaration of Paul Lee in Support of Defendants' Motion for Summary Judgment, dated September 23, 1998 ("Lee Decl."), at PP 1, 3. The editor of the work was Lou Stathis ("Stathis"). During 1994, Alonso was a new assistant editor at DC Comics, whose responsibilities were comprised mostly of clerical and administrative tasks in assisting Stathis. *See* Alsonso Decl. at P 3. According to Alonso, he first became aware of *Dhampire* in early 1996, when he started performing clerical work on the project. *See id.*

In July of 1996, by which time all of the editing on the project had been completed, Stathis became ill, and Alonso took over to supervise the final stages of production. [2] *See id.*; Deposition of Matthew Alonso, dated November 14, 1997, Exhibit B to Declaration of Philip J. Iovieno ("Alonso Dep."), at 12. According to Alonso, at no time during the creation of *Dhampire* did he ever communicate with Collins or Lee about, or supply any ideas or suggestions for, the development of the story or the characters, or the characters' appearance. *See* Alonso Decl., at P 3. Alonso also asserts that he does not recall speaking with Hogan or seeing *Matchsticks* prior to this suit, but that he is certain that he never discussed *Matchsticks* with Stathis, Collins, Lee or anyone else at DC Comics. *See id.* at P 5.

2 Because Stathis died in May of 1997, there is no record of his testimony. Collins Decl. at P 7.

According to Collins, she ran into Stathis, a friend, at an art opening in June of 1994. *See* Collins Decl. P 3. Stathis asked Collins whether she would be interested in authoring a painted graphic novel about vampires that would have a "Gothic feel" and appeal to "Generation X" teenagers. *See id.* Collins had just completed work on a novel entitled *Paint it Black*, which contains a half-human, half-vampire character named Jen, who is referred to in the work as a "dhampire." *See id.*; Defendants' Civil Rule 56.1 Statement ("Defs.' 56.1 Statement"), at P 49; Plaintiffs' Counter-Statement of Material Facts Which are not in Dispute ("Pls.' 56.1 Statement), at P 49; *See* Exhibits to Declarations in Support of Defendants' Motion for Summary Judgment (Defs.' Exhs."), at Exh. 2. Collins immediately suggested the idea of a half-human, half-vampire character based on Jen for the graphic novel, and Stathis, liking the idea, asked Collins to send him a proposal. *See* Collins' Decl. at P 3.

A few days following this meeting, Collins began a partial preliminary proposal, jotting down in a notebook ideas for the story that eventually became *Dhampire*. *See* Defs.' Exhs., at Exh. 3. These notes also contain a list of names, all containing the last name Gaunt paired with variations on "Nicholas," "Natalie," and other first names beginning with "N." According to Collins, she chose the name "Gaunt" as a derivative of the name of a bat-like creature called a "nightgaunt" that appears in the literature of science fiction writer H.P. Lovecraft and because "gaunt" connotes thinness and pallor, qualities associated with the "**undead**." *See* Collins Decl. at P 4. She ultimately chose the first name "Nicholas" for a variety of reasons: she had just viewed the play *Nicholas Nickelby*; "Nick" is another name for the devil; and as a tribute to Jack Nicholson, who also believed his mother was his grandmother. *See id.*

On June 25, 1994, Collins prepared a handwritten draft letter to Stathis setting out her ideas. *See* Defs.' Exhs., at Exh. 5. In this letter, Collins set out the idea of an alienated "slacker" who discovers under hypnosis that the woman he thinks is his mother is really his grandmother and that his real mother is a teenager who was bitten by a vampire when she was pregnant, giving him vampire traits, and who later becomes a vampire after being shot and killed by cops. *See id.* Collins states in the letter that she is considering the titles *Dhampire, Dhampir, Vampire X, Bleake* and *Ghaunt*. *See id.*

On October 2, 1994, Collins forwarded a formal proposal for the work to Stathis. *See* Collins Decl. at P 6. After DC Comics approved the project, Collins created a scene by scene breakdown, and then a script, from her home in Denver, Colorado. *See id.* at PP 6-7. Up until July 1996, Collins worked with Stathis, the editor on the project, although she claims that his role "consisted mainly of fixing and tightening language and improving the flow of the narrative" and that he did not provide her with story ideas or reference materials. *See id.* at P 7. In July of 1996, when Stathis became ill and Alonso took over, the script and most of the artwork had been completed. *See* Collins Decl. at P 7.

DC Comics asked Lee to provide the painted art for *Dhampire* in January 1996. *See* Lee Decl., at P 4. Lee created character sketches based on written descriptions of the characters and a written synopsis of the story that Stathis had provided, as well as photographs that he took of models. *See id.* After DC Comics approved his character sketches, they sent him scene-by-scene breakdowns, from which he created thumbnail sketches. *See id.* Once these sketches were approved, he painted each of the panels in the work. *See id.* Lee claims never to have seen *Matchsticks* prior to this litigation. *See id.* at P 5.

Toward the end of 1994, after Collins submitted to DC Comics the formal proposal for the "one-shot" issue of *Dhampire*, Stathis asked Collins whether she would be interested in developing the graphic novel into a monthly series. *See* Deposition of Nancy Collins, dated July 8, 1998 ("Collins 7/8/98 dep."), Exhibit D to Iovieno Decl., at 6-7. During the next four to six weeks, Collins prepared plot outlines for three or four "story arcs," each of which would result in three or four issues. In these outlines, Gaunt is drawn deeper and deeper into the world of vampires, eventually killing the Iscariot and Natalie. *See id.* at 11; Defs.' Exhs., at Exh. I. After a script for issue two was completed and some artwork for the second issue was drawn, DC Comics canceled the series. *See* Collins 7/8/98 Dep., at 32-34.

III. Discussion

A. Copyright Infringement

To establish a claim of copyright infringement, a plaintiff must prove: "(1) ownership of a valid copyright, and (2) copying of constituent elements of the work that are original." *Feist Publications, Inc. v. Rural Telephone Service Co., Inc.*, 499 U.S. 340, 361, 113 L. Ed. 2d 358, 111 S. Ct. 1282 (1991). Because defendants, for the purpose of this motion, have not contested plaintiffs' ownership of a valid copyright, only the second element is at issue.

Copying may be established "either by direct evidence of copying or by indirect evidence, including access to the copyrighted work, similarities that are probative of copying between the works, and expert testimony." *Castle Rock Entertainment, Inc. v. Carol Pub. Group, Inc.*, 150 F.3d 132, 137 (2d Cir. 1998) (citing *Laureyssens v. Idea Group,*

Inc., 964 F.2d 131, 140 (2d Cir. 1992). The level of similarity needed to establish copying is now commonly referred to as "probative similarity." *See id.; Repp v. Webber*, 132 F.3d 882, 889 n.1 (2d Cir. 1997), *cert. denied*, 142 L. Ed. 2d 40, 119 S. Ct. 52 (1998). Once copying has been established, a plaintiff must next demonstrate that the copying was unlawful by showing that there is a substantial similarity between the protectible elements in the two works. *See Castle Rock*, 150 F.3d at 137; *Williams v. Crichton*, 84 F.3d 581, 587 (2d Cir. 1996).

1. Access

Defendants argue that plaintiffs cannot prove that Collins and Lee, creators of *Dhampire*, ever had access to *Matchsticks*. Both Collins and Lee have submitted declarations stating that they never saw *Matchsticks* until the instigation of this lawsuit. *See* Collins Decl. at P 8; Lee Decl. at P 6. Alonso also submitted a declaration stating that he never provided *Matchsticks* to Collins, Lee or Stathis, and never discussed the work with any of them. *See* Alonso Decl., at P 5.

The editor of *Dhampire*, however, was Lou Stathis, and Alonso, the person at DC Comics to whom Hogan sent *Matchsticks*, was Stathis' assistant during the time that *Dhampire* was created. Alsonso also took over as editor of *Dhampire* after Stathis became ill and is listed as the assistant editor on the work. Moreover, Collins was in contact with Stathis and Alonso over the telephone during the time that she was writing the *Dhampire* script. *See* Deposition of Nancy A. Collins, dated November 13, 1997 ("Collins 11/13/97 Dep."), at 105-08. These facts are sufficient to show a reasonable possibility" of access to *Matchsticks* and, therefore, to place the issue in dispute. *See Sylvestre v. Oswald*, 1993 U.S. Dist. LEXIS 7002, *8, 91 Civ. 5060, 1993 WL 179101, at *3 (S.D.N.Y. May 18, 1993) ("access generally needs to be proved by showing a particular chain of events or 'link' by which the alleged infringer might have gained access to the work"); *Gaste v. Kaiserman*, 863 F.2d 1061, 1067 (2d Cir. 1988) ("access through third parties connected to both a plaintiff and a defendant may be sufficient to prove a defendant's access to a plaintiff's work").

2. Substantial Similarity

It is beyond dispute that copyright protection extends only to the expression of ideas, and not to the ideas themselves. *Williams*, 84

F.3d at 587; *Kregos v. Associated Press*, 3 F.3d 656, 663 (2d Cir. 1993). In applying this often difficult distinction between ideas and expression, courts have frequently looked to the formulation set forth by Judge Learned Hand:

> Upon any work. . .a great number of patterns of increasing generality will fit equally well, as more and more of the incident is left out. The last may perhaps be no more than the most general statement of what the [work] is about, and at times might consist only of its title; but there is a point in this series of abstractions where they are no longer protected, since otherwise the [author] could prevent the use of his "ideas," to which, apart from their expression, his property is never extended.

Nichols v. Universal Pictures Corp., 45 F.2d 119, 121 (2d Cir. 1930); *Warner Bros. Inc. v. American Broadcasting Companies, Inc.*, 654 F.2d 204, 208 (2d Cir. 1981) ("*Warner I*"); *see also* Z. Chafee, *Reflections on the Law of Copyright*, 45 Colum. L. Rev. 503, 515 (1945) ("the line [lies] somewhere between the author's idea and the precise form in which he wrote it down . . .protection covers the 'pattern' of the work. . .the sequence of events, and the development of the interplay of characters").

Similarly, "scenes a faire," which have been described as "scenes that necessarily result from the choice of a setting or situation," *Walker v. Time Life Films, Inc.*, 784 F.2d 44, 50 (2d Cir. 1986), "incidents, characters or settings which are as a practical matter indispensable, or at least standard, in the treatment of a given topic," *Hoehling v. Universal City Studios, Inc.*, 618 F.2d 972, 979 (2d Cir. 1980), and "thematic concepts. . .which necessarily must follow from certain plot situations," *Reyher v. Children's Television Workshop*, 533 F.2d 87, 91 (2d Cir. 1976), are not entitled to copyright protection. *See generally* 3 Melville B. Nimmer & David Nimmer, Nimmer on Copyright § 13.03[B][4], at 13-71 to -73 (1998). For example, the Second Circuit has found the following elements to be non-protectible scenes a faire: "drunks, prostitutes, vermin and derelict cars" in a depiction of policemen in the South Bronx, *Walker*, 784 F.2d at 50, and "electrified fences, automated tours, dinosaur nurseries, and uniformed workers" in a story about a dinosaur zoo, *Williams*, 84 F.3d at 589.

Thus, in comparing two works a court must determine "whether the similarities shared by the works are something more than mere generalized idea[s] or themes." *Walker*, 784 F.2d at 48-49 (citing *Warner I*, 654 F.2d at 208). The works must share a similarity of expression, such as "similarities of treatment, details, scenes, events and characterization," *Reyher*, 533 F.2d at 91, or a similarity in their "total concept and feel." *Williams*, 84 F.3d at 589. [3]

3 The Second Circuit has stated that looking at the total "look and feel" of a work is particularly appropriate in an action involving children's works. *Williams*, 84 F.3d at 589. Although the works at issue here are aimed at young adults, the same principal would appear equally applicable, as comic books generally lack the complexity in plot and character of adult works such as novels.

In determining whether two works are substantially similar, courts in this circuit have applied the "ordinary observer test" and asked "whether an average lay observer would recognize the alleged copy as having been appropriated from the copyrighted work." *Warner I*, 654 F.2d at 208 (citing *Ideal Toy Corp. v. Fab-Lu Ltd.*, 360 F.2d 1021, 1022 (2d Cir. 1966)). Where a work contains elements that are both protectible and non-protectible, this analysis has been described as the discerning ordinary observer test. *See Williams*, 84 F.3d at 588; *Knitwaves, Inc. v. Lollytogs Ltd. (Inc.)*, 71 F.3d 996, 1002 (2d Cir. 1995). Pursuant to this test, a court must "attempt to extract the unprotectible elements from [its] consideration and ask whether the protectible elements, standing alone, are substantially similar." *Knitwaves*, 71 F.3d at 1002; *Williams*, 84 F.3d at 588. Even when two works are dissimilar in many respects, substantial similarity between them may still be found where their similarities are important in the overall context, whether qualitatively or quantitatively. *See Williams*, 84 F.3d at 588.

Even in applying the ordinary observer or discerning ordinary observer test, however, a court must examine the "total concept and feel" of the work. *Knitwaves*, 71 F.3d at 1003. Moreover, even a compilation of unprotectible elements may enjoy copyright protection when those elements are arranged in an original manner. *See id.* at 1003-04 (quoting *Feist*, 499 U.S. at 362); *Softel, Inc. v. Dragon*

Medical and Scientific Communications, Inc., 118 F.3d 955, 964 (2d Cir. 1997).

In determining whether characters are similar, a court looks at the "'totality of [the characters'] attributes and traits' as well as the extent to which the defendants' characters capture the 'total concept and feel' of figures in [plaintiff's work]." *Walker*, 784 F.2d at 50 (quoting *Warner Bros. v. American Broadcasting Co.*, 720 F.2d 231, 241 (2d Cir. 1983) ("*Warner II*")). The Second Circuit has provided the following guidance in the analysis of whether one character infringes another:

> what the character thinks, feels, says and does and the descriptions conveyed by the author through the comments of other characters in the work episodically fill out a viewer's understanding of the character. At the same time, the visual perception of the character tends to create a dominant impression against which the similarity of a defendant's character may be readily compared, and significant differences readily noted.

> Ultimately, care must be taken to draw the elusive distinction between a substantially similar character that infringes a copyrighted character despite slight differences in appearance, behavior, or traits, and a somewhat similar though non-infringing character whose appearance, behavior, or traits, and especially their combination, significantly differ from those of a copyrighted character, even though the second character is reminiscent of the first one.

Warner II, 720 F.2d at 241-42.

A stock character or basic character type, however, is not entitled to copyright protection. *Robinson v. Viacom Intel, Inc.*, 93 Civ. 2539, 1995 WL 417076, at *9 (S.D.N.Y. Jan. 4, 1995); *Sinicola v. Warner Bros.*, 948 F. Supp. 1176, 1185 (E.D.N.Y. 1996). "No character infringement claim can succeed unless plaintiff's original conception sufficiently developed the character, and defendants have copied this development and not merely the broader outlines." *Smith v. Weinstein*, 578 F. Supp. 1297, 1303, *aff'd mem.*, 738 F.2d 419 (2d Cir. 1984); *see also Nichols*, 45 F.2d at 121 ("the less developed the characters, the less they can be copyrighted; that is the penalty an author must bear for marking them too indistinctly").

Substantial similarity is generally a question of fact for a jury. *See Hoehling*, 618 F.2d at 977. Summary judgment is appropriate on this issue, however, where "the similarity concerns only noncopyrightable elements of plaintiff [sic] work or no reasonable trier of fact could find the works substantially similar." *Williams*, 84 F.3d at 587 (quoting *Walker*, 784 F.2d at 48).

3. Comparison of the works

Plaintiffs assert that *Matchsticks* and *Dhampire* share the following elements: (1) both works contain a half-human, half-vampire main character named Nicholas Gaunt, who is a young white male with "pale skin, a medium build, dark and tired eyes, dark hair that is scraggly, short and unkempt"; (2) both characters seek to uncover the truth about their origins and both learn about their origins through flashbacks or memories; (3) both characters are faced with the choice of pursuing good or evil; (4) both characters are indoctrinated into the forces of evil by killing; (5) both characters have a "sinister genealogy"; (6) both characters have a developing romance; (7) both works use similar imagery, such as religious symbolism, biblical allusions and the use of doors to see into the past; and (8) both works have a "macabre" feel, including scary characters and dark, haunted scenes.

Most of these similarities, however, are unprotectible ideas and themes that do not represent any original elements of plaintiffs' work. The two works share a similar basic underlying idea: they both involve a half-vampire character who is on a quest that leads him to discover his origins. Almost all of the remaining similarities between the works are unprotectible themes and concepts that flow predictably from this idea. A half-vampire, half-human character would necessarily have a "sinister genealogy." The quest of a half-vampire who is searching for his origins would predictably involve a struggle and ultimate choice between good and evil, as the very essence of the character and the story is that such character has a "dual nature," and the use of flashback or memory is the most logical way to portray events from that character's past. The fact that the characters become indoctrinated into the forces of evil by killing is a similarly unprotectible theme that is not uncommon to horror or science fiction literature.

Although all of these components are unoriginal, and therefore, unprotectible elements, plaintiffs could still prevail on a claim for copyright infringement if the way in which the two works express these ideas is substantially similar or these elements have been combined in an original way. *See Walker,* 784 F.2d at 50 (scenes a faire copyrightable only to extent they are "given unique. . .expression"). After a careful examination of the works, however, I find that the differences in plaintiffs' and defendants' treatment of these ideas, including the differences in their total look and feel, the interactions of the characters and the plot are so pronounced, that no reasonable jury could find that the works are substantially similar.

a. Setting, "total concept and feel"

Plaintiffs are correct that both works have a "macabre feel," involving dark scenes, scary characters and violence. The works are extremely different however, in their setting and "total concept and feel." *Matchsticks* is a black-and-white comic book set in the year 2017, which is portrayed as a dark fantasy world. The artwork is crude and scratchy and has an "underground" look to it, and the tone is irreverent and, at times, sarcastic and angry. The work is inhabited by strange futuristic characters, such as Maxwell Niphe and Inquisitor Hargroves, some of whom have technology incorporated into their bodies or wear robot-like armor. The work skips quickly among multiple story lines and subplots involving these different characters, shifting to and from Gaunt, members of the Church Group at St. Patrick's Cathedral, Fenris' home at the Asgard Estate, and Maxwell Niphe at his unidentified lair. The work appears to incorporate inside jokes and hidden symbolism and is quite difficult to understand on a first reading.

Dhampire, in contrast, is a color painted graphic novel that presents a world that is much more realistic. It is set in the present day, and the characters are realistically drawn; even the vampires look like real people who have sprouted fangs and pointed ears. The story is much more linear than the one in *Matchsticks,* and it focuses exclusively on Gaunt's present-day quest to find his father and flashbacks to Gaunt's childhood and his mother's past.

b. Characters

The most obvious similarity between the main characters in *Matchsticks* and *Dhampire* is that they share the same name: Nicholas Gaunt. This shared trait, by itself, is insufficient to establish substantial similarity between the characters. *See CK Co. v. Burger King*

Corp., 1994 U.S. Dist. LEXIS 13934, 92 Civ. 1488, 1994 WL 533253, at *8 (S.D.N.Y. Sept. 30, 1994), *aff'd*, 122 F.3d 1055 (2d Cir. 1995). It is, however, a significant similarity. In addition, both Gaunts are half-vampire and half-human. [4] This characteristic is clearly a non-protectible idea that is in the public domain. [5] In addition, the way in which the two Gaunts become half-vampires is different in the two works. *Dhampire*'s Gaunt has vampire characteristics because his mother was bitten by a vampire when she was pregnant. *Matchstick*'s Gaunt, in contrast, has a vampire father and, according to plaintiffs, contains latent vampire genes.

4 Defendants contend that there is nothing in *Matchsticks* to indicate that Gaunt is half-vampire. Although there is no explicit statement to that effect anywhere in the work, the story suggests in multiple places that Gaunt is the son of Fenris, who by all accounts appears to be some sort of vampire. Although no mention is made of Gaunt's mother, it is a reasonable inference that Gaunt is a half-vampire.

5 According to Slavonic folklore, a dhampire was the product of a union between a vampire and his widow. Such dhampires were effective in detecting and destroying their vampire families and often made a living as vampire slayers. *See* Collins Decl. at P 13; Defs' Exhs., at Exh. 8. This idea has been expressed in popular culture as well. For example, in 1973, Marvel Comics' *Tomb of Dracula* introduced the comic book character Blade, who is a half-human, half-vampire vampire hunter; Blade starred in his own comic book series from July 1994 to April 1995. *See* Collins Decl., at P 13; Reply Declaration of Nancy A. Collins in Further Support of Defendants' Motion for Summary Judgment, at P 2, Exhs. A, B attached thereto. In addition, prior to the events in this lawsuit, Collins, the author of *Dhampire*, completed work on a novel containing a character named Jen, who was a half-human, half-vampire who acquired his vampire traits because his pregnant mother was bitten by a vampire. *See* Collins Decl., at P 3.

Both characters are white males who appear to be in their early twenties. Both have thin-to-medium builds, pale skin, dark messy hair and a slovenly appearance. Despite these similarities, which are characteristics common to a great many "Generation X" post-adolescents, the two characters are drawn quite differently. Plaintiffs' Gaunt, although he changes somewhat from scene to scene, has an oval face with a long nose; his hair is usually pictured as a bushy clump on the side of his head, and he wears a jacket with a large collar with a box-like pattern and similar cuffs. Defendants' Gaunt has a heart-shaped, angular face, with pronounced cheekbones and hair that hangs in long strands down the sides of his face and comes to a widow's peak in the middle of his forehead; he has tattoos on both arms and usually wears a black leather motorcycle jacket.

The interactions between the characters are also quite different. Defendants' character has a clinical relationship with a psychiatrist who attempts to help him, a troubled relationship with the woman he thought was his mother and who resented having to raise him, and a romantic relationship with Tanith, who accompanies him on his quest. Unlike plaintiffs' character, he has no contact with his biological father and minimal interaction with his vampire father.

Plaintiffs' character, in contrast, interacts on a personal, human level only with Stanz, the man who raised him after the death of his mother, and despite plaintiffs' assertion to the contrary, experiences no romantic relationships. The work is filled with strange characters, such as the several-thousand-year-old Maxwell Niphe, and the seemingly evil Inquisitor Hargroves. Gaunt has no interaction with many of these characters; the extent of his relationship with the remainder is that they attempt to kill or capture him.

c. Sequence of events, plot

In addition, the sequence of events of the characters' discovery of their origins is very different. Sent a note and a key to a hotel room at the beginning of *Matchsticks*, plaintiff's character is thrown into a mystery, and he uncovers the truth about his heritage and takes the steps necessary to becoming a vampire through the attempts of Fenris, his father, to kill or capture him. At first, Fenris sends Kat to kill Gaunt; it is through Gaunt's killing Kat that his memories about the murder of his mother and uncle are triggered and he is inspired to go to Albany, his home town. Gaunt never expresses any doubts about his own identity or familial origins; he appears to be motivated by the desire to find out the identity of the person who murdered his mother and uncle and who sent Kat to kill him in turn. While Gaunt is in Albany, Zodiac, who is also allied with Fenris, also attempts to kill him. This event causes Gaunt to visit Stanz's house, where he again experiences memories from his childhood and engages in a confrontation with members of the Inquisition Group. Gaunt finally learns that Fenris is his father after Fenris dispatches Sharkey and

Angel to capture him. Gaunt engages in a violent confrontation with Fenris, with each displaying their martial arts abilities, that ends with Gaunt killing Fenris and vowing never to join him.

In *Dhampire*, by contrast, Gaunt is not pursued by anyone. He is obviously depressed, alienated and suicidal; the focus of the work is his quest to uncover the root of psychological problems, which he discovers is due to his vampire genealogy. Gaunt is motivated to discover the truth about his past after being convinced to undergo hypnosis by a psychiatrist who believes that the source of his despair lies in his past. Gaunt searches out the woman he believes is his mother, who reveals that Natalie is his real mother. Tanith suggests that Gaunt travel to the town where he was born; visiting a graveyard in that town, Gaunt encounters the **undead** Natalie, who reveals his true history and identity and later tells him that he can choose whether to become one of the **undead**. Unlike plaintiffs' character, who kills when attacked or captured by his father and his creatures, defendants' character kills innocent people in order to purposefully become a full-fledged vampire.

d. Other elements

Finally, plaintiffs point to other similar elements between the works. The use of imagery of blood, religious symbolism such as crosses and allusions to the bible are unprotectible scenes a faire without which any vampire work would be incomplete. *Dhampire* utilizes this religious imagery in a minor way: a character uses a cross to scare away a vampire -- a standard use of such image in vampire lore -- and the name of Gaunt's birthplace is Bethlehem. *Matchsticks*, in contrast, has a subtext of anti-religious imagery and phrases running through the work that could be read as an attack on organized religion. For example, the Inquisition Group reads as a sinister parody of the Catholic Church, dispatching violent warriors around the world to kill and wreck havoc. [6]

6 In one scene, for example, members of the Inquisition Group's Swiss Armour Guard discuss how they "rolled over Bosnia" slaughtering "blood and souls for the mother church," with the "s" in "souls" depicted as a dollar sign. In another scene, a scantily clad woman in a nun's habit performs torture on an altar boy; she wears a belt that says "Souvenir of the Brides of Christ Wedding Chapel."

Finally, plaintiffs point to a few remaining similar elements, such as the use of the symbolism of doors. These remaining features, however, amount to no more than "random similarities" between the works and are of little importance in the works. *See Williams*, 84 F.3d at 590;

Because the similarities between *Matchsticks* and *Dhampire* relate only to unprotectible ideas and scenes a faire, and the similarities in their expression are so greatly outweighed by their differences, I find that no reasonable trier of fact could find the works substantially similar. *See Arden v. Columbia Pictures Inds., Inc.*, 908 F. Supp. 1248 (S.D.N.Y. 1995) (summary judgment appropriate where two works telling the story of man trapped in a repeating day not substantially similar); *Robinson*, 1995 WL 417076, at *11 (no substantial similarity between two works about the interplay between a contemporary family and a 1950s era television family); *Denker v. Uhry*, 820 F. Supp. 722 (S.D.N.Y. 1992), *aff'd*, 996 F.2d 301 (2d Cir. 1993) (no substantial similarity between two works about an elderly white Jewish person requiring the assistance of a black helper who is initially disliked and later becomes a friend); *Reyher*, 533 F.2d at 93 (summary judgment appropriate because idea of lost child describing mother as most beautiful woman in the world and then reuniting with mother, who is actually unattractive, not expressed in substantially similar manner in two children's works); *cf. Lone Wolf McQuade Assoc. v. CBS Inc.*, 961 F. Supp. 587 (S.D.N.Y. 1997) (reasonable jury could conclude that characters with numerous similarities are substantially similar); *Twentieth Century-Fox Film Corp. v. MCA, Inc.*, 715 F.2d 1327 (9th Cir. 1983) (material issue of fact as to whether expression of plaintiff's ideas was copied).

B. Misappropriation

Plaintiffs claim that defendants misappropriated their novel idea for a comic book "which has been entirely devoted to a main character who is half-human, half-vampire and the particular struggles and the specific problems presented by this dual nature," in particular a character who lacks knowledge about his identity, is driven to discover his past, and struggles between good and evil. New York courts recognize claims for misappropriation of ideas where the following conditions are satisfied: (1) the requisite legal relationship exists between the parties and (2) the idea is novel and concrete. *See McGhan v. Ebersol*, 608 F. Supp. 277, 284 (S.D.N.Y. 1985).

The test for novelty is a stringent one: the idea must "show genuine novelty and invention, and not merely a clever or useful adaptation of existing knowledge." *Paul v. Haley*, 183 A.D.2d 44, 588 N.Y.S.2d 897, 903 (2d Dep't 1992); *Murray v. National Broadcasting Co., Inc.*, 844 F.2d 988 (2d Cir. 1988) (idea for a sitcom involving an intact, nonstereotypical African-American family not novel even though such idea had never been portrayed on television before). Even where an idea is novel, however, a misappropriation claim will be defeated if a defendant can show that she independently created the idea. *See Paul*, 588 N.Y.S.2d at 905; *AEB & Assocs. Design Group, Inc. v. Tonka Corp.*, 853 F. Supp. 724, 734 (S.D.N.Y. 1994) (no recovery where party "arrived on its own initiative or by wholly independent means at a concept similar to that devised by the party seeking recovery"); *McGhan*, 608 F. Supp. at 286 (plaintiff cannot claim an idea is novel if defendant has already used the idea).

Defendants have effectively rebutted the presumption that they misappropriated plaintiffs' idea for a comic book centered around the struggles of a half-vampire, half-human character who is driven to understand his origins and struggles between good and evil. Collins filed a declaration that she originally discussed the idea of creating a graphic painted novel with a Gothic feel centered around a half-vampire character with Stathis in June of 1994. *See* Collins Decl. at P 3; Collins 11/13/97 Dep. Defendants have submitted excerpts from a novel Collins authored prior to that time, which features a dhampire character who gained his vampire traits after his mother was bitten by a vampire while he was in utero and who served as the inspiration for Gaunt in *Dhampire*. Defs.' Exhs., at Exh. 2; Collins Decl. at P 3. In addition, defendants have submitted a draft of a letter dated June 25, 1994, that Collins wrote to Stathis, in which she sets out her ideas for *Dhampire*: a story of an "alienated, death-obsessed Generation X slacker" who discovers under hypnosis that his mother is really his grandmother and his mother was a teenager bitten by a vampire while she was pregnant, giving him vampire traits, and who ends up becoming a killer, being shot by cops and then coming back as a vampire. All of these events happened prior to August 1994, the earliest time that Hogan could have contacted DC Comics. *See* Hogan Dep., at 119, 139, 142-44.

Thus, defendants have come forward with "convincing documentary evidence establishing independent creation" of the ideas contained in *Dhampire*. *cf. Langman Fabrics v. Graff Californiawear, Inc.*, 160 F.3d 106 (2d Cir. 1998) (defendant whose evidence of independent creation presented only "undocumented assertions" of persons associated with defendants failed to rebut plaintiff's prima facie case of copying).

IV. Conclusion

For the reasons set forth above, defendants' motion for summary judgment is granted. The clerk is directed to close the case.

So Ordered:

Shira A. Scheindlin

U.S.D.J.

Dated: New York, New York

January 25, 1998

AMERICAN AMUSEMENT MACHINE ASSOCIATION,
AMUSEMENT & MUSIC OPERATORS ASSOCIATION, INDIANA AMUSEMENT & MUSIC OPERATORS ASSOCIATION, SHAFFER DISTRIBUTING COMPANY, CLEVELAND COIN MACHINE EXCHANGE INC, NAMCO CYBERTAINMENT INC, B J NOVELTY INC. - FOR THEMSELVES AND AS REPRESENTATIVES OF A CLASS OF OWNERS, OPERATORS, DISTRIBUTORS AND MANUFACTURERS OF CURRENCY-OPERATED AMUSEMENT MACHINES, Plaintiffs,

vs.

COTTEY, JACK - FOR THEMSELVES IN THEIR OFFICIAL
CAPACITIES AS MARION COUNTY PROSECUTOR AND SHERIFF FOR MARION COUNTY, RESPECTIVELY, AND AS REPRESENTATIVES OF THE CLASS OF PERSONS EMPOWERED TO ENFORCE GENERAL ORDINANCE NO. 72,2000, PETERSON, BART, BARKER, JERRY L - FOR THEMSELVES, IN THEIR OFFICIAL CAPACITIES AS MAYOR AND CHIEF OF POLICE FOR THE CITY OF INDIANAPOLIS, RESPECTIVELY, AND AS REPRESENTATIVES OF THE CLASS OF PERSONS EMPOWERED TO ENFORCE GENERAL ORDINANCE NO. 72,2000, KENDRICK, TERI, IN HER OFFICIAL CAPACITY AS THE DESIGNATED CITY PROSECUTOR OF THE CITY OF INDIANAPOLIS, Defendants.

CAUSE NO. IP 00-1321-C H/G

UNITED STATES DISTRICT COURT FOR THE SOUTHERN DISTRICT OF INDIANA, INDIANAPOLIS DIVISION

115 F. Supp. 2d 943
2000 U.S. Dist. LEXIS 15076

October 11, 2000, Decided

US DISTRICT COURT JUDGE DAVID F. HAMILTON

ENTRY ON MOTION FOR PRELIMINARY INJUNCTION

Introduction and Summary

The First Amendment does not prohibit states from restricting children's access to pornography even though adults' access to the same sexually explicit materials may not be restricted. See *Ginsberg v.*

New York, 390 U.S. 629, 20 L. Ed. 2d 195, 88 S. Ct. 1274 (1968). This case presents questions about the extension of this rule of First Amendment law to video games with images of graphic violence. Indianapolis General Ordinance No. 72-2000 restricts the display and operation of coin-operated amusement machines (primarily video games) deemed "harmful to minors" if they include either "strong sexual content" or "graphic violence," as those terms are defined more specifically in the Ordinance. Under the Ordinance, children may not play or watch such games without a parent's permission.

Plaintiffs are in the business of manufacturing, distributing, or displaying video games. They have no quarrel with the Ordinance's restriction on children's access to games with "strong sexual content." Plaintiffs contend, however, that the Ordinance's restrictions on games with "graphic violence" are content-based restrictions on speech that violate the First Amendment and that the Ordinance is unconstitutionally vague. Plaintiffs seek preliminary injunctive relief against its enforcement.

The first issue here is whether violent video games are forms of expression protected by the First Amendment at all. At this preliminary injunction stage of the case, the court concludes that at least some video games are expression entitled to First Amendment protection.

The second broad issue is whether a local government may restrict children's access to games with graphic violence, just as *Ginsberg* shows a government may restrict access to games with explicit sexual content. The court finds for several reasons that plaintiffs are unlikely to show that the Ordinance's restrictions on children's access to games with graphic violence violate the First Amendment. First, the City has shown that it has important and legitimate reasons to be concerned about violent video games causing harm to children. Second, the court is not persuaded there is any principled constitutional difference between sexually explicit material and graphic violence, at least when it comes to providing such material to children. Third, the Ordinance is carefully tailored to address the potential harm to children without infringing upon other First Amendment interests. The Ordinance does not bar or significantly limit adults from using the games in question, it does not engage in viewpoint discrimination, it does not limit the expression of ideas or other messages, and it authorizes only civil enforcement mechanisms.

In short, the Ordinance reflects a careful, reasonable, and limited extension of the principles applied in *Ginsberg* to protect children from pornography. The court also finds that plaintiffs are unlikely to prevail on their vagueness challenge to the Ordinance. The court therefore denies plaintiffs' motion for preliminary injunction. This entry sets forth the court's findings of fact and conclusions of law pursuant to Fed. R. Civ. P. 52 and 65.

Factual Background

I. *The Ordinance*

On July 10, 2000, the City-County Council of the City of Indianapolis and Marion County adopted General Ordinance No. 72 regarding the operation and display of currency-operated amusement machines ("video games"). The Ordinance restricts children's access to video games containing graphic violence or strong sexual content by regulating the establishments that offer video games to the public. [1]

---

1 The full text of Ordinance 72, including the preamble, is set forth in the attached Exhibit A.

For constitutional purposes, the most important parts of the Ordinance are the definitions for games that are "harmful to minors." Those definitions trigger the substantive prohibitions of the Ordinance on the display of such games:

> *Harmful to minors* means an amusement machine that predominantly appeals to minors' morbid interest in violence or minors' prurient interest in sex, is patently offensive to prevailing standards in the adult community as a whole with respect to what is suitable material for persons under the age of eighteen (18) years, lacks serious literary, artistic, political or scientific value as a whole for persons under the age of eighteen (18) years, and:
>
> (1) Contains graphic violence; or
>
> (2) Contains strong sexual content.

Graphic violence means an amusement machine's visual depiction or representation of realistic serious injury to a human or human-like being where such serious injury includes amputation, decapitation, dismemberment, bloodshed, mutilation, maiming or disfiguration.

Strong sexual content means the visual depiction or representation by an amusement machine of nudity or explicit human sexual behavior by any human or human-like being in one or more of the following forms: masturbation; deviate sexual conduct; sexual intercourse; or, fondling of genitals.

Nudity means an amusement machine's visual depiction or representation of human male or female genitals, pubic area or buttocks with less than a fully opaque covering, or of a female breast with less than a fully opaque covering of any part of the nipple, or the showing of covered male genitals in a discernibly turgid state.

City-County General Ordinance No. 72-2000, amending Revised Code of the Consolidated City of Indianapolis and Marion County § 831-1. For purposes of the Ordinance, a minor is any unemancipated person under the age of 18. *Id.*

Section 831-5 of the City's Code, as amended by the Ordinance, sets forth the substantive prohibitions that apply to "registrants," who operate five or more video games in one location:

(h) It shall be unlawful for a registrant, a registrant's agent, or an employee of an amusement location knowingly to allow a minor who is not accompanied by the minor's parent, guardian or custodian to operate in the amusement location an amusement machine that is harmful to minors.

(i) It shall be unlawful for a registrant to operate an amusement location unless each amusement machine that is harmful to minors in the amusement location displays a conspicuous sign indicating that the machine may not be operated by a minor under eighteen (18) years of age unless the minor is accompanied by his or her parent, guardian, or custodian. If amusement machines that are harmful to minors are displayed together in an area separate from amusement machines that are not harmful, a single conspicuous sign in that area or at the entrance to that area may be used to mark the group of machines for purposes of this subsection.

(j) It shall be unlawful for a registrant to make available to patrons any amusement machine that is harmful to minors within ten (10) feet of an amusement machine that is not harmful. It shall further be unlawful for a registrant not to separate amusement machines that are harmful to minors from other machines by some form of partition, divider, drape, barrier, panel, screen, or wall that completely obstructs the view of persons outside the partitioned area of the playing surface or display screen of the machines that are harmful to minors. It shall be unlawful for a registrant, registrant's agent, or employee of an amusement location to allow a minor who is not accompanied by his or her parent, guardian, or custodian into the partitioned area. [2]

2 The three subsections of the Ordinance quoted in the text apply to "registrants," who are licensed operators of establishments with five or more games in one location. Parallel provisions apply to "exhibitors" of video games, who operate locations with four or fewer games. The principal distinction between "registrants" and "exhibitors" concerns the manner in which each type of establishment is required to organize and monitor the physical space where the games are displayed. See §§ 831-5(h)-(*l*), 831-6(f)-(i).

Violations of the Ordinance are punishable by civil fines under Section 103-3 of the Code. The minimum fine for a violation is $ 200. No more than one violation may be assessed on any one day. For multiple violations, a registrant or exhibitor may lose the right to make available to the public any machines that are "harmful to minors." The City may also suspend or revoke an amusement location's registration in some circumstances. See §§ 831-5(k)-(*l*), 831-6(i), 831-9.

The record includes an unusually extensive legislative history for a local ordinance. Councillor Rozelle Boyd introduced an early version of the Ordinance to the City-County Council on April 10, 2000, which was referred to the Rules and Public Policy Committee. Ex. P-61. At two meetings the Committee debated the proposal and heard extensive public comment from industry representatives and community interest groups. Exs. P-51, P-52. In addition, several reports on the subject of children and violence in the media were made available to the Committee members. Ex. P-64. In response to comments on the original proposal, the Committee made several substantive changes and sent the amended proposal to the full City-County Council. Ex. P-52. The Council passed the Ordinance on July 10, 2000, and the Mayor of Indianapolis signed the legislation on July 17, 2000. Ex. P-53. [3]

3 The Ordinance was to take effect on September 1, 2000. However, through an agreement reached between the parties after this action was filed, city officials agreed not to enforce the Ordinance until 24 hours after this court rules on plaintiffs' motion for a preliminary injunction.

The preamble to the Ordinance invokes the City's "compelling interests in protecting the well-being of minors, in protecting parents' authority to shield their minor children from influences that the parents find inappropriate or offensive, and in reducing juvenile crime." The preamble then sets forth the need for and purpose of the Ordinance by: (1) noting that "courts have recognized that minors are affected by and may be protected from patently offensive sex-related material;" (2) asserting that "recent academic literature corroborates the finding of earlier studies that violent video games produce psychological effects in minor children and that prolonged exposure to violent video games increases the likelihood of aggression in minor children," citing a particular study that also reviewed past research; (3) referring to "growing evidence of the harmful effects of violent video games" that had led Congress and the Federal Trade Commission to investigate such matters; (4) citing testimony before a congressional committee to the effect that fourth through eighth graders report spending an average of from half an hour to two and a half hours a week playing video games in arcades; and (5) asserting that parents are less able in public places than in the home to control the levels of violence and sexual content to which their children are exposed.

II. *Evidence about Video Games*

Coin-operated video games are an interactive form of entertainment. Each game is usually a stand-alone, self-contained machine consisting of both hardware and software. The player manipulates manual controls, such as guns, buttons, joy sticks, or steering wheels, in order to affect an imaginary computer-generated action sequence displayed on a screen. In the City's live demonstration at the hearing, the player participated in the action as a sniper firing an electronic rifle at "enemies" in a game called "Silent Scope 2." In a game called "Mortal

Kombat 3," the player controlled a martial arts fighter engaged in combat against computer-controlled opponents.

The record identifies six commonly recognized categories of video games: "action-adventure" games, puzzle games, sports games, driving games, fighting games, and shooting games. The categories are convenient but not exhaustive or mutually exclusive. Nearly all games contain some sort of scoring mechanism by which a player can measure his or her progress in the game and compare his or her playing skills to the skills of others. In a fighting game, the player might score points based on the time it takes to defeat an opponent or the difficulty level of the fighting match. In an action-adventure game, a player might score points by accomplishing a certain set of tasks in the face of various obstacles.

At the hearing on plaintiffs' motion for a preliminary injunction, an art director from a video game development company described the typical game development process. As one might imagine, a new video game begins as a creative concept in the minds of the game developers. Teams of artists draw sketches of the characters and create "story boards" that depict the action sequences of the game. The story line and themes of the game help guide the development of this "concept art." Computer programmers then take the concept art and create digital versions of the characters and the background scenes. The characters and scenes are then fully animated, and audio engineers add sound and music to the games.

The visual and audio presentation is meant to be interesting as well as informative in the sense that it provides cues that help guide the player through various stages of the game. Visual and audio effects are also used as "rewards" for skillful and successful play. In addition, when no one is playing the game, most video games operate in an "attract mode" -- essentially advertising themselves to prospective players. In the "attract mode," the screen may show excerpts from the game, give instructions as to how the game is played, or introduce the characters and story line incorporated into the game.

The plaintiffs' game development witness further testified that video games are continuously increasing in complexity. Many of today's games include three-dimensional simulated environments and full motion video similar to the technology used in computer-animated feature films. From beginning to end, the running time to complete a game can be eight hours or more. Further specifics about video games and the research about their effects are set forth in discussion of specific issues.

III. *The Parties*

The seven plaintiffs in this action seek to protect their own interests as well as the interests of a class of businesses whose interests would be similarly affected by enforcement of the challenged provisions of the Ordinance. (At this point no motion for class certification has been filed.) Plaintiffs Namco Cybertainment, Inc. and B.J. Novelty, Inc. own and operate amusement machines in the City of Indianapolis. The Ordinance directly regulates these two plaintiffs. Plaintiffs Shaffer Distributing Company and Cleveland Coin Machine Exchange, Inc. distribute entertainment machines in the City of Indianapolis. They seek to ensure that sales of their products are not hindered by the Ordinance. Plaintiffs American Amusement Machine Association, Amusement & Music Operators Association, and the Indiana Amusement & Music Operators Association are trade organizations seeking to protect the interests of members whose businesses are likely to be affected by the Ordinance.

Defendants in this action are various officials of the City of Indianapolis and Marion County who have responsibility for enforcement of the Ordinance. Defendant Bart Peterson is the Mayor of Indianapolis. Defendant Teri Kendrick is the designated city prosecutor. Defendant Jack Cottey is the Sheriff for Marion County, and defendant Jerry Barker is the Chief of Police of the Indianapolis Police Department. All named defendants have been sued only in their official capacities, and all are referred to collectively here as "the City."

Discussion

I. *The Issues and Claims*

The City wrote the Ordinance with a close eye on First Amendment issues and the prospect of a challenge like this one. The City contends first that video games simply are not a form of expression protected under the First Amendment. Several courts reached that conclusion with respect to earlier, less sophisticated video games in the early 1980s. Assuming that such games are protected at all under the First Amendment, the City in its drafting tried to follow the reasoning of *Ginsberg v. New York*, 390 U.S. 629, 20 L. Ed. 2d 195, 88 S. Ct. 1274 (1968), which upheld similar restrictions on children's access to pornography as reasonable measures to protect children from harm. The City contends there is no principled constitutional distinction between pornography and graphic violence, at least with respect to children. In writing the Ordinance, the City also made a careful and deliberate effort to take the standard for unprotected obscenity as to adults and to adapt it to graphic violence for children. See *Miller v. California*, 413 U.S. 15, 24, 37 L. Ed. 2d 419, 93 S. Ct. 2607 (1973).

Plaintiffs respond that video games, at least the more elaborate games now in circulation, qualify as protected expression under the First Amendment. Plaintiffs therefore contend the Ordinance is an unconstitutional content-based restriction on protected speech. Plaintiffs also claim that the rule of *Ginsberg v. New York* is limited to material of a sexual nature and that the Ordinance could be constitutional only if the City could show it uses the least restrictive possible means to serve a compelling governmental interest, which plaintiffs contend would require definitive proof that violent video games in fact cause harm to children. As a separate but related claim for injunctive relief, plaintiffs also contend that the Ordinance is unconstitutionally vague -- that it fails to provide the ordinary citizen with adequate notice of the prohibited conduct and fails to cabin the discretion of law enforcement personnel. II. *Preliminary Injunction Standard*

To obtain a preliminary injunction, plaintiffs must show (1) a reasonable likelihood of success on the merits, (2) irreparable harm if the preliminary injunction is denied, and (3) the inadequacy of any remedy at law. See *Grossbaum v. Indianapolis-Marion County Building Auth.*, 100 F.3d 1287, 1291 (7th Cir. 1996). If this threshold showing is made, the court balances the harm to plaintiffs if the preliminary injunction is wrongly denied against the harm to the defendant if the injunction is wrongly granted. In the final step of the equitable analysis, the court must consider the public interest by weighing the effect that either granting or denying the injunction will have on nonparties. See *Grossbaum*, 100 F.3d at 1291; *Erickson v. Trinity Theatre, Inc.*, 13 F.3d 1061, 1067 (7th Cir. 1994); *Abbott Laboratories v. Mead*

Johnson & Co., 971 F.2d 6, 12 (7th Cir. 1992); *Roland Machinery Co. v. Dresser Industries, Inc.*, 749 F.2d 380, 386-88 (7th Cir. 1984).

Where plaintiffs assert a violation of their free speech rights, such claims ordinarily satisfy at least the minimum requirements for irreparable harm and inadequacy of legal remedies. As in most free speech cases, therefore, if plaintiffs could show they were likely to prevail on their constitutional claims, they would be entitled to a preliminary injunction.

III. *Video Games as Protected Expression*

The threshold issue is whether video games are forms of expression entitled to any protection at all under the First Amendment. In the early 1980s, most courts examining the issue concluded that the video games of that era were not protected by the First Amendment. See, *e.g., America's Best Family Showplace Corp. v. City of New York*, 536 F. Supp. 170, 173-74 (E.D.N.Y. 1982) (finding that video games were "pure entertainment" not protected by the First Amendment because there was no "element of information or some idea being communicated"); *Malden Amusement Co. v. City of Malden*, 582 F. Supp. 297, 299 (D. Mass. 1983) (adopting *America's Best* analysis); *Marshfield Family Skateland, Inc. v. Town of Marshfield*, 389 Mass. 436, 450 N.E.2d 605, 609-10 (Mass. 1983) (rejecting First Amendment challenge to town's total prohibition on coin-activated amusement devices; court considered evidence of "Ms. Pac-Man," "Tron," "Donkey Kong," "Zaxxon," and "Kangaroo"), *appeal dismissed*, 464 U.S. 987, 78 L. Ed. 2d 675, 104 S. Ct. 475 (1983); *Caswell v. Licensing Comm'n*, 387 Mass. 864, 444 N.E.2d 922, 926-27 (Mass. 1983) (finding no First Amendment protection for video games where city denied license for automatic amusement devices; court considered evidence of "Space Invaders"); *City of Warren v. Walker*, 135 Mich. App. 267, 354 N.W.2d 312, 316-17 (Mich. App. 1984) (holding that ordinance restricting children under age 17 from playing video games did not violate First Amendment).

The reasoning of the Supreme Judicial Court of Massachusetts reflects these courts' approaches to the relatively new medium in the 1980s. In 1983, the Massachusetts court stated:

> From the record before us, it appears that any communication or expression of ideas that occurs during the playing of a video game is purely inconsequential. Caswell has succeeded in establishing only that video games are more technologically advanced games than pinball or chess. That technological advancement alone, however, does not impart First Amendment status to what is an otherwise unprotected game.

Caswell, 444 N.E.2d at 927 (rejecting analogies to movies and television as entertainment).

However, these courts in the 1980s did not foreclose the possibility that further development of video games might transform them into a medium of protected expression. Later in the same year, the Massachusetts court re-examined and followed *Caswell*, but also emphasized that Caswell's result was fact-sensitive and not intended to foreclose all debate on the issue of video games as speech. The court cautioned: "We recognize that in the future video games which contain sufficient communicative and expressive elements may be created." *Marshfield Family Skateland*, 450 N.E.2d at 609-10; see also *Tommy & Tina Inc. v. Department of Consumer Affairs*, 117 Misc. 2d 415, 459 N.Y.S.2d 220, 226-27 (N.Y. Sup. Ct. 1983) (finding that video games considered in the case were not speech but leaving open the possibility that "games . . . of a different nature" may be entitled to First Amendment protection), *aff'd*, 95 A.D.2d 724, 464 N.Y.S.2d 132 (N.Y. App. Div. 1983), *aff'd mem.*, 62 N.Y.2d 671, 476 N.Y.S.2d 290, 464 N.E.2d 988 (N.Y. 1984).

It appears that few courts squarely addressed the issue during the 1990s, which was a period of substantial innovation in the video game industry. In 1991 the Seventh Circuit upheld a local ordinance that prohibited minors from playing video games during school hours. The court declined to decide whether video games are protected by the First Amendment and commented:

> On the basis of the complaint alone, we cannot tell whether the video games at issue here are simply modern day pinball machines or whether they are more sophisticated presentations involving storyline and plot that convey to the user a significant artistic message protected by the first amendment. Nor is it clear whether these games may be considered works of art. To hold on this record that *all* video games -- no matter what their content -- are *completely* devoid of artistic value would require us to make an assumption

entirely unsupported by the record and *perhaps* totally at odds with reality.

Rothner v. City of Chicago, 929 F.2d 297, 303 (7th Cir. 1991) (emphasis in original). In *Rothner* the court assumed for purposes of its decision that the games might have included protected expression. The court then found that the ordinance still amounted to a reasonable restriction on the time, place, and manner of expression. See *id.* Whether video games can be protected speech remains undecided in the Seventh Circuit and apparently in other circuits as well. See *Miller v. City of South Bend*, 904 F.2d 1081, 1098-99 (7th Cir. 1990) (*en banc*) (Posner, J., concurring) (suggesting that video games fall in a "gray area" and that government has a greater scope for regulation in this area which may be outside the boundaries of the First Amendment), *rev'd sub nom. Barnes v. Glen Theatre, Inc.*, 501 U.S. 560, 115 L. Ed. 2d 504, 111 S. Ct. 2456 (1991).

Plaintiffs in this case argue that the once-predicted future of video games has arrived, that the video games of the year 2000 have gone far beyond the simple displays in "Space Invaders" and "Pac-Man," and that many of today's games are highly interactive versions of movies and storybooks, replete with digital art, music, complex plots, and character development. The City argues that the limitations of the early medium have not been transcended and that, fundamentally, video games are still most closely analogous to mechanical pinball machines or shooting galleries at a local fair.

As a general matter, video games will be protected under the First Amendment only if they include sufficient communicative, expressive, or informative elements to fall at least within the outer limits of constitutionally protected speech. The Supreme Court has never articulated a precise test for determining how the First Amendment protects a given form of expression. Instead, the Court has stated generally: "Each medium of expression . . . must be assessed for First Amendment purposes by standards suited to it, for each may present its own problems." *Southeastern Promotions, Ltd. v. Conrad*, 420 U.S. 546, 557, 43 L. Ed. 2d 448, 95 S. Ct. 1239 (1975); see also David B. Goroff, *The First Amendment Side Effects of Curing Pac-Man Fever*, 84 Colum. L. Rev. 744 (1984) (analyzing the medium and arguing that video games are entitled to First Amendment protection). Any given form of entertainment, activity, or interaction may or may not be protected under the First Amendment. Rather than using these labels, the court finds it more productive to discuss the actual evidence presented by the parties.

Plaintiffs' evidence about the expressive components of video games centered on the "Gauntlet" series of action-adventure video games. The series includes Gauntlet Legends and Gauntlet Legacy, which were both released within the last three years. These games are currency-operated "amusement machines" as that term is defined in the Ordinance.

The Gauntlet Legacy story line deals with a fantasy world consisting of eight "realms" and an "underworld." The eight realms are ruled by a powerful wizard named Sumner, while the underworld is ruled by the principal villain of the story, Skorne. In the background story, Sumner's younger brother, Garm, accidentally opened a portal between the eight realms and the underworld. Skorne and his forces used the portal to invade the eight realms and disrupt Sumner's peaceful rule. Vanquishing the forces of the underworld from each of the eight realms appears to be the goal of the game, and, as best as can be deciphered from the record, a player participates in the action as one of eight "heroes" who can assist Sumner in attempting to defeat the underworld's "eight great abominations." The players travel to each realm in search of "items of legend" that will assist them in their task to recover the keys to the underworld and eventually to defeat the forces of Skorne once and for all.

Plaintiffs did not demonstrate a video game from the Gauntlet series, and the court does not have any information about whether the series includes graphic violence or strong sexual content for purposes of the Ordinance. There is also some ambiguity as to how much of the detailed story line is actually communicated to the players and as to how this communication takes place. However, the City did not attempt to rebut plaintiffs' description of the action-adventure games.

Without any attempt to assess artistic merit, the court finds that the visual art and the description of the action-adventure games in the record support plaintiffs' contention that at least some video games contain protected expression. It is difficult for First Amendment purposes to find a meaningful distinction between the Gauntlet game's ability to communicate a story line and that of a movie, television show, book, or -- perhaps the best analogy -- a comic book.

Certainly the distinction cannot be simply that the game is interactive. The Internet is an interactive medium and receives First Amendment protection. See *Reno v. ACLU*, 521 U.S. 844, 868-69, 138 L. Ed. 2d 874, 117 S. Ct. 2329 (1997). Town hall meetings and some theatrical performances are interactive, and their expression is also protected. [4]

4 Some fantasy adventure books are also "interactive" in that the reader make choices at critical points in the narrative and then flips to a page where the story continues based on the reader's decision. Not all readers make the same choices, and they reach different endings -- similar to the different outcomes of the video games. Moreover, it is not difficult to imagine that a reader of a book based on Gauntlet's characters and its imaginary realms could have a discussion with an avid player of the Gauntlet video games about the plot and characters.

As a further indication that at least some video games contain protected forms of expression, it would be theoretically possible for a law to engage in "viewpoint discrimination" in regulating video games. One can imagine a law requiring that, in games involving conflict and/or combat of some type, the player not be associated with forces of evil, darkness, or authoritarianism. In the opening sequence of "Silent Scope 2," for example, the player adopts the role of a sniper whose mission is to shoot enemy "terrorists" in a scene set in London. The fact that it is possible even to consider a "viewpoint" of "good guys" and "bad guys" in these games is a significant indication that there are at least some aspects of plot and character that may be entitled to at least some degree of First Amendment protection. The City properly concedes as much. Tr. 105-06.

The City's evidence on the issue of video games as speech focused on fighting and shooting games, including a video tape containing edited footage from six games: "Ultimate Mortal Kombat 3," "Mace: The Dark Age," "Maximum Force," "Time Crisis II," "Silent Scope," and "The House of the Dead 2." See Ex. 17. At the hearing, the City asserted that the video games shown in Exhibit 17 contained "graphic violence" as defined by the Ordinance. See Tr. 52.

In the first two games on the video tape, the player attempts to help his character survive and win one-on-one combat by executing various fighting tactics. The characters engage in hand-to-hand combat and use an assortment of weapons. "Ultimate Mortal Kombat 3" displays spurts of blood as blows are landed, and it appears that the fights end when one of the combatants is finally killed.

The remaining four games on the City's video tape are shooting games played from the first person perspective. In these "first person shooter" games, the view displayed on the screen is the view through the eyes of a gun-carrying character that the player controls. Of these four games "The House of the Dead 2" is the most graphic. The "plot" in "The House of the Dead 2" is that a town has been over-run by zombie-like characters who have killed many of the town's inhabitants. The player adopts the persona of "James," who is responding to the emergency. The zombies are "**undead**" human figures who are already substantially decayed and disfigured when James encounters them. The zombies attack James. James responds by shooting them. When shot, the **undead** die again in dramatic fashion. In some cases, the chest cavity explodes in a shower of blood, ribs, and gore, while in other cases the target is decapitated. The court observed at least one character whose entire upper torso appeared to have been severed from the lower half of the figure. [5]

5 "The House of the Dead 2" displays a "Parental Advisory Warning" which informs the viewer: "This Game is Classified/Life-Like Violence/Strong." The rating is the product of a voluntary industry program. See Exs. P-68, P-69 (describing the rating system).

In "Silent Scope 2," a game the City demonstrated live at the hearing, the player shoots a mounted gun at designated targets. The game is another "first person shooter" game. In other words, the screen simulates the scene as viewed from the perspective of an actual sniper using a rifle with a scope. The plot aspects are minimal, though not non-existent. The game amounts to electronic target practice on images of people. [6]

6 The evidence indicates that some of the more violent games include switches and settings that the exhibitor and/or the player may adjust. For

example, "Silent Scope 2" was demonstrated on the "mild" violence setting, as it was found at an arcade. There is a suggestion that other games have off/on "gore" switches.

Based on the evidence in this record, the court finds that at least some contemporary video games include protected forms of expression. The court cannot deny a preliminary injunction based on the City's sweeping theory that video games simply do not fall within the scope of the First Amendment. The court has no difficulty determining that any speech elements of "Silent Scope 2," "The House of the Dead 2," and several of the other games described in the record are relatively inconsequential -- perhaps even so inconsequential as to remove the game from the protection of the First Amendment. However, at least some games are protected by the First Amendment.

The nature of the Ordinance itself also cuts against the City's suggestion that video games can never be an expressive medium. Courts in *America's Best, Caswell,* and *Rothner* dealt with either licensing ordinances or other regulations that applied to all video games as a monolithic class. In this case, the City has singled out certain games for regulation based on their content: either "strong sexual content" or depictions of "graphic violence." It would be incongruous to conclude both that video games can be meaningfully distinguished based on their sexual and/or violent content, and that video games as a medium completely lack the capacity to communicate any *other* message, idea, or feeling that falls within the protection offered by the First Amendment. Considering the content-based nature of the Ordinance, the possibility of viewpoint discrimination in the medium, and the unchallenged description of action-adventure games, the protected content of some video games goes beyond their "strong sexual content" or their depictions of "graphic violence."

In finding that video games may contain at least some expressive content protected by the First Amendment, the court does not mean to suggest that video games are essential vehicles of political speech or fine art. Not all protected expression lies at the core of the First Amendment. For example, in *Barnes v. Glen Theatre, Inc.,* the Supreme Court found that several earlier cases supported the conclusion that the "nude dancing of the kind sought to be performed here is expressive conduct within the outer perimeters of the First

Amendment, though we view it as only marginally so." 501 U.S. 560, 565-66, 111 S. Ct. 2456, 115 L. Ed. 2d 504 (1991) (plurality opinion); accord, *City of Erie v. Pap's A.M.*, 529 U.S. 277, 288, 120 S. Ct. 1382, 1391, 146 L. Ed. 2d 265 (2000) (plurality opinion). Thus, even if, as the City suggests, video games can be labeled "low value" speech, they are entitled to protection under the expansive reach of the First Amendment. The court cannot deny a preliminary injunction based on the City's sweeping theory that video games are not protected expression.

IV. *Regulating Children's Exposure to "Graphic Violence"*

The conclusion that at least some video games are protected by the First Amendment does not mean the City is powerless to regulate "graphic violence" in the games offered to children. The Constitution permits government to impose restrictions on speech in limited circumstances. Laws that arguably restrict speech are analyzed under a variety of First Amendment standards. Several can be rejected at the outset as inapplicable to the Indianapolis Ordinance.

First, the Ordinance does not regulate one of the categories of "unprotected" speech that the government has broad power to regulate as to adults. See *R.A.V. v. City of St. Paul*, 505 U.S. 377, 383-84, 120 L. Ed. 2d 305, 112 S. Ct. 2538 (1992) (identifying obscenity, fighting words, and defamation as types of speech government can regulate because of "their distinctively proscribable content"); *Brandenburg v. Ohio*, 395 U.S. 444, 447, 23 L. Ed. 2d 430, 89 S. Ct. 1827 (1969) (no protection for words that incite imminent lawless action).

Second, the City's asserted purpose in passing the Ordinance -- protecting children from exposure to games with graphic violence and strong sexual content -- makes it clear that the City is directly regulating the dissemination of this material and not merely the "secondary effects" that result from having video games physically located in certain neighborhoods. See *Reno v. ACLU*, 521 U.S. 844, 867-68, 138 L. Ed. 2d 874, 117 S. Ct. 2329 (1997) (making this distinction in regard to regulation of offensive speech on the Internet); cf. *City of Renton v. Playtime Theatres, Inc.*, 475 U.S. 41, 48, 89 L. Ed. 2d 29, 106 S. Ct. 925 (1986) (upholding zoning ordinance that limited locations for adult movie theaters where purpose of the ordinance was to protect the city's retail trade, maintain property values, and protect the city's neighborhoods).

Third, the Ordinance is not a content-neutral attempt to regulate solely the time, place, or manner of minors' access to video games. See, *e.g., Rothner v. City of Chicago*, 929 F.2d at 303. Instead, the Ordinance regulates video games based on their sexual and/or violent content.

The parties vigorously contest the standard that should apply here. Plaintiffs contend that the Ordinance amounts to a content-based restriction on speech that calls for the strictest possible scrutiny under the First Amendment. To meet this strict standard, plaintiffs claim that the City would need to show that the Ordinance uses the least restrictive possible means to serve a compelling governmental interest. Plaintiffs interpret "strict scrutiny" to mean that the City cannot prove it has a compelling interest in this case without definitive social science research establishing that playing violent currency-operated video games in fact causes children to engage in harmful aggressive behavior.

The City disagrees. In *Ginsberg v. New York* and in later cases, the Supreme Court has recognized that psychological protection of children is a compelling interest even without such definitive proof of actual harm. See 390 U.S. at 639-42 (upholding restriction on distribution of pornography to children in the face of conflicting evidence about whether it had harmful effects on children). Based on *Ginsberg*, the City argues that it need not show definitive proof of harmful effects, so long as it has a reasonable basis for concluding there may be such harmful effects. Given that legitimate basis for regulation, the City contends, the Ordinance is carefully tailored to serve that interest without infringing other First Amendment interests. As explained below, the court agrees with the City.

A. *The First Amendment Rights of Children*

The City has built the constitutional foundation for the Ordinance on *Ginsberg v. New York*, 390 U.S. 629, 20 L. Ed. 2d 195, 88 S. Ct. 1274 (1968). In *Ginsberg* a store owner was prosecuted under a statute that prohibited the sale to minors of any magazine containing pictures that depicted "nudity, sexual conduct or sado-masochistic abuse and which is harmful to minors." 390 U.S. at 647. The Supreme Court upheld the statute against a First Amendment challenge. The Court reasoned that the state had the power to define obscenity in a variable manner -- one definition that applies to adults and a broader definition that applies to children. This approach has often been described as "variable obscenity."

The Court began its analysis by noting that (1) the so-called "girlie" magazines involved in the case were not obscene for adults, (2) the statute in question did not prohibit the sale of the magazines to adults, and (3) because the issue was not presented, it was assumed that the magazines were in fact "harmful to minors" within the definition of the statute. *Id.* at 634-35. There was no doubt that the First Amendment would have protected adults' access to the magazines, but the Supreme Court upheld the restriction on access for children. Justice Brennan wrote for the Court:

> We do not regard New York's regulation in defining obscenity on the basis of its appeal to minors under 17 as involving an invasion of such minors' constitutionally protected freedoms. Rather [the statute] simply adjusts the definition of obscenity "to social realities by permitting the appeal of this type of material to be assessed in terms of the sexual interests . . ." of such minors. *Mishkin v. State of New York*, 383 U.S. 502, 509, 16 L. Ed. 2d 56, 86 S. Ct. 958; *Bookcase, Inc. v. Broderick*, [18 N.Y.2d 71, 218 N.E.2d 668, 671, 271 N.Y.S.2d 947]. That the State has power to make that adjustment seems clear, for we have recognized that even where there is an invasion of protected freedoms "the power of the state to control the conduct of children reaches beyond the scope of its authority over adults . . . ." *Prince v. Massachusetts*, 321 U.S. 158, 170, 88 L. Ed. 645, 64 S. Ct. 438.

Id. 390 U.S. at 638.

As in the case of obscenity laws that apply to adults, see *Miller v. California*, 413 U.S. 15, 37 L. Ed. 2d 419, 93 S. Ct. 2607 (1973), the *Ginsberg* Court did not require definitive proof of harm:

> Obscenity is not protected expression and may be suppressed without a showing of the circumstances which lie behind the phrase "clear and present danger" in its application to protected speech. *Roth v. United States*, [354 U.S. 476, 1 L. Ed. 2d 1498, 77 S. Ct. 1304,]

486-87. To sustain state power to exclude material defined as obscenity by [the New York statute] requires only that we be able to say that it was not irrational for the legislature to find that exposure to material condemned by the statute is harmful to minors. In *Meyer v. State of Nebraska*, [262 U.S. 390, 400, 67 L. Ed. 1042, 43 S. Ct. 625], we were able to say that children's knowledge of the German language "cannot reasonably be regarded as harmful." That cannot be said by us of minors' reading and seeing sex material. To be sure, there is no lack of "studies" which purport to demonstrate that obscenity is or is not "a basic factor in impairing the ethical and moral development of . . . youth and a clear and present danger to the people of the state." But the growing consensus of commentators is that "while these studies all agree that a causal link has not been demonstrated, they are equally agreed that a causal link has not been disproved either." We do not demand of legislatures "scientifically certain criteria of legislation." *Noble State Bank v. Haskell*, 219 U.S. 104, 110, 55 L. Ed. 112, 31 S. Ct. 186. We therefore cannot say that [the New York Statute], in defining the obscenity of material on the basis of its appeal to minors under 17, has no rational relation to the objective of safeguarding such minors from harm.

390 U.S. at 641-43.

Plaintiffs' First Amendment challenge to the Ordinance in this case is based ultimately on the premise that children have a First Amendment right to play video games, including those depicting graphic violence, without their parents' permission. Surely the plaintiffs have no *independent* First Amendment right to sell their entertainment services to children without the parents' permission.

Ginsberg shows, however, that the Court examines regulation of material that is arguably "harmful to minors" under a standard less strict, at least as a practical matter, than the presumption of unconstitutionality applied to most content-based restrictions. See, e.g., *Simon & Schuster, Inc. v. Members of New York State Crime Victims Bd.*, 502 U.S. 105, 115, 116 L. Ed. 2d 476, 112 S. Ct. 501 (1991) (presuming unconstitutionality and applying strict scrutiny to strike down "Son of Sam" statute designed to prevent convicted criminal from profiting by selling the story of his crime). Under this standard, the government may restrict minors' access to some speech that is protected for adults.

Other Supreme Court decisions show that children have rights under the First Amendment, but that those rights are not as broad as those of adults. Both *Tinker v. Des Moines Independent Sch. Dist.*, 393 U.S. 503, 21 L. Ed. 2d 731, 89 S. Ct. 733 (1969), and *West Virginia State Bd. of Educ. v. Barnette*, 319 U.S. 624, 87 L. Ed. 1628, 63 S. Ct. 1178 (1943), for example, demonstrate that children have significant First Amendment rights.

In *Tinker*, the Supreme Court held that a school could not punish a student for expressing his political opposition to the Vietnam War by wearing a black armband in school. 393 U.S. at 506-09. "Students in school as well as out of school are 'persons' under our Constitution. They are possessed of fundamental rights which the State must respect, just as they themselves must respect their obligations to the State." *Id.* at 511.

Similarly, in *Barnette* the Court held that a student could not be punished for refusing to pledge allegiance to the flag and to the United States. 319 U.S. at 640-42 (1943). "If there is any fixed star in our constitutional constellation, it is that no official, high or petty, can prescribe what shall be orthodox in politics, nationalism, religion, or other matters of opinion." *Id.* at 642.

Outside the school context, which raises its own set of issues, the Court's decision in *Erznoznik v. City of Jacksonville*, 422 U.S. 205, 45 L. Ed. 2d 125, 95 S. Ct. 2268 (1975), also recognized that children have a First Amendment right of access to some materials -- in that case, movies -- even if the movies display nudity. The Court recognized, however, that those rights would not extend to materials deemed "obscene as to minors," as in *Ginsberg*. 422 U.S. at 212-13. Similarly, in *Sable Communications, Inc. v. FCC*, 492 U.S. 115, 126, 106 L. Ed. 2d 93, 109 S. Ct. 2829 (1989), the Court struck down a federal law banning all "dial-a-porn" telephone messages but recognized that a law blocking only children from receiving such messages would be constitutional. The majority recognized the limited First Amendment rights of children: "there is a compelling interest in protecting the physical and psychological well-being of minors. This interest extends to shielding minors from the influence of literature that is not obscene by adult standards." *Id.* at 126; see also *id.* at 134 (Brennan, J., dissenting in part) ("To be sure, the Government has a strong interest in protecting children against exposure to pornographic material that might be harmful to them.").

The limits of children's First Amendment rights are also evident in *Miller v. California*, 413 U.S. 15, 37 L. Ed. 2d 419, 93 S. Ct. 2607 (1973), in which the Supreme Court established the standard for obscenity as to adults. The Court was sharply divided over that standard for adults, but an overwhelming majority of the Court recognized that distribution of sexually oriented materials to children raised a different set of questions. See 413 U.S. at 47 (Brennan, J., dissenting) (noting that case did not present any issue about "state power to regulate the distribution of sexually oriented material to juveniles"); *id.* at 27 (majority opinion) (pointing out dissent's implicit concession with respect to sexual material for children).

Board of Education of Island Trees v. Pico, 457 U.S. 853, 73 L. Ed. 2d 435, 102 S. Ct. 2799 (1982), also demonstrates the limits on children's First Amendment rights. The Court considered the First Amendment implications of a school board's decision to remove several controversial books from the school library. All the books remained available to children in bookstores and through other channels. The Court did not agree on a majority opinion. However, the Justices who found that the school board might have violated the First Amendment acknowledged that the school board was free to remove books because they were deemed "vulgar" or because they were deemed psychologically or intellectually inappropriate for the age group. 457 U.S. at 871 (plurality opinion of Brennan, J.); *id.* at 880 (Blackmun, J., concurring). Similarly, all justices agreed that if the school board removed books because of the ideas expressed in them, that would violate the First Amendment. See *id.* at 907 (Rehnquist, J., dissenting); *id.* at 870-71 (plurality opinion); *id.* at 877-78 (Blackmun, J., concurring). [7]

7 Both the reality of and the limits on children's First Amendment rights are also evident in *Prince v. Massachusetts*, 321 U.S. 158, 170, 88 L. Ed. 645, 64 S. Ct. 438 (1944), which held that a state could prohibit a child from distributing religious literature on public streets: "the power of the state to control the conduct of children reaches beyond the scope of its authority over adults, as is true in the case of other freedoms." *Prince* also explained *Meyer v. Nebraska*, 262 U.S. 390, 67 L. Ed. 1042, 43 S. Ct. 625 (1920), as having guarded children's rights to receive teaching in languages other than English. See 321 U.S. at 166.

The Supreme Court has not adopted a broad theory of children's First Amendment or other constitutional rights, nor has it demarked precise boundaries for those rights. See also *Goss v. Lopez*, 419 U.S. 565, 574, 42 L. Ed. 2d 725, 95 S. Ct. 729 (1975) (recognizing children's due process rights with respect to suspension or expulsion from public school, citing *Tinker* and *Barnette); In re Gault*, 387 U.S. 1, 13, 18 L. Ed. 2d 527, 87 S. Ct. 1428 (1967) (adapting adults' procedural rights in criminal cases to juvenile delinquency proceedings; "neither the Fourteenth Amendment nor the Bill of Rights is for adults alone"). This court need not undertake such an ambitious project to decide the pending motion for preliminary injunction. It is sufficient for the present to observe that children's First Amendment rights are undeniably narrower than adults' rights, and that *Ginsberg* establishes a framework for regulating a narrow range speech that is protected as to adults, but harmful as to minors.

Indianapolis wrote its Ordinance with *Ginsberg* in mind, and there are several important similarities indicating that *Ginsberg* provides the proper standard of review here.

First, as New York did in *Ginsberg*, the City relies on both its "independent interest in the well-being of its youth" and on "the principle that 'the parents' claim to authority in their own household to direct the rearing of their children is basic in the structure of our society.'" See *Reno v. ACLU*, 521 U.S. at 865, quoting *Ginsberg*, 390 U.S. at 639. The Supreme Court has consistently recognized such interests as substantial, and it has done so without requiring social science research definitively proving the danger of harm to children.

Second, just as the New York law in *Ginsberg* did not materially limit adults' access to the pornographic materials in question, the City's Ordinance also does not significantly limit adult access to video games containing graphic violence. See *American Booksellers v. Webb*, 919 F.2d 1493, 1509 (11th Cir. 1990) (upholding ordinance barring public display of materials deemed obscene as to children because it did not substantially limit adults' access to materials); *Crawford v. Lungren*, 96 F.3d 380, 387-88 (9th Cir. 1996) (upholding law barring sale of pornographic material in unattended vending machines; law did not significantly restrict adults' access to such materials); *Upper Midwest Booksellers Ass'n v. City of Minneapolis*, 780 F.2d 1389, 1394-95 (8th Cir. 1985) (upholding ordinance requiring that pornographic magazines be displayed for sale in sealed packages with opaque covers; ordinance did not substantially impair adults' access to regulated material); *M.S. News Co. v. Casado*, 721 F.2d 1281, 1288-89 (10th Cir. 1983) (upholding ordinance requiring that pornographic magazines be displayed for sale behind "blinder" covers on racks; ordinance also did not substantially impair adults' access to regulated materials). [8]

> 8 Plaintiffs have suggested in passing that the Ordinance might "burden" adults by creating a "peep show" stigma for adults who want to play video games with graphic violence or strong sexual content. There is no indication here, however, of any effect more burdensome than the fact that bars serving primarily alcohol by the drink do not admit children, or that adult bookstores are restricted to adults. In fact the evidence shows that about three-fourths of video games in Indianapolis are in bars where children already are not allowed. See Tr. 126; Pl. Dep. Ex. 9. The Ordinance does not even apply to such locations. See § 831-1.

Third, also like the New York law in *Ginsberg*, the Ordinance does not prevent parents who so desire from allowing their children to be exposed to the regulated material, either sexual material as in *Ginsberg* or sexual content or graphic violence in video games in this case. In other words, the Ordinance does not impose a total ban on access even as to children. In *Ginsberg* the Court noted that the New York law similarly allowed parents to permit their children to have access to the materials in question. 390 U.S. at 639 & n.7; cf. *Reno v. ACLU*, 521 U.S. at 878 (lack of exception for parental consent imposed heavier burden on government to justify restrictions on indecent expression on the Internet).

Fourth, the Ordinance attempts to regulate only transactions in a commercial setting where it is reasonable to expect the seller to (1) physically segregate games that are harmful to minors, (2) effectively monitor the regulated games, and (3) verify the customer's age. Commercial exhibition of coin-operated video games is similar in this respect to selling magazines as in *Ginsberg*, and different from the Internet, telephone calls, and cable channels, which are discussed below with respect to government attempts to impose broad restrictions affecting adults because age verification presented a significant problem.

Fifth, the record demonstrates that many, perhaps most, video games contain only the barest minimum of protected speech, whereas magazines (at issue in *Ginsberg*) can lie much closer to the core of the First Amendment.

In light of these strong parallels, *Ginsberg* establishes the proper framework for deciding plaintiffs' First Amendment challenge to the Ordinance. The practical difference between the *Ginsberg* framework and the plaintiffs' interpretation of "strict scrutiny" lies in whether the City is required to prove that video games with graphic violence in fact cause harm to minors, or whether, as in *Ginsberg*, the City may rely on its compelling interest in the welfare of minors to legislate narrowly in a field where the available social science data reflects some arguable uncertainty as to the actual harm caused by video games. The applicable standard of scrutiny does not have a substantial effect on the outcome of the other First Amendment issues here. [9]

9 Plaintiffs argue that the Ordinance regulates only willing providers and willing players who pay to play, so that there is no issue of a captive or unwilling audience. In *Ginsberg*, Justice Stewart's concurring opinion provided the answer to this point. He drew on the Court's precedents dealing with captive audiences and wrote: "I think a State may permissibly determine that, at least in some precisely delineated areas, a child -- like someone in a captive audience -- is not possessed of that full capacity for individual choice which is the presupposition of First Amendment guarantees. It is only upon such a premise, I should suppose, that a State may deprive children of other rights -- the right to marry, for example, or the right to vote -- deprivations that would be constitutionally intolerable for adults." 390 U.S. at 649-50.

B. *Plaintiffs' Arguments for Strict Scrutiny*

Plaintiffs rely on several recent Supreme Court decisions to argue that the Ordinance should be subjected to "strict scrutiny," meaning the City would have the burden of showing the Ordinance is necessary to promote a compelling interest and that it has chosen the least restrictive means to further that interest. See, *e.g., United States v. Playboy Entertainment Group, Inc.*, 529 U.S. 803, 812, 146 L. Ed. 2d 865, 120 S. Ct. 1878, 1886 (2000) (applying strict scrutiny to the "signal bleed" provisions of the Telecommunications Act of 1996); *Reno v.*

ACLU, 521 U.S. 844, 868, 138 L. Ed. 2d 874, 117 S. Ct. 2329 (1997) (applying "most stringent review" to Communications Decency Act's restrictions on indecent and patently offensive Internet communications); *Sable Communications of California, Inc. v. FCC*, 492 U.S. 115, 126, 106 L. Ed. 2d 93, 109 S. Ct. 2829 (1989) (applying strict scrutiny to prohibition of indecent telephone messages).

Plaintiffs contend that under strict scrutiny, the City must prove as a matter of fact that it has a compelling interest in restricting children's access to violent video games. In plaintiffs' view, that would require definitive proof from controlled social science research that playing coin-operated arcade video games in fact causes harmful aggressive behavior. Neither the cited cases nor others impose such a burden on the City in this case.

In *Sable Communications, Playboy Entertainment Group*, and *Reno v. ACLU* the Court took for granted the government's assertion that it had a compelling interest in protecting children from exposure to sexually explicit material that was constitutionally protected with respect to adults. See *Playboy Entertainment Group*, 120 S. Ct. at 1886-87 (citing *Ginsberg* and recognizing government had compelling interest in protecting children from explicit sexual material, but means used to serve it reached too broadly and interfered with adults' rights); *Reno v. ACLU*, 521 U.S. at 875 (same); *Sable Communications*, 492 U.S. at 126 (same). All three decisions plainly indicated that measures restricting *only* children's access to the material would have been constitutional. *Playboy Entertainment Group*, 120 S. Ct. at 1886-87; *Reno v. ACLU*, 521 U.S. at 878-79 (noting that additional refinements of statute might also be needed, such as exception for "valued" messages and parental consent); *Sable Communications*, 492 U.S. at 126. None of the three decisions indicated that a government would need definitive research results to prove harm before imposing content-based restrictions on children's access to material that could reasonably be deemed harmful to them. The difficult problem in each of those three cases, which is not presented here, was that the technology of each medium made it difficult to restrict children's access without also restricting adults' access to the same material.

In *Sable Communications*, the Supreme Court reviewed federal legislation banning all so-called "dial-a-porn" telephone services offering prerecorded sexually oriented messages. The Court upheld the ban as applied to dial-a-porn messages that were obscene by adult standards, but it struck down the ban as applied to messages that were "indecent" but not obscene as to adults. See 492 U.S. at 126. The asserted purpose of the federal statute was to prevent children from being exposed to indecent telephone messages, but the statute criminalized all indecent communications made by telephone. The government's theory was that the age of the caller could not be determined over the telephone, so the only effective way to limit children's access was to limit everyone's access. See *id.* at 122-23, 128-29. Thus, the statute placed a total ban on adult access to indecent messages -- a form of expression the First Amendment protects as to adults. In striking down the prohibition, the Court reaffirmed *Ginsberg* but wrote:

> Sexual expression which is indecent but not obscene is protected by the First Amendment; and the federal parties do not submit that the sale of such materials to adults could be criminalized solely because they are indecent. The Government may, however, regulate the content of constitutionally protected speech in order to promote a compelling interest if it chooses the least restrictive means to further the articulated interest. We have recognized that there is a compelling interest in protecting the physical and psychological well-being of minors. This interest extends to shielding minors from the influence of literature that is not obscene by adult standards. *Ginsberg v. New York*, 390 U.S. 629, 639-640, 20 L. Ed. 2d 195, 88 S. Ct. 1274 (1968); *New York v. Ferber*, 458 U.S. 747, 756-757, 73 L. Ed. 2d 1113, 102 S. Ct. 3348 (1982). The Government may serve this legitimate interest, but to withstand constitutional scrutiny, "it must do so by narrowly drawn regulations designed to serve those interests without unnecessarily interfering with First Amendment freedoms. *Hynes v. Mayor of Oradell*, 425 U.S. [610], at 620; *First National Bank of Boston v. Bellotti*, 435 U.S. 765, 786, 55 L. Ed. 2d 707, 98 S. Ct. 1407 (1978)." *Schaumburg v. Citizens for a Better Environment*, 444 U.S. 620, 637, 63 L. Ed. 2d 73, 100 S. Ct. 826 (1980). It is not enough to show that the Government's ends are compelling; the means must be carefully tailored to achieve those ends.

Id. 492 U.S. at 126. Applying this standard to the ban on indecent communications, the Court held that the statute was "not a narrowly tailored effort to serve the compelling interest in preventing minors from being exposed to indecent telephone messages." *Id.* at 131.

Thus, *Sable Communications* teaches that where government regulation of material harmful to children sweeps too broadly and unduly restricts the First Amendment rights of adults, strict scrutiny will likely be fatal to the challenged restrictions. As to adults, the regulation of indecent phone messages was simply a content-based restriction, and it failed strict scrutiny because it significantly affected *adults'* First Amendment interests. See *id.* (finding that the statute "has the invalid effect of limiting the content of adult telephone conversations to that which is suitable for children to hear."). In *Ginsberg*, by contrast, the Court explicitly found that the New York statute did not restrict adult access to the magazines.

United States v. Playboy Entertainment Group, Inc. and *Reno v. ACLU* are distinguishable from *Ginsberg* and this case on similar grounds. In both cases, the challenged statutes went beyond the government's asserted -- and legitimate -- interest in limiting minors' access to certain speech and significantly restricted adult access to protected communication. In *Playboy Entertainment Group*, the Court found: "To prohibit this much speech is a significant restriction on communication between speakers and willing adult listeners, communication which enjoys First Amendment protection." 529 U.S. at 812, 120 S. Ct. at 1886 (assessing regulation of adult-oriented cable television stations whose video and audio signals, even when scrambled, could sometimes be heard or seen).

Similarly, when examining regulation of indecent speech on the Internet, the Court found that the statute "effectively suppresses a large amount of speech that adults have a constitutional right to receive and to address to one another. That burden on adult speech is unacceptable if less restrictive alternatives would be at least as effective in achieving the legitimate purpose that the statute was enacted to serve." *Reno v. ACLU*, 521 U.S. at 874. Thus, as in *Sable Communications*, the burden on adult speech was a significant factor in both the analysis and outcome of *Playboy Entertainment Group* and *Reno v. ACLU*. In both this case and *Ginsberg*, by contrast, there simply is no appreciable burden on adults' access to video games with strong sexual content or graphic violence. Cf. *Reno v. ACLU*, 521 U.S. at 864-66 (identifying significant differences between the Communications Decency Act and the statute upheld in *Ginsberg*).

Plaintiffs also rely on *Erznoznik v. City of Jacksonville*, 422 U.S. 205, 45 L. Ed. 2d 125, 95 S. Ct. 2268 (1975), which presented a somewhat different problem. A local ordinance prohibited drive-in movie theaters from showing any film containing nudity when the screen was visible from a public street or public place. The Court found that the ordinance was so broad that it violated the First Amendment rights of both adults and children:

> In this case, assuming the ordinance is aimed at prohibiting youths from viewing the films, the restriction is broader than permissible. The ordinance is not directed against sexually explicit nudity, nor is it otherwise limited. Rather, it sweepingly forbids display of all films containing *any* uncovered buttocks or breasts, irrespective of context or pervasiveness. Thus it would bar a film containing a picture of a baby's buttocks, the nude body of a war victim, or scenes from a culture in which nudity is indigenous. The ordinance also might prohibit newsreel scenes of the opening of an art exhibit as well as shots of bathers on a beach. Clearly all nudity cannot be deemed obscene even as to minors. See *Ginsberg v. New York*, 390 U.S. 629, 20 L. Ed. 2d 195, 88 S. Ct. 1274 (1968). Nor can such a broad restriction be justified by any other governmental interest pertaining to minors. Speech that is neither obscene as to youths nor subject to some other legitimate proscription cannot be suppressed solely to protect the young from ideas that a legislative body thinks unsuitable for them. In most circumstances, the values protected by the first amendment are no less applicable when the government seeks to control the flow of information to minors.

422 U.S. at 213-14; see also *Cinecom Theaters Midwest States, Inc. v. City of Fort Wayne*, 473 F.2d 1297, 1301-02 (7th Cir. 1973) (finding a nearly identical drive-in movie ordinance unconstitutional on similar grounds). The problem with the ordinance in *Erznoznik* was that it swept too broadly. When government regulates speech based on content that is protected as to *both* minors and adults, an asserted interest in protecting the welfare of minors will not justify the law.

In summary, *Ginsberg* remains good law. Neither *Playboy Entertainment Group, Reno v. ACLU, Sable Communications*, nor *Erznoznik* required the Court to grapple directly with *Ginsberg*, and none of these cases undermined the holding of *Ginsberg* or the standard the Court applied to restrictions on material that was obscene as to minors. The City's regulation of children's access to video games on the basis of their strong sexual content, for example, appears to call for a relatively straightforward application of Ginsberg's standards. This conclusion is consistent with the standard applied by the Supreme Court in *Playboy Entertainment Group, Reno v. ACLU*, and *Sable Communications*, where the Court expressly recognized the government's "compelling interest in protecting the physical and psychological well-being of minors," which extended to "shielding minors from the influence of literature that is not obscene by adult standards." 492 U.S. at 126. The Court plainly indicated in *Sable Communications* that it would have upheld a law barring children's access to "dial-a-porn" services if the ban had applied only to children, see *id.* at 128-31, and the same applies to the other two cases.

Ginsberg demands more from a statute than mere rationality: The government must have a compelling interest and the regulation must be carefully tailored to advance that interest. However, neither *Ginsberg* nor any other case requires the government, when it regulates speech to serve a compelling interest in the well-being of children, to provide definitive scientific proof that the restricted material in fact causes psychological harm to children.

C. *Evidence on Potential Harm to Minors*

To fall within the reasoning of *Ginsberg*, the City must have had a reasonable basis for believing the Ordinance would protect children from harm and the Ordinance must be limited in scope to such material. In *Ginsberg* the Supreme Court acknowledged there was "no lack of 'studies' which purport to demonstrate that obscenity is or is not 'a basic factor in impairing the ethical and moral development of . . . youth and a clear and present danger to the people of the state.'" 390 U.S. at 641-42, quoting New York's legislative finding. The Court noted that a causal link between pornography and adverse effects on children had not been proved or disproved. The Court then concluded: "We do not demand of legislatures "scientifically certain criteria of legislation." *Id.* at 642-43, quoting *Noble State Bank v. Haskell*, 219 U.S. 104, 110, 55 L. Ed. 112, 31 S. Ct. 186 (1911).

Plaintiffs contend the City lacks an adequate basis for its claim that violent video games are "harmful to minors." Pl. Reply Br. at 1-6. The social science data in the record reflect some uncertainty, but the data also indicate that the City had a soldily reasonable basis for enacting the Ordinance. The Ordinance's legislative history also makes it clear that the Ordinance is the product of considered legislative judgment as to both the problem and the means chosen to address it.

The preamble to the Ordinance and the City's brief cite prominently a recent study examining the effects of violent video games on aggression-related variables, and reviewing evidence from other studies, as well. See Craig A. Anderson & Karen E. Dill, *Video Games and Aggressive Thoughts, Feelings, and Behavior in the Laboratory and in Life*, 78 J. Personality & Soc. Psychol. 772 (2000) (reproduced as Ex. P-55). Anderson and Dill conducted two studies. The first was a correlational study which used questionnaires to examine the relationship between long-term exposure to violent video games and several outcome variables, including aggressive behavior. The second was a laboratory experiment where participants were exposed to either a violent or non-violent video game and then participated in a separate game that provided the opportunity to exhibit aggressive behavior toward a competitor. Ex. P-55 at 9-11. The authors concluded:

> The present research demonstrated that in both a correlational investigation using self-reports of real-world aggressive behaviors and an experimental investigation using a standard, objective laboratory measure of aggression, *violent video game play was positively related to increases in aggressive behavior*. In the laboratory, college students who played a violent video game behaved more aggressively toward an opponent than did students who had played a nonviolent video game. Outside the laboratory, students who reported playing more violent video games over a period of years also engaged in more aggressive behavior in their own lives. Both types of studies -- correlational -- real delinquent behaviors and experimental -- laboratory aggressive behaviors have their strengths and weaknesses. The convergence of findings across such disparate methods lends considerable strength to the main hypothesis that exposure to violent video games can increase aggressive behavior. Though the existence of a violent video game effect cannot be unequivocally established on the basis of one pair of studies, this particular pair adds considerable support to prior work, both empirical and theoretical. When combined with what is known about other types of media violence effects, most notably TV violence (e.g., Eron et al., 1987; Huesmann & Miller, 1994), *we believe that the present results confirm that parents, educators, and society in general should be concerned about the prevalence of violent video games in modern society, especially given recent advances in the realism of video game violence.*

Id. at 33-34 (emphasis added).

Anderson and Dill cautioned that: (1) empirical research on video game violence is sparse, (2) the methodologies of some older studies could be improved upon, (3) additional studies would be helpful, and (4) any causal statements would be premature. See, *e.g., id.* at 22 ("It could be that the obtained video games violence links to aggressive and nonaggressive delinquency are wholly due to the fact that highly aggressive individuals are especially attracted to violent video games.").

Plaintiffs seize on these reasonable concessions to discount the relevance of Anderson's and Dill's work. The City, however, relies on the report only for what it is: one study that provides at least an indication that "concern about the potentially deleterious consequences of playing violent video games is not misplaced." *Id.* at 36.

Plaintiffs find at least two additional major faults with the Anderson and Dill studies. First, the studies did not specifically analyze the effects of coin-operated video games as opposed to home video games. Second, Anderson and Dill found correlations to aggressive behavior -- not necessarily to *harmful* aggressive behavior. Plaintiffs therefore contend that the City could not reliably determine that coin-operated amusement machines video games are a "real" problem. After all, say plaintiffs, aggressive behavior on a football field is "encouraged." Tr. 81.

These arguments are not persuasive. Although home and arcade platforms for video games are different, that does not mean that studies of one are irrelevant to the other. Similarly, the more numerous studies on children's exposure to violence in other, older media -- such as television violence -- remain relevant to the question of the effects of video game violence. See generally Report of the Federal Trade Commission, App. A, *A Review of Research on the Impact of Violence in Entertainment Media* (Sept. 2000) (reproduced as Ex. P-13) (discussing both television violence and violent video games in a review of research on "entertainment media violence"). Considering the similarities and differences between video games and television or movies, Anderson and Dill suggest that video games, due to their unique characteristics as an interactive media, may well pose a greater danger than either violent television or violent movies:

> In a sense, violent video games provide *a complete learning environment for aggression*, with simultaneous exposure to modeling, reinforcement, and rehearsal of behaviors. This combination of learning strategies has been shown to be more powerful than any of these methods used singly (Barton, 1981; Chambers & Ascione, 1987; Loftus & Loftus, 1983).

Ex. P-55 at 37 (emphasis added). In a video game, the player is not the passive viewer of violence on the screen. The player is instead the agent actually causing the increasingly realistic and violent action on the screen.

As for plaintiffs' proposed requirement of studies that definitively show a causal relationship between exposure to violent video games and actually harmful aggression, it is completely unremarkable that an academic study would use proxy variables to stand in for measures of actual, harmful aggression. The prospect of controlled experiments with human subjects that could result in aggression inflicting actual harm raises a few ethical issues, to put it mildly. Surely the constitutionality of a law does not depend on whether such experiments have been conducted.

The City was entitled to assess how such limitations in the data should affect the weight of the studies. In fact, members of the Rules and Public Policy Committee were provided with a copy of a paper that pointed out flaws and limitations of the experimental studies. See Jeffrey Goldstein, *Effects of Electronic Games on Children* (March 2000) (reproduced in Exhibit P-64).

Beyond the Anderson and Dill studies, the City has submitted additional evidence indicating that it was reasonable for the City-County Council to conclude that some violent video games are likely to be "harmful to minors." For example, Exhibit P-64 is a compilation of material distributed to several members of the Rules and Public Policy Committee while the Ordinance was under consideration. Included in the packet were statements by Dr. David Walsh and Dr. Jeanne B. Funk, both of whom had provided testimony to the Senate Commerce Committee. Dr. Walsh, relying in part on the work of Anderson and Dill, called for additional research and concluded that "the concern about the impact of violent video games is justified." David Walsh, *Interactive Violence and Children*, Testimony before the United States Senate Commerce Committee (March 21, 2000) (reproduced in Exhibit P-64). Dr. Funk identified, from a theoretical perspective, several ways in which "playing violent video games could develop and prime aggressive thought networks." See Jeanne B. Funk, *The Impact of Interactive Violence on Children*, Testimony before the United States Senate Commerce Committee (March 21, 2000) (reproduced in Exhibit P-64).

Just after the City enacted the Ordinance, the American Academy of Pediatrics, the American Medical Association, the American Psychological Association, the American Academy of Child and Adolescent Psychiatry, and the American Academy of Family Physicians issued a Joint Statement on the public health aspects of violence in the media, including video games. The Joint Statement, which is Exhibit P-70, provides substantial support for the City's concerns about the effects of violent video games. In response to entertainment industry arguments that there is no proof that violent entertainment causes aggressive behavior and that children know the difference between fantasy and reality, the medical organizations said the industry was wrong on both counts:

> At this time, well over 1000 studies -- including reports from the Surgeon General's office, the National Institute of Mental Health, and numerous studies conducted by leading figures within our medical and public health organizations -- our own members -- point overwhelmingly to a causal connection between media violence and aggressive behavior in some children. The conclusion of the public health community, based on over 30 years of research, is that viewing entertainment violence can lead to increases in aggressive attitudes, values and behavior, particularly in children.

Ex. P-70. Specifically about video games, the medical organizations said: "Although less research has been done on the impact of violent interactive entertainment (video games and other interactive media) on young people, *preliminary studies indicate that the negative impact may be significantly more severe than that wrought by television, movies, or music*. More study is needed in this area, and we urge that resources and attention be directed to this field." *Id.* (emphasis added). A copy of the full Joint Statement is attached to this opinion as Exhibit B.

Thus, even if the debate over violence in video games and its harmful effects on children has not been resolved definitively, the City's evidence shows that the Ordinance is based on far more than mere legislative conjecture and surmise. Cf. *Eclipse Enterprises, Inc. v. Gulotta*, 134 F.3d 63, 66 (2d Cir. 1997) (striking down law regulating sale of crime trading cards to children after finding that government's findings were based on "sheer surmise"). [10]

10 According to the evidence submitted by plaintiffs, "[a] majority of the investigations into the impact of media violence on children find that there is a high *correlation* between exposure to media violence and aggressive and at times violent behavior. . . . Regarding *causation*, however, the studies appear to be less conclusive." Report of the Federal Trade Commission, App. A, *A Review of Research on the Impact of Violence in Entertainment Media*, at 1 (Sept. 2000) (reproduced as Ex. P-13) (emphasis in original).

Requiring the City to produce definitive proof of a causal connection between violent video games and psychological or physical harm to children would come very close to holding that graphic violence could never be regulated. Social phenomena such as violent behavior by children are explained by a multitude of factors. As the Supreme Court said in *Ginsberg*, "We do not demand of legislatures 'scientifically certain criteria of legislation.'" 390 U.S. at 642-43. In fact, under plaintiffs' standard, the outcome of *Ginsberg* should have been different, for there certainly was nothing approaching definitive proof of harmful effects on children from exposure to sexually explicit materials. Yet plaintiffs contend they do not challenge *Ginsberg*, and surely there is no doubt that the result would be the same in *Ginsberg* today, even in the absence of definitive proof that exposure to pornography causes psychological harm to children.

D. *The City's Adaptation of the Miller v. California Obscenity Standard*

The City's Ordinance was written carefully in light of both *Ginsberg* and the Supreme Court's current definition of adult obscenity as set forth in *Miller v. California*, 413 U.S. 15, 24, 37 L. Ed. 2d 419, 93 S. Ct. 2607 (1973). In *Miller*, the Supreme Court held that obscenity for adults is confined to "works which depict or describe sexual conduct," and that any attempt to regulate obscenity must be "limited to works which, taken as a whole, appeal to the prurient interest in sex, which portray sexual conduct in a patently offensive way, and which, taken as a whole, do not have serious literary, artistic, political, or scientific value." *Id.* at 24. To reduce the vagueness inherent in the open-ended term "patently offensive," however, the Court also required the proscribed conduct to be "specifically defined by the applicable state law." *Id.*; see also *Reno v. ACLU*, 521 U.S. at 873 (discussing the inadequacy of the Communications Decency Act's definitions as compared to the *Miller* guidelines).

In an actual prosecution for violation of an obscenity statute that uses the *Miller v. California* guidelines, the trier of fact decides as questions of fact whether the material in question appeals to the "prurient interest" and whether the material is "patently offensive." See *Pope v. Illinois*, 481 U.S. 497, 500, 95 L. Ed. 2d 439, 107 S. Ct. 1918 (1987). These questions of fact are determined by reference to contemporary community standards. See *Smith v. United States*, 431 U.S. 291, 293, 300-01, 52 L. Ed. 2d 324, 97 S. Ct. 1756 (1977). A different standard applies to determine the social value of an allegedly obscene work: "The proper inquiry is not whether an ordinary member of any given community would find serious literary, artistic, political, or scientific value in allegedly obscene material, but whether a reasonable person would find such value in the material, taken as a whole." *Pope v. Illinois*, 481 U.S. at 500-01. Under the reasonable person standard, a work need not obtain majority approval to merit First Amendment protection. *Id.* The inquiry into social value is considered "particularly important" because it "allows an appellate court to impose some limitations and regularity on the definition by setting, as a matter of law, a national floor for socially redeeming value." *Reno v. ACLU*, 521 U.S. at 873.

The City's Ordinance modifies the *Miller* standard in two principal ways. First, the Ordinance rephrases the *Miller* standard in terms of minors rather than the community as a whole. Second, the Ordinance treats "graphic violence" in video games as a form of obscenity as to children. Plaintiffs contend that the City's two departures from *Miller* are constitutionally fatal to the Ordinance. Plaintiffs read the Supreme Court's obscenity jurisprudence, including *Miller* and *Ginsberg*, as strictly limited to material with sexually erotic content. The City contends that the state's interest in the well-being of children allows it to regulate children's access to graphic violence in video games as long as the regulation identifies a narrow range of violent material that is so morbid, offensive, and lacking in other value that it is harmful to children and unprotected by the First Amendment. This section and the next address these two important departures from *Miller* and *Ginsberg*.

The Ordinance adapts Miller's "prurient interest," "patently offensive," and "societal value" prongs so that a video game is "harmful to minors" and is regulated by the Ordinance if it:

> predominantly appeals to minors' morbid interest in violence or minors' prurient interest in sex, is patently offensive to prevailing standards in the adult community as a whole with respect to what is suitable material for persons under the age of eighteen (18) years, lacks serious literary, artistic, political or scientific value as a whole for persons under the age of eighteen (18) years, and:
>
> (1) Contains graphic violence; or
>
> (2) Contains strong sexual content.

§ 831-1.

As required under the *Miller* guidelines, the Ordinance also contains specific definitions of both "strong sexual content" and "graphic violence" for these purposes. The definition of "strong sexual content," as well as the definition of "nudity," closely mirror the wording of the Indiana obscenity statutes. See Ind. Code §§ 35-49-1-5, 35-49-1-9, 35-49-2-2(1). To define "graphic violence," the City relied heavily on the standards used by the video game industry as part of a voluntary rating system. See Exs. P-68, P-69. The final version of the Ordinance defines graphic violence as "an amusement machine's visual depiction or representation of realistic serious injury to a human or human-like being where such serious injury includes amputation, decapitation, dismemberment, bloodshed, mutilation, maiming or disfiguration." § 831-1.

Adapting the *Miller* standard to children does not appear to be controversial in and of itself. Several states, including Indiana, have adapted the *Miller* standard to define sexual material that is "obscene as to minors." Moreover, courts have upheld such statutes as essentially updated and more refined versions of the variable obscenity standard the Supreme Court reviewed and upheld in *Ginsberg v. New York. See, e.g., American Booksellers v. Webb*, 919 F.2d 1493, 1503 & n.18 (11th Cir. 1990) ("Nothing in *Miller* casts any doubt on the constitutional viability of a variable standard of obscenity for minors based upon a *Ginsberg*-like adaptation of the current Supreme Court standard for determining adult obscenity."); accord, *American Booksellers Ass'n v. Virginia*, 882 F.2d 125, 127 & n.2 (4th Cir. 1989) (upholding statute prohibiting display of sexually explicit material where children could examine it; statute used *Miller* standards modified for children); *M.S. News Co. v. Casado*, 721 F.2d 1281, 1286-87 (10th Cir. 1983) ("We reject the argument that the use of the *Miller* test rendered the ordinance overbroad or vague."). Thus, a modified *Miller* standard has become a common way for states to regulate sexual material that is obscene as to minors but protected speech as to adults.

E. *Treating "Graphic Violence" as a Form of Obscenity as to Minors*

Plaintiffs do not challenge the Ordinance's treatment of sexually explicit video games as "harmful to minors, " but do contend that the First Amendment prohibits the City from taking these principles that apply to children's access to sexual pornography and extending them to video games that include "graphic violence." Plaintiffs assert (1) that the Supreme Court and the Seventh, Eighth, and Second Circuits have rejected any effort to extend the concept of obscenity as to minors beyond sexual material to include graphic violence; (2) that extension of the concept of obscenity as to minors to graphic violence is not warranted as a matter of constitutional law; and (3) that any such extension could not be limited and would devolve into broad censorship of protected expression on the theory it is "harmful to minors."

The City concedes that no court has ever reached a holding that directly favors this step. However, the City also points out correctly that no court has rejected such a careful attempt to extend these principles to graphic violence. The City contends that the reasoning and policy of the "obscenity as to minors" cases extend to graphic violence and that courts can effectively limit the extension of those cases to graphic violence without opening a door to broad censorship.

1. *Drawing the "Obscenity" Line at Sexual Content in Prior Cases*

The Supreme Court has often said that the standard for obscenity with respect to adults is limited to sexual materials. In *Reno v. ACLU*, for example, the Court noted that the *Miller* definition of obscenity "is limited to 'sexual conduct,'" which the court distinguished from the Communications Decency Act, which also included "excretory activities" and "organs" of both a sexual and excretory nature. 521 U.S. at 846. In *Erznoznik*, the Court explained that the local ordinance ban on display of "nudity" in drive-in theaters in view of public streets was too broad because not all nudity was obscene even as to minors: "under any test of obscenity as to minors not all nudity would be proscribed. Rather, to be obscene 'such expression must be, in some significant way, erotic.'" 422 U.S. at 214 n. 10. In *Cohen v. California*, 403 U.S. 15, 29 L. Ed. 2d 284, 91 S. Ct. 1780 (1971), the Court struck down a man's conviction for disturbing the peace based on his wearing of a jacket with the words "Fuck the Draft" in a courthouse. The Court held that the expression was not obscene within its First Amendment jurisprudence. The Court explained that a state could not prohibit expression as obscene unless it was "in some significant way, erotic." 403 U.S. at 20.

Similarly, in *Cinecom Theaters Midwest States, Inc. v. City of Fort Wayne*, 473 F.2d 1297, 1301-02 (7th Cir. 1973), which was essentially a precursor to *Erznoznik*, the Seventh Circuit said that a prohibition on nudity at drive-in theaters in view of public streets was too broad even as to children because not all nudity was obscene even as to minors. Although the ordinance in *Cinecom Theatres* did not include a restriction on violent movies, the Seventh Circuit quoted with approval the Fifth Circuit's language striking down a law restricting drive-in movies "depicting excessive brutality and criminal violence." The Fifth Circuit had written about that law: "While we recognize the interest of society in protecting children, we find even the child's freedom of speech too precious to be subjected to the whim of the censor." *Interstate Circuit, Inc. v. City of Dallas*, 366 F.2d 590, 598-99 (5th Cir. 1966), *vacated on other grounds*, 391 U.S. 53, 20 L. Ed. 2d 415, 88 S. Ct. 1649 (1968).

This court has considered these statements by the Supreme Court and Seventh Circuit carefully, and in context. This court is not persuaded that any of these statements foreclose the City's attempt to treat graphic violence, as defined and limited in the Ordinance, as a form of variable obscenity as to children. *Reno, Erznoznik*, and *Cohen* did not present any issue with respect to violence. It would be reading too much into that language in the opinions to conclude that the Court had considered and rejected the theory advance by the City in this case. See *R.A.V. v. City of St. Paul*, 505 U.S. 377, 386-87 n.5, 120 L. Ed. 2d 305, 112 S. Ct. 2538 (1992) ("It is of course contrary to all traditions of our jurisprudence to consider the law on this point conclusively resolved by broad language in cases where the issue was not presented or even envisioned."). This is especially true in First Amendment cases, where broad theories and conceptual labels are far more slippery than the facts of the cases and the results the Supreme Court actually reached. See *id.* at 383-84 (noting that many of the Court's broad statements about "unprotected" forms of speech cannot be taken literally). [11]

11 Plaintiffs point out that in the most recent Supreme Court decision dealing with violence as a form of obscenity, *Winters v. New York*, 333 U.S. 507, 508, 92 L. Ed. 840, 68 S. Ct. 665 (1948), the Court struck down the statute, which prohibited sale of written materials "principally made up of criminal news, police reports, or accounts of criminal deeds, or pictures, or stories of deeds of bloodshed, lust or crime . . . ." Under plaintiffs' theory in this case, the Court should have struck down the statute by finding simply that violence cannot be "obscene." Instead, however, the Court struck down the statute on overbreadth and vagueness grounds, without hinting that violence could *never* be deemed "obscene."

As for the Seventh Circuit's approval in *Cinecom Theatres* of the Fifth Circuit's language in *Interstate Circuit*, this court has no doubt that the Dallas ordinance in question would fail any modern standard requiring reasonable specificity in defining the restricted content of the violence depicted. Vague references to "brutality, criminal violence or depravity," see 366 F.2d at 592, reach far too broadly into constitutionally protected expression even as to children. They also do not recognize the essential safe harbors under the *Miller* standard for material, for example, that does not depict violence in a "patently offensive way," or for works which, taken as a whole, have serious literary, artistic, political, or scientific value for children. For example, it might be difficult to study the history of the modern civil rights movement without information, and perhaps even some depictions, about "excessive brutality and criminal violence" aimed at non-violent protesters. This court does not believe, however, that the Seventh Circuit's comment in *Cinecom Theatres* was intended or should be understood as a blanket rejection of any future, more carefully drafted and better researched effort to protect children from exposure to forms of graphic violence.

Plaintiffs draw their strongest support from recent decisions by the Eighth and Second Circuits rejecting attempts to regulate children's access to some material with violent content. In both cases, the courts declared the laws facially unconstitutional.

In *Video Software Dealers Ass'n v. Webster*, 968 F.2d 684 (8th Cir. 1992), a Missouri statute restricted the rental or sale of video cassettes depicting "violence." The statute included an adaptation of the *Miller* standards for obscenity. It limited the statute to materials, which, taken as a whole and applying contemporary community standards, had "a tendency to cater or appeal to morbid interests in violence" for persons under the age of 17, which depicted violence in a way which was patently offensive to the average person applying contemporary adult community standards with respect to what is suitable for persons under the age of 17, and which, taken as a whole, lacked serious literary, artistic, political, or scientific value for persons under the age of 17. *Id.* at 687.

The fatal flaw was that the Missouri statute contained no definition of the key concept -- "violence." The Eighth Circuit concluded that the absence of any reasonably precise statutory definitions, such as *Miller* requires with respect to sexual expression for purposes of adult obscenity, rendered the statute unconstitutional on its face. *Id.* at 689-91 ("Nothing less than rewriting the statute to include a definition of violence would begin to remedy the statute's vagueness.").

As plaintiffs point out, however, the Eighth Circuit also began its analysis by explicitly rejecting Missouri's contention that the violent videos targeted by the statute could be treated as "obscene" for children as an extension of *Ginsberg v. New York*:

> Obscenity, however, encompasses only expression that "depict[s] or describe[s] sexual conduct." *Miller v. California*, 413 U.S. at 24; see *Roth*, 354 U.S. at 487; *Erznoznik v. City of Jacksonville*, 422 U.S. [at 213 n.10] (expression must be erotic to be obscene). Material that contains violence but not depictions or descriptions of sexual conduct cannot be obscene. [*Sovereign News Co. v. Falke*, 448 F. Supp. 306, 394 (N.D. Ohio 1977).] Thus, videos depicting only violence do not fall within the legal definition of obscenity for either minors or adults.

968 F.2d at 688. Because violent videos could not be equated with sexually obscene videos, the court found that *Ginsberg* did not supply the appropriate standard of review. The Eighth Circuit applied strict scrutiny to the statute as a content-based restriction on protected speech, and the statute flunked the test. *Id.* at 689, citing *Sable Communications*, 492 U.S. at 126, as providing the applicable standard.
12

12 A third ground for the Eighth Circuit's decision was that the Missouri statute authorized penalties even if the merchant did not know the person renting a violent video was under 17. The court viewed a knowledge element as necessary both because the statute was "quasi-criminal in nature" and because such an element is an appropriate requirement in any statute that chills the exercise of First Amendment Rights. 968 F.2d at 690. The City's Ordinance in this case requires proof of knowledge that the player is under age.

The Second Circuit reached a similar result in *Eclipse Enterprises, Inc. v. Gulotta*, 134 F.3d 63 (2d Cir. 1997), which struck down a local law making it a crime to distribute to minors, among other things, "any trading card which depicts a heinous crime, an element of a heinous crime, or a heinous criminal and which is harmful to minors." *Id.* at 64. The asserted purposes of the trading card law were to protect the psychological well-being of children and to combat juvenile crime. *Id.* at 67. The definition of "harmful to minors" was patterned after the *Miller* obscenity standard, and the local legislative body took the additional step of specifically defining "heinous crimes" as murder, assault, kidnaping, arson, burglary, robbery, rape, or other sexual offense. *Id.* at 64, 67.

The Second Circuit found that violence could not be equated with obscenity, treated the law as a content-based restriction on protected speech, and held it unconstitutional under strict scrutiny. *Id.* at 66-67. The court noted that only obscenity, defamation, fighting words, and direct incitement of lawless action have been recognized as unprotected speech, and then said: "We decline any invitation to expand these narrow categories of speech to include depictions of violence." *Id.* at 66. Turning to whether the law was narrowly tailored to serve the government's compelling interest, the Second Circuit declared that the local government had failed to show the law was either necessary or effective. The court simply found no evidence to support the contention that the crime trading cards were either harmful to minors or contributed juvenile crime. *Id.* at 68. The court added:

> Moreover, there has been no showing why trading cards should be singled out for regulation in preference to other material that is no less noxious. For example, books found in the County library and, at least according to one teacher, used in the classroom, contain descriptions of crimes and criminals no different from the information and depictions found in the crime trading cards.

Id.

Video Software Dealers and *Eclipse Enterprises* provide the strongest support for plaintiffs' challenge to the Indianapolis Ordinance. However, both decisions recognized that a narrower statute focused on violent expression might survive First Amendment scrutiny. The Eighth Circuit wrote: "In this case, we need not decide whether states can legitimately proscribe dissemination of material depicting violence to minors because Missouri's statute cannot survive strict scrutiny. * * * A more precise law limited to slasher films and specifically defining key terms would be less burdensome on protected expression." *Video Software Dealers*, 968 F.2d at 689. Similarly, the Second Circuit wrote that it was not deciding whether "carefully delimited and properly tailored restrictions on distribution of non-obscene but otherwise harmful speech to minors, especially younger minors, can ever pass the strict scrutiny test." *Eclipse Enterprises*, 134 F.3d at 67.

In a thoughtful concurring opinion in *Eclipse Enterprises*, Judge Griesa described some of the extraordinarily depraved crimes depicted in some of the trading cards. However, he also recognized that some of the cards regulated by the law, such as cards dealing with presidential assassinations, criminal trials, and the careers of famous criminals depicting what might be found "in any widely circulated news articles or historical works" could not be prohibited as to adults or minors. 134 F.3d at 70-71. Judge Griesa found that the law had not been drafted with the kind of specificity referred to in *Miller* and *Reno v. ACLU*. Judge Griesa therefore recognized but did not try to answer the "surely debatable" question whether a law dealing with depictions of violence and crime could be drafted to meet constitutional standards. *Id.* at 71-72.

The Seventh Circuit has often instructed district courts in this circuit to give respectful consideration to the views of other circuits, but not to abdicate our responsibilities to give the parties before our courts the benefit of our independent judgment. See, *e.g., Colby v. J.C. Penney Co.*, 811 F.2d 1119, 1123 (7th Cir. 1987), citing 1B Moore's Federal Practice P 4.02[1], at 14-16 (2d ed. 1984). This court has tried to do so with respect to the Second and Eighth Circuits' decisions. This court has no quarrel at all with the result in either *Video Software Dealers* or *Eclipse Enterprises.* Both laws were written so broadly that they failed any applicable First Amendment standard. However, with respect to the courts' broader statements that the *Ginsberg* variable obscenity standard for children cannot be extended to violence, this court is not persuaded. Neither opinion offers any reasoned or principled basis for distinguishing between sexual content and violence in evaluating whether children's access to graphic violence may be restricted as material "harmful to minors."

To support the view that "variable obscenity" cannot extend to violence, the Eighth Circuit cited the general comments of the Supreme Court quoted above, which did not directly address the issue of violence. See 968 F.2d at 688. The Eighth Circuit also cited *Sovereign News Co. v. Falke*, 448 F. Supp. 306, 394 (N.D. Ohio 1977), for the proposition that material that "contains violence but not depictions or descriptions of sexual conduct cannot be obscene." The cited portion of *Falke* offered as support for that proposition only the same general comments by the Supreme Court, and it is no more persuasive in this respect. In addition, the court in *Falke* was dealing with a statute that was breathtakingly broad. See 448 F. Supp. at 398-400 (including as "harmful to minors" material that depicted "extreme or bizarre violence, cruelty, or brutality"). The broader statements in the opinion are not persuasive when applied to a more carefully drafted and better researched effort like the Ordinance in this case. In *Eclipse Enterprises*, the Second Circuit panel opinion also did not offer a reasoned explanation for declining to treat violence as a variety of variable obscenity as to children within the reasoning of *Ginsberg.* See 134 F.3d at 66-67.

Accordingly, this court does not believe the question of extension of "obscenity as to minors" to reach "graphic violence" is controlled by prior case law, at least in this circuit.

2. *Extending "Obscenity as to Minors" to Graphic Violence*

The First Amendment allows the state to restrict children's access to sexually explicit material, but does it forbid any comparable effort to restrict access to the most extreme and graphic violence? This court believes the answer is no. The court bases this answer on the reasoning of *Ginsberg*, which is based on the protection of children and which remains viable today, and on the lack of any persuasive, principled basis for distinguishing between graphic violence and explicit sexual content in terms of potential harm to children.

Ginsberg was based on the state's important and substantial interests in safeguarding the psychological well-being of children and enabling the exercise of parental responsibility. See 390 U.S. at 639-42. Courts have repeatedly reaffirmed those interests as a legitimate foundation for laws regulating children's access to some forms of speech. In addition to the cases discussed above, see *New York v. Ferber*, 458 U.S. 747, 756-57, 73 L. Ed. 2d 1113, 102 S. Ct. 3348 (1982), and *ACLU v. Reno*, 217 F.3d 162, 173 (3d Cir. 2000). The Eleventh Circuit has described the protection of children as "one of government's most profound obligations." *American Booksellers v. Webb*, 919 F.2d 1493, 1495 (11th Cir. 1990) (upholding statute barring public display of sexually explicit materials deemed "harmful to minors"). Even the cases striking down overly broad attempts to regulate children's access to certain forms of speech took pains to recognize that government has a compelling interest in protecting children from material that is harmful to them. See *Sable Communications*, 492 U.S. at 126; *Erznoznik*, 422 U.S. at 212.

Justice Brennan's broad description of the state's interest for the Court in *Ginsberg* is not limited strictly to sexual material. A state's power to regulate indecent or harmful material for children, while still significantly limited by children's First Amendment rights, can extend beyond the regulation of sexual material upheld in that case. The focus of the case was harm to the ethical and moral development of children. See *Ginsberg v. New York*, 390 U.S. at 640-41.

In fact, the case for regulating children's access to graphic violence is, if anything, stronger than the case for regulating children's access to explicit sexual material. In *Ginsberg* the Supreme Court was presented with extensive evidence to show that exposure to explicit sexual material either was or was not psychologically harmful to children. See 390 U.S. at 642-43 & n.10. Professor Ross, who has been critical of courts' efforts dealing with both types of restrictions, has observed: "In contrast to the dearth of support for the notion that sexually explicit speech is harmful, substantial social science research conducted over several decades lends support to the allegation that violent speech may lead some children to violent attitudes or actions." Catherine J. Ross, *Anything Goes: Examining the State's Interest in Protecting Children from Controversial Speech*, 53 Vand. L. Rev. 427, 505 (2000). In her next sentence, Professor Ross points out that the research on violent speech is "not uncontroverted." *Id.* Nevertheless, given Ginsberg's holding that legislatures are entitled to act reasonably to protect children in the face of inconclusive social science evidence about the danger of harm, the accumulation of research on the effects of violence in the media in recent decades provides ample basis for allowing states to take action similar to that taken with respect to sexual materials. See Joint Statement attached as Exhibit B.

Plaintiffs argue that sex is different from violence because violence has always been a prominent element of our culture, as reflected in our literature and art. Plaintiffs refer to the violence in *The Iliad*, for example, and they remind the court of some extraordinarily graphic violence depicted in paintings by the masters. Consider paintings of Salome being presented the head of John the Baptist on a platter, or paintings of the martyrdom of Saint Stephen or Saint Sebastian. The same could also be said, however, of sex. Consider Aristophanes' comic play *Lysistrata*, for example, or Shakespeare's *Othello*, or classical statues and paintings depicting the rape of the Sabines. For that matter, even *Romeo and Juliet* has plenty of both sex and violence, and it is taught in required high school English classes.

Plaintiffs also suggest that our culture's taboos with respect to sexual material are simply more universal and more firmly established than those with respect to violence. As a question of history, that is far from clear. Professor Saunders has traced the history of government efforts to regulate obscenity. He has shown that the concept was very broad in the 18th and early 19th centuries, including profanity and blasphemy, as well as descriptions or depictions of violence and sex. See Kevin W. Saunders, *Media Violence and the Obscenity Exception to the First Amendment*, 3 Wm. & Mary Bill of Rts. J. 107, 116-27 (1994), discussing sources cited in *Roth v. United States*, 354 U.S. 476, 1 L. Ed. 2d 1498, 77 S. Ct. 1304 (1957), to support the conclusion that obscenity, however defined, should not be protected by the First Amendment. Professor Saunders also found examples in which both sexual and violent materials were treated as obscene in the 19th and early 20th centuries. He notes in his later book, for example, that in 1884, New York enacted a statute that regulated as "obscene" materials with "pictures and stories of deeds of bloodshed, lust or crime," and that other states passed similar statutes. Kevin W. Saunders, Violence as Obscenity: Limiting the Media's First Amendment Protection 113-18 (1996). An Indiana statute enacted in 1895 applied to both sex and violence. It banned the distribution of "any paper, book, or periodical, the chief feature or characteristic of which is the record of commission of crime, or to display by cut or illustration of crimes committed, or the acts or pictures of criminals, desperadoes, or of men or women in lewd and unbecoming positions or improper dress." 1895 Ind. Acts 230.

From the perspective of the year 2000, of course, it is easy to smile knowingly at the vague and broad prohibitions of those earlier laws treating depictions of both violence and sex as obscenity. However, if history and tradition should, as plaintiffs contend, guide the courts in limiting the concept of obscenity, those older statutes' vagueness and breadth by modern standards provide no basis for concluding they are irrelevant today in determining whether to draw a constitutional line, with respect to children, between sex and violence. The restrictions on sexual material in most of those older statutes and ordinances also would not survive modern First Amendment analysis, but the history of such restrictions obviously helped persuade the Supreme Court to preserve the First Amendment exception for a narrow category of sexually explicit material.

The restrictions on sexual material have been the principal focus of obscenity litigation for the past half-century. However, the Supreme Court has never squarely held that all attempts to restrict depictions of violence -- especially when children are the audience -- must violate the First Amendment. As discussed above, the Court's decisions offer no persuasive basis for expecting that a carefully drafted law restricting children's access to graphic violence in video games could never survive a First Amendment challenge.

3. *Limits on the Extension of Obscenity to Violence*

The plaintiffs' strongest argument against extending the reasoning of *Ginsberg* to graphic violence is the difficulty in drawing lines. Plaintiffs suggest that if research results on "harm to children" that are less than definitive are enough to justify censorship, the same logic will quickly be extended to such obviously protected but arguably harmful matters as anti-religious expression, "witchcraft," or depictions of inequality among racial groups or social classes. See Pl. Reply Br. at 9. With these possibilities in mind, plaintiffs defend drawing a line at sexual obscenity precisely, and simply, because the rationale that supports extending *Ginsberg* to reach graphic violence would otherwise be too difficult to limit. In addition, allowing government to regulate violent video games suggests that government could choose to regulate graphic violence in other media -- books, television, and movies are obvious examples.

Plaintiffs' concerns about a slippery slope are important, but they fail to take into account other anchors that should prevent a slide into obviously unconstitutional censorship in the name of protecting children from asserted harms. Any law that attempts to regulate material as "harmful to minors" under *Ginsberg* must meet several requirements that serve to limit the scope of permissible government regulation. First, as shown above, the government may not substantially limit adult access to the regulated material. Second, in acting to protect the well-being of children, the government must provide the safe harbors under the adapted *Miller* standard for those materials that have serious literary, artistic, political, or scientific value as a whole, that are not patently offensive, and that are not directed to children's morbid interest in violence. Third, the government cannot discriminate based on the viewpoint of the proscribed material. The Indianapolis Ordinance was drafted with careful attention paid to these major limiting principles.

The limiting principles that were built into the Ordinance to make it constitutional would make it difficult to impose sweeping restrictions on children's access to violence in media other than video games.

Playboy Entertainment Group, Reno v. ACLU, and *Sable Communications*, for example, illustrate that some media are extremely difficult to regulate even when the state asserts an interest in protecting children -- primarily because it would be difficult to restrict access for children without affecting the protected rights of adults. The third prong of the *Miller* standard -- the societal value prong -- also stands in the way of regulating violence in other media. For example, under a law attempting to limit children's access to graphic violence in books, television, and movies, the government would have to show that the particular book, television program, or movie "lacked serious literary, artistic, political or scientific value as a whole for persons under the age of eighteen (18) years." That would be a difficult burden to meet as applied to those media. In fact, the Ordinance may be constitutional as applied to some extremely violent video games precisely because the expressive elements of those video games are so inconsequential -- especially as compared to significant elements of protected expression present in books, television, and movies.

The difficulty of providing a specific definition of the prohibited material and the difficulty of meeting the "patently offensive" prong of *Miller* also limit the reach of the variable obscenity doctrine as applied to violence. The City has crafted a reasonably objective definition of graphic violence by listing specific serious injuries (decapitation, dismemberment, maiming, etc.). The limits of the variable obscenity doctrine restrict the scope of permissible regulation to material that is both defined in a sufficiently objective way and patently offensive. In other words, not every depiction of an assault is patently offensive with respect to children. The range of activity covered by the term "assault" indicates that the term may not be specific enough to equate with the specific sexual activity identified in *Miller*. Attempts to regulate in content areas other than graphic violence or sex are likely to encounter similar difficulties in adequately defining the proscribed material.

Another important parallel between the statute upheld in *Ginsberg* and the Ordinance also limits the danger of falling down the slippery slope toward unconstitutional censorship: The Ordinance is not a viewpoint-based restriction. The definition of "graphic violence" applies without regard for any viewpoint that might be expressed. The safe harbors created by the other *Miller* factors -- patently offensive, appealing to morbid interest, and no redeeming value --

pose no greater threat of viewpoint discrimination with respect to violence than they do with sexual content. Thus, even if the violence in a video game is completely justified and shows the forces of good prevailing over the forces of evil in a fantastic battle, it is still regulated.

Any attempt to regulate children's access to material based on the viewpoint of proscribed material would raise serious constitutional questions and move the regulation outside the bounds of the variable obscenity doctrine. Even obscenity and "fighting words," which are usually described as simply outside all First Amendment protection, cannot be subjected to viewpoint-based discrimination. See *R.A.V. v. St. Paul*, 505 U.S. at 383-84, 391 (striking down city's attempt to regulate "hate speech" because "the First Amendment does not permit St. Paul to impose special prohibitions on those speakers who express views on disfavored subjects.").

Plaintiffs' expressed fears about the danger that any restriction on children's access to violent video games would inevitably lead to sweeping restrictions on other media are not persuasive in light of experience with restrictions on children's access to sexual content. Such restrictions have scarcely "cleansed" literature, films, and television, for example, of sexual themes and content.

The slippery slope argued by plaintiffs obviously deserves close attention. However, the doctrine of variable obscenity as to children and the careful drafting of the Indianapolis Ordinance provide several anchors to prevent a slide down that slope. The doctrine is self-limiting not because it is restricted to sexual material, but because it still holds laws to strict requirements before they can survive First Amendment challenge. New York's statute met the demanding requirements outlined in *Ginsberg*. Indianapolis' attempt to regulate children's access to video games containing graphic violence meets the requirements in this case, as adapted by *Miller* and as adapted for graphic violence.

F. *The Ordinance's Use of One Age Standard*

Plaintiffs also contend the Ordinance violates the First Amendment because it fails to accommodate the different maturity levels of older and younger children. Common sense shows there are differences between seven year olds and seventeen year olds when it comes to

Undead in the Federal Courts

material with strong sexual content or graphic violence. As plaintiffs maintain, the violent material appropriate for young children and the violent material appropriate for older teenagers may be significantly different. Thus, in applying the third-prong of the adapted *Miller* standard, which is whether there is any serious literary, artistic, political, or scientific value for children, for example, it may be important to know whether the "reasonable minor" is an older child, a younger child, or some hypothetical "average child." The limited record before the court at this time does not contain much evidence either supporting or contradicting the claim that older minors are harmed less (or more) than younger children by exposure to graphic violence in video games as defined by the Ordinance. [13]

> 13 One option available to the City would have been to regulate access to violent video games according to one or more additional age categories. Plaintiffs also contend that distinguishing among age groups would be unduly burdensome and call for even more arbitrary line-drawing. The original draft of the Ordinance took that approach, but it was amended in committee to use only one age standard after objections were raised by the video game industry.

While plaintiffs maintain that any "solution" to the problem of different maturity levels would be inadequate, some cases address the issue of treating children as a group under a modified *Miller* standard. In the context of sexual material, some courts have concluded that "'if a work is found to have serious literary, artistic, political or scientific value for a legitimate minority of normal, older adolescents, then it cannot be said to lack such value for the entire class of juveniles taken as a whole.'" *American Booksellers v. Webb*, 919 F.2d 1493, 1505 (11th Cir. 1990), quoting *American Booksellers Ass'n v. Virginia*, 882 F.2d 125, 127 (4th Cir. 1989). [14]

> 14 In the context of adult obscenity, the Supreme Court has noted that "the mere fact that only a minority of a population may believe a work has serious value does not mean the 'reasonable person' standard would not be met." *Pope v. Illinois*, 481 U.S. 497, 501 n.3, 95 L. Ed. 2d 439, 107 S. Ct. 1918 (1987).

From the City's perspective, the Eleventh and Fourth Circuits' approach is problematic. It leaves younger children with less than an appropriate level of protection and may severely frustrate the purpose of the Ordinance. The court agrees. No matter where an age line is drawn, it would be possible to point to a "legitimate minority" of children just under the age limit for whom the prospect of harm would not be significant. If any age limit can be defeated by showing such a "legitimate minority" of children just a little bit younger, then no age limit could survive constitutional scrutiny.

A second approach to the problem appears in *Ginsberg* itself. In addressing the New York statute, the Supreme Court gave no indication that treating all children identically is unconstitutional when a state regulates material under a variable obscenity theory. All adults are treated as an undifferentiated group under the *Miller* standard, just as all children under 17 were treated as one group in *Ginsberg*. The City has chosen that approach in this case, and it survives scrutiny under *Ginsberg*. This court also sees no constitutional difference between drawing the line on an 18th birthday instead of a 17th birthday.

G. *Plaintiffs' Challenges to the Operational Aspects of the Ordinance*

Plaintiffs also request relief from the provisions of the Ordinance that impose different requirements on large and small locations, require physical separation of harmful video games from other video games, and impose monitoring requirements on owners and operators to ensure that no unaccompanied minor can view or operate the regulated video games. See §§ 831-1, 831-5, 831-6. Plaintiffs contend that these "operational" provisions of the Ordinance are internally inconsistent and unnecessarily burdensome. As a result of these alleged drafting failures, the Ordinance is said to present a "trap" that is insufficiently tailored to serve the City's asserted interests in protecting children and empowering parents. Plaintiffs have not shown that these operational aspects of the Ordinance are likely to make it unconstitutional.

First, the Ordinance directly furthers the City's compelling interests by limiting, but not banning, children's access to the regulated material. Alternative approaches to regulation that would be equally effective in preventing children from viewing and operating harmful games would not materially broaden anyone's access to protected speech. Compare *United States v. Playboy Entertainment Group*, U.S. at , 120 S. Ct. at 1887 (finding statute that significantly burdened adults' access to protected speech failed to use a plausible, less restrictive alternative and that "Government cannot ban speech if targeted blocking is a feasible and effective means of furthering its compelling interests.").

Second, the court disagrees with the plaintiffs' characterization of several of the provisions as overly burdensome, as explained below. Third, many of the detailed "operational aspects" of the Ordinance are difficult to evaluate in a facial challenge to the Ordinance. Fourth, the court disagrees with plaintiffs' assertion that the Ordinance stigmatizes adult use of violent video games to the point where the regulations unconstitutionally burden adults' right of access to these games. See *American Booksellers v. Webb*, 919 F.2d at 1501-02 (upholding regulations on display of material that is harmful to minors and finding the indirect burden on adults' First Amendment right to access the material was insignificant). For all of these reasons, the court will not enjoin the challenged operational provisions of the Ordinance. See §§ 831-1, 831-5, 831-6.

More specifically, plaintiffs contend that the Ordinance irrationally requires larger establishments both to create a physically partitioned area and to maintain ten feet of separation between all video games that are harmful to minors and those that are not harmful. Plaintiffs reason that if a physical wall divides the harmful games from the other games, the additional ten-foot barrier serves no purpose -- that it is essentially just a punishment for having any violent games at the establishment. If all establishments comply by building partitions with solid walls, that argument might have more force. However, the Ordinance also authorizes less expensive (and more permeable) barriers, which many establishments might choose as their means to comply. A ten-foot separation from the partitioned area would still serve a purpose by helping to prevent any temptation to "jump" the barrier.

In addition, the spacing requirements are open to a different interpretation. For example, where an amusement location creates a partitioned area for harmful games, the ten-foot spacing requirement can reasonably be read to apply to require measurement through the entrance to the partitioned area. Under this reading, harmful games and non-harmful games could co-exist on opposite sides of the same solid wall. Plaintiffs' argument on this point does not support a facial challenge.

With respect to the monitoring requirements imposed by the Ordinance, plaintiffs argue that the rules regarding "incidental views" and parental supervision/permission will be unworkable in practice. Plaintiffs envision owners, operators, and enforcement officials running around with stop watches and tape measures to ensure that parents remain within five feet of their children and that no minor ever has more than a thirty second exposure to the regulated games. These scenarios are both far-fetched and almost completely avoidable. See *American Booksellers v. Webb*, 919 F.2d at 1507 ("Since this is a facial challenge, we cannot, as appellees seem to suggest, consider the constitutional propriety of the most onerous methods of compliance which a broad reading of [the statute] could possibly require.").

Plaintiffs complain the Ordinance will burden them because they will be required to have an employee physically on the site to monitor the ages of players on games deemed "harmful to minors." The coin-operated games now are typically left unattended. The requirement that games deemed "harmful to minors" be attended is no more burdensome than laws that effectively prohibit sale of sexually explicit magazines or alcoholic beverages in unattended vending machines. See, *e.g., American Booksellers v. Webb*, 919 F.2d at 1506-08 (upholding ordinance barring public display of materials deemed obscene as to children); *Crawford v. Lungren*, 96 F.3d 380, 387-88 (9th Cir. 1996) (upholding law barring sale of adult-oriented publications in unattended vending machines). This requirement does not render the Ordinance unconstitutional.

The "incidental view" provision that applies to "exhibitors" is obviously a reasonable accommodation for those smaller establishments that are not required to erect a physical partition between games "harmful to minors" and other games. See § 831-6(h). If the owner of a small establishment finds it too difficult to prevent minors from viewing the screens of regulated games, the owner certainly could choose to create a partitioned area and then not allow minors in that area. In addition, state courts may reasonably decide that the Ordinance's knowledge requirement applies to the incidental view provision. Under such an interpretation, the thirty second limit would serve as notice that once an owner knows that a child is viewing a regulated game, the owner needs to do something about it immediately.

Similarly, if owners find it too difficult to monitor parents' supervision of their children, they can follow the Ordinance's alternative procedure and require all parents to give express permission as provided in the Ordinance. See § 831-1 (defining "accompanied by"). Once a parent has given express permission, the parent would be free to roam about the establishment or even to leave the child on his own. The fact that a parent's permission "expires" at the end of each day raises no serious constitutional issue. A longer-term parental permission would not address the City's concern that the type of video games a particular establishment has on its premises may change over time without parents' knowledge.

Plaintiffs also challenge the provision of the Ordinance that completely bans amusement machines deemed harmful to minors on "public property." § 831-7. The City has responded that where it acts in a proprietary capacity rather than in its regulatory capacity, the First Amendment gives it considerably more (but not unlimited) latitude to choose who may use that property. See generally *International Society for Krishna Consciousness, Inc. v. Lee*, 505 U.S. 672, 678, 120 L. Ed. 2d 541, 112 S. Ct. 2701 (1992). In any event, the City has presented evidence that "there are not now nor have there recently been" any games regulated by the Ordinance on public property. Ex. P-66 (Harris Aff. P 2). Thus, no games are threatened with immediate removal under Section 831-7 and plaintiffs have not come forward with any evidence showing that anyone has applied, or will apply, to place any of the restricted games on public property. Because no one claims to be threatened with irreparable injury by the enforcement of Section 831-7, the court declines to consider the issue at this preliminary injunction stage.

V. *Vagueness*

Plaintiffs also contend that the Ordinance is unconstitutionally vague. The void-for-vagueness doctrine addresses the due process concern that "legislative enactments must articulate terms 'with a reasonable degree of clarity' to reduce the risk of arbitrary enforcement and allow individuals to conform their behavior to the requirements of the law." *Gresham v. Peterson*, 225 F.3d 899, 907, 2000 WL 1231066, at *7 (7th Cir. 2000), quoting *Roberts v. United States Jaycees*, 468 U.S. 609, 629, 82 L. Ed. 2d 462, 104 S. Ct. 3244 (1984), and *Kolender v. Lawson*, 461 U.S. 352, 357, 75 L. Ed. 2d 903, 103 S. Ct. 1855 (1983). However, "a state statute should not be deemed facially invalid unless it is not readily subject to a narrowing construction by the state courts." *Erznoznik v. City of Jacksonville*, 422 U.S. 205, 216, 45 L. Ed. 2d 125, 95 S. Ct. 2268 (1975). If a reasonable interpretation by a state court could cure the constitutional problem, a federal court should not hold a potentially vague statute unconstitutional. *Gresham v. Peterson*, 225 F.3d 899, 2000 WL 1231066, at *7.

The degree of drafting precision demanded by the Constitution depends on the nature of the law. *Gresham v. Peterson* dealt with another Indianapolis ordinance enforceable by civil fines that was challenged on First Amendment grounds. The Seventh Circuit noted that "laws imposing civil rather than criminal penalties do not demand the same high level of clarity," but also found that this lowered burden is "mitigated" by the fact that a more stringent vagueness test applies to enactments that potentially interfere with free speech. *Id.* at *8. Plaintiffs argue that a heightened First Amendment vagueness threshold applies, and the City asserts that it has greater leeway in defining civil violations. Suffice it to say that "it is . . . essential that legislation aimed at protecting children from allegedly harmful expression -- no less than legislation enacted with respect to adults -- be clearly drawn and that the standards adopted be reasonably precise." *Interstate Circuit, Inc. v. City of Dallas*, 390 U.S. 676, 689, 20 L. Ed. 2d 225, 88 S. Ct. 1298 (1968), quoting *People v. Kahan*, 15 N.Y.2d 311, 206 N.E.2d 333, 335, 258 N.Y.S.2d 391 (1965) (Fuld, J., concurring). The Ordinance meets that standard.

A. *The Modified Miller Standard*

Complementing their argument that the *Miller* standard is restricted exclusively to regulation of sexual material, plaintiffs argue that the *Miller* standard is unconstitutionally vague as applied to graphic violence. Plaintiffs claim that the owners and operators of amusement locations are left with no guidance on the meaning of "morbid interest in violence," "patently offensive," and "suitable material" as they attempt to segregate games that are "harmful to minors." Plaintiffs support that argument with the deposition of Deputy Mayor David Harris, who was asked to explain or define the terms "morbid interest in violence" and what is "suitable material" for children. Harris declined to offer a definition or explanation without consulting with the City's lawyers. Based on that testimony, plaintiffs argue that if the City's enforcement officials cannot understand those terms without consulting lawyers, they do not provide fair notice to plaintiffs and other video game operators as to what is regulated.

As explained above, the City's adaptation of the *Miller* standard is appropriate under the First Amendment. The Court is not persuaded by plaintiffs' secondary attack on vagueness grounds. Even if it is true, for example, that a given community can more readily agree on which sexual material is inappropriate for children than on which graphically violent material is inappropriate (though plaintiffs offer no evidence to support this assertion), that would not make the *Miller* standard unworkable *per se*. It would simply narrow the scope of permissible regulation to that particular subset of violent material where there is an acceptable level of agreement.

Plaintiffs' argument based on the Harris testimony is based on a misunderstanding of how the *Miller* standard works in practice. First, the law must identify with reasonable specificity the particular types of depictions that are prohibited, which the Indianapolis Ordinance does in its definition of "graphic violence." The other prongs of the modified *Miller* standard then work together to provide three analytically distinct "safe harbors" for material that contains "graphic violence." Those harbors are safe for material that either does not predominantly appeal to minors' morbid interest in violence, or that is not "patently offensive" to prevailing standards in the community, or that nevertheless has serious literary, artistic, political, or scientific value as a whole for persons under 18 years old.

The Supreme Court has explained with respect to obscenity for adults that the three *Miller* prongs work together to "limit the uncertain sweep of the obscenity definition." See *Reno v. ACLU*, 521 U.S. at 873. Similarly here, the entire standard works as an integrated "safety valve" to save from regulation some of those video games that contain graphic violence and strong sexual content. Thus, even if the court credited plaintiffs' argument that "morbid interest in violence" is in some way less precise than "prurient interest in sex," the standard as a whole retains the required precision. We have achieved a rough peace with the *Miller* standard as applied to sexual obscenity for adults, and it appears also to be constitutionally serviceable as adapted to regulate graphic violence in video games played by children.

For example, the three modified *Miller* prongs would presumably protect games like Gauntlet Legacy even if the game contains some graphic violence. The City apparently agrees: "By definition, the Ordinance steers clear of any video game that in fact contains the type of extensive plot, character development and narrative that plaintiffs attempt to ascribe to some games." Def. Br. at 11; see also *id.* at 4 ("The Ordinance does not apply to every game that displays 'graphic violence' or 'strong sexual content.'"). The Ordinance is consistent with this interpretation. [15]

> 15 For example, a video hockey game might include a fight during which a player's face is cut and his nose is broken. If the scene could be construed to show "bloodshed" or "disfiguration" realistically, it would appear to meet the Ordinance's definition of graphic violence. However, the modified *Miller* standard should save the game from regulation because the graphic violence in the game is not likely to be "patently offensive," and/or a video hockey game probably "predominantly appeals" to children's interest in hockey, not their "morbid interest in violence."

The plaintiffs also argue more specifically that the Ordinance's "patently offensive" prong is particularly suspect under a vagueness analysis. Under the *Miller* standard (or a modified version), the objectionable material must be specifically defined, and the test for whether the material is "patently offensive" refers specifically to the objectionable portion of the work in question. The issue is not whether the work as a whole is patently offensive. See *American Booksellers v. Webb*, 919 F.2d at 1503 n.18. Plaintiffs here argue that, because the Ordinance identifies "graphic violence" as the proscribed material in a clause separate from the clause that sets forth the "patently offensive" prong of the *Miller* standard, the Ordinance is unconstitutional as written because it fails to require "that graphic violence be depicted in a patently offensive way." Pl. Reply Br. at 19.

On its face the Ordinance is susceptible to plaintiffs' proposed interpretation, which would render it unconstitutional. However, the court is also confident that the Supreme Court of Indiana could and would easily construe the Ordinance to include the requirement that the graphic violence itself be "patently offensive." "We have regularly said that courts have an 'overriding obligation to construe our statutes in such a way as to render them constitutional if reasonably possible. . . .'" *Brownsburg Area Patrons Affecting Change v. Baldwin*, 714 N.E.2d 135, 141 (Ind. 1999), quoting *A Woman's Choice-East Side Women's Clinic v. Newman*, 671 N.E.2d 104, 111 (Ind. 1997) (Dickson, J., concurring); *Burris v. State*, 642 N.E.2d 961, 968 (Ind. 1994) ("[A] statute is accorded every reasonable presumption supporting its validity."), citing *Brady v. State*, 575 N.E.2d 981 (Ind. 1991); see also Ind. Code § 35-49-2-2 (identifying the proscribed material in a separate clause).

B. *The Definition of "Graphic Violence"*

Plaintiffs also claim that the Ordinance's definition of graphic violence is unconstitutionally vague. As already noted, the Ordinance's formulation of graphic violence is reasonably objective and is not far afield from the proscribed conduct and various states of nudity that are used to define sexual obscenity as to minors. [16] The drafters of the Ordinance chose to define the proscribed content according to the *specific* types of injury inflicted on the characters and depicted in the game. If one of the listed injuries is depicted or represented, it will qualify as graphic violence. Perhaps one can quibble at the margins about the exact meaning of "mutilation" or "disfiguration," but the terms are "reasonably precise." See *Interstate Circuit, Inc. v. City of Dallas*, 390 U.S. at 689. In addition, it was reasonable to focus on the injuries that are depicted rather than the conduct that causes the injuries. Cf. *Miller v. California*, 413 U.S. 15, 25, 37 L. Ed. 2d 419, 93 S. Ct. 2607 (1973) (suggesting that definitions of adult obscenity could include representations or descriptions of "ultimate sexual acts, normal or perverted, actual or simulated" and of "masturbation, excretory functions, and [lewd] exhibition of the genitals").

16 The key terms upheld in *Ginsberg*, although a product of their time, certainly were not inherently more precise than the specific types of injury listed in the Ordinance. See *Ginsberg v. New York*, 390 U.S. 629, 645-46, 20 L. Ed. 2d 195, 88 S. Ct. 1274 (1968) (reproducing statute's definitions of nudity, sexual conduct, sexual excitement, and sado-masochistic abuse).

Moreover, even if the definition of graphic violence could be interpreted in a broad, open- ended manner, a state court could provide a reasonable narrowing construction that would render the Ordinance constitutional in some applications. See *Gresham v. Peterson*, 225 F.3d 899, 2000 WL 1231066, at *7. For example, to the extent that the word "including" implies that the definition of graphic violence offers an incomplete list of the proscribed "serious injuries," a state court could easily determine that the list is exclusive. See *id.* at *8. Similarly, this court need not decide whether a human-like alien's green ooze counts as "bloodshed." 17 These decisions can and should be made by the Indiana courts. Because the City has met its obligation to define with reasonable specificity the violent material it seeks to regulate, plaintiffs are unlikely to succeed on their claim that the definition is unconstitutionally vague.

17 At least some video games have switches that allow the player or the exhibitor to choose from among several colors of "blood."

Conclusion

It would be an odd conception of the First Amendment and "variable obscenity" that would allow a state to prevent a boy from purchasing a magazine containing pictures of topless women in provocative poses, as in *Ginsberg*, but give that same boy a constitutional right to train to become a sniper at the local arcade without his parent's permission. The plaintiffs have not shown they are reasonably likely to succeed on their claims that the Indianapolis Ordinance violates the First Amendment or is unconstitutionally vague. Accordingly, the plaintiffs' motion for a preliminary injunction is denied.

So ordered.

Date: October 11, 2000

DAVID F. HAMILTON, JUDGE

United States District Court

Southern District of Indiana

EXHIBIT A

CITY-COUNTY GENERAL ORDINANCE NO. 72, 2000

Proposal No. 239, 2000

PROPOSAL FOR A GENERAL ORDINANCE to regulate the conduct of persons who own or operate places of business which contain amusement machines and/or video games, in such a manner that restricts and prohibits access to amusement machines and/or video games which are deemed harmful to minors, and to prohibit such amusement machines and/or video games on public property.

WHEREAS, Marion County and the City of Indianapolis have compelling interests in protecting the well-being of minors, in protecting parents' authority to shield their minor children from influences that the parents find inappropriate or offensive, and in reducing juvenile crime; and

WHEREAS, our courts have recognized that minors are affected by and may be protected from patently offensive sex-related material; and

WHEREAS, recent academic literature corroborates the finding of earlier studies that violent video games produce psychological effects in minor children and that prolonged exposure to violent video games increases the likelihood of aggression in minor children (see Craig A. Anderson & Karen E. Dill, Video Games and Aggressive Thoughts, Feelings, and Behavior in the Laboratory and in Life, 78 J. of Personality and Soc. Psychol. 772 (2000) (summarizing past research and noting that the "positive association between violent video games and aggressive personality is consistent with a developmental model in which extensive exposure to violent video games . . . contributes to the creation of an aggressive personality" and concluding that "the present data indicate that concern about the potentially deleterious consequences of playing violent video games is not misplaced")); and

WHEREAS, growing evidence of the harmful effects of violent video games has led Congress to investigate the impact of these games on minor children (see Hearing on "The Impact of Interactive Violence on Children," United States Senate Comm. on Commerce, Science & Transportation, 106th Cong. (March 21, 2000) ("Hearing"); see also Majority Staff of Senate Comm. on the Judiciary, 106th Cong., Children, Violence and the Media: A Report for Parents and Policy Makers (Sept. 14, 1999)), and has led President Clinton to ask the Federal Trade Commission to investigate the marketing of violent video games to minor children (see Letter from William J. Clinton, President, to Janet Reno, Attorney General of the United States, and Robert Pitofsky, Chairman, Federal Trade Commission (June 1, 1999)); and

WHEREAS, producers and retailers of video games agree that "the best control is parental control" (see Statement of the Video Software Dealers Association in conjunction with Hearing, above); and

WHEREAS, testimony before Congress indicates that fourth through eighth graders report spending an average of from half an hour to two-and-a-half hours playing video games in arcades each week (see Hearing, above, Testimony of Jeanne B. Funk, Ph.D., clinical child psychologist); and

WHEREAS, parents are less able in public places than in the home to control the level of violence and sexual content to which their minor children are exposed; now, therefore,

BE IT ORDAINED BY THE CITY-COUNTY COUNCIL OF THE CITY OF INDIANAPOLIS AND OF MARION COUNTY, INDIANA:

SECTION 1. Section 831-1 of the "Revised Code of the Consolidated City and County," regarding definitions, hereby is amended by the deletion of the language which is stricken-through, and by the addition of the language which is underscored, to read as follows:

Sec. 831-1. Definitions.

As used in this chapter, the following terms shall have the meanings ascribed to them in this section.

Accompanied by for purposes of subsections 831-5(h), 831-5(i), 831-5(j), 831-6(f), 831-6(g), and 831-6(h), means that the parent, guardian, or custodian of the minor either:

> (1) Is within five feet of the minor at all times while the minor is operating the amusement machine; or,
>
> (2) Has appeared in person with the minor at the amusement location or place of business containing amusement machines on that day and has given his or her permission for the exhibitor or registrant or an employee of the exhibitor or registrant to place on the back of the minor's hand or wrist a clearly visible, non-transferable designation such as a stamp or wrist band signifying that the parent, guardian, or custodian has consented to allow the minor to operate amusement machines that are harmful to minors.

Amusement location means any public room or area in the city which contains five (5) or more amusement machines; however, amusement locations shall not include premises which are licensed (as defined in IC 7.1-1-3-20) for the sale of alcoholic beverages and where entry is limited to persons who are eighteen (18) years of age or older.

Amusement machine means a currency-operated machine or device, including a machine or device operated by tokens, cards, points, or other currency-like means, offered to the public as a game or amusement, the object of which is to achieve a high or low score based on the skill of the player, including, but not limited to, video games, pool or billiard tables and pinball machines. Such a machine or device designed and used exclusively for the vending of merchandise of a tangible nature shall not be deemed an amusement machine.

Exhibitor means a person who owns or operates a place of business in the city where four (4) or fewer amusement machines are located; however, the provisions of this chapter shall not apply to an exhibitor's place of business which is licensed (as defined in IC 7.1-1-3-20) for the sale of alcoholic beverages and where entry is limited to persons who are eighteen (18) years of age or older.

Graphic violence means an amusement machine's visual depiction or representation of realistic serious injury to a human or human-like being where such serious injury includes amputation, decapitation, dismemberment, bloodshed, mutilation, maiming or disfiguration.

Harmful to minors means an amusement machine that predominantly appeals to minors' morbid interest in violence or minors' prurient interest in sex, is patently offensive to prevailing standards in the adult community as a whole with respect to what is suitable material for persons under the age of eighteen (18) years, lacks serious literary, artistic, political or scientific value as a whole for persons under the age of eighteen (18) years, and:

(1) Contains graphic violence; or,

(2) Contains strong sexual content.

Incidental view means a minor's view for fewer than thirty (30) seconds of the playing surface or screen of an amusement machine.

Knowingly means having general knowledge of, or reason to know, or a belief or ground for belief that warrants further inspection or inquiry of both:

(1) The character and content of the visual representations of the amusement machine; and,

(2) The age of the person operating or seeking to operate the amusement machine, provided, however, that an honest mistake shall constitute an excuse from liability hereunder if the defendant made a reasonable bona fide attempt (including but not limited to asking for legal photo identification) to ascertain the true age of the minor.

Minor means a person under the age of eighteen (18) years. This definition does not apply to a minor who has obtained a court decree pursuant to IC 31-34-20-6.

Not harmful means an amusement machine that is not harmful to minors.

Nudity means an amusement machine's visual depiction or representation of human male or female genitals, pubic area or buttocks with less than a fully opaque covering, or of a female breast with less than a fully opaque covering of any part of the nipple, or the showing of covered male genitals in a discernibly turgid state.

Parent, guardian or custodian means and includes a person who has legal custody of the ~~child~~ minor and is the ~~child's~~ minor's:

(1) Natural parent;

(2) Stepparent, adoptive parent or custodian as those terms are defined by IC 35-42-4-7;

(3) Guardian as defined by IC 29-3-1-6; or

(4) Other adult who has been appointed by a court to care for a [O>child<O] minor;

but, for purposes of subsections 831-5(e), 831-5(f) and 831-5(g) and subsections 831-6(c), 831-6(d) and 831-6(e), shall not include an exhibitor, or owner or operator of an amusement location with respect to a [O>child<O] minor who is present in the exhibitor's, owner's or operator's place of business.

Pool or billiard table means a table used for any form of the games commonly referredto as pool or billiards and includes any table of any size, the top of which is surrounded by an elastic ledge or cushion and which is designed or used to play any game which consists of impelling balls by means of sticks or cues.

[EDITOR'S NOTE: TEXT WITHIN THESE SYMBOLS [O> <O] IS OVERSTRUCK IN THE SOURCE.]

[O> <O]

Public property means all buildings and areas within Marion County that are owned, operated, or leased as lessee, by the City of Indianapolis, Marion County, a city or county department, a city-county agency, or a township, including but not limited to the Department of Parks and Recreation, but does not include property for which the City of Indianapolis, Marion County is the lessor.

Registrant in this chapter means a person registered with the controller under this chapter as the owner or operator of an amusement location in the city.

Strong sexual content means the visual depiction or representation by an amusement machine of nudity or explicit human sexual behavior by any human or human-like being in one or more of the following forms: masturbation; deviate sexual conduct; sexual intercourse; or, fondling of genitals.

SECTION 2. Section 831-5 of the "Revised Code of the Consolidated City and County," regarding operation of amusement locations, hereby is amended by the deletion of the language which is stricken-through, and by the addition of the language which is underscored, to read as follows:

Sec. 831-5. Operation of amusement locations; violations.

(a) All amusement locations shall be kept in a clean, healthful and sanitary condition at all times and the controller shall have the power to determine if such room or rooms are kept in a clean, healthful and sanitary condition and for such purpose, when desired, have the assistance of any law enforcement agency or the Health and Hospital Corporation of Marion County. If the controller shall determine, by a law enforcement agency or the division of buildings of the Health and Hospital Corporation of Marion County, that an unsanitary condition exists within an amusement location or on property immediately adjacent to the amusement location, which property is under the control of the amusement location owners or their lessee or lessor, the controller shall have the power to suspend the amusement location registration until such unsanitary condition is rectified.

(b) No registrant under this chapter shall permit persons to congregate in a disturbing manner within an amusement location or on parking areas or other property immediately adjacent to or normally used for purposes of parking for an amusement location which property is under the control of the amusement location owner or owners or their lessee or lessor. A violation of this provision shall be sufficient grounds for the revocation of the amusement location registrations by the controller.

(c) No registrant under this chapter, or registrant's employee, shall violate any state statute or city ordinance, or allow any other person to commit such violation, within an amusement location or on parking areas or other property immediately adjacent to or normally used for purposes of parking for an amusement location which property is under the control of the amusement location owner or owners or their lessee or lessor. A violation of this provision shall be sufficient grounds for the revocation of the amusement location registrations by the controller.

(d) All employees of a registrant under this chapter shall be eighteen (18) years of age or older.

(e) It shall be unlawful for a person to allow a ~~child~~ minor under sixteen (16) years of age who is subject to the compulsory school attendance laws of the state and who is not accompanied by the ~~child's~~ minor's parent, guardian or custodian to be present in an amusement location between the hours of 7:00 a.m. and 3:30 p.m. on a day when such ~~child'~~ minor's school is in session.

(f) It shall be unlawful for a person to allow a ~~child~~ minor to be present in an amusement location after the hours established by state statute or city ordinance for juvenile curfew unless such ~~child~~ minor is accompanied by the ~~child's~~ minor's parent, guardian or custodian, or an adult specified by the ~~child's~~ minor's parent, guardian or custodian.

an amusement location unless a sign is conspicuously posted inside the location which provides that no ~~child~~ minor under sixteen (16) years of age may be present in an amusement location between the hours of 7:00 a.m. and 3:30 p.m. on a day when the ~~child's~~] minor's school is in session unless accompanied by the ~~child's~~ minor's parent, guardian or custodian, and that no ~~child~~ minor may be present in an amusement location in violation of the curfew established by state statute or city ordinance.

(h) It shall be unlawful for a registrant, a registrant's agent, or an employee of an amusement location knowingly to allow a minor who is not accompanied by the minor's parent, guardian or custodian to operate in the amusement location an amusement machine that is harmful to minors.

(i) It shall be unlawful for a registrant to operate an amusement location unless each amusement machine that is harmful to minors in the amusement location displays a conspicuous sign indicating that the machine may not be operated by a minor under eighteen (18) years of age unless the minor is accompanied by his or her parent, guardian, or custodian. If amusement machines that are harmful to minors are displayed together in an area separate from amusement machines that are not harmful, a single conspicuous sign in that area or at the entrance to that area may be used to mark the group of machines for purposes of this subsection.

(j) It shall be unlawful for a registrant to make available to patrons any amusement machine that is harmful to minors within ten (10) feet of an amusement machine that is not harmful. It shall further be unlawful for a registrant not to separate amusement machines that are harmful to minors from other machines by some form of partition, divider, drape, barrier, panel, screen, or wall that completely obstructs the view of persons outside the partitioned area of the playing surface or display screen of the machines that are harmful to minors. It shall be unlawful for a registrant, registrant's agent, or employee of an amusement location to allow a minor who is not accompanied by his or her parent, guardian, or custodian into the partitioned area.

(k) It shall be unlawful for a registrant to make available to patrons any amusement machine that is harmful to minors if the registrant has been cited for three (3) or more violations of Section 831-5(h), (i), (j), or (k) of this Code in any twelve-month period in the preceding three (3) years.

(l) One or more violations of Section 831-5(h), (i), (j), or (k) of this Code may serve as grounds for suspension or revocation of the amusement location's registration, pursuant to the authority vested in the controller and procedures prescribed in Chapter 801 of this Code. Three (3) or more violations of Section 831-5(h), (i), (j), or (k) of this Code, however, shall require revocation of the amusement location's registration, subject to the notice and hearing requirements of Chapter 801. For the purposes of this subsection, no more than one violation shall be deemed to have occurred on any one day.

SECTION 3. Section 831-6 of the "Revised Code of the Consolidated City and County," regarding operation of amusement machines by exhibitors, hereby is amended by the deletion of the language which is stricken-through, and by the addition of the language which is underscored, to read as follows:

Sec. 831-6. Operation of amusement machines by exhibitors; violations.

(a) No exhibitor or exhibitor's employee shall permit persons to congregate in a disturbing manner on the premises of the exhibitor's place of business.

(b) No exhibitor or exhibitor's employee shall violate any state statute or city ordinance, or allow any other person to commit such violation on the premises of the exhibitor's place of business.

(c) It shall be unlawful for an exhibitor or the exhibitor's employee to allow a ~~child~~ minor under sixteen (16) years of age who is subject to the compulsory school attendance laws of the state and who is not accompanied by the ~~child's~~ minor's parent, guardian or custodian to operate an amusement machine in the exhibitor's place of business between the hours of 7:00 a.m. and 3:30 p.m. on a day when such [O>child's<O] minor's school is in session.

(d) It shall be unlawful for an exhibitor or the exhibitor's employee to allow a ~~child~~ minor to operate an amusement machine in the exhibitor's place of business after the hours established by state statute or city ordinance for juvenile curfew unless such ~~child~~ minor is accompanied by the ~~child's~~] minor's parent, guardian or custodian, or an adult specified by the ~~child's~~ minor's parent, guardian or custodian.

(e) It shall be unlawful for an exhibitor to have amusement machines in his or her place of business unless a sign is conspicuously posted near any amusement machines which provides that no ~~child~~ minor under sixteen (16) years of age may operate an amusement machine between the hours of 7:00 a.m. and 3:30 p.m. on a day when the ~~child's~~ minor's school is in session unless accompanied by the ~~child's~~ minor's parent, guardian or custodian, and that no ~~child~~ minor who is in violation of the curfew established by state statute or city ordinance may operate an amusement machine.

(f) It shall be unlawful for an exhibitor, an exhibitor's agent, or an exhibitor's employee knowingly to allow a minor who is not accompanied by the minor's parent, guardian or custodian to operate in the exhibitor's place of business an amusement machine that is harmful to minors.

(g) It shall be unlawful for an exhibitor to make available to patrons in his or her place of business amusement machines that are harmful to minors unless each amusement machine that is harmful to minors displays a conspicuous sign indicating that the machine may not be operated by a minor under eighteen (18) years of age unless the minor is accompanied by his or her parent, guardian, or custodian. If amusement machines that are harmful to minors are displayed together in an area separate from amusement machines that are not harmful, a single conspicuous sign in that area or at the entrance to that area may be used to mark the group of machines for purposes of this subsection.

(h) It shall be unlawful for an exhibitor to make available to patrons any amusement machine that is harmful to minors within ten feet of an amusement machine that is not harmful. It shall further be unlawful for an exhibitor, exhibitor's agent, or exhibitor's employee to allow a minor who is not accompanied by his or her parent, guardian, or custodian to view, with the exception of an incidental view, the playing surface or screen of a game that is harmful to minors.

(i) It shall be unlawful for an exhibitor to make available to patrons any amusement machine that is harmful to minors if the exhibitor has been cited for three (3) or more violations of Section 831-6(f), (g), (h), or (i) of the Code in any twelve-month period in the preceding three (3) years.

SECTION 4. Chapter 831 of the "Revised Code of the Consolidated City and County," regarding amusement machine locations, hereby is amended by the addition of a NEW Section 831-7, regarding harmful games on public property, to read as follows:

Sec. 831-7. Harmful games on public property.

It shall be unlawful for an registrant or exhibitor to make available on public property any amusement machine that is harmful to minors.

SECTION 5. Section 831-7 of the "Revised Code of the Consolidated City and County," regarding inspections and reports of violations, upon the passage of this ordinance shall be RENUMBERED as "Section 831-8."

SECTION 6. Section 831-8 of the "Revised Code of the consolidated City and County," regarding enforcement and penalties, hereby is amended by the deletion of the language which is stricken-through, and by the addition of the language which is underscored, to read as follows:

Sec. 831-89. Enforcement and penalties.

A person who violates any provision of this chapter shall be punishable as provided in section 103-3 of the Code; provided, however, the fine imposed for such violation shall not be less than two hundred dollars (\$ 200.00), that for the purpose of assessing fines no more than one violation shall be deemed to have occurred on any one day, and that each day that an offense continues shall constitute a separate violation. The fines assessed for violations of this chapter shall be deposited with the law enforcement agency that caused the violation to be filed, if any.

SECTION 7. The expressed or implied repeal or amendment by this ordinance of any other ordinance or part of any other ordinance does not affect any rights or liabilities accrued, penalties incurred, or proceedings begun prior to the effective date of this ordinance. Those rights, liabilities, and proceedings are continued, and penalties shall be imposed and enforced under the repealed or amended ordinance as if this ordinance had not been adopted.

SECTION 8. Should any provision (section, paragraph, sentence, clause, or any other portion) of this ordinance be declared by a court of competent jurisdiction to be invalid for any reason, the remaining provision or provisions shall not be affected, if such remaining provisions can, without the invalid provision or provisions, be given the effect intended by the Council. To this end, the provisions of the ordinance are severable.

SECTION 9. This ordinance shall be in effect September 1, 2000.

The foregoing was passed by the City-County Council this 10th day of July, 2000, at 9:17 p.m.

ATTEST:

/s/

Dr. Beurt SerVaas

President, City-County Council

/s/

Suellen Hart, Clerk, City-County Council

Presented by me to the Mayor this 13th day of July, 2000, at 10:00 a.m.

/s/

Suellen Hart, Clerk, City-County Council

Approved and signed by me this 17th day of July, 2000

/s/

Bart Peterson, Mayor

STATE OF INDIANA, MARION COUNTY

CITY OF INDIANAPOLIS

SS:

I, Suellen Hart, Clerk of the City-County Council, Indianapolis, Marion County, Indiana, do hereby certify the above and foregoing is a full, true, and complete copy of Proposed No. 239, 2000, a Proposal for GENERAL ORDINANCE, passed by the City-County Council on the 10th day of July, 2000, by a vote of 27 YEAS and 0 NAYS, and was retitled General Ordinance No. 72, 2000, which was signed by the Mayor on the 17th day of July, 2000, and now remains on file and on record in my office.

WITNESS my hand and the official seal of the City of Indianapolis, Indiana, this 17th day of July, 2000.

[SEAL]

/s/

Suellen Hart, Clerk, City-County Council

EXHIBIT B

Joint Statement on the Impact of Entertainment Violence on Children Congressional Public Health Summit July 26, 2000

We, the undersigned, represent the public health community. As with any community, there exists a diversity of viewpoints -- but with many matters, there is also consensus. Although a wide variety of viewpoints on the import and impact of entertainment violence on children may exist outside the public health community, within it, there is a strong consensus on many of the effects on children's health, well-being and development.

Television, movies, music, and interactive games are powerful learning tools, and highly influential media. The average American child spends as much as 28 hours a week watching television, and typically at least an hour a day playing video games or surfing the Internet. Several more hours each week are spent watching movies and videos, and listening to music. These media can, and often are, used to instruct, encourage, and even inspire. But when these entertainment media showcase violence -- and particularly in a context which glamorizes or trivializes it -- the lessons learned can be destructive.

There are some in the entertainment industry who maintain that 1) violent programming is harmless because no studies exist that prove a connection between violent entertainment and aggressive behavior in children, and 2) young people know that television, movies, and video games are simply fantasy. Unfortunately, they are wrong on both counts.

At this time, well over 1000 studies -- including reports from the Surgeon General's office, the National Institute of Mental Health, and numerous studies conducted by leading figures within our medical and public health organizations -- our own members -- point overwhelmingly to a causal connection between media violence and aggressive behavior in some children. The conclusion of the public health community, based on over 30 years of research, is that viewing entertainment violence can lead to increases in aggressive attitudes, values and behavior, particularly in children.

Its effects are measurable and long-lasting. Moreover, prolonged viewing of media violence can lead to emotional desensitization toward violence in real life.

The effect of entertainment violence on children is complex and variable. Some children will be affected more than others. But while duration, intensity, and extent of the impact may vary, there are several measurable negative effects of children's exposure to violent entertainment. These effects take several forms.

-- Children who see a lot of violence are more likely to view violence as an effective way of settling conflicts. Children exposed to violence are more likely to assume that acts of violence are acceptable behavior.

-- Viewing violence can lead to emotional desensitization towards violence in real life. It can decrease the likelihood that one will take action on behalf of a victim when violence occurs.

-- Entertainment violence feeds a perception that the world is a violent and mean place. Viewing violence increases fear of becoming a victim of violence, with a resultant increase in self-protective behaviors and a mistrust of others.

-- Viewing violence may lead to real life violence. Children exposed to violent programming at a young age have a higher tendency for violent and aggressive behavior later in life than children who are not so exposed.

Although less research has been done on the impact of violent interactive entertainment (video games and other interactive media) on young people, preliminary studies indicate that the negative impact may be significantly more severe than that wrought by television, movies, or music. More study is needed in this area, and we urge that resources and attention be directed to this field.

We in no way mean to imply that entertainment violence is the sole, or even necessarily the most important factor contributing to youth aggression, anti-social attitudes, and violence. Family breakdown, peer influences, the availability of weapons, and numerous other factors may all contribute to these problems. Nor are we advocating restrictions on creative activity. The purpose of this document is descriptive, not prescriptive; we seek to lay out a clear picture of the pathological effects of entertainment violence. But we do hope that by articulating and releasing the consensus of the public health community, we may encourage greater public and parental awareness of the harms of violent entertainment, and encourage a more honest dialogue about what can be done to enhance the health and well-being of America's children.

/s/
Donald E. Cook, MD
President
American Academy of Pediatrics

/s/
Clarice Kestenbaum, MD
President
American Academy of Child & Adolescent Psychiatry

/s/
Bruce Bagly, MD
President
American Academy of Family Physicians

/s/
L. Michael Honaker, Ph. D.
Deputy Chief Executive Officer
American Psychological Association

/s/
Dr. E. Ratcliffe Anderson, Jr. MD
Executive Vice President
American Medical Association

American Amusement Machine Association, et al., Plaintiffs-Appellants,

v.

Teri Kendrick, et al., Defendants-Appellees.

No. 00-3643

UNITED STATES COURT OF APPEALS FOR THE SEVENTH CIRCUIT

244 F.3d 572
2001 U.S. App. LEXIS 4371

December 1, 2000, Argued
March 23, 2001, Decided

BEFORE CIRCUIT JUDGES POSNER, WOOD, and WILLIAMS,

OPINION BY JUDGE POSNER

The manufacturers of video games and their trade association seek to enjoin, as a violation of freedom of expression, the enforcement of an Indianapolis ordinance that seeks to limit the access of minors to video games that depict violence. Denial of a preliminary injunction has precipitated this appeal.

The ordinance defines the term "harmful to minors" to mean "an amusement machine that predominantly appeals to minors' morbid interest in violence or minors' prurient interest in sex, is patently offensive to prevailing standards in the adult community as a whole with respect to what is suitable material for persons under the age of eighteen (18) years, lacks serious literary, artistic, political or scientific value as a whole for persons under" that age, and contains either "graphic violence" or "strong sexual content." "Graphic violence," which is all that is involved in this case (so far as appears, the plaintiffs do not manufacture, at least for exhibition in game arcades and other public places, video games that have "strong sexual content"), is defined to mean "an amusement machine's visual depiction or representation of realistic serious injury to a human or human-like being where such serious injury includes amputation, decapitation, dismemberment, bloodshed, mutilation, maiming or disfiguration [disfigurement]."

The ordinance forbids any operator of five or more video-game machines in one place to allow a minor unaccompanied by a parent, guardian, or other custodian to use "an amusement machine that is harmful to minors," requires appropriate warning signs, and requires that such machines be separated by a partition from the other machines in the location and that their viewing areas be concealed from persons who are on the other side of the partition. Operators of fewer than five games in one location are subject to all but the partitioning restriction. Monetary penalties, as well as suspension and revocation of the right to operate the machines, are specified as remedies for violations of the ordinance.

The ordinance was enacted in 2000, but has not yet gone into effect, in part because we stayed it pending the decision of the appeal. The legislative history indicates that the City believes that participation in violent video games engenders violence on the part of the players, at least when they are minors. The City placed in evidence videotapes of several of the games that it believes violate the ordinance.

Although the district judge agreed with the plaintiffs that video games, possibly including some that would violate the ordinance, are "speech" within the meaning of the First Amendment and that children have rights under the free-speech clause, he held that the ordinance would violate the amendment only if the City lacked "a reasonable basis for believing the Ordinance would protect children from harm." He found a reasonable basis in a pair of empirical studies by psychologists which found that playing a violent video game tends to make young persons more aggressive in their attitudes and behavior, and also in a larger literature finding that violence in the media engenders aggressive feelings. The judge also ruled that the ordinance's tracking of the conventional standard for obscenity eliminated any concern that the ordinance might be excessively vague.

Having decided that the ordinance did not violate the plaintiffs' constitutional rights, the district judge did not consider the other criteria that might bear on the decision to grant or deny a preliminary injunction. In this appeal too, the parties argue only over whether the ordinance is legal, tempting us to treat this as if it were an appeal from a final judgment in favor of the defendants. We shall consider at the end of the opinion whether there is any occasion for further proceedings in the district court.

The ordinance brackets violence with sex, and the City asks us to squeeze the provision on violence into a familiar legal pigeonhole, that of obscenity, which is normally concerned with sex and is not protected by the First Amendment, while the plaintiffs insist that since their games are not obscene in the conventional sense they must receive the full protection of the First Amendment. Neither position is compelling. Violence and obscenity are distinct categories of objectionable depiction, Winters v. New York, 333 U.S. 507, 518-20, 92 L. Ed. 840, 68 S. Ct. 665 (1948); United States v. Thoma, 726 F.2d 1191, 1200 (7th Cir. 1984) ("depictions of torture and deformation are not inherently sexual and, absent some expert guidance as to how such violence appeals to the prurient interest of a deviant group, there is no basis upon which a trier of fact could deem such material obscene"); State v. Johnson, 343 So. 2d 705, 709-10 (La. 1977), and so the fact that obscenity is excluded from the protection of the principle that government may not regulate the content of expressive activity (as distinct from the time, place, or manner of the activity) neither compels nor forecloses a like exclusion of violent imagery. This would be obvious if a pornographer were to argue that because violence is "like" obscenity yet has not yet been placed on the list of expressive forms that can be regulated on the basis of their content, see, e.g., R.A.V. v. City of St. Paul, 505 U.S. 377, 382-84, 120 L. Ed. 2d 305, 112 S. Ct. 2538 (1992); DiMa Corp. v. Town of Hallie, 185 F.3d 823, 827 (7th Cir. 1999), obscenity should be struck from the list.

We shall discover some possible intersections between the concerns that animate obscenity laws and the concerns that animate the Indianapolis ordinance as we proceed, but in general the concerns are different. The main worry about obscenity, the main reason for its proscription, is not that it is harmful, which is the worry behind the Indianapolis ordinance, but that it is offensive. A work is classified as obscene not upon proof that it is likely to affect anyone's conduct, but upon proof that it violates community norms regarding the permissible scope of depictions of sexual or sex-related activity. Miller v. California, 413 U.S. 15, 24, 37 L. Ed. 2d 419, 93 S. Ct. 2607

(1973); United States v. Moore, 215 F.3d 681, 686 (7th Cir. 2000); United States v. Langford, 688 F.2d 1088, 1091 (7th Cir. 1982); United States v. Loy, 237 F.3d 251, 262 (3d Cir. 2001). Obscenity is to many people disgusting, embarrassing, degrading, disturbing, outrageous, and insulting, but it generally is not believed to inflict temporal (as distinct from spiritual) harm; or at least the evidence that it does is not generally considered as persuasive as the evidence that other speech that can be regulated on the basis of its content, such as threats of physical harm, conspiratorial communications, incitements, frauds, and libels and slanders, inflicts such harm. There are people who believe that some forms of graphically sexual expression, not necessarily obscene in the conventional legal sense, may incite men to commit rape, or to disvalue women in the workplace or elsewhere, see, e.g., Catharine A. MacKinnon, Only Words (1993); but that is not the basis on which obscenity has traditionally been punished. No proof that obscenity is harmful is required either to defend an obscenity statute against being invalidated on constitutional grounds or to uphold a prosecution for obscenity. Offensiveness is the offense.

One can imagine an ordinance directed at depictions of violence because they, too, were offensive. Maybe violent photographs of a person being drawn and quartered could be suppressed as disgusting, embarrassing, degrading, or disturbing without proof that they are likely to cause any of the viewers to commit a violent act. They might even be described as "obscene," in the same way that photographs of people defecating might be, and in many obscenity statutes are, included within the legal category of the obscene, Miller v. California, supra, 413 U.S. at 25; Pope v. Illinois, 481 U.S. 497, 501 n. 4, 95 L. Ed. 2d 439, 107 S. Ct. 1918 (1987); United States v. Langford, supra, 688 F.2d at 1091 n. 3, even if they have nothing to do with sex. In common speech, indeed, "obscene" is often just a synonym for repulsive, with no sexual overtones at all.

But offensiveness is not the basis on which Indianapolis seeks to regulate violent video games. Nor could the ordinance be defended on that basis. The most violent game in the record, "The House of the Dead," depicts zombies being killed flamboyantly, with much severing of limbs and effusion of blood; but so stylized and patently fictitious is the cartoon-like depiction that no one would suppose it "obscene" in the sense in which a photograph of a person being decapitated might be described as "obscene." It will not turn anyone's stomach. The basis of the ordinance, rather, is a belief that violent video games cause temporal harm by engendering aggressive attitudes and behavior, which might lead to violence.

This is a different concern from that which animates the obscenity laws, though it does not follow from this that government is helpless to respond to the concern by regulating such games. Protecting people from violence is at least as hallowed a role for government as protecting people from graphic sexual imagery. Chaplinsky v. New Hampshire, 315 U.S. 568, 572-73, 86 L. Ed. 1031, 62 S. Ct. 766 (1942), permits punishment of "fighting words," that is, words likely to cause a breach of the peace--violence. See also R.A.V. v. City of St. Paul, supra, 505 U.S. at 386, 391-92. Such punishment is permissible "content based" regulation, and in effect Indianapolis is arguing that violent video games incite youthful players to breaches of the peace. But this is to use the word "incitement" metaphorically. As we'll see, no showing has been made that games of the sort found in the record of this case have such an effect. Nor can such a showing be dispensed with on the ground that preventing violence is as canonical a role of government as shielding people from graphic sexual imagery. The issue in this case is not violence as such, or directly; it is violent images; and here the symmetry with obscenity breaks down. Classic literature and art, and not merely today's popular culture, are saturated with graphic scenes of violence, whether narrated or pictorial. The notion of forbidding not violence itself, but pictures of violence, is a novelty, whereas concern with pictures of graphic sexual conduct is of the essence of the traditional concern with obscenity.

There is a hint, though, that the City is also concerned with the welfare of the game-playing children themselves, and not just the welfare of their potential victims. This concern is implicit in the City's citation of Ginsberg v. New York, 390 U.S. 629, 639-43, 20 L. Ed. 2d 195, 88 S. Ct. 1274 (1968), which holds that potential harm to children's ethical and psychological development is a permissible ground for trying to shield them from forms of sexual expression that fall short of obscenity. See also FCC v. Pacifica Foundation, 438 U.S. 726, 749-50, 57 L. Ed. 2d 1073, 98 S. Ct. 3026 (1978). Ginsberg upheld a statute that forbade any representation of nudity that "(i) predominantly appeals to the prurient, shameful or morbid interest of minors, and (ii) is patently offensive to prevailing standards in the adult community as a whole with respect to what is suitable material for minors, and (iii) is utterly without redeeming social importance for minors." 390 U.S. at 633. In the present setting, concern with the welfare of the child might take two forms. One is a concern with the potential psychological harm to children of being exposed to violent images, and would be unrelated to the broader societal concern with violence that was the primary motivation for the ordinance. Another, subtler concern would be with the consequences for the child incited or predisposed to commit violent acts by exposure to violent images. In Hoctor v. U.S. Dept. of Agriculture, 82 F.3d 165, 168 (7th Cir. 1996), we noted that the Animal Welfare Act requires secure containment of dangerous animals in part because if they escape and injure a human being they are likely to be killed. A child who is caught and punished for committing a violent act suffers, much as his victim does--indeed, one purpose of punishment is to inflict on the criminal suffering commensurate with that of his victims, either to deter him or others from committing such crimes or (in retributive theory) because it is considered just that he should suffer as his victims do. Obscenity statutes, too, might be thought concerned not just with offensiveness, or with third-party effects (the thrust of the Indianapolis pornography ordinance, a precursor of the present ordinance, invalidated in American Booksellers Association, Inc. v. Hudnut, 771 F.2d 323 (7th Cir. 1985), aff'd without opinion, 475 U.S. 1001 (1986)), but also with the potential harm to the consumer of obscenity, especially a child who might be disturbed by graphic sexual images or suffer psychological harm--and thus Ginsberg. See also Osborne v. Ohio, 495 U.S. 103, 111, 109 L. Ed. 2d 98, 110 S. Ct. 1691 (1990).

If the community ceased to find obscenity offensive, yet sought to retain the prohibition of it on the ground that it incited its consumers to commit crimes or to engage in sexual discrimination, or that it interfered with the normal sexual development of its underage consumers, a state would have to present a compelling basis for believing that these were harms actually caused by obscenity and not pretexts for regulation on grounds not authorized by the First Amendment. The Court in Ginsberg was satisfied that New York had sufficient grounds for thinking that representations of nudity that would not constitute obscenity if the consumers were adults were

harmful to children. We must consider whether the City of
Indianapolis has equivalent grounds for thinking that violent video
games cause harm either to the game players or (the point the City
stresses) the public at large.

The grounds must be compelling and not merely plausible. Children
have First Amendment rights. Erznoznik v. City of Jacksonville, 422
U.S. 205, 212-14, 45 L. Ed. 2d 125, 95 S. Ct. 2268 (1975); Tinker v.
Des Moines Independent School District, 393 U.S. 503, 511-14, 21 L.
Ed. 2d 731, 89 S. Ct. 733 (1969). This is not merely a matter of
pressing the First Amendment to a dryly logical extreme. The
murderous fanaticism displayed by young German soldiers in World
War II, alumni of the Hitler Jugend, illustrates the danger of allowing
government to control the access of children to information and
opinion. Now that eighteen-year-olds have the right to vote, it is
obvious that they must be allowed the freedom to form their political
views on the basis of uncensored speech before they turn eighteen,
so that their minds are not a blank when they first exercise the
franchise. And since an eighteen-year-old's right to vote is a right
personal to him rather than a right to be exercised on his behalf by
his parents, the right of parents to enlist the aid of the state to shield
their children from ideas of which the parents disapprove cannot be
plenary either. People are unlikely to become well-functioning,
independent-minded adults and responsible citizens if they are raised
in an intellectual bubble.

No doubt the City would concede this point if the question were
whether to forbid children to read without the presence of an adult
the Odyssey, with its graphic descriptions of Odysseus's grinding out
the eye of Polyphemus with a heated, sharpened stake, killing the
suitors, and hanging the treacherous maidservants; or The Divine
Comedy with its graphic descriptions of the tortures of the damned;
or War and Peace with its graphic descriptions of execution by firing
squad, death in childbirth, and death from war wounds. Or if the
question were whether to ban the stories of Edgar Allen Poe, or the
famous horror movies made from the classic novels of Mary
Wollstonecraft Shelley (Frankenstein) and Bram Stoker (Dracula).
Violence has always been and remains a central interest of
humankind and a recurrent, even obsessive theme of culture both
high and low. It engages the interest of children from an early age, as
anyone familiar with the classic fairy tales collected by Grimm,

Andersen, and Perrault are aware. To shield children right up to the age of 18 from exposure to violent descriptions and images would not only be quixotic, but deforming; it would leave them unequipped to cope with the world as we know it.

Maybe video games are different. They are, after all, interactive. But this point is superficial, in fact erroneous. All literature (here broadly defined to include movies, television, and the other photographic media, and popular as well as highbrow literature) is interactive; the better it is, the more interactive. Literature when it is successful draws the reader into the story, makes him identify with the characters, invites him to judge them and quarrel with them, to experience their joys and sufferings as the reader's own. Protests from readers caused Dickens to revise Great Expectations to give it a happy ending, and tourists visit sites in Dublin and its environs in which the fictitious events of Ulysses are imagined to have occurred. The cult of Sherlock Holmes is well known. Most of the video games in the record of this case, games that the City believes violate its ordinances, are stories. Take once again "The House of the Dead." The player is armed with a gun--most fortunately, because he is being assailed by a seemingly unending succession of hideous axe-wielding zombies, the living dead conjured back to life by voodoo. The zombies have already knocked down and wounded several people, who are pleading pitiably for help; and one of the player's duties is to protect those unfortunates from renewed assaults by the zombies. His main task, however, is self-defense. Zombies are supernatural beings, therefore difficult to kill. Repeated shots are necessary to stop them as they rush headlong toward the player. He must not only be alert to the appearance of zombies from any quarter; he must be assiduous about reloading his gun periodically, lest he be overwhelmed by the rush of the zombies when his gun is empty.

Self-defense, protection of others, dread of the "**undead**," fighting against overwhelming odds--these are all age-old themes of literature, and ones particularly appealing to the young. "The House of the Dead" is not distinguished literature. Neither, perhaps, is "The Night of the Living Dead," George A. Romero's famous zombie movie that was doubtless the inspiration for "The House of the Dead." Some games, such as "Dungeons and Dragons," have achieved cult status; although it seems unlikely, some of these games, perhaps including some that are as violent as those in the record, will become cultural icons. We are in the world of kids' popular culture. But it is not lightly to be suppressed.

Although violent video games appeal primarily to boys, the record contains, surprisingly, a feminist violent video game, "Ultimate Mortal Kombat 3." A man and a woman are dressed in vaguely medieval costumes, and wield huge swords. The woman is very tall, very fierce, and wields her sword effortlessly. The man and the woman duel, and the man is killed. Another man appears--he is killed too. The woman wins all the duels. She is as strong as the men, she is more skillful, more determined, and she does not flinch at the sight of blood. Of course, her success depends on the player's skill, and the fact that the player, whether male or female, has chosen to be the female fighter. (The player chooses which fighter to be.) But the game is feminist in depicting a woman as fully capable of holding her own in violent combat with heavily armed men. It thus has a message, even an "ideology," just as books and movies do.

We are not persuaded by the City's argument that whatever contribution to the marketplace of ideas and expression the games in the record may have the potential to make is secured by the right of the parent (or guardian, or custodian--and does that include a babysitter?) to permit his or her child or ward to play these games. The right is to a considerable extent illusory. The parent is not permitted to give blanket consent, but must accompany the child to the game room. Many parents are too busy to accompany their child to a game room; most teenagers would be deterred from playing these games if they had to be accompanied by mom; even parents who think violent video games harmful or even edifying (some parents want their kids to develop a shooter's reflexes) may rather prevent their children from playing these games than incur the time and other costs of accompanying the children to the game room; and conditioning a minor's First Amendment rights on parental consent of this nature is a curtailment of those rights.

The City rightly does not rest on "what everyone knows" about the harm inflicted by violent video games. These games with their cartoon characters and stylized mayhem are continuous with an age-old children's literature on violent themes. The exposure of children to the "girlie" magazines involved in the Ginsberg case was not. It seemed obvious to the Supreme Court that these magazines were an adult invasion of children's culture and parental prerogatives. No such argument is available here. The City instead appeals to social science to establish that games such as "The House of the Dead" and "Ultimate Mortal Kombat 3," games culturally isomorphic with (and often derivative from) movies aimed at the same under-18 crowd, are dangerous to public safety. The social science evidence on which the City relies consists primarily of the pair of psychological studies that we mentioned earlier, which are reported in Craig A. Anderson & Karen E. Dill, "Personality Processes and Individual Differences--Video Games and Aggressive Thoughts, Feelings, and Behavior in the Laboratory and in Life," 78 J. Personality & Soc. Psych. 772 (2000). Those studies do not support the ordinance. There is no indication that the games used in the studies are similar to those in the record of this case or to other games likely to be marketed in game arcades in Indianapolis. The studies do not find that video games have ever caused anyone to commit a violent act, as opposed to feeling aggressive, or have caused the average level of violence to increase anywhere. And they do not suggest that it is the interactive character of the games, as opposed to the violence of the images in them, that is the cause of the aggressive feelings. The studies thus are not evidence that violent video games are any more harmful to the consumer or to the public safety than violent movies or other violent, but passive, entertainments. It is highly unlikely that they are more harmful, because "passive" entertainment aspires to be interactive too and often succeeds. When Dirty Harry or some other avenging hero kills off a string of villains, the audience is expected to identify with him, to revel in his success, to feel their own finger on the trigger. It is conceivable that pushing a button or manipulating a toggle stick engenders an even deeper surge of aggressive joy, but of that there is no evidence at all.

We can imagine the City's arguing that it would like to ban violent movies too, but that either this is infeasible or the City has to start somewhere and should not be discouraged from experimenting. Experimentation should indeed not be discouraged. But the City makes neither argument. Its only expressed concern is with video games, in fact only video games in game arcades, movie-theater lobbies, and hotel game rooms. It doesn't even argue that the addition of violent video games to violent movies and television in the cultural menu of Indianapolis youth significantly increases whatever dangers media depictions of violence pose to healthy character formation or peaceable, law-abiding behavior. Violent video games played in public places are a tiny fraction of the media violence to which modern American children are exposed. Tiny--and judging from the record of this case not very violent compared to what is available to children on television and in movie theaters today. The characters in the video games in the record are cartoon characters, that is, animated drawings. No one would mistake them for photographs of real people--another difference between this case and Ginsberg. The idea that a child's interest in such fantasy mayhem is "morbid"--that any kid who enjoys playing "The House of the Dead" or "Ultimate Mortal Kombat 3" should be dragged off to a psychiatrist--gains no support from anything that has been cited to us in defense of the ordinance.

Ginsberg did not insist on social scientific evidence that quasi-obscene images are harmful to children. The Court, as we have noted, thought this a matter of common sense. It was in 1968; it may not be today; but that is not our case. We are not concerned with the part of the Indianapolis ordinance that concerns sexually graphic expression. The video games at issue in this case do not involve sex, but instead a children's world of violent adventures. Common sense says that the City's claim of harm to its citizens from these games is implausible, at best wildly speculative. Common sense is sometimes another word for prejudice, and the common sense reaction to the Indianapolis ordinance could be overcome by social scientific evidence, but has not been. The ordinance curtails freedom of expression significantly and, on this record, without any offsetting justification, "compelling" or otherwise.

It is conceivable though unlikely that in a plenary trial the City can establish the legality of the ordinance. We need not speculate on what evidence might be offered, or, if none is offered (in which event a permanent injunction should promptly be entered), what amendments might bring the ordinance into conformity with First Amendment principles. We have emphasized the "literary" character of the games in the record and the unrealistic appearance of their "graphic" violence. If the games used actors and simulated real death and mutilation convincingly, or if the games lacked any story line and were merely animated shooting galleries (as several of the games in the record appear to be), a more narrowly drawn ordinance might survive a constitutional challenge.

That we need not decide today. The plaintiffs are entitled to a preliminary injunction. Not only have they shown a strong likelihood of ultimate victory should the City persist with the case; they will suffer irreparable harm if the ordinance is permitted to go into effect, because compliance with it will impose costs on them of altering their facilities and will also cause them to lose revenue. And given the entirely conjectural nature of the benefits of the ordinance to the people of Indianapolis, the harm of a preliminary injunction to the City must be reckoned slight, and outweighed by the harm that denying the injunction would impose on the plaintiffs. The judgment is therefore reversed, and the case remanded with instructions to enter a preliminary injunction.

Reversed and Remanded, with Instructions.

OSCAR RUIZ, Petitioner,

v.

JANIE COCKRELL, Director, Texas
Department of Criminal Justice,
Institutional Division, Respondent.

2:00-CV-0296

UNITED STATES DISTRICT COURT FOR
THE NORTHERN DISTRICT OF TEXAS,
AMARILLO DIVISION

2003 U.S. Dist. LEXIS 14978

August 29, 2003, Decided
August 29, 2003, Filed

U.S. MAGISTRATE JUDGE CLINTON E. AVERITTE

REPORT AND RECOMMENDATION TO DENY PETITION
FOR A WRIT OF HABEAS CORPUS

Petitioner OSCAR RUIZ has filed with this Court a Petition for a
Writ of Habeas Corpus by a Person in State Custody challenging his
conviction out of the 26TH Judicial District Court of Williamson
County, Texas, for the felony offense of aggravated assault, enhanced
with prior felonies. For the reasons hereinafter expressed, the United
States Magistrate Judge is of the opinion petitioner's application for
federal habeas corpus relief should be DENIED.

I.

PROCEDURAL HISTORY

On October 3, 1996, in Cause No. 96-376-K26, styled *The State of
Texas vs. Oscar Ruiz,* petitioner was convicted of the felony offense of
aggravated assault and sentenced to fifty (50) years imprisonment in
the Texas Department of Criminal Justice, Institutional Division. *Ex
parte Ruiz,* App. No. 44,044-02 at 141-145.

Petitioner appealed his conviction to the Court of Appeals for the Third District of Texas who affirmed petitioner's conviction in an unpublished opinion on September 17, 1998. *Id.* at 146-158; *Ruiz v. State*, 1998 Tex. App. LEXIS 5897 (Tex.App. -- Austin 1998, pet.ref'd). Petitioner filed a petition for discretionary review which was refused by the Texas Court of Criminal Appeals on April 14, 1999. *Ruiz v. State*, No. 4270991720-98 (Tex.Crim.App. January 13, 1999).

On May 23, 2000, petitioner filed a state application for a writ of habeas corpus challenging the instant conviction. *Ex parte Ruiz*, App. No. 44,044-02 at 3-132. On July 12, 2000, the Texas Court of Criminal Appeals denied petitioner's application without written order on findings of the trial court without a hearing. *Id.* at cover.

On September 6, 2000, petitioner filed the instant application for federal habeas relief with this Court challenging his conviction and sentence.

II.

PETITIONER'S ALLEGATIONS

Petitioner appears to contend he is being held in violation of the Constitution and laws of the United States for the following reasons:

> 1. The evidence was insufficient to support a conviction because the evidence did not show that petitioner used his hands, feet a crowbar or a tire tool as a deadly weapon during the commission of the offense;
>
> 2. The trial court erred by denying a motion for mistrial after the prosecutor made improper jury arguments during the punishment phase of trial;
>
> 3. Petitioner's Fifth Amendment rights were violated because the prosecution did not prove its case beyond a reasonable doubt;
>
> 4. Petitioner was denied due process when the judge accepted the deadly weapon verdict which was erroneous;
>
> 5. The Third Judicial District Court of Appeals abused their discretion in affirming the conviction;
>
> 6. The trial court violated the Fourteenth Amendment when it allowed amendment of the indictment by the prosecutor's oral motion;

7. The affirmative finding of a deadly weapon was erroneous;

8. Petitioner was denied a fair trial because he was convicted upon an erroneous jury charge;

9. The Third Judicial District Court of Appeals abused their discretion in applying the standards set forth in *Kitchens v. State* and *Fuller v. State*, which cases can be distinguished;

10. Petitioner's Fifth Amendment rights were violated because he was convicted of two offenses;

11. The indictment was fundamentally defective and therefore the trial court had no jurisdiction;

12. Petitioner was denied effective assistance of counsel;

13. Petitioner was denied effective assistance of appellate counsel;

14. The trial court lacked jurisdiction to try petitioner in the indictment because petitioner was not admonished he could waive the indictment;

15. The trial court erred in allowing Barbara Ortiz to testify in the punishment phase of trial and this prejudiced petitioner;

16. The prosecution knowingly suborned and used perjured testimony;

17. The trial court erred when it admitted witness opinion testimony since it invaded the province of the jury and was prejudicial to petitioner;

18. Petitioner was deprived of proper notice in the indictment in violation of Texas Constitution, Art. I, Sec. 1019. The prosecution engaged in misconduct by eliciting inflammatory testimony from witnesses in violation of petitioner's due process rights;

20. The prosecution further engaged in misconduct by eliciting witness testimony outside the scope of the witness's knowledge; and

21. Texas Penal Code § 22.02 is vague and/or unconstitutional in not putting petitioner on adequate notice to prepare a defense.

III.

EXHAUSTION OF STATE COURT REMEDIES

Section 28 U.S.C. § 2254 states, as relevant to this proceeding:

(b)(1) An application for a writ of habeas corpus on behalf of a person in custody pursuant to the judgment of a State court shall not be granted unless it appears that--

> (A) the applicant has exhausted the remedies available in the courts of the State; or
>
> (B)(I) there is an absence of available State corrective process; or
>
> (ii) circumstances exist that render such process ineffective to protect the rights of the applicant.

(2) An application for a writ of habeas corpus may be denied on the merits, notwithstanding the failure of the applicant to exhaust the remedies available in the courts of the State.

(3) . . .

c) An applicant shall not be deemed to have exhausted the remedies available in the courts of the State, within the meaning of this section, if he has the right under the law of the State to raise, by any available procedure, the question presented.

28 U.S.C. § 2254. The exhaustion doctrine set forth in section 2254 requires that the state courts be given the initial opportunity to address and, if necessary, correct alleged deprivations of federal constitutional rights in state cases. *Castille v. Peoples*, 489 U.S. 346, 349, 109 S. Ct. 1056, 1059, 103 L. Ed. 2d 380 (1989). The doctrine serves "to protect the state courts' role in the enforcement of federal law and prevent disruption of state judicial proceedings." *Rose v. Lundy*, 455 U.S. 509, 518, 102 S. Ct. 1198, 1203, 71 L. Ed. 2d 379 (1982).

> Under our federal system, the federal and state courts are equally bound to guard and protect rights secured by the Constitution. Because it would be unseemly in our dual system of government for a federal district court to upset a state court conviction without an opportunity to the state courts to correct a constitutional violation, federal courts apply the doctrine of comity, which teaches that one court should defer action on causes properly within its jurisdiction until the courts of another sovereignty with concurrent powers, and already cognizant of the litigation, have had an opportunity to pass upon the matter.

Id. (brackets, internal quotation marks, and citations omitted). To have exhausted his state remedies, a habeas petitioner must have *fairly presented* the *substance* of his federal constitutional claims to the state courts. *Nobles v. Johnson*, 127 F.3d 409, 420 (5th Cir. 1997), *cert. denied*, 523 U.S. 1139, 118 S. Ct. 1845, 140 L. Ed. 2d 1094 (1998). This requires that any federal constitutional claim presented to the state courts be supported by the same factual allegations and legal theories upon which the petitioner bases his federal claims. *Picard v. Connor*, 404 U.S. 270, 276, 92 S. Ct. 509, 512, 30 L. Ed. 2d 438 (1971). Further, in order to satisfy the federal exhaustion requirement, petitioner must fairly present to the highest state court each constitutional claim he wishes to assert in his federal habeas petition. *Skelton v. Whitley*, 950 F.2d 1037, 1041 (5th Cir.), *cert. denied sub nom. Skelton v. Smith*, 506 U.S. 833, 113 S. Ct. 102, 121 L. Ed. 2d 61 (1992); *Richardson v. Procunier*, 762 F.2d 429, 431 (5th Cir. 1985); *Carter v. Estelle*, 677 F.2d 427, 443 (5th Cir. 1982), *cert. denied*, 460 U.S. 1056, 103 S. Ct. 1508, 75 L. Ed. 2d 937 (1983). In the state of Texas, the Court of Criminal Appeals in Austin, Texas is the highest court which has jurisdiction to review a petitioner's confinement. Tex. Code Crim. Proc. Ann. art. 44.45 (Vernon 1999). Claims may be presented to that court through an application for a writ of habeas corpus, *see* Tex. Code Crim. Proc. Ann. art. 11.01 et seq. (Vernon 1999), or on direct appeal by a petition for discretionary review.

In the instant case, respondent has argued petitioner has failed to exhaust his second claim, that the trial court erred by denying a motion for mistrial after the prosecutor made improper jury arguments during the punishment phase of trial. Specifically, respondent avers that while petitioner presented this claim in his direct appeal, petitioner failed to raise the claim in his petition for discretionary review or his state habeas application, and as such, the claim is barred from federal review. A review of the record shows respondent to be correct and accordingly, it is the opinion of the undersigned Magistrate Judge that petitioner's second ground is procedurally barred from federal habeas review.

Because petitioner has filed a federal petition raising both exhausted and unexhausted grounds, it is a mixed petition and is subject to summary dismissal in order that petitioner may present the unexhausted grounds to the Texas Court of Criminal Appeals. *See Rose v. Lundy*, 455 U.S. 509, 510, 102 S. Ct. 1198, 71 L. Ed. 2d 379 (1982); *Wilder v. Cockrell*, 274 F.3d 255 n.2 (5th Cir. 2001); *Graham v. Johnson*, 168 F.3d 762, 777-78 (5th Cir.1999), *cert. denied*, 529 U.S. 1097, 120 S. Ct. 1830, 146 L. Ed. 2d 774 (2000). If, however, petitioner were to return to the Texas Court of Criminal Appeals to present his unexhausted ground, that court would dismiss petitioner's state habeas application without review of the merits for abuse-of-the-writ. *See Ex parte Barber,* 879 S.W.2d 889, 891 n. 1 (Tex.Crim.App. 1994) (announcing the state's strict application of abuse-of-the-writ doctrine). The Fifth Circuit has ruled that the Texas courts' application of the abuse of writ doctrine is an adequate, independent state ground barring federal habeas review. *Fearance v. Scott,* 56 F.3d 633, 642 (5th Cir.), *cert. denied,* 515 U.S. 1153, 115 S. Ct. 2603, 132 L. Ed. 2d 847 (1995). [1] Federal review of a habeas claim is procedurally barred when the last state court to consider the claim denies relief based on a state procedural bar. *Harris v. Reed,* 489 U.S. 255, 262, 109 S. Ct. 1038, 1043, 103 L. Ed. 2d 308 (1989). Moreover, where a state court relies on a procedural bar to deny relief, a prisoner may not thereafter obtain federal habeas relief without showing cause for the default, and prejudice resulting therefrom. *Coleman v. Thompson,* 501 U.S. 722, 750, 111 S. Ct. 2546, 2565, 115 L. Ed. 2d 640 (1991). [2] In order to show prejudice, petitioner must show the result of the proceeding would have been different. *Smith v. Dixon,* 14 F.3d 956, 974 (5th Cir. 1994), *cert. denied* 513 U.S. 841, 115 S. Ct. 129, 130 L. Ed. 2d 72 (1995). Petitioner has not made such a showing and thus his second claim related to prosecutorial misconduct is procedurally barred from federal corpus review. *See Vega v. Johnson,* 149 F.3d 354, 362 (5th Cir. 1998), *cert. denied,* 525 U.S. 1119, 119 S. Ct. 899, 142 L. Ed. 2d 899 (1999).

1 This ruling came after the Texas Court of Criminal Appeal's decision in *Ex Parte Barber,* 879 S.W.2d 889, 892 (Tex.Crim.App. 1994), *cert. denied,* 513 U.S. 1084, 115 S. Ct. 739, 130 L. Ed. 2d 641 (1995). Prior to the decision in *Barber,* the Texas abuse doctrine was not regularly and strictly applied. *Lowe v. Scott,* 48 F.3d 873, 876 (5th Cir.), *cert. denied,* 515 U.S. 1123, 115 S. Ct. 2278, 132 L. Ed. 2d 282 (1995), cited in *Fearance,* 56 F.3d at 642.

2 It is acknowledged that the state court has not dismissed a habeas petition presented by petitioner on the unexhausted grounds presented herein. However, based upon the holdings of *Ex parte Barber* and *Fearance,* this Court assumes such would occur. The only other alternative would be to dismiss the instant mixed petition because it presents both exhausted and unexhausted claims but to do so would be more detrimental to petitioner in that no ruling on his exhausted grounds would be reached.

Therefore, it is the opinion of the Magistrate Judge that while petitioner has not exhausted, in state court, one of the issues presented herein, this cause should not be dismissed for failure to exhaust, but instead, should be decided on the merits as to the exhausted claims. The unexhausted claim relating to prosecutorial misconduct, the undersigned finds to be procedurally barred.

IV.

STANDARD OF REVIEW

This case was filed subsequent to the April 24, 1996 effective date of the Antiterrorism and Effective Death Penalty Act of 1996 (AEDPA) and so the standards of review set forth in the AEDPA apply to this case. *Lindh v. Murphy*, 521 U.S. 320, 326, 117 S. Ct. 2059, 2063, 138 L. Ed. 2d 481 (1997); *Williams v. Cain*, 125 F.3d 269, 274 (5th Cir. 1997). Consequently, petitioner may not obtain relief in this Court with respect to any claim adjudicated on the merits in the state court proceedings unless the adjudication of the claim:

> (1) resulted in a decision that was contrary to, or involved an unreasonable application of, clearly established Federal law, as determined by the Supreme Court of the United States; or
>
> (2) resulted in a decision that was based on an unreasonable determination of the facts in light of the evidence presented in the State court proceeding.

28 U.S.C. § 2254(d). Further, all factual determinations made by a state court shall be presumed to be correct and such presumption can only be rebutted by clear and convincing evidence presented by petitioner. 28 U.S.C. § 2254(e).

Petitioner has filed one (1) state habeas application in the Texas Court of Criminals Appeals relating to Cause No. 96-376-K26. The Court of Criminal appeals denied such application in *Ex parte Ruiz*, App. No. 44,044-02 on July 12, 2000 without written order on the findings of the trial court without a hearing. The ruling of the Texas Court of Criminal Appeals on the grounds presented constitute an adjudication of petitioner's claims on the merits. *Bledsue v. Johnson*, 188 F.3d 250, 257 (5th Cir. 1999).

V.

MERITS

Federal habeas corpus will not lie unless an error was so gross or a trial so fundamentally unfair that the petitioner's constitutional rights were violated. In determining whether an error was so extreme or a trial so fundamentally unfair, this Court must review the putative error at issue, looking at the totality of the circumstances surrounding the error for a violation of the petitioner's constitutional rights. Based upon a review of the state court records the pleadings of record with this Court, it is the opinion of the Magistrate Judge that petitioner has failed to show he is being unlawfully detained in violation of the Constitution and laws of the United States.

1.

Sufficiency of the Evidence

The state appellate court considered a sufficiency of the evidence issue on direct appeal. Their opinion summarizes the evidence at trial.

> Barbara Ortiz testified that she was a good friend of Arleen Ruiz, appellant's wife. About 8:00 p.m. on May 17, 1996, Ortiz met Arleen and appellant at the Gold Post Bar in Round Rock. Shortly after she arrived, all three of them left the bar because of an apparent argument between appellant and his wife, the nature of which was unclear to Ortiz because of the noise in the bar. As they walked to their parked cars, appellant hit or knocked his wife to the ground and began to kick her with his feet and hit her with his hands. Ortiz tried to push appellant away from his wife and two men arrived to restrain appellant. Ortiz and Arleen Ruiz immediately went to the front of the bar where Ortiz used the outside telephone to call 911 and summon the police. Ortiz observed appellant driving his car around the bar several times before he parked. He then approached his wife with a crowbar in his hand and threatened to kill her. Arleen fled inside the bar and was followed by appellant.

> Arleen Ruiz testified that she and appellant had separated but that he had stayed with her the night before the alleged assault. They went to the Gold Post Bar together on May 17, 1996. They were to meet Ortiz there. Arleen explained that some "guys" came into the bar and apparently appellant thought one of them knew Arleen. Appellant's mood changed and he became upset. Jealousy had been

a problem in their marriage. Shortly after Ortiz arrived, appellant was ready to leave. As they walked to their car, appellant turned and slapped Arleen, knocking her to the ground. He began hitting her with his hands and feet and kicking her in the body, on her side and legs. Arleen described appellant as being very strong and engaged in construction work.

Arleen described how two men and Ortiz were finally able to restrain appellant. She ran to the front of the bar where Ortiz called the police. Appellant then began driving around the bar and kept asking Arleen to get in the car but she refused. Appellant parked his car and came towards Arleen with "something" in his hand. He began yelling, "I'm going to kill you, bitch." Arleen fled into the bar and tried to reach the back door. Several of her cousins were in the bar and when appellant entered the room some four or five men struggled to wrestle appellant to the floor. Thereafter, the police arrived and removed appellant. Arleen described her pain and her injuries, including a scar on her leg where appellant kicked her with his work boots.

The bartender, Richard Ontiveros, testified that Arleen came running into the bar with appellant in full pursuit with a crowbar or tire tool raised above his head. Over the sound of the music, appellant could be heard yelling, "I am going to kill you, bitch." He made this threat three times before six men were able to take him to the floor. Ontiveros explained that appellant was a very strong man and very upset. Ontiveros testified that appellant seemed capable, with the crowbar, of causing death or serious bodily injury to Arleen. Ontiveros observed that after the police arrived they had a difficult time in removing appellant from the bar.

Round Rock Police Officer Jim Weber was the second officer on the scene after he heard a report that a man with a crowbar was chasing his wife. Weber found appellant on the bar floor struggling aggressively while five men held him down. Weber and Officer Thomason struggled to properly handcuff appellant, but were only able to handcuff him in the front as he was "very, very strong." Appellant continued to resist as they removed him from the bar. They were unable to lay him over the back of a car because of appellant's strength and the aggressive use of his feet. When other officers arrived, Weber went to obtain some flex-cuffs for appellant's feet, but when he returned appellant had been sprayed with pepper spray and was calm. While appellant struggled with the police, Ortiz heard him yell, "If I get out, I'm going to kill you, Arleen." Officer Weber, trained in the use of force, testified that appellant was capable of causing death or serous bodily injury to Arleen Ruiz and his hands or feet or a crowbar or tire iron.

Ruiz v. State, slip op. at 5.

After reviewing the evidence offered at trial in a light most favorable to the verdict, the undersigned is of the opinion that the Court of Appeals' finding of sufficient evidence was correct, and finds the evidence sufficient to support the verdict of guilty in this case. The undersigned specifically finds the evidence sufficient on the issue of defendant's threat to kill his wife and his exhibition of the crowbar/tire tool when making that threat.

2.

Trial Court Error

This allegation, charging improper prosecutorial final argument, was decided on direct appeal. That decision, finding any error to have been cured by a jury instruction to disregard, correctly adjudicated the claim. A jury is presumed to have followed instructions given to it by the court. *Galvan v. Cockrell*, 293 F.3d 760, 765 (5th Cir. 2002). It cannot be said that any error occurred and further, in light of the jury instruction, petitioner has failed to establish that any juror disregarded the Court's instruction. No prejudice has been shown.

3.

Fifth Amendment Rights Violation Not Proved Beyond a Reasonable Doubt

This claim is difficult to understand. Petitioner says he is not challenging sufficiency of the evidence, but in actuality, he is. In any event, as set forth under ground number one above, the evidence was sufficient to support the verdict.

4.

Denied Due Process When Judge Accepted Deadly Weapon Verdict

This ground basically restates ground number three. Petitioner's allegation is without merit. The evidence clearly was sufficient for the jury to determine that petitioner's use and intended use of the crowbar/tire tool constituted a deadly weapon.

5.

Third Judicial District Court of Appeals Abused Discretion in Affirming Conviction

This ground is basically a restatement of grounds three and four, and is without merit.

6.

Trial Court Violated Fourteenth Amendment When It Allowed Amendment of Indictment by the Prosecutor's Oral Motion

Petitioner does not appear to argue that an oral motion to amend an indictment was improper procedure and thus violative of his Constitutional rights, but that the addition of the language "tire tool" confused the defense and the jury as to what the alleged deadly weapon was. As stated by the Third Court of Appeals of Texas,

> The trial court in its jury charge tracked the indictment and in its application paragraph submitted both theories of assault and required that the jury find that appellant used a deadly weapon, a hand or feet or a crowbar or tire tool, before it could find appellant guilty of aggravated assault as alleged in the indictment and finding that a deadly weapon 'namely, hands or feet or a crowbar or a tire iron was used or exhibited' during the commission of the offense. When different theories of the offense are submitted to the jury in the disjunctive, a general verdict is sufficient of the evidence supports one of the theories. [cites omitted] The same reasoning would apply to the submission in the disjunctive of the nature of the deadly weapon used or exhibited during the commission of the offense.

Ruiz v. State, slip op. at 5. The state court's interpretation of what constitutes an offense under state law is not open to reinterpretation on federal habeas review. *Weeks v. Scott*, 55 F.3d 1059, 1063 (5th Cir. 1995). Petitioner's claim is without merit.

7.

Affirmative Finding of a Deadly Weapon was Erroneous

Petitioner's allegations under this ground are merely a restatement of his allegations under grounds three, four, and five. For the reasons set forth above, petitioner's claims are without merit.

8.

Petitioner was Denied Fair Trial Because He was Convicted Upon an Erroneous Jury Charge

Under this ground, petitioner again attempts to reargue grounds three, four, five, and seven. It appears to the undersigned that petitioner is attempting to say that the evidence showed he committed two separate assaults rather than one assault. Even if petitioner is correct and he committed an assault initially by knocking his wife to the ground and kicking her with his work boots while she lay on the ground, and then terminated that offense, only to return to the lounge and threaten to kill his wife with the crowbar/tire tool, petitioner has failed to show how he was harmed by the state prosecuting him for only one aggravated assault rather than two. In addition, any argument petitioner makes that the jury charge authorized conviction based upon use of a tire iron while the indictment alleged a tire tool, does not, in the opinion of the undersigned, constitute a variance. Even if it did, it would not be the type of variance which would render the trial fundamentally unfair.

9.

Third Judicial District Court of Appeals Abused Their Discretion in Applying Standards set forth in *Kitchens v. State* and *Fuller v. State*

It appears petitioner is again arguing the trial record evinces that two distinct offenses were committed in this case and as such, the application of *Kitchens* and *Fuller* was misplaced. Petitioner seems to argue that the caselaw allows presentation of alternative pleadings of differing methods of committing one offense but that such is inapplicable in his case because there were two distinct offenses. This ground is without merit.

10.

Petitioner's Fifth Amendment rights Violated Because He was Convicted of Two Offenses

Under this ground, petitioner merely reargues the two offenses versus one offense as presented in grounds eight and nine above. As discussed previously, the ground is without merit.

11.

Indictment fundamentally Defective and Trial Court Had no Jurisdiction

Petitioner argues that the indictment violates Texas law. Specifically, Article 21.24 of the Code of Criminal Procedure, that he received inadequate notice of the offense charged and of the allegation of a deadly weapon. Petitioner represents his argument of a variance between the word "tire tool" and "tire iron." State law violations are not cognizable in federal habeas corpus. *West v. Johnson*, 92 F.3d 1385, 1404 (5th Cir. 1996), *cert. denied*, 520 U.S. 1242, 117 S. Ct. 1847, 137 L. Ed. 2d 1050 (1997). This ground is without merit.

12.

Petitioner was Denied Effective Assistance of Counsel

Under this ground, petitioner lists nine instances in which he contends counsel was ineffective. Petitioner complains that counsel failed to file any motion to quash the indictment or a motion to sever the two separate assaults. Again, the one offense versus two offenses has been discussed above, and petitioner's contentions in that regard are without merit. Consequently, there was no ineffective assistance of counsel with respect to those issues.

Petitioner also alleges counsel was ineffective because counsel allegedly failed to object to:

   a) inflammatory opinions by witnesses;

   b) the charge;

   c) testimony regarding petitioner's being jealous;

   d) testimony regarding two unknown individuals; and

   e) to the prosecutor's statement regarding the capability of the tire iron/tire tool to cause death.

It does not appear to the undersigned that any of the matters about which petitioner contends counsel should have lodged objections were matters which either an objection could be properly lodged or about which the failure to object could not be considered trial strategy. In any event, petitioner has failed to show any prejudice as a result of counsel's failure to object to any of the items listed above.

Petitioner also alleges in general fashion that counsel was ineffective for failing to investigate the case, for failing to see character witnesses, for failing to establish a lawyer-client relationship, for failing to object to the verdict, for failing to object to certain extraneous offenses, and for not filing motions. None of these grounds are adequately set forth, as ineffective assistance of counsel claims, to entitle petitioner to relief.

None of petitioner's allegations of ineffective assistance of counsel are meritorious, and petitioner's ground alleging ineffective assistance of counsel should be denied.

13.

Petitioner Denied Effective Assistance of Appellate Counsel

Under this ground, petitioner alleges appellate counsel was ineffective for the following reasons:

> 1) Counsel did not speak with the victim;
>
> 2) Counsel did not obtain a record for the defendant to file a pro se brief;
>
> 3) Counsel did not raise the following issues:
>
> > a) failure to charge **undeadly** conduct;
> >
> > b) failure to file motion to quash; and
> >
> > c) did not correct the state's brief.

All of petitioner's allegations of ineffective assistance of appellate counsel are without merit. The appellate issues raised and addressed by the Texas Court of Appeals reflect counsel to have acted effectively in the representation of petitioner.

14.

Trial Court Lacked Jurisdiction to Try Petitioner in the Indictment Because Petitioner was not Admonished He Could Waive Indictment

Under this ground, petitioner argues the trial court lacked jurisdiction because the trial court failed to admonish petitioner that he could waive the presentation of the case to the Grand Jury. Since this case was indicted by the Grand Jury, petitioner's claim that the trial court failed to admonish him about waiver of the indictment is meritless.

15.

Trial Court Erred in Allowing Barbara Ortiz to Testify in the Punishment Phase of Trial and This Prejudiced Petitioner

Under this ground, petitioner complains that the witness Barbara Ortiz was impermissibly allowed to testify regarding prior assaults that petitioner committed against his wife during the sentencing phase. Article 37.07, Sec. 3(a), Tex. Code Crim. Pro., allows evidence of unadjudicated offenses and bad acts to be presented during the punishment phase of trial. As such, petitioner's prior assault history against his wife would have been admissible during the sentencing phase, and the testimony in that regard did not deprive petitioner of his constitutional rights.

16.

The Prosecution Knowingly Suborned and Used Perjured Testimony

Petitioner's allegation the state suborned perjury is totally without substance or merit. Contradictory testimony from witnesses, inconsistencies within a witness' testimony, and conflict between reports, written statements and the trial testimony of witnesses do not, standing alone, constitute perjury. *Koch v. Puckett*, 907 F.2d 524, 531 (5th Cir. 1990). Aside from his bald allegation, petitioner's has made no showing that the state knowingly offered any perjured testimony.

17.

Trial Court Erred When it Admitted Witness Opinion Testimony Since it Invaded the Province of the Jury and was Prejudicial to Petitioner

The complained-of testimony involved testimony by a police officer regarding his opinion as to whether the tire tool was capable of causing death, and the testimony of witness Ortiz and the victim, Arleen Ruiz, regarding whether petitioner was attempting to kill his wife. Petitioner has failed to enunciate why such testimony should not have been admitted. He has failed to cite authority for his argument. The evidence appears to be permissible witness testimony, and petitioner's ground of error is without merit.

18.

Petitioner was Deprived of Proper Notice in the Indictment in Violation of Texas Constitution, Art. I, Sec. 10.

Under this ground, petitioner's argument is that the indictment was faulty, in that it alleged more than one offense. This ground has previously been addressed, and ground number eighteen is without merit and should be denied.

19.

Prosecution Engaged in Misconduct by Eliciting Inflammatory Testimony From Witnesses in Violation of Petitioner's Due Process Rights

Under this ground, petitioner alleges the prosecution coaxed witnesses into testifying to inflammatory matters. The trial court record does not reflect any such impermissible actions by the prosecution. Moreover, as stated in the trial court's findings of fact and conclusions of law citing *Ex parte Dutchover*, 779 S.W.2d 76 (Tex.Crim.App. 1989), the improper admission of evidence at trial may not be raised in state habeas corpus. Therefore, as argued by respondent, such argument is procedurally barred herein.

20.

Prosecution Further Engaged in Misconduct by Eliciting Witness Testimony Outside the Scope of the Witness's Knowledge

This ground is similar, if not identical, to ground number nineteen. For the reasons stated above, it also is without merit.

21.

Texas Penal Code § 22.02 is Vague and/or Unconstitutional in not Putting Petitioner on Adequate Notice to Prepare a Defense.

As stated supra, state law violations are not cognizable in federal habeas corpus.*West v. Johnson*, 92 F.3d 1385, 1404 (5th Cir. 1996), *cert. denied*, 520 U.S. 1242, 117 S. Ct. 1847, 137 L. Ed. 2d 1050 (1997).

Petitioner's allegation that the Texas Penal Code is unconstitutional is without merit.

VI.

RECOMMENDATON

It is the RECOMMENDATION of the United States Magistrate Judge to the United States District Judge that the petition for a writ of habeas corpus filed by petitioner OSCAR RUIZ be DENIED.

VII.

INSTRUCTIONS FOR SERVICE and NOTICE OF RIGHT TO OBJECT

The United States District Clerk is directed to send a file-marked copy of this Report and Recommendation to petitioner by certified mail, return receipt requested, and to respondent's attorney of record by regular U.S. mail or other agreed means.

Any party may file objections to this Report and Recommendation within fourteen (14) days after its date of filing. 28 U.S.C. § 636(b); Rule 8(b)(3) of the Rules Governing Section 2254 Cases in the United States District Courts. *See* Fed. R. Civ. P. 5(b); 6(e). Any such objections shall be made in the form of a written pleading entitled "Objections to Report and Recommendation" and shall specifically identify the portions of the findings, conclusions, or recommendation to which objection is made, setting out fully the basis for each objection. Petitioner shall file the written objections with the United States District Clerk and serve a copy of such objections to all other parties. Petitioner's failure to timely file written objections to the proposed findings, conclusions, and recommendation contained in the original Report and Recommendation shall bar her, except upon grounds of plain error, from attacking on appeal the unobjected-to proposed factual findings and legal conclusions set forth in this report and accepted by the district court. *Douglass v. United Services Auto. Ass'n*, 79 F.3d 1415, 1428-29 (5th Cir. 1996).

IT IS SO RECOMMENDED.

ENTERED this 29th day of August 2003.

JOYCE MARIE MOORE, et al.
VERSUS
TANGIPAHOA PARISH SCHOOL
BOARD, et al.

CIVIL ACTION NO. 65-15556 SEC. "B"(1)

UNITED STATES DISTRICT COURT FOR
THE EASTERN DISTRICT OF LOUISIANA

2008 U.S. Dist. LEXIS 35238

April 30, 2008, Decided
April 30, 2008, Filed

UNITED STATES DISTRICT JUDGE IVAN L. R. LEMELLE

ORDER AND REASONS

Before the Court is Plaintiffs' Motion for Further Relief and Evidentiary Hearing In re: Alden Foster (Rec. Doc. No. 534). After review of the pleadings and applicable law and for the reasons that follow,

IT IS ORDERED that Alden Foster shall be hired as the head football coach at Amite High School.

BACKGROUND

The matter before this Court, *Joyce Marie Moore, et. al. v. Tangipahoa Parish School Board, et. al.,* is a forty-three year old school desegregation case, attempting seeking to rid the Tangipahoa School System of the vestiges of *de jure* school segregation. Despite the age of this case, myriad issues remain ripe for review. However, the scope of this order solely addresses the Tangipahoa Parish School Board's decision not to hire Mr. Alden Foster as head coach of the Amite High School football team.

A. 40-60 Ratio

As part of this Court's initial injunctive ruling in the 1960s in *Joyce Marie Moore, et. al. v. Tangipahoa Parish School Board, et. al.,* the Court ordered the Tangipahoa School Board ("the Board") to make affirmative attempts to desegregate its public schools and make all good faith efforts to eradicate the vestiges of *de jure* segregation. As part of its affirmative duty to make good faith efforts to desegregate its schools and eradicate the vestiges of de jure segregation therein, the parties convened, obtaining assistance and recommendation of professors from Tulane University, New York University and the University of Oklahoma, and agreed upon the set of "Objective Criteria" to be used in hiring job applicants after the Board reached a 40-60 ratio of African-American and Caucasian employees. [1]

1 The 40-60 ratio represents a systemwide faculty-staff ratio of 40% of African-American to 60% Caucasian.

On May 15, 1975, a partial settlement agreement was reached between the Tangipahoa Parish School System and Plaintiffs. The agreement indicated that qualified African-American educators would be employed and assigned so as to achieve a systemwide faculty staff ratio of 40% African-American and 60% Caucasian (40-60 ratio). This 40-60 ratio required the School Board to make special efforts to increase the number of African-American teachers employed at the high school level. The parties agreed that as vacancies arise in the categories of: high school principals, agricultural teachers, band directors, vocal music teachers, coaches, athletic directors, and central office administrators, the school system would be required to appoint African-Americans to fill such vacancies so that the 40-60 ratio could be achieved.

On June 19, 1975, the Court approved the settlement agreement with respect to the above specific categories. [2] The June 19, 1975 order of the Court mandated, "[a]s vacancies arise in the [select categories listed in the text] the school system will appoint black educators to fill them so that the 40-60 ratio is achieved . . ." With regard to the hiring of African-American coaches before the 40-60 ratio is achieved, the Court issued an order on August 12, 1976, stating the following: "[f]irst it will be noted that this provision of the order (which merely reflected the parties' agreement) does not make the matter of filling the two positions with black educators discretionary with the school board. . . The clause is mandatory. It says in effect, that only black coaches will be hired until the 40-60 ratio is achieved within each of the categories." (emphasis added)

2 Judge Rubin signed the June 19, 1975 Court order approving of the settlement terms.

On July 5, 1977, Judge Rubin signed a court order holding the School System in contempt for its failure to meet the criteria for the hiring of coaches. [3] In that order the school system was ordered to meet the 40-60 ratio of coaches prior to the 1977-78 school year. In paragraph 4 of the order, the Court stated that: "4) after the ratio has been achieved, any coaching vacancy that causes the ratio of black coaches to fall below 40% shall be filled by a coach of the Black race."

3 A n April 1, 1977 order details three Caucasian applicants were hired as head football coaches after entry of the June 19, 1975 order.

In paragraph 9 of the order the court stated:

9) Notwithstanding anything to the contrary in the court's May 12, 1977 order, compliance with the 40-60 ratio shall be achieved in all coaching positions without regard to whether they are high school positions or otherwise. After compliance has been achieved, then effective for the 1978-79 school year, there shall be two groups of coaching positions, high school and others, and a 40-60 ratio shall be achieved in each, but no coach shall be discharged or relieved of coaching responsibility in either group to accomplish that result; it shall be attained by filling positions that occur in normal attrition.

In 1977, the Court instated a compliance officer to ensure compliance with the desegregation orders of the Court. The Court directed Defendant School Board "to designate one individual who shall be personally responsible to the Court for ensuring compliance with the responsibilities detailed in the June 19, 1975 order of the court . . . The compliance officer specified . . . shall not only be responsible for ensuring compliance with the June 19, 1975 Order, but shall be responsible for ensuring compliance with all orders and mandates issued by the court in this matter. . ."

On June 19, 1979, Judge Collins issued an order, which stated the following:

"The Employment Criteria for Administrators, Supervisors, and
Teachers are revised and approved by the defendant School Board
on April 17, 1979, and submitted by letter from Defendants'
counsel dated May 10, 1979, are approved for use. In those
employment categories where previous court ordered ratios have
been achieved, defendants are free to use the criteria in its
employment decisions without regard to the racial ratios."

"Approval of the criteria, however, is without prejudice to Plaintiffs'
right to raise in subsequent proceedings issues of discriminatory
impact of the criteria. The School shall retain the rating forms of
job applicants and shall maintain records to show each applicant's
name, race address and position sought."

Until the 40-60 ratio was achieved in the employment categories
where it was required, the court mandated that qualified African-
Americans be hired. But once the 40-60 ratio was achieved, the
School system could then use the objective criteria as the basis for its
selection of job applicants.

When Alden Foster, a qualified football coach, applied for the
position of Amite High School Head Football Coach in 2007, he was
rejected for the position; instead, the position was awarded to
Caucasian, Mr. Mark Vining, at the Tangipahoa Parish School Board
meeting of January 23, 2007. On February 13, 2007, Compliance
Officer, Arlene Guerin, notified Louis Joseph, Superintendent of the
Board, that she would commence an investigation regarding the
hiring of the Amite High School Head Football Coach. On May 15,
2007, Ms. Guerin notified Board counsel that she had completed her
initial investigation. She found that the Tangipahoa School System
had not met the previously agreed upon 40-60 ratio.

Plaintiffs contend that the failure to hire Alden Foster, a recent
"Coach of the Year" from adjoining St. Helena Parish, and a graduate
of Amite High School, who holds a Masters Degree in Secondary
Education, demonstrates continued racial discrimination. The only
head football coach hired in Tangipahoa Parish after the court's
mandate to desegregate the school system occurred decades ago
when this court issued an order directing the removal of a Caucasian
Coach hired in violation of the Court's orders, fined School Board
members individually, and ordered the School Board to hire an
African-American head football coach. The court-ordered African-

American coach has been the only African-American head football coach hired in the past four decades of this case. [4] The record establishes that Tangipahoa Parish School Officials initially responded to the Court's school desegregation orders by eliminating all African-American football coaches from the system. There is no question that this Court regarded their actions as reflective of a dual system. The Court responded with an extensive order and held school officials in contempt for their failure to appoint an African-American head football coach. There have been no other African-American head football coaches hired since this Court's order. When the Defendant was hiring only Caucasian head football coaches in 1977, the Court ordered the removal of the Caucasian coach hired at Hammond High School and the appointment of an African-American person.

4 The Compliance Officer has testified that the only African-American head football coach ever hired by the Board was the one that this Court ordered the Board to hire.

Prior to filing proceedings before this court, the Plaintiffs requested the designated Compliance Officer to investigate the matter of Alden Foster, an African-American applicant for the head football coach position at Amite High School. The Compliance Officer recommended that Alden Foster be hired as head football coach due to the subjective nature of the objective criteria used and the premature commencement of the use of the criteria as the 40-60 ratio had never been achieved.

Since this series of orders and occurrences, Defendant Board has presented no credible evidence that the 40-60 ratio was achieved in the category of high school coaches. As such, the Board prematurely commenced the use of the objective criteria in its hiring practices. Defendant's conclusory summaries of compliance with the 40-60 ratio do not represent adequate documentation and evidence that said ratio has been met; the underlying evidence informing such summaries is required, yet absent from the record. As a result of the Board's failure to substantiate its claim that it met the 40-60 ratio, it should have followed court orders to hire qualified African-American applicants, such as Mr. Foster, until the 40-60 ratio was met. The court orders noted above were violated when the Board failed to hire

Alden Foster, a highly qualified African-American applicant for the Amite High School head football coaching position.

B. Objective Criteria

The Objective Criteria used by the board for hiring purposes is scored as follows with a maximum of 100 points:

10 points	Past Performance (An evaluation by previous employer or if a student teacher, the final college past performance form)
10 points	Educational and Professional Background
20 points	Communication Skills (Determined by evaluating an essay written by applicant)
10 points	Teaching Experience
25 points	Personal Interview
10 points	Transcript
6 points	N.T.E. scores
9 points	Major and Minor Fields

At least 55 points from the total 100 points, Past Performance, Personal Interview and the Communication sections are all subjective factors. These factors are subject to interpretation and can be manipulated. The actual scoring mechanism for some portions of the exam are complicated and cumbersome and do not seem to have sound basis for their use. For instance, the procedure for evaluating an applicant's past performance report involves a reference from a past employer in which he evaluates the applicant, but unbeknownst to this past employer, the Board subsequently assigns a point value to various categories. Such a requirement proves obscure and unnecessarily muddles the process. Credible evidence was received from Mr. Foster's prior employment evaluator indicates that had he been aware of this scoring rubric, Mr. Foster would have received higher evaluations. The Board did not present clear and convincing evidence to refute this.

The total points accumulated for sixteen items are divided by sixteen in order to arrive at an average of the applicant's past performance. If the applicant's average score is between 0-.9, he will receive an "unsatisfactory" score and will be awarded 0 points in this category. If the applicant's average score is between 1.0-3.9, he or she will receive the "needs improvement" score and will be awarded 1 point in this category. If the applicant's average score is between 4.0-7.9 he or she will receive a "satisfactory" score and will be awarded 4 points in this category. If the applicant's score is between 8. 0 and 9. 9, he or she will receive an "above average" score and will be awarded 8 points in the category and if he or she scores a 10 he or she will receive an "outstanding" score and be awarded 10 points.

An applicant's average may only be 3 points less than his or her fellow applicant, but he or she could be given a score as much as 6 points less (i.e. if an applicant scores a 7.9 he or she will only get 4 points; whereas if an applicant scores a 10 he or she will get 10 points). This difference between 7.9 and 10 points is less than 3 points however in the points to be awarded the difference is 6 points.

Board witnesses at the hearing could not explain the basis for some of the scoring at issue. For instance, Foster's handwriting style score was highly subjective, and subject to questionable interpretation and utility. The Compliance Officer recommended that the criteria should be reevaluated to remove as much potential bias from this selection process as possible and the scoring of some sections should be revised.

The Board argues it has encountered problems over the years in obtaining applications from minority applicants, specifically African-Americans. It further contends that there is no significant difference between the number of applicants hired from within the school district and outside of same, where the criteria for hiring was used, The Board contends the difference along racial lines is negligible and thereby indicative of no disparate impact. Conversely, the Board's admission that it has been difficult to attract minority teacher applicants could also indicate that use of the questioned criteria for over 29 years has over that time adversely and increasingly impacted minority recruitment and hiring, as reflected here.

On May 23, 2007, Plaintiffs filed Plaintiffs' Motion for Further Relief and Evidentiary Hearing In re: Alden Foster (Rec. Doc. No. 534). Plaintiffs allege that the Board illegally discriminated against Alden Foster, a teacher and football coach employed by the St. Helena Parish School System and an applicant for a teaching and head football coaching position at Amite High School. With this motion, Plaintiffs seek to enjoin the Board and affirmatively require it to hire

Alden T. Foster as a teacher and head football coach at Amite High School.

Plaintiffs' motion regarding Alden Foster was specifically authorized by the court in its order allowing limited conditional use of the objective criteria. The court specifically reserved Plaintiffs' right to raise issues regarding discriminatory application and/or discriminatory impact of the criteria. These issues represent the content of the Alden Foster motion.

Plaintiffs assert that the absence of an African-American head football coach and the complete failure of school officials to appoint such a coach represents yet another vestige of the dual system. Defendant School Board fails to justify its hiring decision here with clear and convincing evidence. Plaintiffs also allege that the Board's longstanding usage of the court-approved Objective Criteria had a discriminatory impact on Mr. Foster.

The Board asserts that based on this Court's previous ruling defining membership in Plaintiffs' class, Mr. Foster cannot be a member of said class because it is comprised of African-American school children and their parents. *Joyce Marie Moore, et al v. Tangipahoa Parish School Board*, 594 F.2d 489, 491 (5th Cir. 1989). Because Mr. Foster is not a member of Plaintiffs' class and Plaintiffs' counsel of record do not represent Mr. Foster, Mr. Foster lacks standing to assert an employment discrimination claim in the above-captioned matter. The Board also argues that Mr. Foster failed to state an employment discrimination cause of action under which injunctive relief could legally be granted.

DISCUSSION

A. STANDING

Defendant Board claims that no standing exists that would permit the adjudication of Alden Foster's claim. Defendant asserts that in *Joyce Marie Moore, et al v. Tangipahoa Parish School Board*, 625 F.2d 33 (5th Cir. 1980) ("Moore II"), the Fifth Circuit addressed the identical issue. Defendant further avers that the underlying relief Plaintiffs seek to address is substantively distinct from *Joyce Marie Moore, et al v. Tangipahoa Parish School Board*, 594 F.2d 489 (5th Cir. 1979)("Moore I") where Plaintiffs had standing to protest school desegregation reductions in force, an employment consequence common in school desegregation cases, and the Board's alleged discriminatory conduct toward teachers it already employed.

In *Moore II*, Elizabeth Moulds, a Caucasian female teacher, unsuccessfully applied on three separate occasions for a principal position in Tangipahoa Parish. The Board rejected Ms. Moulds and hired a Caucasian male using the objective criteria for the district. The Fifth Circuit affirmed the district court ruling in *Moore II*, that Ms. Moulds lacked standing to file a motion pursuant to Fed. R. Civ. P. 71 seeking to enforce the January 27, 1977 order against the school board "because the order was issued to eliminate the racially biased method of selecting principals and to achieve the ultimate goal of the suit, a unitary system." 625 F.2d at 34. Fed. R. Civ. P. 71 states, "[w]hen an order is made in favor of a person who is not a party to the action that person may enforce obedience to the order by the same process as if a party . . ." While Rule 71 allows non-parties to enforce orders made in their favor, it cannot be adopted by one to enforce an order in an action where he or she has no standing. The Fifth Circuit further explained that "[a] party has standing only if the interest she seeks to vindicate is arguably within the zone of interests to be protected or regulated by the . . . constitutional guarantee in question." *Id.*

Mr. Foster's claim is precisely within the zone of interests which this Court's orders seek to protect. In order to comply with the Court's objective of achieving a unitary school system, the Board was required to hire qualified African-American applicants until a 40-60 ratio could be met. Although not a party to the matter, Alden Foster represents a qualified African-American applicant whom the Court ordered that the Board hire in order to reach a 40-60 ratio that would then trigger the use of the objective criteria in hiring. Fed. R. Civ. P. 71 explicitly permits non-parties, such as Alden Foster, to enforce orders made in their favor so long as standing exists. Unlike the interests of Ms. Moulds, a Caucasian female applicant in *Moore II*, an African-American applicant seeking a teaching position within the Tangipahoa School System represents the non-party zone of interests protected by the series of orders issued by the court, which would lead to the 40-60 ratio set by court and parties as desirable and necessary achieving a unitary school system. Therefore, Mr. Foster has standing to file the motion before the Court.

Defendant asserts that *Moore II* stands for the premise that an individual employee's employment discrimination, whether political or racial in nature, cannot properly be maintained as part of the above-captioned proceeding because said claim should be properly alleged in separate litigation. This proves to be an over extension of what the *Moore II* represents. In *Moore II,* the Fifth Circuit affirmed the district court ruling that Ms. Mould's interest in freedom from politically-inspired employment decision did not implicate the same constitutional guarantees which require the establishment and maintenance of a racially neutral, unitary school system. This holding distinguishes the fact pattern before the Court from that of *Moore II,* and provides further support for the finding that Mr. Foster does enjoy standing to enforce this action.

Defendant also relies on *Moore I* as the basis for its assertion that Mr. Foster's allegations should be brought under a separate lawsuit because in the present circumstances there was no school segregation reduction in force or no discriminatory treatment in an effort to make Mr. Foster resign from an employment position he already had in Tangipahoa Parish. In *Moore I,* The Fifth Circuit explicitly states, "[o]n this appeal we are concerned solely with the claims of eight black teachers that they were discharged, demoted, or discriminated against by the defendant school board in a manner denying them their constitutional and Jefferson County/Singleton III rights." 594 F.2d at 491. While *Moore I* does not provide support for the Alden Foster's claims as an applicant, it most certainly does not bar the claims of new applicants. *Moore I* simply addresses the claims of eight teachers who were discriminated against by the Board while in positions they already held in Tangipahoa. The limited scope of this particular appeal does not limit the myriad future actions permitted under Fed. R. Civ. P. 71 that may be invoked to enforce the court's orders and primary objective of ensuring a unitary school system exists.

As additional support for the assertion that Mr. Foster's allegations should be brought under a separate suit, Defendant erroneously relies upon *U.S. v. Coffeeville Consolidated School District,* 513 F.2d 244, (5th Cir. 1975). In *U.S. v. Coffeeville,* teachers' interest in continued employment within the system was at issue, and the school district was ordered to develop and implement an objective criteria to ensure the requisite reduction in the work force would not be discriminatory. *Id.* at 249. However, in the case at bar the obligation of the Board extends beyond simply guarding against discrimination in the work force. The Court ordered the Board to hire qualified African-American applicants until the 40-60 ratio could be obtained, and then to use the objective criteria for hiring, a form of prospective relief. For these reasons, Defendant's challenge of Alden Foster's standing fails.

B. TITLE VII

On November 15, 2007, this Court issued an order directing parties to file memoranda briefing whether under *Tolbert v. U.S.*, 916 F.2d 245 (5th Cir. 1990) individuals are required to exhaust administrative remedies before pursuing judicial relief when making Title VII claims. In *Tolbert v. U.S.*, a federal employee waged an employment discrimination claim against a federal agency employer. The Fifth Circuit held that a claimant who chose to pursue administrative review of federal agency's denial of his or her claim was required to exhaust that remedy before filing civil action in federal court. *Id.* In *Love v. Pullman*, the Fifth Circuit asserted, "[a] person claiming to be aggrieved by a violation of Title VII of the Civil Rights Act of 1964, may not maintain a suit for redress in federal district court until he has first unsuccessfully pursued certain avenues for administrative relief. 404 U.S. 522, 523, 92 S. Ct. 616, 30 L. Ed. 2d 679 (1972).

Plaintiffs state that no Title VII matters are pending before this court that require the exhaustion of administrative remedies. Instead, Plaintiffs have presented an employment discrimination claim arising out of violation of the orders of this court. The case of *Tolbert v. United States* does not apply to these circumstances, which involve a 42 U.S.C. § 1983 school desegregation class action enforcing rights of African-American children and their parents and the subsequent enforcement of orders emanating therefrom. Because Alden Foster's interests are within the zone of interests protected by the orders of this court, the employment discrimination issue invokes the required enforcement of the Court's previous order.

Moreover, Defendant's argument that the Court should not grant Plaintiffs' request for relief regarding Alden Foster because Foster filed a Title VII complaint with EEOC is defeated by Congressional intent of Title VII. In *Johnson v. Railway Exp. Agency, Inc.*, 421 U.S.

454, 459, 95 S.Ct. 1716, 1720, 44 L. Ed. 2d 295 (1975), the United States Supreme Court asserted:

> "the aggrieved individual clearly is not limited to Title VII in his search for relief. '[T]he legislative history of Title VII manifests a congressional intent to allow an individual to pursue independently his rights under both Title VII and other applicable state and federal statutes.' *Alexander v. Gardner-Denver Co.*, 415 U.S. 36, 48, 94 S.Ct., 1011, 1019, 39 L. Ed. 2d 147 (1974). In particular, Congress noted 'that the remedies available to the individual under Title VII are co-extensive with the indiv(i)dual's right to sue under the provisions of the Civil Rights Act of 1866, 42 U.S.C. § 1981, and that the two procedures augment each other and are not mutually exclusive.'" H.R.Rep. No. 92-238, p.19 (1971), *U.S. Code Cong. & Admin. News*, 1972, pp. 2137, 2154. *See also* S.Rep.No. 92-415, p.24 (1971). Later, in considering the Equal Employment Opportunity Act of 1972, the Senate rejected an amendment that would have deprived a claimant of any right to sue under §1981. 118 Cong. Rec. 3371-3373 (1972).

Title VII does not preempt or stay actions to obtain relief available from employment discrimination under other civil rights laws, including 42 U.S.C. §§ 1981 and 1983 as applied under the Fourteenth Amendment.

While the law necessitates the exhaustion of administrative remedies in order to maintain a suit for redress in federal district court in Title VII actions, such an exhaustion is rightfully inapplicable to Alden Foster's claim. As previously noted, the claims of Alden Foster consist of a motion filed to benefit a non-party whose interest are within the zone of protected interests of the court's orders. Although Defendant implores the Court to require a separate Title VII action addressing Alden Foster's claims, Plaintiffs' Motion for Further Relief and Evidentiary Hearing in re: Alden Foster (Rec. Doc. No. 534) was properly filed under Fed. R. Civ. P. 71. It does not represent a new or separate lawsuit seeking redress as a result of a Title VII violation. As such, no legal support exists that would require the exhaustion of administrative remedies of a Fed. R. Civ. P. 71 motion.

C. Authority of the Court to Provide Proper Remedy to Post Desegregation Discrimination

In *Brown v. Board of Ed. Of Topeka, Shawnee County, Kan.,* 347 U.S. 483, 74 S.Ct. 686, 98 L.Ed. 873 (1954) (*"Brown I"*) and *Brown v. Board of Education,* 349 U.S. 294, 75 S.Ct. 753, 99 L.Ed 1083, 71 Ohio Law Abs. 584 (*"Brown II"*), the Supreme Court denounced the existence of a segregated dual school system. In order to purge the vestiges of segregated dual school systems, school boards are "charged with the affirmative duty to take whatever steps necessary to convert to a unitary system in which racial discrimination would be eliminated root and branch." *Swann v. Charlotte-Mecklenburg Bd. Of Ed.,* 402 U.S. 1, 26, 91 S.Ct. 1267, 28 L.Ed.2d 554 (1971); *Graham v. Evangeline Parish School Board,* 223 F.R.D. 407, 412 (W.D.La. 2004). This obligation requires the court to review school board actions to ensure that each one " will further rather than delay conversion to a unitary, nonracial nondiscriminatory school system." *Monroe v. Board of Comm'rs of Jackson,* 391 U.S. 450, 459, 88 S.Ct. 1700, 20 L.Ed.2d 733.

The present matter involves a forty-three year old school § 1983 school desegregation case, in which the Defendant has not complied with the Court's orders that seek to create a unitary school system. Desegregation decrees and the judicial supervision of compliance therewith proves forward looking and intrusive. *See Bd. Of Educ. Of Oklahoma v. Dowell,* 498 U.S. 237, 248-249, 111 S. Ct. 630, 112 L. Ed. 2d 715 (1991); *see also* Brian J. Sutherland, *Killing Jim Crow and the*

Undead *Nondelegation Doctrine with Privately Enforceable Federal Regulations,* 29 Seattle Univ. L. R. 917, 936 n. 155 (2006). Section 1983 claims warrant the use of prospective injunctive relief to remedy an existing controversy, prevent its recurrence, or end a continuing violation of federal law. *See State Board of Chiropractic Examiners v. Stjernholm,* 935 P.2d 959 (Colo. 1997); *see also Nicolas v. Rhode Island,* 160 F.Supp. 2d 229 (D.R.I. 2001), order *aff'd,* 37 Fed. Appx. 3 (1st Cir. 2002). As such, the Court has ordered that qualified African-Americans be hired until a 40-60 ratio is achieved. In this matter, Defendant Board has failed to comply with the court's order affirming the consent decree binding parties to reach a 40-60 ratio. Consequently, the appropriate remedy to address the non-compliance with hiring requirements is to enforce the requirement of the Board to hire the qualified African-American applicant, Mr. Foster, which will necessarily result in the termination of the Caucasian coach head football coach hired by the Board. As part of the antidote to the societal afflictions caused by segregation and discrimination, "innocent persons" may be called upon to "share the burden". *Id.*, *quoting Franks v. Bowman Transportation Co.*, 424 U.S. 747, 777, 96 S. Ct. 1251, 1270, 47 L. Ed. 2d 444 (1976). "Race-conscious remedial action may be necessary" to eliminate the vestiges of prior discrimination. *Wygant v. Jackson Bd. Of Educ.*, 476 U.S. 267, 280-281, 106 S.Ct 1842, 1850, 90 L.Ed.2d 260, 277 (1986). In the case at bar, the Court must enforce its prior orders requiring the hiring of qualified African-Americans until a 40-60 ratio is achieved before permitting the use of the objective criteria. As such, the remedial action of terminating Mr. Mark Vining, the Caucasian coach hired instead of Mr. Alden Foster, is necessary in order to enforce compliance with the prospective relief previously granted. [5]

5 In addition to desegregation, prospective relief is generally used in court-ordered affirmative action programs favoring minorities with respect to new hires and promotions. Michael Pritchett, *No Retrenchment in Affirmative Action: The Tension Between Civil Rights Laws and Layoffs*, 50 Missouri L. Rev. 663, 675 (1985).

Defendant's unilateral acts in violation of court order cannot undermine this Court's determination requiring the hiring of Alden Foster and the termination of the present Head Football Coach. Defendant cannot circumvent the Court's ability to provide prospective remedies by simply re-characterizing said relief as reverse-discrimination through its unilateral decision to hire a Caucasian Head Football Coach instead of adhering to the prospective remedies set forth by the Court. Hiring Alden Foster as Head Football Coach demonstrates necessary and overdue compliance with the court's previous orders and prescribed prospective remedy.

D. Disparate Impact of the Criteria on Alden Foster

The court specifically reserved Plaintiffs' right to raise issues regarding discriminatory application and/or discriminatory impact of the criteria. Plaintiffs have done so by filing a motion for injunctive relief. Notwithstanding the improper use of the objective criteria, this criteria was resulted in a disparate impact on Alden Foster.

In traditional disparate impact claims, a plaintiff may establish a prima facie case of disparate treatment by proving that he or she is a member of a protected classification and was qualified for an available employment opportunity that he or she did not receive. *Texas Dep't of Community Affairs v. Burdine,* 450 U.S. 248, 253-54, 101 S. Ct. 1089, 67 L. Ed. 2d 207 (1981). A disparate impact claim does not require a demonstration of racial animus or intent. Under a Title VII [6] disparate treatment analysis, a plaintiff may establish a prima facie case using statistics alone if statistics show "gross disparity" in the treatment of workers based on discriminatory factors, such as race. *Page v. U.S. Industries, Inc.,* 726 F.2d 1038, 1046 (5th Cir. 1984). Using such evidence, a plaintiff must show: (1) membership in a minority group; (2) an application for an open job or promotion for which he or she was qualified; (3) rejection; and (4) the employer promoted or hired a non-minority for the job or continued to seek non-minority applicants for the position applied for by the plaintiff. *Id.* However, if the statistical disparity shown by the plaintiff's evidence is insufficient alone to establish a prima facie case of disparate treatment, a plaintiff "may get over this hurdle by combining statistics with historical, individual or circumstantial evidence." *Id.* In order to rebut a prima facie case of disparate treatment, defendant must discredit plaintiff's evidence or provide a nondiscriminatory explanation for apparently discriminatory result. *Id.*

6 As previously stated, this action does not stem from Title VII. However, the Title VII disparate treatment or disparate impact analysis assists in informing this Court's evaluation of the actions taken by the Board.

In the case at bar, Defendant asserts that the lack of African-American coaches resulted from the decline in the number of qualified black applicants for teaching positions. However, Defendant's rebuttal misses the bull's eye as it fails to address the precise issue before the court regarding disparate impact, which is how the use of the Objective Criteria resulted in disparate impact. Simply pointing to the decline in the number of applicants does not address the relevant question of the disparate impact caused by the use of Objective Criteria.

In *Griggs v. Duke Power Co.,* the Supreme Court concluded that if an employer could not show that its facially neutral policy was job-related and consistent with business necessity, its practice would be prohibited. 401 U.S. 424, 91 S. Ct. 849, 28 L. Ed. 2d 158 (1971); Joseph A. Seiner, *Disentangling Disparate Impact and Disparate Treatment: Adapting the Canadian Approach,* 25 Yale L. & Pol'y Rev. 95, 100 (2006). While *Griggs* invoked Title VII and the case before the court is a §1983 school desegregation case, the disparate impact theory used in *Griggs* provides further support for the Plaintiffs' right previously reserved by this Court to raise issues regarding disparate impact. Defendant cannot demonstrate how using certain aspects of the objective criteria, such as handwriting evaluation, proves to be a "business necessity" or even relevant to a football coaching position. Moreover, the objective criteria, a facially neutral policy, used has resulted in a disparate impact in hiring African-American football coaches, as illustrated through the claim raised by a qualified applicant, Mr. Alden Foster. In fact, an African-American has not been hired for a head football coaching position since last ordered by this Court decades ago. Due to the failure the Board to take the necessary actions to comply with court order, this Court must take action to guard against disparate impact in hiring and to assist with the creation a unitary system.

CONCLUSION

The use of racial classifications are justified by the compelling state purpose to create a unitary school system. [7] Forty-three years after this case was filed, the interest of achieving this goal has not dissipated. Rather, achieving a unitary school system remains a preeminent community concern. This record contains more than just a mere citation to prior societal discrimination. Rather, the record contains convincing evidence of prior discrimination by the Board, which necessitated the series of orders of the court to address the vestiges of de jure segregation. *See Wygant v. Jackson Bd. of Educ.,* 476 U.S. 267, 106 S.Ct. 1842, 90 L. Ed. 2d 260 (1986). The passage of time does not discharge the Board of its duty to comply with court orders or pardon it from its duty to ensure that the vestiges of the dual school system resulting from de jure segregation are eradicated. This Court cannot continue to allow the Tangipahoa School Board's interpretation of "all deliberate speed" to further eschew the attainment of a unitary school system.

7 The prospective remedies of Affirmative Action may be upheld as long as they are supported by a compelling state purpose.

Accordingly, IT IS ORDERED that Alden Foster shall be hired as the head football coach at Amite High School.

New Orleans, Louisiana, this 30th day of April, 2008.

/s/ Ivan L. R. Lemelle

IVAN L. R. LEMELLE

UNITED STATES DISTRICT JUDGE

IN RE TROY ANTHONY DAVIS

CASE NO. CV409-130

UNITED STATES DISTRICT COURT FOR THE SOUTHERN DISTRICT OF GEORGIA, SAVANNAH DIVISION

2010 U.S. Dist. LEXIS 87340

August 24, 2010, Decided
August 24, 2010, Filed

U.S. DISTRICT JUDGE WILLIAM T. MOORE, JR.,

ORDER

Before the Court is Petitioner Troy Anthony Davis's Petition for a Writ of Habeas Corpus. (Doc. 2.) This petition was originally filed with the United States Supreme Court and has been transferred to this Court, pursuant to 28 U.S.C. § 2241(b), with instructions to "receive testimony and make findings of fact as to whether evidence that could not have been obtained at the time of the trial clearly establishes petitioner's innocence." [1] In re Davis, 557 U.S. , 130 S. Ct. 1, 1, 174 L. Ed. 2d 614 (2009). This Court has conducted the hearing. (See Docs. 82, 83.) For the reasons that follow, the Court concludes that while executing an innocent person would violate the United States Constitution, Mr. Davis has failed to prove his innocence. Accordingly, the petition is DENIED.

[1] The jurisdictional effects of this transfer, especially with respect to appeal, are unclear. According to the Revision Notes of 28 U.S.C. § 2241:

> Subsection (b) was added to give statutory sanction to orderly and appropriate procedure. A circuit judge who unnecessarily entertains applications which should be addressed to the district court, thereby disqualifies himself to hear such matters on appeal and to that extent limits his usefulness as a judge of the court of appeals. The Supreme Court and Supreme Court Justices should not be burdened with applications for writs cognizable in the district courts.

This text suggests that petitions are transferred to avoid burdening the Supreme Court. Functionally, then, this Court is operating as a magistrate for the Supreme Court, which suggests appeal of this order would be directly to the Supreme Court. However, this Court has been unable to locate any legal precedent or legislative history on point.

BACKGROUND

This case involves the shooting of Savannah Police Department ("SPD") Officer Mark Allen MacPhail. In the early hours of August 19, 1989, Officer MacPhail was working a part-time security job when he came to the assistance of a homeless man, whom had been assaulted in the parking lot of a Burger King restaurant. As Officer MacPhail neared the commotion, one of the three men responsible for the assault gunned him down.

An earlier shooting at a party in the Cloverdale neighborhood of Savannah also plays a role in this case. [2] Here, an individual shot at a car as it was leaving the party, striking one of its occupants in the face. Because this case centers on eyewitness testimony, the Court presents the facts in the manner in which they were provided by those who witnessed these events.

> [2] By recounting the facts of the Cloverdale shooting, the Court does not mean to suggest that the validity of that conviction is tied to the validity of Mr. Davis's conviction for the murder of Officer MacPhail. See infra Analysis Part III.C.iv. Rather, the Court details those facts because they are necessary to understand the events of August 19, 1989 and the subsequent investigation and trial, during which the State bootstrapped the conviction for the Cloverdale shooting to Mr. Davis's conviction for the MacPhail murder.

I. THE INVESTIGATIONS

At 11:29 p.m. on August 18, 1989, the SPD received a 911 call from a resident in the Cloverdale neighborhood informing them that several shots had been fired. (Resp. Ex. 30, Disk 1 at 00:14.) The police received several more reports of gunfire, and an officer was dispatched to investigate. At 12:17 a.m. on August 19, 1989, an officer was informed that a local hospital had admitted Mr. Michael Cooper to treat a gunshot wound he received in the Cloverdale neighborhood. (Id. at 03:37, 09:12.) The police visited Mr. Cooper in the hospital and obtained a description of the shooter: a young, tall, African-American male wearing a white batman shirt, a black hat, and shorts. (Id. at 11:01.)

At 1:09 a.m. on August 19, 2010, the SPD received a 911 call from an employee at the Thunderbird Inn, located across the Street from the Burger King on Oglethorpe Avenue. [3] (Id. at 22:56.) The caller informed the police that an individual had been shot in the Burger King parking lot and that she saw two African-American males running from the scene in the direction of the Trust Company Bank building. One minute later, the SPD received another 911 call informing the police that the shooting victim was a police officer. (Id. at 24:13.) At 1:16 a.m., the SPD received a second call from the Thunderbird employee, informing them that she saw two men run from the Burger King parking lot towards the Trust Company Bank building, that both were wearing shorts, and that one was wearing a tank top t-shirt. (Id. at 30:38.) The caller did not identify the color of the shorts or the tank top. The limited description was quickly relayed to the responding officers, who immediately began searching for similarly dressed individuals. (Id. at 38:03.) Meanwhile, the officers at the scene secured the area and began interviewing potential witnesses. (Resp. Ex. 30 at 13-14.) The following relevant witness statements were secured during the investigations.

3 For reference, a hand drawn diagram of the Burger King parking lot and surrounding area is provided in the appendix to this order. The diagram is from the police file (Resp. Ex. 30 at 375) and is not to scale.

A. Harriett Murray's First Statement

At 2:27 a.m. on August 19, 1989, Ms. Harriett Murray provided the police with a statement concerning the MacPhail shooting. (Pet. Ex. 32-U at 1.) In the early hours of August 19, 1989, Ms. Murray was sitting in front of the Burger King restaurant with Mr. Larry Young. (Id.) Mr. Young went to the nearby convenience store to purchase cigarettes and beer. (Id.) While Mr. Young was returning from the store to the Burger King parking lot, Ms. Murray noticed that he was arguing with another individual, who was following him. (Id.) Ms. Murray also noticed two other individuals, approaching from the direction of the Trust Company Bank building, who were following Mr. Young. (Id.)

Walking away from the individuals, Mr. Young repeatedly told the group that he was not going to fight them. (Id.) Ms. Murray heard one individual tell Mr. Young not to walk away and threaten to shoot him. (Id.) The individual then started digging down his shirt. (Id.) As the three individuals converged on Mr. Young, one produced a gun. (Id.) Unaware of the weapon, Mr. Young continued to walk away from the trio. (Id.) As Mr. Young approached a van parked at the Burger King drive-through window, the armed individual struck Mr. Young in the head with what Ms. Murray believed was the butt of the weapon. (Id. at 1-2.) Mr. Young then fled toward the drive-through window, and began beating on the van and the window, asking for someone to call the police. (Id. at 1.)

Next, Ms. Murray observed a police officer approaching the three individuals, who were now fleeing, telling them to 'hold it." (Id. at 1-2.) As the officer closed to within five feet, the individual with the firearm turned and aimed the weapon at the officer. (Id. at 2.) The weapon did not discharge when the individual first pulled the trigger. (Id.) As the officer reached for his gun, the individual shot him in the face. (Id.) Wounded, the officer fell to the ground, at which point the gunman fired two or three additional rounds at the officer and then continued running. (Id.) Ms. Murray then found Mr. Young and assisted him in tending to his head wound. (Id.)

Ms. Murray described the gunman as having medium-colored skin with a narrow face, high cheekbones, and a fade-away haircut. (Id.) She estimated him to be between twenty-four to thirty years old, four inches taller than the officer, and approximately one hundred and thirty pounds. (Id.) Ms. Murray recalls the gunman as wearing a white shirt and dark colored pants. (Id.)

B. Larry Young

At 3:10 a.m. on August 19, 1989, the police obtained a statement from Mr. Young concerning the MacPhail shooting. (Pet. Ex. 32-N at 1.) Mr. Young informed the police that, during the early hours of August 19, 1989, he was sitting in the Burger King parking lot drinking beer with his girlfriend, Ms. Murray. (Id. at 2.) When the couple drank their last beer, Mr. Young went to the Time-Saver [4] convenience store to get more beer. [5] (Id.) As Mr. Young was returning, an African-American male wearing a yellow t-shirt began asking him for one of the beers that Mr. Young just purchased. (Id. at 2, 5.) When Mr. Young informed the individual that he could not have a beer, the individual began using foul language toward Mr. Young. (Id. at 2.) As Mr. Young continued walking back toward the Burger King, the individual in the yellow t-shirt followed him, continuing the verbal altercation. (Id.) As he approached the Burger King parking lot, Mr. Young noticed a second African-American male slipping through the fence separating the convenience store parking lot from the Trust Company Bank property. (Id.) Soon, Mr. Young realized that he was being followed by a third individual. (Id.)

4 Different witnesses refer to this convenience store as either the Time-Saver or Penny-Saver.

5 The convenience store is located to the west of the Burger King, on the same side of Oglethorpe Avenue as the Burger King. (Pet. Ex. 32-N at 1.)

As Mr. Young entered the Burger King parking lot, he observed Ms. Murray and two gentlemen sitting with her quickly get up and flee the area. (Id.) Mr. Young now realized that he was cornered and resumed arguing with the individual in the yellow t-shirt. (Id.) As Mr. Young was focused on the individual in the yellow t-shirt, he was hit in the head by a second person. (Id. at 2-3.) A stunned and fearful Mr. Young ran toward the Burger King drive-through window, seeking help. (Id. at 3.) When he was at the window, Mr. Young heard one gunshot, which caused him to duck for cover behind a van waiting at the window. (Id. at 8.) Eventually, he ran to the building's front entrance and entered the building. (Id. at 3.)

Mr. Young informed the police that the individual in the yellow t-shirt was around twenty to twenty-one years old, five feet nine inches tall, and one hundred and fifty-eight pounds. (Id. at 5-6.) The individual had short hair, no facial hair, and lighter brown skin. (Id. at 6.) When describing his clothes, Mr. Young stated that the yellow t-shirt was a tank-top and that the individual was wearing "lam" pants. (Id.) Mr. Young stated that he definitely recognized the individual in the yellow t-shirt. (Id. at 5.)

Mr. Young described the individual who assaulted him as about twenty-two to twenty-three years old, five feet eleven inches tall, and one hundred and seventy-two pounds. (Id. at 7.) Mr. Young could not remember the individual's facial features or skin color (id.), but believed that he might be able to recognize him if he saw him again (id. at 5). He did state that the individual was wearing a white hat and a white t-shirt with "some kind of print on it." (Id. at 7.) Mr. Young could not remember anything about the third individual because that person was only in the background and was not directly involved in the altercation. (Id.)

C. Antoine Williams

At 3:22 a.m. on August 19, 1989, the police took a statement from Mr. Antoine Williams concerning the MacPhail shooting. (Pet. Ex. 32-00 at 1.) At about 1:00 a.m. that morning, Mr. Williams was pulling into the Burger King parking lot to begin his shift at the restaurant. (Id.) As he was parking, he noticed three men following one individual, who was walking across Fahm Street toward the Burger King parking lot. (Id.) As they drew closer, Mr. Williams could tell that two of the individuals were arguing. (Id.) He overheard the individual being followed say that he did not want to fight anyone and that the three others should go back to where they were. (Id.) As the group came between his car and the drive-through window, one of the individuals ran up and slapped the man being followed in the head with a gun. (Id.)

When Mr. Williams looked the other way, he saw a police officer coming from behind a van waiting at the Burger King drive-through window. (Id.) The officer was running towards the individual with the firearm. (Id.) The two unarmed individuals were already running away, and the individual with the gun was trying to stick it back in his pants. (Id.) According to Mr. Williams, the assailant appeared to panic as the officer was approaching and he was unable to conceal the gun. (Id. at 1-2.) When the officer closed to within approximately fifteen feet, the assailant turned and shot the officer. (Id.) After falling to the ground, it appeared that the officer was trying to regain his footing when the gunman shot him three more times. (Id. at 2.) After firing the fourth shot, the gunman fled from the scene. (Id.)

Mr. Williams described the gunman as approximately twenty to twenty-three years old, six feet two inches to six feet four inches tall, and one hundred and eighty pounds. (Id.) Mr. Williams believed that the gunman was wearing a blue or white t-shirt, and dark jeans. (Id.) He explained that the dark shade of tint on his car's windows may have affected his ability to distinguish the exact color of the gunman's t-shirt. (Id. at 2-3.) Mr. Williams then described the gun used in the shooting as a rusty, brownish colored revolver. (Id. at 3.) Mr. Williams did state that he believed he could identify the gunman if he saw him again. (Id.) When asked to describe the other three individuals, Mr. Williams could not provide any details because he was focused on the gunman. (Id.)

D. Dorothy Ferrell's First Statement

At 4:14 a.m. on August 19, 1989, Ms. Dorothy Ferrell provided a statement to the police concerning the MacPhail shooting. (Pet. Ex. 32-Y at 1.) Ms. Ferrell informed the police that, during the early hours of August 19, 1989, she was descending the stairs at the Thunderbird Inn, located directly across Oglethorpe Avenue from the Burger King, when she saw a bloodied individual in the Burger King parking lot. (Id.) Next, Ms. Ferrell observed a police officer walk across the parking lot, yelling at a group of people. (Id.) While two of the individuals fled, one reached into his shorts, produced a firearm, and shot the officer. (Id.) The wounded officer fell to the ground, at which point the gunman fired three additional shots and then fled the scene. (Id.)

Ms. Ferrell also recalls that, at around 6:00 p.m. on August 18, 1989, the same officer directed the gunman to leave the Burger King property. (Id.) The gunman was wearing the same clothes during both incidents--a white t-shirt with writing, dark colored shorts, and a white hat. (Id. at 1-2.) She described the shooter as approximately six feet tall with a slender build and medium-light colored skin. (Id. at 2.) Ms. Ferrell was pretty sure that she could identify the gunman if she saw him again. (Id.)

E. Anthony Lolas

At 5:20 a.m. on August 19, 1989, the police took a statement concerning the MacPhail shooting from United States Air Force Lieutenant Colonel Anthony Lolas. (Resp. Ex. 30 at 110.) Lt. Col. Lolas informed the police that at approximately 1:01 a.m. he was lying down in the back seat of a van waiting at the Burger King drive-through window when a man started banging on the vehicle, asking for the police. (Id.) As he was rising from the seat, Lt. Col. Lolas heard one gunshot, quickly followed by two additional shots. (Id.) Turning toward the direction of the gunshots, Lt. Cal. Lolas saw someone in a striped jumpsuit running toward the front of the Burger King. (Id.) Then, Lt. Cal. Lolas focused on an individual in a white t-shirt, whose arm was surrounded by smoke. (Id. at 110-11.) After firing the shots, the gunman fled to the northwest. (Id.) Lt. Col. Lolas stated that he had no doubt that the individual in the white t-shirt was the shooter. (Id. at 111.)

Lt. Col. Lolas never saw the shooter's face, but described him as an African-American male, approximately six feet tall, and around one hundred and seventy pounds. (Id.) The shooter was wearing a white t-shirt with very dark pants. (Id.)

F. Matthew Hughes

At 5:49 a.m. on August 19, 1989, Mr. Matthew Hughes provided the police with a statement concerning the MacPhail shooting. (Id. at 115.) Mr. Hughes was seated directly behind the driver's seat in a van waiting at the Burger King drive-through when an individual came up to the driver's side window. (Id.) Mr. Hughes could not hear what the man was saying, but noticed a severe cut over his right eye. (Id.) Next, Mr. Hughes heard a pop from the direction of the parking lot. (Id.) He did not think much of it until the other passengers told him there was something going on in the parking lot. (Id.) As Mr. Hughes turned to look, he heard two more popping sounds. (Id.) Once he was facing the direction of the sounds, he saw an African-American male in a light colored t-shirt standing over the body of a white individual. (Id.) After the shooting, the African-American male ran toward the Trust Company Bank building. (Id. at 116-17.)

Mr. Hughes described the individual in the light colored t-shirt as an African-American male with a slender to medium build, approximately five feet seven inches to five feet nine inches tall. (Id.) The individual wore dark shorts, a light colored baseball cap, and a light colored t-shirt, with either short or no sleeves. (Id.) Mr. Hughes also saw a second individual running toward the Trust Company Bank building, who was much closer to that building than the man in the light colored t-shirt. (Id.) This individual was skinny, dressed in all dark clothes, and appeared to be carrying a gym bag. (Id.)

G. Eric Biggins

At 5:57 a.m. on August 19, 1989, the police obtained a statement from Mr. Eric Riggins concerning the MacPhail shooting. (Id. at 118.) Mr. Riggins was seated in the second row, behind the driver's seat, in a van waiting at the Burger King drive-through window when an individual came to the driver's side window calling for someone to phone the police. (Id.) After a few seconds passed, Mr. Biggins heard a single gunshot. (Id.) Turning toward the direction of the gunshot, Mr. Riggins observed a man falling to the ground. (Id.) An individual, standing five feet from the man on the ground, raised his hand and fired two more shots. (Id.) Mr. Riggins recalls that the gunman never completely stopped running to fire the shots and fled towards the Trust Company Bank building. (Id. at 118-19.)

Mr. Riggins described the shooter as a slim, African-American male, approximately five feet ten inches tall and one hundred and sixty pounds. (Id. at 118.) The gunman was wearing a light colored shirt, dark shorts, and a baseball cap, the color of which Mr. Riggins could not recall. (Id.) Beyond the shooter, Mr. Riggins saw a second, taller male running towards the Trust Company Bank building. (Id.)

H. Steven Hawkins

At 6:10 a.m. on August 19, 1989, Mr. Steven Hawkins provided the police with a statement concerning the MacPhail shooting. (Id. at 129.) Mr. Hawkins was seated in the middle of the third row of a van waiting at the Burger King drive-through window when an individual came up to the driver's side window asking for someone to call the police. (Id.) Soon thereafter, Mr. Hawkins heard three popping sounds from the parking lot. (Id.) Turning to look in the direction of the noise, Mr. Hawkins saw an African-American teenager, who was skinny, approximately six feet tall, and was wearing a white shirt with black shorts or pants, running across the parking lot. (Id.)

I. Steven Sanders

At 5:15 a.m. on August 19, 1989, the police obtained a statement from Mr. Stephen Sanders concerning the MacPhail shooting. (Id. at 112.) Mr. Sanders was seated in a van waiting at the Burger King drive-through window when he observed one African-American male strike another African-American male in the parking lot. (Id.) The man who had been hit ran to the van, asking for someone to call the police while banging on the hood of the vehicle. (Id.) It was at this time that Mr. Sanders heard a gunshot. (Id.) Turning toward the noise, Mr. Sanders observed an African-American male wearing a white shirt and black shorts standing in front of an individual who was falling forward. (Id.) The male in the white shirt shot at the individual two more times and then start running, with a second individual in a black outfit, toward the Trust Company Bank building. (Id. at 112-13.) Mr. Sanders informed the police that he would not be able to recognize the two fleeing men, except by their clothing. (Id. at 113.)

J. Robert Grizzard

At 6:07 a.m. on August 19, 1989, Mr. Robert Grizzard provided a statement to the police concerning the MacPhail shooting. (Id. at 130.) Mr. Grizzard was seated in a van waiting at the Burger King drive-through window when he observed two men running from the parking lot toward the front of the building. (Id.) Looking in the direction from which the men fled, Mr. Grizzard saw one man hit another on the side of his face. (Id.) The assaulted individual then staggered to the van and asked for someone to call the police. (Id.) Looking back toward the parking lot, Mr. Grizzard observed a police officer with a baton moving toward the assailant. (Id.) As the officer closed in on the assailant, the assailant fired as many as four shots at the officer. Once the officer fell to the ground, the shooter fled. (Id.) Mr. Grizzard remembered only that the shooter was wearing a hat. (Id. at 130-31.) Mr. Grizzard informed the police that he would not be able to identify the shooter. (Id. at 131.)

K. Mark Wilds

At 6:40 a.m. on August 19, 1989, the police obtained a statement from Mr. Mark Wilds concerning the Cloverdale shooting. (Id. at 194.) Mr. Wilds was driving away from the Cloverdale party with Messrs. Lamar Brown, Benjamin Gordon, and Joseph Blige when someone fired at their vehicle from the bushes. (Id.) Mr. Wilds believed that the weapon used was a thirty-eight caliber. (Id.) Later, at 845 p.m. on August 19, 1989, Mr. Wilds amended his statement to include an identification of Mr. Davis as one who attended the Cloverdale party. (Id. at 195.)

L. Joseph Blige

At 7:10 a.m. on August 19, 1989, Mr. Blige provided the police with a statement concerning the Cloverdale shooting. (Id. at 196.) He informed the police that he was leaving the Cloverdale party in Mr. Wilds's vehicle, along with Messrs. Brown, Gordon, and Michael Cooper, when someone started shooting at them from behind some bushes. (Id.) There were between four and five people standing behind the bushes when the shooting began. (Id.) One bullet struck Mr. Cooper, whom Mr. Wilds subsequently drove to the hospital. (Id.)

M. Benjamin Gordon

At 7:47 a.m. on August 19, 1989, the police obtained a statement from Mr. Benjamin Gordon concerning the Cloverdale shooting. (Id. at 198.) Mr. Gordon informed the police that, as he was leaving the Cloverdale party in Mr. Wilds's vehicle with Messrs. Brown, Cooper, and Blige, someone on the corner fired multiple shots at the vehicle, hitting Mr. Cooper. (Id.) The shooter was wearing a white batman shirt and a dark colored pair of jeans. (Id.) Mr. Gordon remembered seeing the gunman earlier at the party, by the pool. (Id.) Mr. Gordon believed that the individual was angry at Mr. Gordon and his friends because they were from another neighborhood and the girls were talking mostly to them. (Id. at 198-99.) Later that evening, Mr. Gordon walked to the Burger King because he heard that an officer had been shot. (Id. at 199.)

N. Lamar Brown

At 6:00 p.m. on August 19, 1989, Mr. Lamar Brown provided the police with a statement concerning the Cloverdale shooting. (Id. at 207.) According to Mr. Brown, he was leaving the Cloverdale party in Mr. Wilds's vehicle, along with Messrs. Gordon, Blige, and Cooper, when someone started shooting at them from the corner. (Id.) The shooter was dark skinned with short hair, between five feet nine inches and five feet ten inches tall, and around one hundred and fifty-nine pounds. (Id. at 208.) The gunman was wearing a batman shirt, black pants, and a black hat. (Id.) Mr. Brown did not remember seeing this individual at the party. (Id.)

Later that evening, Mr. Brown was passing time with Messrs. Wilds, Gordon, and Blige in the Yamacraw neighborhood when he heard gunshots. (Id. at 209-10.) After the shooting, Mr. Brown observed two individuals running toward the Trust Company Bank building, into the Yamacraw neighborhood. (Id. at 209.) One was running a short distance behind the other. (Id. at 210.) Due to the darkness, Mr. Brown could not see any identifying features on either individual. (Id.)

O. Sylvester "Red" Coles's First Statement

At 8:52 p.m. on August 19, 1989, Mr. Sylvester "Red" Coles gave a statement to the police concerning the MacPhail shooting. (Id. at 143.) Mr. Coles was standing outside of Charlie Brown's pool room with Messrs. Troy Davis and Darrell Collins when he started arguing with someone passing through the parking lot. (Id. at 143-44.) Mr. Coles continued to argue with the individual as he walked toward the Burger King restaurant, followed by Messrs. Davis and Collins. (Id.) Mr. Coles stated that, when they were near the restaurant's drive-through window, Mr. Davis hit the individual in the head with a pistol. (Id.)

As the individual ran off shouting, a police officer came out of the Burger King restaurant and told Messrs. Coles and Davis to "hold it." (Id.) Mr. Coles stood in the middle of the parking lot while Mr. Davis ran past him toward the Trust Company Bank building. (Id.) After the officer, nightstick in hand, ran past Mr. Coles toward Mr. Davis, Mr. Coles heard a gunshot. (Id.) Upon hearing the shot, Mr. Coles began running toward the Trust Company Bank building. (Id.) As he was fleeing, Mr. Coles turned around and saw the police officer falling to the ground. (Id. at 145.) Mr. Coles ran past the pool room to his sister's house in Yamacraw Village. (Id. at 143-44.)

Mr. Coles informed the police that he had seen Mr. Davis with a firearm earlier that evening at the pool room. (Id. at 145.) The gun was black, with a short barrel and brown wooden handle. (Id.) Mr. Coles stated that he thought Mr. Davis was wearing a short sleeve t-shirt and orange cut off shorts, but could not really remember. (Id. at 146.)

P. Darrell Collins's First Statement

At 11:30 p.m. on August 19, 1989, the police obtained a statement from Mr. Darrell Collins. (Id. at 148.) Mr. Collins informed the police that, on the evening of August 18, 1989, he went to a pool party in Cloverdale with Messrs. Eric Ellison and Davis. (Id.) The trio was leaving the party when Messrs. Collins and Ellison stopped to talk to girls, while Mr. Davis continued to walk toward the street corner. (Id.) When Mr. Davis was almost to the corner, the occupants of an approaching car were leaning out of the vehicle's windows, cussing and throwing things. (Id.) Mr. Davis shot at the vehicle as it passed the corner where he was standing using a short barreled, black gun with a brown handle. (Id. at 149.)

After the shooting, Messrs. Collins and Ellison returned to Mr. Ellison's house. (Id. at 148.) After spending some time at Mr. Ellison's home, the pair were on their way to purchase gas for the vehicle when they passed Mr. Davis, who was walking on the side of the road. (Id.) Mr. Davis joined them and they went to the Time-Saver. (Id.)

Once at the Time-Saver, Messrs. Collins and Ellison stood by the vehicle while Mr. Davis walked over to Charlie Brown's pool room, located adjacent to the Time-Saver, and engaged Mr. Coles in conversation. (Id. at 148-49.) Soon thereafter, an argument between Mr. Coles and a second individual broke out. (Id. at 149.) As the argument moved toward the Burger King parking lot, Mr. Coles was followed by Mr. Davis, who was, in turn, followed by Mr. Collins. (Id.)

As the group entered the Burger King parking lot, Mr. Davis slapped the individual they had been following in the head. (Id.) Mr. Collins then noticed a police officer advancing toward the commotion. (Id.) Upon observing the officer, Mr. Collins turned around and started walking back toward the gas station. (Id.) While he was returning to the station, Mr. Collins heard a single gunshot, which caused him to start running. (Id.) When Mr. Collins arrived at the gas station, he rejoined Mr. Ellison, who drove Mr. Collins home. He informed the police that, on the night of the MacPhail shooting, Mr. Davis was wearing blue or black shorts, and a white t-shirt with writing on the front. (Id.)

Q. Jeffrey Sams's First Statement

On August 20, 1989, Mr. Jeffrey Sams provided a statement to the police concerning the Cloverdale shooting. (Id. at 161.) Mr. Sams informed the police that, on August 18, 1989, he was at a party in the Cloverdale neighborhood, where he saw Mr. Davis. (Id.) After he heard some guys arguing at the party, he decided to take his car home and walk back to the party. (Id.) As he was walking back, Mr. Sams was picked up by Mr. Ellison, whose vehicle was also occupied by Messrs. Davis and Collins. (Id.) Mr. Ellison then drove the group to the Time-Saver. (Id.) After visiting the store, the group went to Charlie Brown's pool room. (Id.) After shooting a few games of pool, Mr. Sams returned to the car, where he stayed until Messrs. Ellison and Collins returned. (Id.)

R. Jeffrey Sapp

At 2:30 on August 21, 1989, Mr. Jeffrey Sapp provided a statement to the police concerning the MacPhail shooting. (Id. at 166.) Between 2:00 and 3:00 p.m. on August 19, 1989, Mr. Davis was riding a bicycle when he stopped to talk with Mr. Sapp. (Id.) Mr. Davis asked Mr. Sapp if he heard about a shooting. (Id.) After Mr. Sapp told Mr. Davis that he heard an officer had been shot, Mr. Davis confessed that he was the shooter. (Id.) Mr. Davis then recounted how Mr. Coles got into a fight with another individual, whom Mr. Davis slapped in the face with a pistol. (Id.) The police officer then appeared from behind a van, told Mr. Davis to stop, and reached for his firearm. (Id.) Mr. Davis told Mr. Sapp that he shot the officer because the officer was reaching for his firearm. (Id.) Mr. Sapp stated that he did not believe Mr. Davis's story. (Id.)

S. Eric Ellison

On August 21, 1989, the police obtained a statement from Mr. Eric Ellison. (Id. at 156.) Mr. Ellison informed the police that, on the evening of August 18, 1989, he and Mr. Collins were driving to a party in the Cloverdale neighborhood when they passed Mr. Davis, who was walking to the same party. (Id.) They picked up Mr. Davis and continued to Cloverdale. (Id.) Once they arrived, the group parted ways. (Id. at 156-57.) When Mr. Ellison left the pool area at the back of the home, he observed an argument in the front yard between two groups of people, which involved some shouting and cursing. (Id.) A few minutes later, Mr. Ellison saw Mr. Davis leave the party in a truck, only to return within five to ten minutes. (Id. at 157.)

As Messrs. Ellison and Collins were in the front yard speaking with some girls, Mr. Ellison noticed an automobile driving by with an individual leaning out of a passenger's side window, yelling derogatory comments. (Id.) When the car neared the corner, Mr. Ellison heard between four and five gunshots. (Id.) The gunfire prompted Mr. Ellison to leave the party with Mr. Collins. (Id.) As Mr. Ellison was leaving, he saw Mr. Davis close to the corner where the shots were fired. (Id.) Mr. Davis asked Mr. Ellison to be taken to the Yamacraw neighborhood. (Id.) Having agreed, Mr. Ellison was driving the three toward Yamacraw when he passed Mr. Jeffery Sams, who was walking back to the party. (Id.) Mr. Sams got into the vehicle, and the four drove off toward Yamacraw. (Id.)

At the direction of Mr. Davis, Mr. Ellison drove to a convenience store. (Id. at 158.) After going into the store, the group went to the adjacent pool room to shoot pool. (Id.) The group separated while playing pool. Finishing his last game, Mr. Ellison was leaving the pool room when he heard three gunshots. (Id.) As he got into his car, where Mr. Sams was already located, Mr. Collins approached and entered the vehicle. (Id. at 159.) Mr. Ellison then drove home, where he remained until he had to report to work at 10:00 a.m. (Id.)

T. Monty Holmes

At 2:11 p.m. on August 22, 1989, Mr. Monty Holmes provided a statement to the police regarding the MacPhail shooting. (Id. at 169.) Mr. Holmes stated that, on the morning of August 19, 1989, Mr. Davis came to his home and confessed to shooting Officer MacPhail. (Id.) Mr. Davis told Mr. Holmes that he shot the officer because he thought the officer was reaching for his firearm. (Id.) Mr. Holmes thought the confession was a joke. (Id.)

U. Craig Young

At 2:28 p.m. on August 22, 1989, the police obtained a statement from Mr. Craig Young. (Id. at 211.) Mr. Craig Young informed the police that Mr. Davis told him that he had gotten into an argument with Mr. Mike Wilds at the Cloverdale party. (Id.) Mr. Craig Young recalls Mr. Wilds's vehicle being shot at and hearing that Mr. Davis was the shooter. (Id.)

According to Mr. Craig Young, he was walking home with Mr. Sapp on the morning of August 19, 1989, when Mr. Sapp informed him that Mr. Davis claimed to have shot the police officer. (Id. at 212.) As the two separated, Mr. Craig Young observed Mr. Davis slowly riding a bicycle down the street. (Id.)

V. Harriett Murray's Second Statement

At 6:11 p.m. on August 24, 1989, Ms. Murray provided the police with a second statement concerning the MacPhail shooting. (Pet. Ex. 32-V at 1.) In this statement, Ms. Murray identified Mr. Davis as Officer MacPhail's murderer from a photographic lineup. (Id. at 1-2.) She also identified Mr. Coles as the individual in a yellow shirt who grabbed Mr. Young's arm, causing Mr. Young to turn around. (Id.) It was at this time that the individual in the white shirt--Mr. Davis--struck Mr. Young with the gun. (Id. at 1.) Ms. Murray stated that the individual in the yellow shirt was heavier than the individual in the white shirt, whom she estimated was between 135 and 155 pounds. (Id.)

W. Sylvester "Red" Coles's Second Statement

At 7:55 p.m. on August 24, 1989, Mr. Coles provided a second statement to the police concerning the MacPhail shooting. (Resp. Ex. 30 at 147.) In this statement, Mr. Coles admits that he was carrying a gun on the night Officer MacPhail was shot. (Id.) Specifically, Mr. Coles carried a chrome, long barreled, thirty-eight caliber revolver in the waistline of his pants. (Id.) Mr. Coles no longer had the gun on him when he started the argument because he had given it to Mr. Sapp for safekeeping while Mr. Coles was playing pool. (Id.)

X. Darrell Collins's Second Statement

At 9:03 a.m. on August 25, 1989, the police obtained a second statement from Mr. Collins. (Id. at 150.) In this statement, Mr. Collins tells the police that he, Messrs. Ellison, Sams, and Davis were all in the car as they drove to the Time-Saver. (Id.) When Mr. Ellison went inside Charlie Brown's pool room, Mr. Coles took a firearm from his pants and placed it on the front seat of Mr. Ellison's vehicle. (Id.) Not wanting the gun in the car, Mr. Collins took it and hid it in some bushes on the side of the building. (Id.) Mr. Collins described the gun as long barreled and chrome with a brown handle. (Id.) Also, he informed the police that he had seen Mr. Davis with the gun used in the Cloverdale shooting at least twice, once two weeks prior to that shooting and once after that shooting. (Id. at 151.)

Y. Jeffrey Sams's Second Statement

At 4:06 p.m. on August 25, 1989, Mr. Sams provided a second statement to the police concerning the MacPhail shooting. (Id. at 164.) Mr. Sams informed the police that, when he was sitting by himself in Mr. Ellison's car, Mr. Coles placed a gun in the front seat of the vehicle. (Id.) According to Mr. Sams, Mr. Collins immediately picked up the gun and removed it from the car. (Id.) Mr. Sams recalled the gun as being shiny, but could not remember if it had a long or short barrel. (Id.)

Z. Antoine Williams's Second Statement

At 1:16 p.m. on August 30, 1989, Mr. Williams provided the police with a second statement. (Pet. Ex. 32-PP at 1.) In this statement, he identified Mr. Davis as the individual who shot the officer. (Id.) Mr.

Williams was about sixty percent sure in his identification. (Id.) He had not read about the case in the newspaper, or heard about it on the radio or television. However, Mr. Williams did see a picture of Mr. Davis on a wanted poster at work, which he thought looked like the gunman. (Id. at 1-2.) He stated that he would not be able to identify any of the other individuals involved in the incident. (Id. at 2.)

Also, Mr. Williams informed the police that the individual who slapped the man was the same individual who shot the officer. (Id. at 1.) And, he stated that the gunman was wearing either a white or blue shirt, but that he had difficulty distinguish between these colors due to the dark tint on his car windows. (Id. at 2.) However, Mr. Williams stated that the tint would not have prohibited him from distinguishing yellow from either white or blue. (Id.)

AA. Valerie Gordon

At 10:47 a.m. on September 1, 1989, the police obtained a statement from Ms. Valerie Gordon, Mr. Coles's sister. (Resp. Ex. 30 at 175.) Ms. Gordon informed the police that, in the early morning of August 19, 1989, she was sitting on her front porch when she heard gunshots. (Id.) A few minutes later, Mr. Coles ran onto the front porch and sat down in a chair. (Id.) He then informed his sister that he was not sure what was going on, but that there had been a shooting and he thought someone was trying to kill him. (Id. at 175-76.) Mr. Coles changed out of his yellow t-shirt and into a red, white, and blue stripped collared shirt that Ms. Gordon retrieved for him. (Id. at 176.) As Ms. Gordon returned to the front door, she observed a shirtless Mr. Davis standing next to the porch, talking to Mr. Coles. (Id.) Mr. Coles gave Mr. Davis the yellow t-shirt he had previously been wearing, which Mr. Davis then put on. (Id. at 177.) Ms. Gordon informed the police that, after Mr. Davis put on the yellow t-shirt, Mr. Coles left the property and she Went inside the house. (Id.) A few minutes later, she observed Mr. Davis take off the yellow t-shirt, lay it just inside her front door, and exit the property. (Id. at 177-78.)

BB. Dorothy Ferrell's Second Statement

At 10:25 a.m. on September 5, 1989, Ms. Ferrell provided the police with a second statement concerning the MacPhail shooting. (Pet. Ex.

32-Z at 1.) In this statement, Ms. Ferrell identifies Mr. Davis as the individual who shot the officer. (Id.) She stated that, on the night of the MacPhail shooting, Mr. Davis was wearing a white t-shirt with quarter length sleeves and writing on the front, and dark colored shorts. (Id. at 4.) She admitted that she had seen his picture on television once prior to her identification, but stated that her identification was based only on what she observed on August 19, 1989. (Id. at 1-2.) Ms. Ferrell was between eighty and ninety percent sure that Mr. Davis was the shooter. (Id. at 3.)

Also, Ms. Ferrell stated that, prior to her identification, she had seen a photograph of Mr. Davis on the seat of a police car. (Id. at 2.) Ms. Ferrell was speaking to an officer in her neighborhood about events unrelated to the MacPhail shooting when she noticed the photograph on the seat of the officer's vehicle. (Id.) Ms. Ferrell informed the officer that she had witnessed the shooting and that the individual in the photograph was the gunman. (Id.)

II. PROBABLE CAUSE HEARING

On September 8, 1989, Mr. Davis had a probable cause hearing in Chatham County Recorder's Court. (Recorder's Court Transcript at 1.) At the hearing, the State was represented by Chatham County District Attorney Spencer Lawton, and Mr. Davis was represented by Mr. Robert Falligant, Jr. (Id.) At the conclusion of the hearing, the court found that the State presented sufficient evidence to charge Mr. Davis and submitted the case to Chatham County Superior Court. (Id. at 185.) The Court now relates the relevant witness testimony.

A. Larry Young

At the hearing, Mr. Young testified that, in the early hours of August 19, 1989, he was sitting in the Burger King parking lot with Ms. Murray when he walked to the Penny-Saver convenience store to purchase more beer. (Id. at 6-7.) As he was returning to the Burger King, an individual approached him and asked for some beer. (Id. at 8.) When Mr. Young told him no, the individual got upset and started cursing at him. (Id.) Mr. Young continued to walk toward the Burger King and exchange expletives with the individual, who was now following him. (Id.) As he was walking, Mr. Young noticed another individual slip through a fence and circle around the back of the adjacent Trust Company Bank building. (Id. at 9.) By the time Mr. Young reached the Burger King parking lot, he was aware of a third individual following him. (Id. at 9-10.)

When Mr. Young reached the parking lot, he heard one of the individuals say something, which caused the two gentlemen sitting with Ms. Murray to start running. (Id. at 10.) Startled, Mr. Young looked back at his pursuers and noticed that the three had closed in on him, prompting Mr. Young to quicken his pace. (Id.) As he neared the Burger King drive-through, Mr. Young stopped and was confronted by the individual he had been arguing with, who was dressed in a yellow t-shirt. (Id. at 11-12.) Mr. Young was aware that someone was further behind him on his left side, and that someone was closer behind him on his right side, wearing a white t-shirt and a light colored cap. (Id. at 12.)

As Mr. Young was focused on the individual in the yellow t-shirt, someone else struck him on the right side of his head. (Id. at 13-14.) Dazed, Mr. Young ran in between a van waiting at the drive-through and the drive-through window and asked for someone to call the police. (Id. at 14-15.) When Mr. Young was in between the van and the window, he heard a single gunshot. (Id. at 15.) Scared, Mr. Young ran to the front of the building and went inside. (Id. at 16-17.) Once inside, he was joined by Ms. Murray, who helped tend to his wound. (Id. at 17.)

On August 19, 1989, the police showed Mr. Young a photo array of individuals and asked him if he recognized anyone who was involved in his assault. (Id. at 18-19.) Mr. Young incorrectly identified the individual he was arguing with, but stated that he was not sure. (Id. at 19.) A few days later, however, Mr. Young realized his error when he saw Mr. Coles in person at the police station. After seeing Mr. Coles, Mr. Young identified him as the man he was arguing with. (Id. at 19-20.)

On cross-examination, Mr. Young testified that the individual he was arguing with was an African-American male with lighter colored skin than Mr. Young and short hair. (Id. at 30.) The man was approximately five foot eleven inches tall and wore a yellow t-shirt and short pants. (Id. at 30-31.) The individual that struck him was wearing a white t-shirt with printing, black pants, and a white baseball cap. (Id. at 40-41, 43.) Mr. Young was unable to identify the individual who struck him from a photo array. (Id. at 48.)

B. Harriett Murray

At the hearing, Ms. Murray testified that she was drinking beer with Mr. Young in the Burger King parking lot in the early hours of August 19, 1989. (Id. at 53.) Eventually, Mr. Young went to the convenience store to purchase more beer. (Id. at 54.) As Mr. Young was returning, he was being followed by an individual who was arguing with him as he continued toward the Burger King parking lot. (Id.) Ms. Murray also noticed two additional individuals approaching from the adjacent Trust Company Bank building, one farther back than the other. (Id. at 55.)

As Mr. Young neared the Burger King parking lot, the three individuals were converging on him, and one told Mr. Young that he would shoot him and began digging in his pants. (Id.) Upon hearing the threat, the two men sitting with Ms. Murray fled. (Id.) When Mr. Young neared the drive-through lane, he was cornered: the individual in the yellow shirt was on his left and the individual in the white shirt was on his right. (Id. at 56-57.) The third individual was standing five or six feet behind Mr. Young. (Id. at 57.) The individual in the yellow shirt grabbed Mr. Young's arm, causing Mr. Young to look to his left, directly at the individual in the yellow shirt. (Id. at 56.) When Mr. Young turned his head, the individual on Mr. Young's right hit him in the head with the handle of a gun. (Id. at 56, 58.) Ms. Murray described the gun as having a black barrel and brown handle. (Id. at 58.)

After being hit, Mr. Young ran between a van waiting at the drive-through and the drive-through window, crying for someone to call the police. (Id. at 59.) Shortly thereafter, a police officer came running from behind the building. (Id.) Upon seeing the police, the individuals in the yellow shirt and the white shirt began to flee. (Id. at 60.) At this point, Ms.. Murray was not sure where the third individual was located. (Id.) The officer took out his nightstick and told the two remaining individuals to "hold it." (Id.) Both individuals initially slowed down, but when the officer ran past the individual in the yellow shirt and continued toward the individual in the white shirt, the individual in the yellow shirt resumed running toward the

Trust Company Bank building. (Id. at 60-61.) As the officer approached, the individual in the white shirt stopped, waited for the officer to get within five feet, turned, aimed the gun at the officer, and pulled the trigger. (Id. at 61.) The gun did not fire the first time. (Id. at 61-62.) As the officer reached for his own firearm, the individual in the white shirt fired again, this time striking the officer in the face and causing him to fall to the ground. (Id.) The gunman then took two steps forward, fired two or three additional bullets at the fallen officer and fled. (Id. at 62.)

Ms. Murray was shown a photo array the night of the shooting, but could not identify the gunman. (Id. at 64.) Several days later, the police showed her a second photo array, from which she identified Mr. Davis as the man who hit Mr. Young and shot the officer. (Id. at 64-65.)

On cross-examination, Ms. Murray testified that the individual who threatened to shoot Mr. Young and started digging in his pants for a gun was the individual in the white shirt. (Id. at 70-71.) She also stated that the individual in the yellow shirt was a little taller and heavier than Mr. Young, while the individual in the white shirt was taller and thinner than Mr. Young. (Id. at 73.) Also, Ms. Murray recalled that the individual in the white shirt had darker skin than both Mr. Young and the individual in the yellow shirt. (Id. at 72-73.)

C. Sylvester "Red" Coles

At the hearing, Mr. Coles testified that he was playing pool at Charlie Brown's pool room in the early hours of August 19, 1989, when he began arguing with a man coming out of the Time-Saver. (Id. at 96.) The argument started because the man would not give Mr. Coles one of the beers he had just purchased. (Id.) As the argument continued, Mr. Coles pursued the man as he walked toward the Burger King parking lot. (Id. at 96-97.) Messrs. Davis and Collins followed the pair by cutting through the Trust Company Bank property. (Id. at 97.)

As Mr. Coles and the man he was arguing with neared the Burger King drive-through, the man stopped and the two began trading insults face-to-face. (Id. at 98.) While they were arguing, Mr. Coles observed Mr. Davis take up a position lust behind the man and to the man's right, with Mr. Collins remaining somewhere behind Mr.

Davis. (Id. at 98-99.) As the man was looking at Mr. Coles, Mr. Davis hit the man in the head with a small, snub-nose thirty-eight with a black or brown handle. (Id. at 99-100.) Mr. Coles saw the handle of the gun sticking out of Mr. Davis's pants while the two were in the pool room earlier that night. (Id. at 100.)

After being struck by Mr. Davis, the individual ran to the drive-through window, pleading for someone to call the police. (Id. at 100.) Both Messrs. Coles and Davis had turned to start running--Mr. Colas toward the Trust Company Bank building and Mr. Davis closer to Oglethorpe Avenue. (Id.) Soon after they had started running, a police officer came around the Burger King and told them to "hold it." (Id. at 101.) Upon hearing the officer, Mr. Coles turned and stopped. (Id.) The officer ran past Mr. Coles's right side, continuing toward Mr. Davis. (Id.) After the officer had passed him, Mr. Coles heard a single gunshot, which caused him to turn and resume running toward the Trust Company Bank building. (Id. at 101-02.) As he was running, Mr. Coles heard two more gunshots. (Id. at 102.) Mr. Coles stated that he was wearing a yellow t-shirt and blue shorts the night of the shooting, but could not remember what Mr. Davis was wearing. (Id. at 103.)

On cross-examination, Mr. Coles testified that he was five feet eleven inches tall, and weighed between one hundred forty and one hundred forty-five pounds. (Id. at 104-05.) He also admitted to carrying a firearm in the waistline of his shorts earlier that evening, but claimed that he no longer possessed it at the time of the argument. (Id. at 115.) Specifically, he gave the weapon to Mr. Sams because Mr. Coles did not want to carry it into the pool room. (Id. at 116-17.) The weapon, a long-barreled, chrome-plated thirty-eight, was never returned to Mr. Coles. (Id. at 116.)

Also on cross-examination, Mr. Coles stated that he continued running to the Yamacraw neighborhood until he reached the home of his sister, Ms. Valerie Gordon. (Id. at 123.) Mr. Coles had been sitting on his sister's porch for twenty to thirty minutes when a shirtless Mr. Davis approached and asked Mr. Coles for a shirt. (Id. at 127-28.) Mr. Coles gave Mr. Davis the yellow t-shirt that he had been wearing earlier that night-the only spare shirt Mr. Coles had on hand. (Id. at 128-29.)

D. Dorothy Ferrell

At the hearing, Ms. Ferrell testified that, in the early hours of August 19, 1989, she was descending the stairwell of the Thunderbird Motel when she observed some commotion in the Burger King parking lot, which was across Oglethorpe Avenue. (Id. at 131.) Ms. Ferrell saw a police officer tell three African-American males, who were running from the parking lot, to stop. (Id.) One of the men continued to run. (Id.) The second turned and stopped. (Id.) The third man was walking backwards, away from the officer, when he fired a gun at the officer. (Id. at 131, 133.) When the shot was fired, the second man resumed his flight. (Id. at 136.) It took a moment for the officer to fall to the ground. Then, the shooter fired three or four additional bullets at the officer. (Id. at 137-38.)

Ms. Ferrell testified that the gunman was wearing a white t-shirt with some letters or a design on it. (Id. at 138.) She was unable to recall what the other two men were wearing. (Id. at 136-37.) Also, Ms. Ferrell testified that she identified the shooter from a photo array. (Id. at 139-40.)

On cross-examination, Ms. Ferrell testified that she had a good look at the face of the man in the white t-shirt. (Id. at 147.) Ms. Ferrell described the shooter as having a medium build, with lighter colored skin than herself. (Id. at 153-54.) She recalled him having a slim, narrow face with what looked like a slight moustache. (Id. at 148.) However, Ms. Ferrell admitted that she never saw the gunman's face straight on, only from each side. (Id. at 151.) Ms. Ferrell was unable to provide a description of the gun used in the shooting. (Id. at 150.)

Ms. Ferrell also testified that she first saw a picture of the shooter on the front seat of a police cruiser a few days after the shooting, while she was talking to an officer about an unrelated matter. (Id. at 154-55.) She told the officer that she recognized the man in the picture as the individual who shot the officer in the Burger King parking lot. (Id. at 155-56.) Approximately a week after she saw the picture in the police cruiser, Ms. Ferrell indentified the same individual from an array of five photographs. (Id. at 156-57.) She was positive that the man she identified was the shooter, despite the fact that the photograph showed Mr. Davis straight on and she saw only the gunman's profiles on the night of the shooting. (Id. at 157-58.)

E. Jeffery Sapp

At the hearing, Mr. Sapp testified that, at approximately 2:00 or 3:00 p.m. on August 19, 1989, he stopped to talk with Mr. Davis, who was riding a bicycle through the neighborhood. (Id. at 160.) Mr. Davis asked Mr. Sapp if he heard about a shooting. (Id. at 161.) Mr. Sapp acknowledged that he knew about the officer being shot in the Burger King parking lot. (Id.) In response, Mr. Davis stated that he had shot the officer and explained what happened. (Id.)

Mr. Davis explained that Mr. Coles was arguing with an individual, who said something to Mr. Davis. (Id. at 161.) In response, Mr. Davis hit the individual in the face with a pistol, causing him to run to the drive-through window and call for the police. (Id.) Mr. Davis ran at first, but stopped when the officer told him to freeze. (Id.) Mr. Davis then shot the officer when the officer reached for his firearm. (Id.) Thinking that the officer got a good look at his face, Mr. Davis "finished the job." (Id.) Mr. Davis also said that he shot the officer in self-defense. (Id. at 161-62.)

On cross-examination, Mr. Sapp testified that he stopped Mr. Davis to ask him about the shooting at the Cloverdale party. (Id. at 164.) Mr. Davis stated that he did not know who fired the shots at the party, then inquired if Mr. Sapp heard about another shooting. (Id. at 165-66.) Mr. Sapp opined that Mr. Davis confessed to him because they were close friends. (Id. at 167.) Mr. Sapp admitted that he did not believe the confession. (Id. at 169.)

F. Monty Holmes

At the hearing, Mr. Holmes testified that, on August 19, 1989, Mr. Davis visited Mr. Holmes, who had just returned to Savannah, at his home. (Id. at 171-72,) While they were catching up, Mr. Davis mentioned the shooting in the Burger King parking lot. (Id. at 173-74.) Mr. Davis explained that he had been in a quarrel when the police officer appeared. (Id. at 174.) When the officer reached for his gun, Mr. Davis shot him in self-defense. (Id. at 174-75.) Mr. Davis said that, after he shot the officer the first time, he had to finish the job." (Id. at 175.) Mr. Holmes thought Mr. Davis was joking. (Id.)

On cross-examination, Mr. Holmes estimated that the conversation took place at approximately noon and that Mr. Davis rode a bicycle to Mr. Holmes's residence. (Id. at 177.) Mr. Holmes reiterated that he thought Mr. Davis's confession was a joke. (Id. at 178.)

III. THE TRIAL

Mr. Davis was charged with the murder of Officer MacPhail, aggravated assault on Mr. Cooper, obstruction of a law officer, and possession of a gun in commission of a felony. (Trial Transcript at 8.) Mr. Davis pled not guilty and proceeded to trial. The trial occurred in Chatham County Superior Court and lasted from August 19 to 28, 1991. The state presented thirty-four [6] witnesses in its case-in-chief. (Id. at 2-5.) Mr. Davis called five witnesses and testified on his own behalf. (Id. at 5.) After deliberating for approximately two hours, the jury found Mr. Davis guilty on all counts. (Id. at 1508-10.) The Court now relates the relevant witness testimony.

---

6 The Court does not detail every witnesses' testimony, restricting its account to those witnesses whose testimony is cogent to determining this petition.

A. Larry Young

At trial, Mr. Young testified that he was sharing a beer with Ms. Murray in the Burger King parking lot in the early hours of August 19, 1989. (Id. at 797-98.) When the couple finished, Mr. Young walked to the nearby Time-Saver to purchase more beer. (Id. at 798.) As he was returning, a man asked him for one of the newly purchased beers. (Id. at 799.) When Mr. Young refused, the man began cursing at Mr. Young, following him as he walked back toward the Burger King. (Id.) Mr. Young was continuing toward the Burger King parking lot when he noticed a second man following him, this one approaching from the Trust Company Bank property. (Id.) As Mr. Young was entering the Burger King parking lot, the man he was arguing with said something that caused the two gentlemen sitting next to Ms. Murray to flee. (Id.) Mr. Young, however, thought little of it and continued to walk toward the Burger King parking lot. (Id.) As Mr. Young entered the parking lot, he realized that he was now surrounded by three individuals. (Id. at 799-800.) The man he was arguing with was in front of him, and the other two individuals were behind him, one on his right and one on his left. (Id. at 800.)

Of the three men, Mr. Young focused his attention mostly on the man he had been arguing with, who now stood directly in front of him. (Id.) The man in front of him was wearing a yellow shirt and was somewhat slender, tall, and had light brown-skin. (Id. at 800-01.) He could not describe the other two men, but remembered that the individual on his right wore a white t-shirt. (Id. at 801-02.)

Mr. Young did try to keep an eye on all three men. However, soon the man in the yellow shirt made a move toward him, causing Mr. Young to shift his attention solely to this individual. (Id. at 802.) As Mr. Young looked forward, he received a hard blow to his head. (Id.) Dazed, he stumbled toward the drive-through window, where a van was waiting, and asked for help. (Id. at 803-04.) When Mr. Young was at the drive-through window, he heard a single gunshot, causing him to hide behind the van. (Id. at 804.) He then ran to the building's front door. (Id.) Once inside, Mr. Young was rejoined by Ms. Murray, who helped tend to Mr. Young's wound. (Id. at 804-05.)

Mr. Young testified that the person who struck him was definitely not the man in the yellow shirt that he had been arguing with. (Id. at 811.) A few days after the assault, Mr. Young picked an individual out of a photo array that he believed was the man he was arguing with. (Id. at 805.) However, he later saw the man he was arguing with while at the police station. (Id. at 805-06.) Realizing his mistake, Mr. Young informed the police that his earlier identification was incorrect and that the man at the station was the man in the yellow shirt. (Id. at 806.) At trial, Mr. Young testified that he did not recognize Mr. Davis as the man he had been arguing with. (Id. at 813-14.)

On cross-examination, Mr. Young testified that the man he was arguing with might have threatened to shoot him, which caused the gentlemen with Ms. Murray to flee. (Id. at 825.) Mr. Young could not recall the man in the white t-shirt saying anything that night. (Id. at 824-25.) Also, Mr. Young described the man in the white t-shirt as slim, and wearing dark colored shorts and a baseball cap. (Id. at 828.)

Regarding Mr. Young's initial misidentification in the photo array, Mr. Young testified that the photo he first picked out as the man he was arguing with depicted Mr. Davis. (Id. at 831-32.) However, Mr.

Young reiterated that his original identification was incorrect and he had not been arguing with Mr. Davis. (Id. at 832-33.) While Mr. Young was not sure who exactly hit him, he was sure that it was the individual behind him on his right, and not the man he had been arguing with. (Id.)

B. Harriet Murray

Ms. Murray testified at the trial that she was drinking beer with Mr. Young in the Burger King parking lot in the early hours of August 19, 1989. (Id. at 840-41.) After the two finished their last beer, Mr. Young walked to the nearby convenience Store to purchase more. (Id. at 842.) When Mr. Young left, Ms. Murray was joined by two gentlemen who had just disembarked from a bus. (Id. at 842-43.) As Mr. Young returned, Ms. Murray noticed an individual following and harassing Mr. Young. (Id. at 843.) As the pair drew nearer, Ms. Murray noticed two additional individuals following Mr. Young, approaching from the Trust Company Bank property. (Id. at 843-44.) The three men steadily closed in on Mr. Young as he neared the parking lot. (Id. at 844.)

As the group neared the parking lot, an individual in a yellow shirt threatened to shoot Mr. Young. (Id. at 845.) Ms. Murray then saw one of the individuals following Mr. Young start digging in the front of his pants. (Id.) These events caused the two gentlemen with Ms. Murray to flee. (Id.) Worried, she went to the Burger King entrance, which was locked, to ask if someone could call the police. (Id. at 845-46.)

Unable to find help, Ms. Murray turned her attention back to Mr. Young, who was now being confronted by the individual in the yellow shirt. (Id. at 846.) As Mr. Young turned to face the individual in the yellow shirt, an individual in a white shirt, located on Mr. Young's right side, hit Mr. Young on the right side of his face with a brown-handled gun with a black barrel. (Id. at 846-47.) After he received the blow, Mr. Young ran in between a van waiting at the drive-through and the drive-through window, pleading for someone to call the police. (Id. at 848.)

While Mr. Young was at the drive-through window, a police officer entered the parking lot from behind the Burger King restaurant. (Id. at 848.) As the officer was approaching, the individuals in the yellow and white shirts started running. (Id. at 848-49.) The third individual had started running as soon as Mr. Young was hit. (Id.) After the police officer told the two to "hold it," the individual in the yellow shirt slowed. (Id. at 849.) The officer ran past the individual in the yellow shirt and continued toward the individual in the white shirt. (Id.) After the officer ran past him, the individual in the yellow shirt resumed running toward the back of the Trust Company Bank property. (Id.) As the officer chased the individual in the white shirt, nightstick in hand, the individual stopped and looked over his shoulder. (Id. at 850.) When the officer came within five or six feet, the individual in the white shirt turned around, gun in hand, and pulled the trigger. (Id.) The gun did not discharge, but only clicked, causing the officer to reach for his own firearm. (Id.) As the officer was reaching, the individual in the white shirt shot him. (Id.) Reeling from the shot, the officer fell to the ground, at which point the individual in the white shirt took a few steps forward and shot him again. (Id.) After firing his last shot, the individual in the white shirt fled toward the Trust Company Bank building. (Id. at 851.) Ms. Murray then found Mr. Young and helped tend to his wound. (Id.)

Ms. Murray described the individual in the yellow shirt, who had been arguing with Mr. Young, as stocky and slightly taller than Mr. Young with light colored skin. (Id. at 846.) The first time Ms. Murray was shown a photo spread, she did not recognize any of the individuals pictured. (Id. at 861-62.) Later, Ms. Murray was shown a second photo spread, from which she identified Mr. Davis as the man who both hit Mr. Young and shot the officer. (Id. at 862-65.) Ms. Murray testified that she recognized Mr. Davis's photograph because of his narrow face. (Id. at 865.)

On cross-examination, Ms. Murray admitted that she was a little near-sighted and had trouble seeing long distances without her glasses, which she was not sure if she was wearing that night. (Id. at 870.) Also, Ms. Murray was questioned regarding discrepancies between her trial testimony, police statement, and Recorder's Court testimony regarding which individual threatened to shoot Mr. Young and was digging in his shorts. (Id. at 871-79.) Further, Ms. Murray described the man in the yellow shirt as having a chubby face, and taller, stockier, and lighter in skin color than Mr. Young. (Id. at 883.) She recalled that the man in the white shirt was tall and slender with dark colored skin, a narrow face, and a fade-away hair cut. (Id. at 883-84.)

Comparing the individuals in the yellow and white shirts, Ms. Murray testified that the individual in the yellow shirt was shorter, heavier, and lighter in skin color than the individual in the white shirt. (Id. at 885.) Also, Ms. Murray admitted that when she first picked out Mr. Davis's picture from the photo spread, she told the police only that he was one of the three men at the shooting, not that he was the gunman. (Id. at 888-89.)

C. Sylvester 'Red" Coles

Mr. Coles testified at the trial that, in the early hours of August 19, 1989, he was outside of Charlie Brown's pool room when he asked a man passing by for a beer. (Id. at 900.) Mr. Coles began arguing with the individual when he was refused, following him along Oglethorpe Avenue toward the Burger King parking lot. (Id. at 902-04.) Messrs. Davis and Collins were trailing the two, coming around the back of the Trust Company Bank building. (Id.) The three young men converged on the individual with the beer in the Burger King parking lot, Mr. Coles in front of him, Mr. Davis behind the individual to his right, and Mr. Collins in the background. (Id. at 908-09.) As the individual was looking at Mr. Coles, Mr. Davis hit the man on the right side of the head with a black, short-barreled, thirty-eight with a brown handle. (Id. at 908, 912-13.) He recalled seeing Mr. Davis with a gun in the waistline of his pants earlier when they were at the pool room. (Id. at 913.)

After the assault the group scattered: the man who was struck ran to the drive-through window, Mr. Coles ran toward the back of the Trust Company Bank building, and Mr. Davis ran along Oglethorpe Avenue toward the front of the Trust Company Bank property. (Id. at 909.) As they started to run, a police officer appeared from behind the Burger King and ordered everyone to "hold it." (Id. at 910.) Mr. Coles stopped and turned, and the officer ran past him toward Oglethorpe Avenue. (Id. at 910.) As the officer past him, Mr. Coles heard a single gunshot. (Id. at 910-11.) After hearing the first gunshot, he turned and resumed running, at which point he heard two more gunshots. (Id. at 911.) Mr. Coles continued running until he reached his sister's house in the Yamacraw neighborhood. (Id. at 912.)

When Mr. Coles arrived at his sister's house, he changed Out of his yellow t-shirt. (Id. at 914.) Approximately twenty to thirty minutes after Mr. Coles arrived, Mr. Davis appeared at the house. Mr. Davis was not wearing a shirt when he arrived and asked for one to wear. (Id.) Mr. Coles gave Mr. Davis the only other shirt he had at the house--the yellow t-shirt he had been wearing earlier. (Id.) As Mr. Coles was leaving, Mr. Davis put on the yellow t-shirt. (Id. at 915.)

On cross-examination, Mr. Coles admitted that he was carrying a long barreled, thirty-eight caliber revolver on the night of the shooting. (Id. at 927.) During his re-direct examination, Mr. Coles described the firearm as chrome plated, making it silver in color. (Id. at 952.) During cross-examination, Mr. Coles also testified that he had been carrying the revolver in the waist of his pants, but would often leave it in some bushes on the side of the building when he went inside the pool room. (Id. at 927-28.) On the night of the shooting, Mr. Coles gave the gun to Mr. Sams for safekeeping, approximately thirty minutes after Mr. Sams arrived at the pool room. (Id. at 930-31.) Mr. Coles never recovered the weapon. (Id. at 931.)

Also on cross-examination, Mr. Coles testified that he arrived at the pool room at approximately 8:00 p.m. and was not in Cloverdale the evening of the shooting. (Id. at 922-24, 926.) He further testified that he neither threatened to shoot anyone nor heard Mr. Davis speak to the man with the beer. (Id. at 936-37.) Mr. Coles admitted that he did not see Mr. Davis shoot the officer and did not remember what Mr. Davis was wearing on the night of the shooting. (Id. at 930, 942.) Mr. Coles stated that he was five feet eleven inches tall and weighed between one hundred forty-five and one hundred fifty pounds. (Id. at 920.) He explained that he often kept clothes at his sister's house because he liked to change after playing basketball in that neighborhood. (Id. at 924-25.) Mr. Coles admitted that, after leaving his sister's house, he walked back by the Burger King parking lot, then returned to her house. (Id. at 947-48.)

The afternoon after the shooting, Mr. Coles's brother and uncle took him to an attorney, for whom Mr. Coles had occasionally worked. (Id. at 948-49.) After listening to Mr. Coles, the attorney promptly took Mr. Coles to the police station to provide a voluntary statement. (Id. at 949.)

D. Antoine Williams

Mr. Williams testified at the trial that, in the early hours of August 19, 1989, he was arriving for his 1:00 a.m. shift at the Burger King. (Id. at 955-56.) As Mr. Williams was pulling into the parking lot, he noticed three men following one individual, who was telling them he did not want to fight. (Id. at 957-58.) Mr. Williams parked his car facing the drive-through window, where a van was waiting for its order. (Id. at 961.) While the group was between Mr. Williams and the drive-through window, one of the three men ran in front of the lone individual and struck him with a gun. (Id. at 960-61.)

Immediately after the assault, a police officer came from behind the Burger King building, running toward the men and telling them to stop. (Id. at 961-62.) The two men not responsible for the assault took off running, but the third was trying to hide the weapon in his waistline. (Id. at 962.) As the officer came closer and the individual could not hide the gun, the individual shot the officer. (Id.) According to Mr. Williams, the shooting occurred a couple of feet behind him. (Id.) After the shooting, Mr. Williams went inside the Burger King and told his manager to call the police. (Id. at 962-63.)

On August 29, 1989, Mr. Williams was shown a photo spread and asked if he could recognize Officer MacPhail's murderer. (Id. at 963.) Mr. Williams identified Mr. Davis as the man who both hit the individual with the gun and shot the officer. (Id. at 963-64.) Mr. Williams also testified that Mr. Davis was wearing either a white or yellow shirt, contrary to an earlier statement given to the police. (Id. at 958.) Mr. Williams explained that he could not distinguish these colors due to the dark tint on his car's windows. (Id. at 959-60.) However, when Mr. Williams was shown his prior statement, in which he stated that the gunman was wearing either a white or blue shirt, he reaffirmed his prior statement, explaining that he could remember those details better immediately following the shooting. (Id.)

On cross-examination, Mr. Williams stated that the individual who was assaulted was struck on the left side of his head and that Officer MacPhail's murderer was not wearing a hat. (Id. at 967-68.) With respect to the photo spread, Mr. Williams admitted to seeing a wanted poster of Mr. Davis at work prior to being shown the photos and that he was only sixty percent sure that his identification was accurate. (Id. at 970-71.)

E. Steven Sanders

Mr. Sanders testified at the trial that, in the early hours of August 19, 1989, he was a passenger in a van at the Burger King drive-through window. (Id. at 976-77.) While the occupants of the van were placing their orders, Mr. Sanders observed two African-American men walking toward the Burger King building, trailed by two other African-American men. (Id. at 977-78.) As they walked in front of the van, one of the trailing men caught up, pushed one of the leading individuals, and then struck him on the right side of his head with an object. (Id. at 978, 981.) After he was hit, the victim started banging on the hood of the van, asking for help and for someone to call the police. (Id.)

Turning his attention to the assailant, Mr. Sanders observed him start to run through the Burger King parking lot. (Id. at 979.) He then witnessed the attacker shoot a police officer, which was the first time Mr. Sanders noticed the officer. (Id.,) To Mr. Sanders, it appeared that the police officer was already standing in the parking lot, the gunman shooting him as the gunman ran past the officer. (Id. at 979-80.) The officer fell to the ground, at which point the gunman fired several more bullets. (Id.) When he was finished, the shooter fled toward the back of the Trust Company Bank building. (Id. at 980.) Mr. Sanders testified that the gunman was wearing a white t-shirt, dark shorts, and a white hat, and identified Mr. Davis as the individual responsible for both the assault and the murder. (Id. at 983.)

On cross-examination, Mr. Sanders admitted that he initially told the police he would not be able to identify the gunman, except by what he was wearing. (Id. at 984.) He further conceded that he saw a picture of Mr. Davis in the paper the day before he testified. (Id. at 983-84.) Mr. Sanders could identify neither the individual that was struck in the head nor the object used to strike him. (Id. at 986.) Also, Mr. Sanders testified that, after the shooting, he observed a second man, dressed in a black shirt and black pants, run in the same direction as the shooter. (Id. at 988.) This second individual appeared to be trailing the shooter, but not running with him. (Id.)

F. Robert Grizzard

Mr. Grizzard, a staff sergeant in the United States Air Force, testified at the trial that he was at the Burger King drive-through window in the early hours of August 19, 1989 in a van, which he was driving. (Id. at 996-97.) While there, Mr. Grizzard noticed one individual chasing a second across the parking lot toward the Burger King. (Id. at 998.) When the man in front tripped and fell, the pursuer veered off and headed away from the building. (Id. at 998.)

While he was still at the window, Mr. Grizzard again saw the man who had been chasing the individual. (Id.) This time, Mr. Grizzard saw him strike another man in the head. (Id.) The individual who had been struck staggered toward the van's driver's side window, asking for someone to call the police. (Id.) Next, Mr. Grizzard observed a police officer running toward the assailant. (Id.) As the officer approached, the individual aimed a weapon at the officer and fired one shot. Struck by the bullet, the officer fell to the ground, at which point the gunman fired at least one more shot at the officer. (Id.) When he finished shooting, the gunman fled. (Id. at 998-99.) Mr. Grizzard described the weapon as dark in color with a short barrel. (Id. at 1009.)

Mr. Grizzard testified that the gunman was wearing a dark baseball hat and a light colored shirt, the exact color of which he could not recall. (Id. at 999.) However, Mr. Grizzard was sure that the same individual who struck the man on the head shot the officer. (Id.) Mr. Grizzard was unable to identify Mr. Davis as the shooter. (Id. at 1002.)

On cross-examination, Mr. Grizzard reiterated that he did not see what the assailant used to strike the individual. (Id. at 1007-08.) Also, Mr. Grizzard again stated that he would not be able to identify the gunman. (Id.)

G. Dorothy Ferrell

Ms. Ferrell testified at the trial that, on the night of August 18, 1989, she was a guest at the Thunderbird Motel, located across Oglethorpe Avenue from the Burger King. (Id. at 1011-12.) Around 1:00 a.m. on August 19, 1989, she was descending a stairwell at the motel when she heard screaming from the Burger King parking lot. (Id. at 1012-13.) She ran to the sidewalk to get a better view. (Id. at 1013.)

From the sidewalk, she saw three men in the Burger King parking lot. (Id.) As one of the men started running toward the Trust Company Bank property, a police officer entered the parking lot and told the men to stop. (Id. at 1013-14.) As the officer approached, one of the men, who was wearing a light yellow t-shirt, started moving backwards. (Id. at 1014-15.) Then the third man, who was wearing a white t-shirt and dark shorts, shot the officer. (Id. at 1015.) After the officer fell to the ground, the gunman stepped forward, stood over the officer, and fired more bullets at him. (Id. at 1016.) Finished, the gunman ran toward the Trust Company Bank. (Id. at 1016.) At trial, Ms. Ferrell identified Mr. Davis as the individual who shot the officer. (Id. at 1021.)

Ms. Ferrell also testified that, two days after the shooting, she recognized a photograph of Mr. Davis and identified him as the gunman. (Id. at 1021-23.) According to Ms. Ferrell, she was speaking with a police officer about matters unrelated to the MacPhail shooting when she noticed a photograph of Mr. Davis on the front passenger seat of the officer's cruiser. (Id. at 1022.) She informed the officer that she recognized the man in the photograph as Officer MacPhail's murderer. (Id. at 1023.) Ms. Ferrell had not seen any pictures of Mr. Davis prior to that identification. (Id.) A few days later, Ms. Ferrell was shown a photo spread and asked if she recognized the gunman. (Id. at 1024.) Ms. Ferrell again identified Mr. Davis. (Id. at 1024-25.) Ms. Ferrell testified that she was pretty confident in the accuracy of her identification. (Id. at 1027.)

On cross-examination, Ms. Ferrell testified that the individual in the yellow t-shirt was looking straight at the gunman when he fired the first shot. (Id. at 1041.) Ms. Ferrell stated that the gunman passed in front of the Trust Company Bank building while fleeing. (Id. at 1041-42.) She was then impeached with her police statement, in which she claimed that the gunman ran behind the Trust Company yank building. (Id. at 1045-46.) Ms. Ferrell was also questioned on variations between her police statement and trial testimony regarding when the individuals in the yellow and white t-shirts started running. (Id. at 1044-46.) Finally, Ms. Ferrell admitted that the portion of her police statement recounting how Officer MacPhail had run the shooter off the Burger King property earlier in the day was incorrect. (Id. at 1046-48.) She explained that she had not seen Officer MacPhail run the shooter off the property, only some individuals dressed like the shooter. (Id. at 1048.) Ms. Ferrell opined that the inconsistency was due to a misunderstanding by the officer taking her statement. (Id. at 1048-50.)

Also on cross-examination, Ms. Ferrell was challenged regarding her prior descriptions of the shooter. (Id. at 1050-52.) In her police statement, Ms. Ferrell recalled that the shooter was six feet tall with a narrow face and slender build, while she described the shooter as slightly taller than her height--five feet--and with a medium build when she testified in Recorder's Court. (Id. at 1050-51.) In Recorder's Court, Ms. Ferrell testified that the shooter had lighter colored skin than her. (Id.) However, Ms. Ferrell admitted that she and Mr. Davis had about the same skin color, while Mr. Coles's skin color was much lighter that hers. (Id.) Ms. Ferrell did state that she would not describe Mr. Coles's skin color as light, but rather as "red." (Id.) Also, Ms. Ferrell admitted that, despite testifying in Recorder's Court that the shooter had a narrow face, she never saw the shooter face-on, seeing only his left and right profiles. (Id. at 1052-53.) Finally, Ms. Ferrell testified that she saw Mr. Davis on television prior to her identification of his photograph. [7] (Id. at 1053-54.)

---

[7] Ms. Ferrell also admitted during cross-examination that she had a number of prior criminal convictions for shoplifting and trespass. (Id. at 1060-61.)

On redirect-examination, Ms. Ferrell explained a few of the inconsistencies between her various statements. Ms. Ferrell clarified that, in Recorder's Court, she stated the shooter was a little taller than Mr. Davis's attorney, not a little taller than herself. (Id. at 1064-65.) Also, Ms. Ferrell explained that she did not see only left and right profiles of the gunman's face. While she never observed his face straight on, Ms. Ferrell saw enough of the shooter's face at various angles to recognize that he had a narrow face. (Id. at 1066-67.)

H. Darrell Collins

Mr. Collins testified at the trial that he attended a party in the Cloverdale neighborhood with Messrs. Davis and Ellison on the night of August 18, 1989. (Id. at 1115.) When the three arrived at the party, they went to the backyard, where Mr. Collins swam in the pool while Messrs. Ellison and Davis talked with some of the guests. (Id. at 1116-17.) They stayed for approximately an hour and a half. (Id. at 1118.) As the group was walking through the front yard to Mr. Ellison's car, with Mr. Davis in front, a car drove by the house with individuals hanging out of the windows, cursing and throwing items. (Id. at 1118-19.) As the car rounded the corner at the end of the block, Mr. Collins heard gunshots. (Id. at 1120.)

Contrary to his earlier statements, Mr. Collins testified at trial that he did not see who shot at the car. (Id.) The State challenged Mr. Collins with the contents of his August 19, 1989 police statement, which both placed Mr. Davis at the end of the block where the car turned and identified him as the shooter. (Id. at 1120-21.) At trial, Mr. Collins alleged that the police pressured him into identifying Mr. Davis as the Cloverdale shooter by threatening to charge him as an accessory to murder and give him a ten to twelve year prison sentence. (Id. at 1120-21, 1135-37.) Explaining his photo identification of Mr. Davis as the Cloverdale shooter, Mr. Collins testified that he identified Mr. Davis because the police asked if Mr. Collins knew any of the individuals in the photographs. (Id. at 1130.)

After the Cloverdale shooting, Mr. Ellison drove Mr. Collins to Mr. Ellison's home. (Id. at 1121.) Later, Mr. Ellison, accompanied by Messrs. Collins and Sams, were driving to purchase gasoline when they came upon Mr. Davis, who asked for a ride. (Id. at 1122.) Now accompanied by Mr. Davis, Mr. Ellison drove to the gas station, which was adjacent to Charlie Brown's pool room. (Id.) After Mr. Ellison purchased gasoline, he and Mr. Collins went inside the pool room. (Id. at 1123.) Mr. Collins could not recall if Mr. Davis went inside the pool room. (Id.)

Later, Mr. Collins observed Mr. Coles get into an argument with a gentleman in front of the pool room. (Id.) The two continued to argue as they walked in front of the Trust Company Bank building, toward the Burger King parking lot. (Id. at 1224, 1131.) Messrs. Collins and Davis followed the pair, also walking in front of the Trust

Company Bank building. (Id. at 1131.) By the time they reached the parking lot, Mr. Collins was behind the three other individuals. (Id. at 1132.) As they approached the Burger King restaurant, Mr. Davis slapped the individual that Mr. Coles was arguing with on the right side of the face. (Id. at 1124-25.) Mr. Collins did not see anything in Mr. Davis's hand when he dealt the blow. (Id.)

After Mr. Davis slapped the individual, Mr. Collins noticed a police officer standing behind the Burger King building. (Id. at 1125.) As Mr. Collins was turning to exit the parking lot, he saw the officer making motions toward where Mr. Davis assaulted the individual. (Id.) Mr. Collins heard some gunshots as he was walking away, which caused him to start running. (Id. at 1125-26.) He ran back to the pool room, got in Mr. Ellison's car with Messrs. Ellison and Sams, and left the area. (Id. at 1126.) Mr. Collins stated that, on the night of the shootings, Mr. Davis was wearing blue or black shorts and a white t-shirt with writing on it. (Id. at 1128.)

Mr. Collins testified that he did not see Mr. Davis with a firearm on the night of the shooting. (Id. at 1126-27.) Again, the State challenged Mr. Collins with his initial police statement where he described the gun Mr. Davis used at the Cloverdale shooting as short-barreled and black with a brown handle. (Id. at 1127.) Mr. Collins was also challenged with his August 25, 1989 police statement, in which he informed the police that he saw Mr. Davis with the weapon Mr. Davis used in Cloverdale both prior to and after that shooting. (Id. at 1134-35.) Yet, Mr. Collins contended that the police told him what to put in his statement and that his present testimony reflected the truth. (Id.) However, Mr. Collins did testify that, prior to the Cloverdale shooting, he saw Mr. Davis with a gun fitting the description that Mr. Collins provided in his police statement. (Id. at 1128.)

Mr. Collins also claimed to have seen Mr. Coles with a chrome, long-barreled thirty-eight on the night of the shootings. (Id. at 1128-29.) He testified that, when they were at the pool room, Mr. Coles placed his weapon on the seat of Mr. Ellison's car. (Id. at 1129.) Prior to the MacPhail shooting, Mr. Collins took the firearm and placed it on the ground at the end of the pool room building because he did not want it in the vehicle. (Id.)

On cross-examination, Mr. Collins testified that he did not see Mr. Davis argue with anyone at the Cloverdale party, shoot at the vehicle, or even possess a firearm that evening. (Id. at 1139-43.) However, Mr. Collins admitted that he would not have been able to see a gun even if Mr. Davis was carrying one. (Id. at 1140.) Also, Mr. Collins testified that Mr. Coles knew that Mr. Collins placed his weapon next to the building. (Id. at 1148-49.)

Mr. Collins then reiterated that he and Mr. Davis passed in front of the Trust Company Bank building as they walked toward the Burger King parking lot. (Id. at 1151-52.) Mr. Collins could not recall Mr. Coles threatening to shoot anyone. (Id. at 1153.) He also claimed that he did not see anything that happened after Mr. Davis slapped the individual because he had turned to walk back to the pool room. (Id. at 1155-56.) Mr. Collins did not recall Mr. Davis wearing a hat on the evening of the shootings. (Id. at 1158.)

Mr. Collins also reiterated that he was pressured to name Mr. Davis as the Cloverdale shooter. (Id. at 1142-43.) He stated that he was taken to the police station, told that he was a suspect, provided no opportunity to call an attorney, threatened with jail time, and questioned prior to his parents arrival. (Id. at 1143-45.) Mr. Collins was sixteen at the time and claimed that he told the police what they wanted to hear because he was scared and did not want to go to prison. (Id. at 1144-45.)

I. Valerie Coles Gordon

Ms. Gordon testified at the trial that, in the early hours of August 19, 1989, she was sitting on the porch of her Yamacraw neighborhood home when she heard some gunshots. (Id. at 1160-61.) Approximately fifteen to twenty minutes later, Ms. Gordon's brother, Mr. Coles, ran onto the porch. (Id. at 1161.) Mr. Coles immediately slumped over, gasping for breath, causing Ms. Gordon to think that he was hurt. (Id. at 1161-62.) Satisfied that he was uninjured, Ms. Gordon went into the house and laid out three shirts for Mr. Coles to change into. (Id. at 1162.) Ms. Gordon recalls Mr. Coles changing out of the yellow shirt he had been wearing into a blue, red, and white collared shirt. (Id. at 1162-63.) After changing shirts, Mr. Coles left the yellow shirt on the banister. (Id. at 1163-64.)

A few minutes later, Mr. Davis came up to the porch, wearing dark shorts and no shirt. (Id. at 1164-65.) Mr. Coles stepped outside to speak with Mr. Davis, eventually handing him the yellow shirt that Mr. Coles had previously been wearing. (Id.) After handing the yellow shirt to Mr. Davis, Mr. Coles left. (Id. at 1165.) According to Ms. Gordon, Mr. Davis put the shirt on, but quickly took it off and left it by her front door. (Id.) She washed the shirt the next day, later giving it to the police. (Id. at 1165-66.)

On cross-examination, Ms. Gordon admitted that, after arriving on the porch, Mr. Coles stated that he thought someone was trying to kill him. (Id. at 1168.) Ms. Gordon also stated that, prior to Mr. Davis arriving, Mr. Blige came by the house. (Id. at 1171.) Mr. Blige appeared to argue with Mr. Coles, who told him to leave. (Id. at 1171-72.) Ms. Gordon never saw Mr. Davis with a firearm. (Id. at 1174.)

J. Michael Cooper

Mr. Cooper testified that he attended a party in the Cloverdale neighborhood on the evening of August 18, 1989. (Id. at 1179.) Mr. Wilds drove Mr. Cooper to the party, along with Messrs. Blige, Brown, and Gordon. (Id. at 1179-80.) The group arrived at approximately 10:30 p.m. and went to the backyard to hang out by the pool. (Id. at 1181.) While at the party, Mr. Wilds argued with some gentlemen, who were across the street from the party, because the two groups were from rival neighborhoods. (Id. at 1182.) Mr. Cooper remembers seeing Mr. Davis in the area of the group arguing with Mr. Wilds. (Id. at 1182-83.)

Mr. Cooper returned to the pool area, but his group decided to leave and change their clothes because they had been splashed with water. (Id. at 1183.) They told some of the girls that they would be back and walked to Mr. Wilds car. (Id. at 1185.) As they were leaving, Mr. Cooper was in the front passenger seat, hanging out of the window speaking loudly to some girls. (Id. at 1185-86.) As they took a right turn, Mr. Cooper, now fully inside the vehicle, heard several gunshots. (Id. at 1186-87.) One struck Mr. Cooper in the right side of his jaw. (Id. at 1187.) Panicked, Mr. Wilds drove Mr. Cooper to the hospital. (Id.)

On cross-examination, Mr. Cooper admitted that he was intoxicated when he arrived at the party. (Id. at 1190.) He could remember neither how many men Mr. Wilds was arguing with nor whether Mr. Davis was actually a part of that group. (Id. at 1191.) However, Mr. Cooper was sure that Mr. Davis was in the vicinity of the argument. (Id. at 1191-92.) Mr. Cooper testified that he had never met Mr. Davis, and could not think of a reason why Mr. Davis would shoot at him. (Id. at 1192.)

K. Benjamin Gordon

Mr. Gordon testified at the trial that he attended a party in the Cloverdale neighborhood on the evening of August 18, 1989. (Id. at 1194.) Mr. Wilds drove Mr. Gordon to the party, along with Messrs. Blige, Brown and Cooper. (Id. at 1195.) After parking down the street from the party, the group walked through the front yard to the pool in the backyard. (Id. at 1196.) There was not a group of individuals standing near the front of the house when they arrived and nobody spoke to them as they made their way to the backyard. (Id. at 1196.) However, the State confronted Mr. Gordon with his August 19, 1989 police statement, in which he recounted a group of young men asking Mr. Gordon's group if they were from the Yamacraw neighborhood. (Id. at 1196-97.) At trial, Mr. Gordon stated that he could not remember if that happened. (Id. at 1197.)

Once at the party, the group socialized by the pool for some time, speaking with girls before leaving the party because they were bored. (Id. at 1197.) As they were leaving, Mr. Gordon was sitting in the middle of the back seat next to Mr. Bilge, who was hanging out of the window. (Id. at 1197-98.) As they were rounding the corner at the end of the block, someone fired a weapon at the vehicle, one bullet striking Mr. Cooper. (Id. at 1198-99.)

At trial, Mr. Gordon denied seeing the individual who shot at the vehicle. (Id. at 1199-1200.) He was again confronted with his August 19, 1989 police statement, in which he described the shooter as wearing a white, batman t-shirt and dark color jeans. (Id. at 1199-1201.) He had also stated that, earlier at the party, he saw the shooter by the pool. (Id. at 1201) At trial, Mr. Gordon testified that he only told the police that he heard someone in a white, batman t-shirt with dark jeans had been the shooter, not that he actually saw someone wearing those clothes shoot at the car. (Id. at 1200.) Mr. Gordon explained that he did not remember telling the police the information in his statement, which he signed without reviewing. (Id. at 1201-02.)

On cross-examination, Mr. Gordon testified that he was a frightened sixteen-year old when he provided the August 19, 1989 police statement. (Id. at 1202-03.) He explained that he was questioned by the police without having either his parents or a lawyer present. (Id. at 1202.) Mr. Gordon reiterated that he did not see who shot at the vehicle. (Id. at 1203.)

L. Craig Young

Mr. Craig Young testified at the trial that he attended a party in the Cloverdale neighborhood on the evening of August 18, 1989, where he saw Mr. Davis. (Id. at 1207-08.) However, he neither saw Mr. Davis argue nor threaten anyone at the party. (Id. at 1209.) Likewise, Mr. Davis never confessed these actions to him. (Id. at 1209.) While Mr. Craig Young did testify that he heard the gunshots, he did not see the shooter. (Id.)

The State confronted Mr. Craig Young with his previous police statement. (Id. at 1211.) In the statement, he informed the police that Mr. Davis told him at the party that Mr. Davis had gotten into an argument with an individual named "Mike-Mike," but "Mike-Mike" did not give Mr. Davis a reason to start anything. (Id. at 1212-13.) According to the police statement, Mr. Davis joked that he should have "burned one of y'all." (Id. at 1213.) Also, Mr. Craig Young told the police that he observed Mr. Davis cursing at a group of girls who would not talk to Mr. Davis. (Id. at 1213.)

With respect to the police statement, Mr. Craig Young contended that he only repeated what the police told him to say. (Id. at 1212.) He stated that they were yelling at him and coaching him on what to put in his statement. (Id.) Also, Mr. Craig Young stated that he and Mr. Davis had been fighting prior to the questioning and thought the statement was a good way to get back at Mr. Davis. (Id. at 1211.) But now that Mr. Craig Young was on the stand, he was not going to lie about what he saw that night. (Id.)

M. Eric Ellison

Mr. Ellison testified at the trial that he attended a party in the Cloverdale neighborhood on the evening of August 18, 1989. (Id. at 1215.) Mr. Ellison drove Messrs. Collins and Davis to the party. (Id.) Mr. Davis was wearing a white t-shirt with writing on it and dark colored shorts. (Id. at 1216-17.) After they arrived at the party, the three men went straight to the pool in the backyard. (Id. at 1217.) While Mr. Collins swam, Messrs. Ellison and Davis socialized by the pool. (Id.) Mr. Davis left the pool area after eating some food. (Id. at 1217-18.) Messrs. Ellison and Collins decided to leave the party after staying for approximately an hour to an hour and a half. (Id. at 1218.)

As they were walking through the front yard, Mr. Ellison observed an argument between two groups on opposite sides of the street. (Id.) He noticed Mr. Davis standing in the walkway leading to the home where the party was being held. (Id.) As Mr. Ellison was standing in the driveway, he heard shots down the street. (Id. at 1218-19.) Mr. Ellison did not know from where, or at what, the shots were fired. (Id. at 1219.) However, he recalled a vehicle heading in the direction of the gunshots with an individual hanging out of its window. (Id. at 1219-20.)

As Mr. Ellison was walking back to his car, which was parked in the area the shots were fired from, Mr. Davis asked him for a ride back to the Yamacraw neighborhood. (Id. at 1220-21.) At trial, Mr. Ellison could not remember if Mr. Davis approached him from the direction of the gunshots. (Id. at 1221.) However, Mr. Ellison confirmed the truth of his police statement, which stated that Mr. Davis approached from the direction the shots were fired. (Id. at 1221-22.) After waiting for things to settle down, Mr. Ellison drove Messrs. Collins and Davis first to Mr. Ellison's house, where they picked up Mr. Sams, and then to Charlie Brown's pool room. (Id. 1221-23.)

After parking the car, the four men went inside the pool room. (Id. at 1223.) After playing several games of pool, Mr. Ellison was leaving the pool room when he heard gunshots. (Id. at 1223.) Mr. Ellison started to walk back to his car, where Mr. Sams was already in the backseat. (Id.) As Mr. Ellison neared his car, Mr. Collins arrived. (Id. at 1123-24.) Mr. Ellison told Mr. Collins to get in the car, and the three went to Mr. Ellison's home. (Id.) Mr. Ellison did not know what became of Mr. Davis after they arrived at the pool room. (Id. at 1224.)

On cross-examination, Mr. Ellison testified that he did not know who fired the shots at the Cloverdale party. (Id. at 1225.) Also, he did not see Mr. Davis carrying a firearm that night. (Id.)

N. Kevin McQueen

Mr. McQueen testified at trial that Mr. Davis confessed to shooting Officer MacPhail. (Id. at 123132.) The alleged confession occurred while the two were waiting to play basketball in the Chatham County Jail. (Id. at 1230.) According to Mr. McQueen, Mr. Davis asked Mr. McQueen if he knew why Mr. Davis was in jail. (Id.) Mr. McQueen responded that everyone knew why Mr. Davis was in jail. (Id.) Mr. Davis explained that he got into an argument at a party in Cloverdale, which resulted in an exchange of gunfire. (Id. at 1230-31.) After he left the party, Mr. Davis went to his girlfriend's house, located in the Yamacraw neighborhood. (Id. at 1231.) Later, Mr. Davis left his girlfriend's house and walked to the Burger King to eat breakfast. (Id.) While Mr. Davis and a friend were on their way into the restaurant, Mr. Davis noticed someone who owed him drug money. (Id.) As he started arguing with the debtor, a police officer approached. (Id.) Afraid that the officer would connect him with the earlier Cloverdale shooting, Mr. Davis shot the officer first in the face and again as the wounded officer was trying to get up. (Id. at 1231-32.)

On cross-examination, Mr. McQueen admitted that he had seen a story about the shooting on the news and heard about it from other inmates. (Id. at 1239.) Mr. McQueen was not sure what weapon Mr. Davis used to shoot the officer, but recalled that Mr. Davis's friend had a rifle in the trunk of his car. (Id. at 1240.) Mr. McQueen denied having any arguments with Mr. Davis prior to either of them being placed in jail. (Id. at 1241.) Also, Mr. McQueen denied hoping to gain any advantage by testifying on behalf of the State, claiming that he had already been sentenced for his crimes. (Id. at 1242-43.)

O. Jeffery Sapp

Mr. Sapp testified at trial that, on the afternoon of August 19, 1989, he was walking through the Cloverdale neighborhood when he approached Mr. Davis, who was riding a bicycle. (Id. at 1249-50.) Mr. Sapp stopped Mr. Davis and asked him about the shooting at the Cloverdale party. (Id. at 1250.) Mr. Davis denied any knowledge of that shooting but began to discuss the MacPhail shooting. (Id.) Mr. Davis said that Mr. Coles was arguing with an individual, who said something to Mr. Davis that prompted him to hit the individual with a pistol. (Id. at 1250-51.) After Mr. Davis struck the man, a police officer ran toward him and told him to freeze. (Id. at 1251.) When the officer reached for his firearm, Mr. Davis shot him in self-defense. (Id. at 1251-52.)

Mr. Sapp also testified that he fabricated a portion of his police statement and Recorder's Court testimony. (Id. at 1253-55.) Specifically, Mr. Sapp stated that, contrary to his prior statements, Mr. Davis never told him that he had to go back and finish the job because the officer got a good look at Mr. Davis's face. (Id.)

On cross-examination, Mr. Sapp testified that his conversation with Mr. Davis took place at approximately 2:00 to 3:00 p.m. (Id. at 1258.) Mr. Sapp recalled that he did not believe Mr. Davis when he confessed to shooting the officer. (Id. at 1260.) Also, Mr. Sapp explained that his false statements were made for revenge due to a recent feud between he and Mr. Davis. (Id. at 1261-62.)

P. Joseph Washington[8]

> 8 The following witnesses are the relevant witnesses from Mr. Davis's defense at trial.

Mr. Washington, who was incarcerated for armed robbery at the time of trial, testified that he attended a party in the Cloverdale neighborhood on the evening of August 18, 1989. (Id. at 1339-40.) Mr. Washington was unsure what time he arrived at the party. (Id. at 1340.) Mr. Washington recalled seeing Mr. Davis at the Cloverdale party, but not Mr. Coles. (Id. at 1343.) At some point, Mr. Washington left the party to meet a friend named "Wally" in the Yamacraw neighborhood, with whom he planned to return to the party. (Id. at 1340-41.)

Some girls from the party drove Mr. Washington to Yamacraw, dropping him off on the corner of the Burger King property. (Id. at

1341-42.) There, he observed three people arguing while he was waiting for Wally. (Id. at 1342.) Mr. Washington recognized one of the individuals as Mr. Coles. (Id. at 1342-43.) As the argument continued, Mr. Washington saw Mr. Coles hit one of the individuals. (Id. at 1343.) After the assault, a police officer approached the group. (Id.) While Mr. Coles was backing up, he fired a gun at the officer. (Id.) After the shooting, Mr. Washington returned to the party. (Id. at 1344.) Mr. Washington explained that he did not mention observing the incident in the Burger King parking lot in his police statement concerning the Cloverdale shooting because he did not want to get involved. (Id.) In addition, Mr. Washington testified that Mr. Coles has a lighter complexion than Mr. Davis. (Id. at 1345.)

On cross-examination, Mr. Washington contended that he was at the Cloverdale party for both the earlier shooting involving Mr. Cooper and a later shooting involving Sherman Coleman. [9] (Id. at 1345-46.) Also, Mr. Washington testified that he did not remember what time he left the Cloverdale party, how long he waited in the Burger King parking lot, or how long he stayed at the party when he returned. (Id. at 1345-48.) Finally, he could not remember Wally's last name. (Id. at 1347.)

> [9] A second shooting occurred at the Cloverdale party at approximately 1:04 a.m. on August 19, 1989. (Resp. Ex. 30 at 642.) In this shooting, Lamar Brown shot at the party from the window of Mr. Wilds's car as it was passing the party, striking Sherman Coleman in the leg. (Id.) Important to Mr. Washington's credibility is the fact that he claims to be present at both the MacPhail shooting, which occurred at approximately 1:09 a.m., see supra Background Part I, and the Coleman shooting, which occurred at approximately 1:04 a.m. Worse still, is Mr. Washington's testimony that he observed the Coleman shooting after he returned from observing the MacPhail shooting. (Trial Transcript at 1348.)

Q. Tayna Johnson

Ms. Johnson testified at trial that she was at home when she heard gunshots in the early hours of August 19, 1989. (Id. at 1358.) Looking outside, she noticed police lights. (Id.) When she felt it was safe, she walked toward the police lights with her friend, Gail Dunham. (Id. at 1358-59.) As she was walking toward the Burger King, Ms. Johnson was approached by Mr. Coles and an individual named Terry. (Id. at 1359.) Mr. Coles asked if they could walk with the two down the street. (Id. at 1359.) Ms. Johnson agreed, and the group headed toward the Burger King and the police lights. (Id.)

As they approached the Burger King, Mr. Coles did not want to walk into the parking lot. (Id. at 1359-60.) After visiting the Burger King, Ms. Johnson and Mr. Coles walked back to Ms. Johnson's mother's home. (Id. at 1360.) While they were at the house, Mr. Coles asked Ms. Johnson to return to the Burger King and look for police. (Id.) Ms. Johnson returned to the Burger King, spoke with the police, and reported back to Mr. Coles. (Id.)

Ms. Johnson recalls that Mr. Coles was acting very nervous, especially after she informed him that the police were investigating the Burger King shooting. (Id. at 1361.) Also, Ms. Johnson stated that Mr. Coles was wearing a white shirt that evening. (Id. at 1362.) Ms. Johnson also attended the Cloverdale party, where she saw Mr. Coles and Mr. Davis. (Id. at 1364.) She testified that she did not see Mr. Davis argue with anyone while he was at the party. (Id. at 1365.)

On cross-examination, Ms. Johnson admitted that Mr. Coles appeared not to know what happened at the Burger King when he asked her to go and look around. (Id. at 1366.) Also, Ms. Johnson stated that she only saw Mr. Davis on a few occasions while he was at the party, but that she would have heard if he had gotten into an argument. (Id. at 1368-69.)

R. Jeffery Sams

Mr. Sams testified at trial that he attended a party in the Cloverdale neighborhood on the evening of August 18, 1989. (Id. at 1373.) Mr. Sams stayed at the party for fifteen to twenty minutes, then left to take his car home. (Id. at 1373-74.) He saw Mr. Davis at the party. (Id. at 1374.)

After driving his car home, Mr. Sams was walking back to the party when he came upon a vehicle driven by Mr. Ellison. (Id.) Messrs. Collins and Davis were also in the automobile. (Id. at 1374-75.) Mr. Sams joined the group, which then went to Charlie Brown's pool room. (Id. at 1375.) Mr. Sams went inside the pool room for five or ten minutes, then returned to the vehicle to listen to music. (Id. at 1376.) He remembers seeing both Mr. Davis and Mr. Coles inside the pool room. (Id. at 1376.)

While he was sitting in Mr. Ellison's car, Mr. Coles placed a firearm on the front seat. (Id. at 1377.) Almost immediately, Mr. Collins took the weapon and walked toward the side of the pool room. (Id. at 1378.) Soon after, Mr. Sams fell asleep, not waking until after Mr. Ellison drove away from the pool room. (Id. at 1379.) Mr. Sams did not recall seeing Mr. Davis with a gun that night. (Id. at 1379-81.)

On cross-examination, Mr. Sams described the firearm Mr. Coles placed on the front seat as real shiny. (Id. at 1382.) Mr. Sams reiterated that he had never seen Mr. Davis with a firearm. (Id. at 1384.) Finally, Mr. Sams admitted that it was possible for Mr. Davis to have a weapon in the waistline of his pants without it being noticed. (Id.)

S. Virginia Davis

Virginia Davis, Mr. Davis's mother, testified at trial that Mr. Davis went to a party in Cloverdale on the evening of August 18, 1989. (Id. at 1386-87.) He left for the party with Messrs. Ellison, Collins, and Sams. (Id. at 1387.) Ms. Davis also testified that when she woke Mr. Davis for breakfast on the morning of August 19, 1989, he was not acting nervous or in any way out of the ordinary. (Id. at 1388-89.) After breakfast, Mr. Davis stayed at home all day. (Id. at 1389.) Ms. Davis never saw Mr. Davis talking to Mr. Sapp that afternoon. (Id.)

On cross-examination, Ms. Davis stated that Mr. Davis never left her sight from 10:00 a.m. to 4:00 p.m. on August 19, 1989. (Id. at 1395-96.) She also testified that she would have known if Mr. Davis left the property. (Id. at 1399.) Finally, Ms. Davis recalled that Mr. Davis was wearing blue shorts and a multi-colored shirt when he left for the Cloverdale party. (Id. at 1411-12.)

T. Troy Davis

At trial, Mr. Davis took the stand in his own defense. (Id. at 1415.) He testified that he arrived at the Cloverdale party between 10:00 and 10:15 p.m. wearing a pink and purple polo shirt. (Id. at 1416, 1418.) After socializing in the backyard for approximately twenty-five to thirty minutes, Mr. Davis decided to leave the party. (Id. at 1417.) As he was walking, Mr. Davis observed a car speeding down the street. (Id.) The vehicle was rounding the corner at the end of the block when he heard a gunshot. (Id. at 1417-18.) He did not see who fired the gun. (Id. at 1418.)

When Mr. Davis returned home, he changed shirts because his shirt had gotten wet at the party. (Id. at 1418.) Mr. Davis never stated what color shirt he was wearing after he changed clothes. Mr. Davis then went for a ride with Messrs. Collins and Ellison. (Id.) While they were driving, they picked up Mr. Sams, whom they passed walking on the side of the road. (Id. at 1418-19.) The group first drove back by the Cloverdale party, then decided to shoot pool at Charlie Brown's pool room. (Id. at 1419.)

Mr. Davis was waiting to play a game of pool when Mr. Collins told him that Mr. Coles was outside arguing with someone. (Id. at 1420.) After going outside, Mr. Davis decided to follow the arguing pair. (Id. at 1421.) As he neared Mr. Coles, Mr. Davis figured out that Mr. Coles wanted the man to give him some of his beer. (Id.) Mr. Davis told Mr. Coles to just leave the man alone, but Mr. Coles told him to "shut the hell up." (Id. at 1421-22.) Joined by Mr. Collins, Mr. Davis continued following Mr. Colas to see what would happen. (Id. at 1422.)

Mr. Davis, along with Mr. Collins, cut through the back of the Trust Company Bank property on their way to the Burger King parking lot. (Id. at 1422.) As Mr. Coles was about to cross Fahm Street toward the Burger King parking lot, Mr. Davis overheard Mr. Coles threaten to take the life of the man with whom Mr. Coles was arguing. (Id. at 1422-23.) Mr. Davis caught up with Mr. Coles and the individual in the middle of the Burger King parking lot. (Id. at 1423.) According to Mr. Davis, he again pleaded with Mr. Coles to leave the man alone, but was told to shut up. (Id.)

Mr. Davis testified that the individual turned to Mr. Davis and told him to tell Mr. Coles to back off. (Id.) While the individual was focused on Mr. Davis, Mr. Coles slapped him in the head. (Id.) Mr. Davis stated that, after Mr. Coles slapped the individual, Mr. Davis shook his head and started walking away. (Id.) As he was walking, Mr. Davis observed Mr. Collins running, prompting Mr. Davis to start jogging away from the Burger King. (Id.) Looking over his shoulder, Mr. Davis saw a police officer entering the Burger King parking lot. (Id.) When Mr. Davis was crossing back over Fahm Street, toward the Trust Company Bank property, he heard a single gunshot, which caused him to run even faster. (Id. at 1424.) Mr. Davis was running past Charlie Brown's when he heard a few more gunshots. (Id.) As Mr. Davis was entering the Yamacraw neighborhood, Mr. Coles ran past him. (Id.) Thinking Mr. Coles had been shot, Mr. Davis asked him if he was alright, but Mr. Coles continued running and did not respond. (Id.) Mr. Davis then walked home to the Cloverdale neighborhood, arriving sometime before 2:00 a.m. (Id. at 1425.) Mr. Davis testified that he never looked back to see who was firing the weapon. (Id. at 1424.)

According to Mr. Davis, he slept until his mother woke him the next morning. (Id. at 1426.) After he awoke, Mr. Davis showered, ate breakfast, and started performing his weekend chores. (Id. at 1426-27.) Mr. Davis testified that he only saw his neighbor, Ms. Shelley Sams, that afternoon. (Id. at 1427.) He denied both speaking to Mr. Sapp or riding a bicycle in the neighborhood. (Id. at 1431.)

Mr. Davis testified that, at the time of the shooting, he weighed approximately one-hundred and seventy-five pounds. (Id. at 1433.) He denied ever having a fade-away haircut. (Id.) Comparing himself to Mr. Coles, Mr. Davis stated that he was the same height, a little bigger, and had a darker complexion. (Id. at 1434.) While he recognized Mr. McQueen from jail, Mr. Davis denied ever playing basketball or speaking with Mr. McQueen. (Id.)

On cross-examination, Mr. Davis testified that, at the Cloverdale party, he never noticed a group of individuals from Yamacraw talking to girls. (Id. at 1437-39.) He stated that he recognized only five or six people at the party. (Id. at 1439.) Mr. Davis denied shooting at Mr. Wilds's vehicle. (Id. at 1440.) Regarding the events in the Burger King parking lot, Mr. Davis stated that he approached the Burger King parking lot from behind the Trust Company Bank building because he thought it was faster, not because he wanted to approach the man Mr. Coles was arguing with without being seen. (Id. at 1446-48.) Also, Mr. Davis reiterated that it was Mr. Coles who slapped Mr. Young. (Id. at 1451.) He denied shooting the police officer, seeing Mr. Coles at his sister's house later that evening, or speaking to Mr. McQueen while imprisoned in the Chatham County Jail. (Id. at 1453, 1456, 1458-59.)

IV. SUBSEQUENT PROCEEDINGS

A. Motion for New Trial

After he was convicted, Mr. Davis filed a Motion for New Trial. (Doc. 14, Ex. 28.) On February 18, 1992, a hearing on the motion was held in Chatham County Superior Court. (Id.) On March 16, 1992, the court denied Mr. Davis's motion. (Doc. 21 at 15.)

B. Direct Appeal

Mr. Davis appealed his conviction directly to the Georgia Supreme Court. Davis v. State, 263 Ga. 5, 426 S.E.2d 844 (1993). After oral argument, the Georgia Supreme Court unanimously affirmed Mr. Davis's convictions and capital sentence. Id. On November 1, 1993, the Supreme Court of the United States denied Mr. Davis's petition for writ of certiorari. (Doc. 15, Attach. 12.)

C. State Habeas Proceedings

On March 15, 1994, Mr. Davis filed a petition for a writ of habeas corpus in the Georgia Superior Court. (Doc. 15, Attach. 15.) An evidentiary hearing was held on December 16, 1996. (Doc. 16, Attachs. 3-10.) During the hearing, Mr. Davis submitted six affidavits purporting to establish his innocence. [10] (Id., Attach. 3 at 3.) On September 5, 1997, the court denied the petition after reviewing the entire record, including the innocence affidavits. (Doc. 17, Attach. 6.)

10 The six affidavits were from Joseph Washington, Tanya Johnson, Kevin McQueen, Joseph Blige, April Hester, and Lamar Brown. (Doc. 21, App'x 1.) Mr. Davis submitted twenty-seven additional affidavits relating to his other claims, such as ineffective assistance of counsel and the unconstitutionality of the death penalty. (Doc 16, Attachs. 5-10.)

Mr. Davis appealed the denial of his habeas petition to the Georgia Supreme Court. Davis v. Turpin, 273 Ga. 244, 539 S.E.2d 129 (2000). In his application for certificate of probable cause to appeal, Mr. Davis argued that the failure to present additional evidence of innocence was ineffective assistance of counsel and that the new evidence undermined confidence in the guilty verdict. (Doc. 17,

Attach. 8 at 88-96.) However, the Georgia Supreme Court declined to hear this question on appeal. (See id., Attach. 11.) Ultimately, the court affirmed the denial of Mr. Davis's state habeas petition. Davis, 273 Ga. at 249, 539 S.E.2d at 134. On October 1, 2001, the Supreme Court of the United States denied Mr. Davis's petition for writ of certiorari. (Doc. 17, Attach. 25.)

D. Federal Habeas Proceedings

On December 14, 2001, Mr. Davis filed a petition for writ of habeas corpus in federal district court. (Id., Attach. 26.) In support of his petition, Mr. Davis submitted between sixteen and nineteen new innocence affidavits, [11] along with the six innocence affidavits he submitted as part of his state habeas petition. (Compare Doc. 3, Ex. 1, with Doc. 21, Ex. 1.) On March 10, 2003, the district court denied Mr. Davis's request for an evidentiary hearing, which asked the court to receive live testimony from the affiants. (Doc. 17, Attach. 47.) Ultimately, the district court denied Mr. Davis's petition on May 13, 2004. (Doc. 18, Attach. 5.) In denying the petition, the district court did not directly address Mr. Davis's claims of innocence, instead finding Mr. Davis's claims of constitutional error without merit. [12] (Id. at 65.)

---

11 It is not clear how each new affidavit is best characterized. However, the additional substantive affidavits were given by: Monty Holmes, Dorothy Ferrell, Harriett Murray, Larry Young, Antoine Williams, Anthony Hargrove, Shirley Riley, Darold Taylor, Gary Hargrove, Abdus-Salam Karim, Anita Dunham Saddler, Jeffrey Sapp, Michael Cooper, Benjamin Gordon, April Hester Hutchinson, Peggie Grant, Darrell Collins, James Riley, and Daniel Kinsman. (Doc. 3 Ex. 1; Doc. 21, Ex. 1.)

12 In addressing any claim of actual innocence raised by Mr. Davis, the district court concluded that

[A] federal court looks, under the miscarriage of justice exception, to colorable claims of actual innocence for "permission" to address questions of constitutional impropriety asserted in procedurally defaulted claims. If a federal court is satisfied that no constitutional error occurred, however, the "actual innocence" gateway need not be implemented. Ultimately, the state habeas court's analysis

serves as assurance that no constitutional deficiencies exist
in this case so as to merit habeas corpus relief.

(Doc. 18, Attach. 5 at 65.) (citations omitted)).

On September 26, 2006, the Eleventh Circuit Court of Appeals
affirmed the district court's decision. Davis v. Terry, 465 F.3d 1249
(11th Cir. 2006). The Eleventh Circuit did not recognize Mr. Davis's
claim as a substantive one based on actual innocence. Id. at 1251.
Rather, that court identified Mr. Davis as "argu[ing] that his
constitutional claims of an unfair trial must be considered, even
though they are otherwise procedurally defaulted, because he has
made the requisite showing of actual innocence." Id. The Eleventh
Circuit concluded that the question of Mr. Davis's innocence was
immaterial to its inquiry because he conceded that the district court
considered his claims of constitutional error even though they had
been procedurally defaulted. Id. at 1252-53. Therefore, the Eleventh
Circuit only addressed the issue of whether Mr. Davis's claims of
constitutional error failed as a matter of law, not whether he
established a substantive claim of actual innocence. Id. at 1253. On
June 25, 2007, the Supreme Court of the United States denied Mr.
Davis's petition for writ of certiorari. Davis v. Terry, 551 U.S. 1145,
127 S. Ct. 3010, 168 L. Ed. 2d 728 (2007)

E. Extraordinary Motion for New Trial

On July 9, 2007, Mr. Davis failed an extraordinary motion for new
trial in Chatham County Superior Court. (Doc. 19 Attachs. 4-5.) In
the motion, Mr. Davis directly argued that he was innocent and that
new evidence showed Mr. Coles murdered Officer MacPhail. (Id.,
Attach. 4 at 1-2.) In support of his claim, Mr. Davis presented
twenty-six innocence affidavits, the bulk of which were the same
affidavits Mr. Davis presented in his state and federal habeas
petitions. (Id., Table of Appendices at 41-42.) On July 13, 2007, the
court denied Mr. Davis's motion, concluding that, under Georgia law,
the affidavits submitted by Mr. Davis failed to meet the burden
required for a new trial. [13] (Id., Attach. 16 at 3-6.)

13 The state court applied the following six part standard for determining
whether the affidavits submitted by Mr. Davis warranted a new trial:

"(1) [T]hat the evidence has come to his knowledge since the trial; (2) that it was not owing to the want of due diligence that he did not acquire it sooner; (3) that it is so material that it would probably produce a different verdict; (4) that it is not cumulative only; (5) that the affidavit of the witness himself should be procured or its absence accounted for; and (6) that a new trial will not be granted if the only effect of the evidence will be to impeach the credit of a witness."

(Doc. 19, Attach. 16 at 2 (quoting Drake v. State, 248 Ga. 891, 894, 287 S.E.2d 180, 182 (1992)).)

On August 3, 2007, the Georgia Supreme Court granted Mr. Davis's application for a discretionary appeal. Davis v. State, 282 Ga. 368, 651 S.E.2d 10 (2007). After reviewing the innocence affidavits, a divided court affirmed the denial of Mr. Davis's motion, finding the strength of the innocence affidavits insufficient to overturn the jury's verdict. Davis v. State, 283 Ga. 438, 447, 660 S.E.2d 354, 362-63 (2008). The three justices in the minority reasoned that, the trial court should at least "conduct a hearing, to weigh the credibility of Davis's new evidence, and to exercise its discretion in determining if the new evidence would create the probability of a different outcome if a new trial were held." Id. at 450, 660 S.E.2d at 365 (Sears, J., dissenting). On October 14, 2008, the Supreme Court of the United States denied Mr. Davis's petition for writ of certiorari. (Doc. 20, Attach. 16.)

F. Georgia State Board of Pardons and Paroles

Following the denial of his extraordinary motion for new trial, Mr. Davis submitted an application for executive clemency with the Georgia State Board of Pardons and Paroles. (Doc. 20, Attach. 7 at 1.) In reviewing Mr. Davis's case, the Board allowed Mr. Davis's attorneys "to present every witness they desired to support their allegation that there is doubt as to Davis' guilt." (Id., Attach. 13 at 1.) In addition, the Board reviewed "the voluminous trial transcript, the police investigation report and the initial statements of all witnesses." (Id.) Finally, the Board retested some of the physical evidence in the case and interviewed Mr. Davis. (Id.) Following their exhaustive review, the Board concluded that Mr. Davis's showing was insufficient to warrant clemency. (Id.)

G. Application to File Second Habeas Petition

On October 22, 2008, Mr. Davis submitted an application to file a second habeas petition to the Eleventh Circuit. In re Davis, 565 F.3d 810 (11th Cir. 2009). In his application, Mr. Davis argued that his execution would be unconstitutional under the Eighth and Fourteenth Amendments because he is actually innocent of the crime of murder. Id. at 813. In denying the application, a divided Eleventh Circuit panel, relying solely on the affidavit of Benjamin Gordon, concluded that

> Davis has not even come close to making a prima facie showing that his [] claim relies on facts (i) that could not have been discovered previously through the exercise of due diligence, and (ii) that if proven, would "establish by clear and convincing evidence that, but for constitutional error, no reasonable factfinder would have found the applicant guilty of the underlying offense."

Id. at 824 (quoting 28 U.S.C. § 2244 (b) (2) (B)). The dissenter would have granted Mr. Davis's application, reasoning that "where a defendant who can make a viable claim of actual innocence is facing execution, the fundamental miscarriage of justice exception should apply and AEDPA's procedural bars should not prohibit the filing of a second or successive habeas petition." Id. at 831 (Barkett, J., dissenting).

H. Petition for Writ of Habeas Corpus filed in the Supreme Court of the United States

On May 19, 2009, Mr. Davis filed a Petition for Writ of Habeas Corpus within the original jurisdiction of the United States Supreme Court. (Doc. 2.) In the petition, Mr. Davis again argued that his execution would be unconstitutional under both the Eighth and Fourteenth Amendments. (Id. at 28.) On August 17, 2009, the Supreme Court transferred Mr. Davis's petition to this Court with instructions to "receive testimony and make findings of fact as to whether evidence that could not have been obtained at the time of trial clearly establishes [Mr. Davis's] innocence." Davis, 130 S. Ct. at 1. As instructed, this Court held a hearing on June 24, 2010, allowing Mr. Davis to present live witnesses and other evidence supporting his claim of innocence. (Docs. 78, 82, 83.) In addition, the Court directed the parties to brief several issues relating to the cognizability of and appropriate evidentiary burden for a claim for actual innocence. [14] (Doc. 77 at 1-2.)

> 14 The Court discusses the evidence proffered at this proceeding in the analysis section.

ANALYSIS

The Court begins its analysis by considering the cognizability of a freestanding claim of actual innocence. Concluding that the claim is cognizable, the Court then determines the appropriate burden of proof andfrontyar whether Mr. Davis has met that burden.

I. COGNIZABILITY OF FREESTANDING CLAIMS OF ACTUAL INNOCENCE

The Supreme Court recently reiterated that the cognizability of freestanding claims of actual innocence is an open question. Dist. Attorney's Office for Third Judicial Dist. v. Osborne, 557 U.S.   , 129 S. Ct. 2308, 2321, 174 L. Ed. 2d 38 (2009) ("Osborne also obliquely relies on an asserted federal constitutional right to be released upon proof of 'actual innocence.' Whether such a federal right exists is an open question."). While the cognizability of a freestanding claim of actual innocence is an open question, it is not a novel one. The Court considers the present state of the law prior to considering the underlying constitutional question. [15]

> 15 The State of Georgia concedes that it would be unconstitutional to execute an innocent man (Doc. 79 at 2), apparently abandoning its initial arguments to the contrary (see Doc. 21 at 56-62). However, the State now urges this Court to dodge the cognizability issue by finding Mr. Davis's claim insufficient on its merits. (Doc. 79 at 2.) When courts find a Herrera claim insufficient after lengthy factfinding regarding innocence, it is usually because the extensive factifinding was already necessary to determine a Schlup claim, and the Herrera claim can be resolved by reference to the Schlup determination. See House v. Bell, 547 U.S. 518, 126 S. Ct. 2064, 165 L. Ed. 2d 1 (2006). By contrast, this Court has already expended significant resources taking in evidence specifically regarding Mr. Davis's Herrera claim. It will have to expend even more resources to review the evidence and determine the merits of the Herrera claim, which is not facially

insufficient even though it fails upon close examination. The expenditure of those resources can, and should, be avoided if this claim is not cognizable. Accordingly, the Court declines to dodge the question that is squarely before it.

A. Background Case Law

i. Herrera v. Collins

The Supreme Court has discussed the cognizability of a freestanding claim of actual innocence at length only once. See Herrera v. Collins, 506 U.S. 390, 113 S. Ct. 853, 122 L. Ed. 2d 203 (1993). In Herrera, petitioner Leonel Torres Herrera was sentenced to death for the murder of two police officers--Carrisalez and Rucker. 506 U.S. at 394-95. After multiple unsuccessful appeals and collateral attacks, Herrera asserted a freestanding claim of actual innocence in a second federal habeas petition. Id. at 397-98. The district court stayed the execution to hear the claim, but that stay was vacated by the Fifth Circuit Court of Appeals, which held that freestanding claims of actual innocence were not cognizable. Id. Herrera successfully petitioned the Supreme Court for certiorari. Id. at 398.

The factual resolution of the case was as clear as the underlying constitutional question was muddled. And, it was the facts around which the majority congealed. As Justice O'Connor explained, "[d]ispositive to this case, however, is an equally fundamental fact: Petitioner is not innocent, in any sense of the word." Id. at 419 (O'Connor, J., concurring); see also id. at 429 (White, J., concurring); id. at 418-19 (majority opinion) ("[Herrera's] showing of innocence falls far short of that which would have to be made in order to trigger the sort of constitutional claim which we have assumed, arguendo, to exist."). Ultimately, the Court rejected Herrera's claim on the merits by assuming, without deciding, the cognizability of the freestanding claim of actual innocence. Id. at 417-19.

Herrera's guilt was obvious both because of the overwhelming evidence presented at his trial and the weakness of his new evidence of innocence. The proof of guilt at Herrera's trial [16] was ironclad, consisting of physical evidence, Herrera's handwritten confession, and positive eyewitness identifications. [17] Id. Herrera's newly discovered proof of innocence consisted of four dubious affidavits implicating his deceased brother as the murderer. Id. at 396-97. The affidavits were internally inconsistent, composed largely of hearsay, and pointed to a conveniently dead suspect. Id. at 417-19. When the affidavits were "considered in light of the proof of petitioner's guilt at trial," they fell far short of proving that a jury would have found reasonable doubt. Id. at 418. That is, the affidavits did not shift the balance of proof in Herrera's case. See id. at 418 ("That proof, even when considered alongside petitioner's belated affidavits, points strongly to petitioner's guilt.")

16 Herrera was tried for the murder of Carrisalez. Herrera, 506 U.S. at 395. He later pled guilty to the murder of Rucker. Id. at 394.

17 There were two identifications of Herrera, one by Carrisalez's partner and the other by Carrisalez himself, who survived for several days after the shooting. Herrera, 506 U.S. at 394. Herrera's social security card was found at the scene of Rucker's murder, and Rucker's blood and hair were found on Herrera's car, jeans, and wallet. Id. at 394. In addition, Herrera was carrying a handwritten confession when he was arrested. Id. at 394-95.

Because the Supreme Court simply assumed that freestanding claims of actual innocence were cognizable, it became unnecessary for the court to state a concrete position on the issue. Indeed, four Justices provided only suggestive dicta on either side of the question. See id. at 419 (O'Connor, J., concurring); see also id. at 429 (White, J., concurring); Id. at 398-417 (majority opinion). Two Justices expressly stated that the constitution does not recognize the claim. Id. at 427-29 ("There is no basis in text, tradition, or even in contemporary practice (if that were enough) for finding in the Constitution a right to demand judicial consideration of newly discovered evidence of innocence brought forward after conviction.') (Scalia, J., dissenting). Three others explicitly recognized such a claim. Id. at 430-31 (Blackmun, J., dissenting) ('We really are being asked to decide whether the Constitution forbids the execution of a person who has been validly convicted and sentenced but who, nonetheless, can prove his innocence with newly discovered evidence. Despite the State of Texas' astonishing protestation to the contrary, I do not see how the answer can be anything but 'yes.' 11 citation omitted)). In short, two justices denied the existence of the claim, three recognized it, and four stated no express opinion, causing the question of the cognizability of freestanding claims of actual innocence to remain open. See Osborne, 129 S. Ct. at 2321.

While the actual holding of Herrera was narrow, the opinion contains broad, sweeping dicta that sheds some light on considerations relevant to the cognizability of freestanding actual innocence claims. First, those justices doubting or disagreeing with the cognizability of the claim set out several concerns regarding recognizing this right. [18] Herrera, 506 U.S. at 400-04, 411-18. Second, Justices O'Connor and Kennedy, in their concurrence, provided dicta suggesting that they supported the cognizability of the claim and, when paired with the dissents, suggests that a majority of the Herrera court believed that the execution of the innocent violated the Constitution. Id. at 419 (O'Connor, J., concurring). Ultimately, while the dicta of Herrera is meaningful, the most important aspect of Herrera is the question it left unanswered: Are freestanding claims of actual innocence cognizable? Osborne, 129 S. Ct. at 2321.

18 One of the Herrera concerns, that "the passage of time only diminishes the reliability of criminal adjudications," 506 U.S. at 403, has been significantly eroded since Herrera was decided. While it remains true that the reliability of witness testimony will decrease with time as memory fades, the vastly increased importance of forensic science has created an opposite force. Unlike memory, scientific ability improves with time. While forensic science has always played some role in the consideration of cases, the use of scientific evidence has become pervasive since Herrera. Compare Learned Hand, Historical and Practical Considerations Regarding Expert Testimony, 15 Harv. L. Rev. 40 (1901), with Kenworthey Bilz, The Fall of the Confession Era, 96 J. Crim. L. & Criminology 367, 379 (2005) ("The science of DNA testing did not hit the mainstream of criminal investigations until the 1990's in this country, and [this evidence has come to play an increasingly integral part in prosecutions . . . ."), and Paul C. Giannelli, Ake V. Oklahoma: The Right to Expert Assistance in a Post-Daubert, Post-DNA World, 89 Cornell L. Rev. 1305 (2004). Where it is science that allows for increased accuracy, and the new science occurs post-trial, it can be fairly said that the accuracy of the guilt determination increases with time. Examples of such advances include DNA fingerprinting and new knowledge in the science of arson. See Brandon L. Garrett, Judging Innocence, 108 Colum. L. Rev. 55, 56 (2008); David Grann, Trial by Fire: Did Texas Execute an Innocent Man?, The New Yorker (Sept. 7, 2009), available at http://www.newyorker.com/reporting/2009/09/07/090907fa_fact_gran

n?currentPage=all (discussing advances in arson detection science that disproved various forensics associated with arson detection such as the importance of V-shaped burn marks, certain puddle configurations, and low burns on walls and floors). However, in this case, none of the reasons why forensic science would cause an adjudication to become less reliable over time are present.

ii. Schlup v. Delo and House v. Bell

Herrera's progeny address the question only obliquely. See, e.g., House v. Bell, 547 U.S. 518, 126 S. Ct. 2064, 165 L. Ed. 2d 1 (2006); Schlup v. Delo, 513 U.S. 298, 115 S. Ct. 851, 130 L. Ed. 2d 808 (1995). In Schlup v. Delo, Herrera was discussed, but only to contrast its hypothetical freestanding claim of actual innocence to the long-recognized exception to procedural default for a miscarriage of justice. Schlup, 513 U.S. at 315-16. House v. Bell also briefly touched on the question of freestanding claims of actual innocence, assuming that such a claim would exist, but finding that the petitioner had not made a sufficient showing to require consideration of the claim. 547 U.S. at 554-55. Neither case answered the ultimate question of whether there is a right of the innocent to be released upon a showing of actual innocence. As noted above, that question remains open. See Osborne, 129 S. Ct. at 2321. The Court now considers that question.

B. Eighth Amendment

The Eighth Amendment provides that "[e]xcessive bail shall not be required, nor excessive fines imposed, nor cruel and unusual punishments inflicted." [19] U.S. Const. amend. VII. "The Eighth Amendment stands to assure that the State's power to punish is 'exercised within the limits of civilized standards.'" Woodson v. North Carolina, 428 U.S. 280, 288, 96 S. Ct. 2978, 49 L. Ed. 2d 944 (1976) (plurality opinion) (quoting Trop v. Dulles, 356 U.S. 86, 100, 78 S. Ct. 590, 2 L. Ed. 2d 630 (1958) (plurality opinion)). The scope of the Amendment is not static. Its reach is defined by looking beyond historical conceptions to "the evolving standards of decency that mark the progress of a maturing society." Trop, 356 U.S. at 101. "'This is because [t]he standard of extreme cruelty is not merely descriptive, but necessarily embodies a moral judgment. The standard itself remains the same, but its applicability must change as the basic mores of society change.'" Graham v. Florida, 560 U.S.   , 130 S. Ct. 2011, 2021, 176 L. Ed. 2d 825 (2010) (quoting Kennedy v. Louisiana, 554 U.S. 407, 128 S. Ct. 2641, 2649, 171 L. Ed. 2d 525 (2008)) (alterations in original)

19 The Eighth Amendment is applicable to the states through the Fourteenth Amendment. See Kennedy v. Louisiana, 554 U.S. 407, 128 S. Ct. 2641, 2649, 171 L. Ed. 2d 525 (2008).

Recently, the Supreme Court has clarified its Eighth Amendment jurisprudence. See Graham, 130 S. Ct. 2011, 176 L. Ed. 2d 825. In Graham, the Supreme Court divided its Eighth Amendment cases into two classifications: (1) those that "challenge[d] the length of term-of-years sentences given all the circumstances in a particular case" and (2) those "in which the Court implements the proportionality standard by certain categorical restrictions on the death penalty." Id. at 2021-22. The Supreme Court then went further and divided this latter grouping into two subsets, one focusing on the nature of the offense and the other on the characteristics of the offender. [20] Id. at 2022. That latter subset turns on the culpability of a defendant with a certain characteristic [21] that significantly diminishes the offender's culpability. See Roper v. Simmons, 543 U.S. 551, 568, 125 S. Ct. 1183, 161 L. Ed. 2d 1 (2005) As a result of the diminished culpability, the justifications for imposing the death penalty are no longer applicable, rendering the imposition of the death penalty unconstitutional. [22] See id. ("Capital punishment must be limited to those offenders . . . whose extreme culpability makes them 'the most deserving of execution.'" (quoting Atkins v. Virginia, 536 U.S. 304, 319, 122 S. Ct. 2242, 153 L. Ed. 2d 335 (2002))); see Atkins, 536 U.S. at 323.

20 This latter division does not affect the applicable analysis; both subsets apply the approach stemming from Trop, 356 U.S. 86, 78 S. Ct. 590, 2 L. Ed. 2d 630 (plurality opinion). Compare Kennedy, 128 S. Ct. at 2649 (applying Trop analysis to an Eighth Amendment challenge to the punishment of death for child rape), with Roper v. Simmons, 543 U.S. 551, 560-61, 125 S. Ct. 1183, 161 L. Ed. 2d 1 (2005) (applying Trop analysis to an Eighth Amendment challenge to the execution of minors)

21 In addition to personal characteristics, a defendant's culpability is based on the nature of his conduct. See generally Irizarry v. United States, 553 U.S. 708, 128 S. Ct. 2198, 171 L. Ed. 2d 28 (2008)

22 Moreover, where the state attempts to punish an individual who has no culpability at all, the Eighth Amendment prohibits the imposition of any punishment. Robinson v. California, 370 U.S. 660, 667, 82 S. Ct. 1417, 8 L. Ed. 2d 758 (1962). As the Supreme Court explained:

> We hold that a state law which imprisons a person thus afflicted [with an addiction to narcotics] as a criminal, even though he has never touched any narcotic drug within the State or been guilty of any irregular behavior there, inflicts a cruel and unusual punishment in violation of the Fourteenth Amendment. To be sure, imprisonment for ninety days is not, in the abstract, a punishment which is either cruel or unusual. But the question cannot be considered in the abstract. Even one day in prison would be a cruel and unusual punishment for the 'crime' of having a common cold.

Id.

This Eighth Amendment challenge calls into question the permissibility of capital punishment [23] based upon a characteristic of the offender: a total lack of culpability, which is demonstrated through a showing of factual innocence based upon evidence discovered subsequent to a full and fair trial. [24] Graham held that challenges grounded in individual culpability are to be considered using the Trop analysis. 130 S. Ct. at 2021-22. Therefore, the Court applies the Trop analysis here. [25]

23 The Supreme Court has stated that the open question underlying this case extends beyond the capital context. See Osborne, 129 S. Ct. at 2321. However, in Herrera, the assumed right was contingent upon the fact that the case was a capital one. 506 U.S. at 417 ("We may assume, for the sake of argument in deciding this case, that in a capital case a truly persuasive demonstration of 'actual innocence' made after trial would render the execution of a defendant unconstitutional . . . ." (emphasis added)). It is unclear whether that distinction remains good law. See Graham, 130 S. Ct. at 2046 ("Today's decision eviscerates that distinction. 'Death is different' no longer.") (Thomas, J., dissenting). Regardless, the present case is a

capital one, so the Court limits its consideration to capital cases based upon the definition of the assumed right in Herrera.

24 Abstract conceptualizations of this challenge may be clarified by a simple hypothetical. A defendant is convicted of the murder of his child after a full and fair trial, and he is then sentenced to death. Ten years later, the defendant discovers the "murdered" child has been safely living on a remote island, conclusively disproving defendant's guilt. The defendant then goes before the state with his living child, but is denied relief and the state prepares to move forward with his execution. The challenge under these circumstances is whether, in spite of the truly persuasive proof of innocence, the state may proceed with the execution without violating the Eighth Amendment of the United States Constitution.

At one time, such a hypothetical would draw the objection that this factual scenario could never occur because any serious showing of innocence would result in state relief by clemency or state judicial process. This is, the state would always admit its mistake and rectify it. While it remains the case that state officials denying relief under such circumstances would be an extreme rarity, events since Herrera shatter the notion of a perfect "fail safe" system for truly persuasive proof of innocence. See, e.g., Watkins v. Miller, 92 F. Supp. 2d 824, 836 (S.D. Ind. 2000) ("In an effort to keep Jerry Watkins in prison, the state has clung to this theoretical possibility. A close look at this possibility shows it is farfetched, both as a matter of science and in terms of the overall evidence in the case. The theoretical possibility is also completely inconsistent with the theory of the case that the prosecution presented to the jury."); cf. Brandon L. Garrett, Exoneree Post-Conviction Data, http://www.law.virginia.edu/pdf/faculty/garrett/judging_innocence/exonerees_postconviction_dna_testing.pdf (showing that of 225 DNA exonerations, prosecutors opposed vacating the conviction in 22 cases (9.8%)).

25 In reality, the closest cousin of this case is Robinson v. California, 370 U.S. 660, 82 S. Ct. 1417, 8 L. Ed. 2d 758 (1962), holding that any punishment is disproportionate where the convict has no culpability. Robinson analyzed the case using a common sense approach that does not accord with either test recognized in Graham. 130 S. Ct. at 2021-23. Presumably, because Robinson turned on an issue of culpability, if the case were reheard today it would be analyzed under Trop. See Graham, 130 S. Ct. at 2022-23. Accordingly, while common sense and long-held historical views proscribe the punishment of the innocent, see Patterson v. New York, 432 U.S. 197, 208, 97 S. Ct. 2319, 53 L. Ed. 2d 281 (1977) (" [I]t is far worse to convict an innocent man than to let a guilty man go free.'" (quoting In re Winship, 397 U.S. 358, 372, 90 S. Ct. 1068, 25 L. Ed. 2d 368 (1970))); Winship, 397 U.S. at 364 ("It is critical that the moral force of the criminal law not be diluted by a standard of proof that leaves people in

doubt whether innocent men are being condemned."); Coffin v. United
States, 156 U.S. 432, 455-56, 15 S. Ct. 394, 39 L. Ed. 481 (1895); Alexander
Volokh, Guilty Men, 146 U. Pa. L. Rev. 173 (1997) (tracing the concept of
the paramount importance of innocence as far back as ancient Greece), this
Court will go beyond common sense and tradition in this case, and into the
deeper analysis required under Graham.

When addressing categorical challenges under Trop, the proper
approach is a two step inquiry. First, a court "considers 'objective
indicia of society's standards, as expressed in legislative enactments
and state practice' to determine whether there is a national consensus
against the sentencing practice at issue." Id. at 2022 (quoting Roper,
543 U.S. at 572). Second, a court must independently determine
whether the punishment in question violates the constitution based
upon precedent and the court's AN 'understanding and interpretation
of the Eighth Amendment's text, history, meaning, and purpose.'" Id.
at 2022 (quoting Kennedy, 128 S. Ct. at 2650). The societal consensus
presently at issue is whether it would be cruel to allow the execution
on an individual who can clearly establish his innocence of the crime
of conviction based on evidence discovered subsequent to a full and
fair trial.

i. Objective Indicia of Societal Standards

"The analysis begins with objective indicia of national consensus." Id.
at 2023. The Supreme Court has "emphasized that legislation is the
'clearest and most reliable objective evidence of contemporary
values.'" Atkins, 536 U.S. at 323 (quoting Penry v. Lynaugh, 492 U.S.
302, 331, 109 S. Ct. 2934, 106 L. Ed. 2d 256 (1989)). While the
inability of the state to punish an innocent person has long been
recognized, [26] recent state legislation demonstrates increasing
consternation with the execution [27] of innocent convicts. Since
Herrera, forty-seven state [28] and the District of Columbia have
enacted statutes designed to help innocent convicts prove that their
convictions were erroneous. [29] In so doing, the statutes themselves
recognize that their protections will be used to disprove erroneous
jury verdicts and avoid punishment of the innocent. [30] Indeed, if
states were not concerned with preventing punishment of the
wrongfully convicted, it would be difficult to understand why they
would allow validly convicted persons avenues with which to secure
evidence of their innocence. Moreover, over the course of American

history several states have gone further to avoid executing the innocent, adopting over-inclusive solutions by abolishing the death penalty or requiring absolute certainty as to guilt. [31]

26 It has long been established that the constitution prohibits states from punishing the innocent. See, e.g., Herrera, 506 U.S. at 419 (O'Connor, J., concurring) ('I cannot disagree with the fundamental legal principle that executing the innocent is inconsistent with the Constitution."); United States v. U.S. Coin & Currency, 401 U.S. 715, 726, 91 S. Ct. 1041, 28 L. Ed. 2d 434 (1971) (Brennan, J., concurring) ("[T]he government has no legitimate interest in punishing those innocent of wrongdoing."); Robinson, 370 U.S. at 667 ("Even one day in prison would be a cruel and unusual punishment for the 'crime' of having a common cold.") Calder v. Bull, 3 U.S. 386, 388, 1 L. Ed. 648, 3 Dall. 386 (1798) (The Legislature may . . . declare new crimes . . . but they cannot change innocence into guilt; or punish innocence as a crime . . . .").

27 Despite considering this right in the context of capital punishment, the Court looks to the laws of all fifty states regarding the permissibility of post-conviction exoneration to determine societal consensus. Because laws pertaining to the conviction of the innocent usually extend beyond capital convictions, see, e.g., Ariz. Rev. Stat. Ann. 13-4240 (2000); S.C. Code. Ann. § 17-28-30 (2008), the Court has indulged in the assumption that for states without the death penalty, their existing practices regarding post-conviction exoneration would also extend into the capital context were such punishment available. Had the Court limited its review of state law to only those states with the death penalty; it would have found that, of the thirty-five states with the death penalty, only Oklahoma provides no avenues to secure evidence of innocence in the post-conviction setting. See Death Penalty Information Center, States With and Without the Death Penalty, http:// www.deathpenaltyinfo.org/states-and-without-death-penalty. That is, 97.1% of States with a death penalty provide some avenue through which to seek evidence necessary to prove innocence subsequent to a conviction. Whether one limits the inquiry to states with capital punishment, or considers all fifty states, the consensus regarding punishment of the innocent remains constant.

28 The three states that have not enacted modern reforms to ensure that convicts are actually innocent are Massachusetts, Alaska, and Oklahoma. Of these three, only Oklahoma utilizes the death penalty. See Roper, 125 S. Ct. at 1201; Okla. Stat. tit. 21, § 701.10 (2002).

29 The baseline protection enacted involves DNA testing. However, multiple states have enacted laws that allow for additional factfinding procedures regarding the innocence of the convicted, including fingerprint

analysis and other additional forensic testing. Ala. Code § 15-18-200 (2009); Ariz. Rev. Stat. Ann. § 13-4240 (2000); Ark. Code Ann. § 16-112-202 (2001); Cal. Penal Code § 1405 (West 2001); Cola. Rev. Stat. § 18-1-413 (2004); Conn. Gen. Stat. § 54-102kk (2003); Del. Code Ann. tit. 11, § 4504 (2000); D.C. Code § 22-4133 (2002); Fla. Stat. § 925.11 (2006); Ga. Code Ann. § 5-5-41 (2003); Haw. Rev. Stat. § 844D-123 (2005); Idaho Code Ann. § 19-4902 (2010); 725 Ill. Comp. Stat. 5/116-3 (2003); Ind. Code § 35-38-7-5 (2003); Iowa Code § 81.10 (2005); Kan. Stat. Ann. § 21-2512 (2001); Ky. Rev. Stat. Ann. § 422.285 (West 2002); La. Code Crim. Proc. Ann. art. 926.1 (2001); Me. Rev. Stat. tit. 15, § 2137 (2001); Md. Code Ann., Crim. Proc. § 8-201 (West 2001); Mich. Comp. Laws § 770.16 (2000); Minn. Stat. § 590.01 (1999); Miss. Code Ann. § 99-39-5 (1995); Mo. Rev. Stat § 547.035; Mont. Code Ann. § 46-21-110 (2003); Neb. Rev. Stat. § 29-4120 (2001); Nev. Rev. Stat. § 176.0918 (2003); N.H. Rev. Stat. Ann. § 651-D:2 (2004); N.J. Stat. Ann. § 2A:84A-32a (West 2001); N.M. Stat. Ann. § 31-1A--2 (2003); N.Y. Crim. Proc. Law § 440.30(1-a) (McKinney 1994); N.C. Gen. Stat. § 15A-269 (2001); N.D. Cent. Code § 29-32.1-15 (2005); Ohio Rev. Code Ann. § 2953.72 (West 2010); Or. Rev. Stat. § 138.690 (2001); 42 Pa. Cons. Stat. § 9543.1 (2002); R.I. Gen. Laws § 10-9.1-12 (2002); S.C. Code Ann. § 17-28-30 (2008); S.D. Codified Laws § 23-5B-1 (2009); Tenn. Code Ann. § 40-30-304 (2001); Tex. Code Crim. Proc. Ann. art. 64.01 (West 2001); Utah Code Ann. § 78B-9-301 (West 2008); Vt. Stat. Ann. tit. 13, § 5561 (2007); Va. Code Ann. § 19.2-327.1 (2001); Wash. Rev. Code § 10.73.170 (2000); W. Va. Code § 15-2B-14 (2004); Wis. Stat. § 974.07 (2001); Wyo. Stat. Ann. § 7-12-303 (2008).

30 Ala. Code § 15-18-200(e) (3) (2009); Ariz. Rev. Stat. Ann. § 13-4240(B)(1) (2000); Ark. Code Ann. § 16-112-202(6) (B) (2001); Cal. Penal Code § 1405(f)(4)-(5) (West 2001); Colo. Rev. Stat. § 18-1-413(1)(a) (2004); Conn. Gen. Stat. § 54-102kk(b) (4) (2003); Del. Code Ann. tit. 11, § 4504(a) (5) (2000); D.C. Code § 22-4135 (2002); Fla. Stat. § 925.11(1) (a) (2006); Ga. Code Ann. § 5-5-41(c)(3)(C) (2003); Haw. Rev. Stat. § 844D-123(b)(1) (2005); Idaho Code Ann. § 19-4902(e)(1) (2010); 725 Ill. Comp. Stat. 5/122-1 (2003); Ind. Code § 35-38-7-8(4), 35-38-7-19 (2004); Iowa Code § 81.10(7) (e) (2005); Kan. Stat. Ann. § 21-2512(c) (2001); Ky. Rev. Stat. Ann. § 422.285(3)(a) (West 2002); La. Code Crim. Proc. Ann. art. 926.1(B) (1) (2001); Me. Rev. Stat. tit. 15, § 2138(10)(C)(1) (2001); Md. Code. Ann., Crim. Proc. § 8-301 (West 2009); Minn. Stat. § 590.01(1) (2) (1999); Miss. Code Ann. § 99-39-5(1) (e) (1995); Mo. Rev. Stat § 547.037 (2001) Mont. Code Ann. § 46-21-110(1) (c) (2003); Neb. Rev. Stat. § 29-4119, 29-4120(5) (2001); Nev. Rev. Stat. § 176.515(3), 176.0918(3)(b) (2003); N.H. Rev. Stat. Ann. § 651-D:2(I) (b) (2004); N.J. Stat. Ann. § 2A:84A-32a(a)(1)(b) (West 2001); N.M. Stat. Ann. § 31-1A-2(A) (2003); N.Y. Crim. Proc. Law § 440.30(1-a) (McKinney 1994); N.C. Gen. Stat. § 15A-269(b) (2) (2001); N.D. Cent. Code Ann. § 29-32.1-01(1) (e), 29-32.1-15(1) (2005); Ohio Rev. Code Ann. § 2953.71(L) (West 2010); Or. Rev. Stat. § 138.692 (1)(a)(A)(ii) (2001); 42 Pa. Cons. Stat. § 9543.1(c)(2)(i) (2002); R.I. Gen. Laws § 10-9.1-

11(c) (2002); S.C. Code Ann. § 17-28-30 (A), (B) (2008); S.D. Codified Laws § 23-5B-1(9)(b) 23-5B-16 (2009); Tenn. Code Ann. § 40-30-304(4) (2001); Tex. Code Crim. Proc. Ann. art. 64.04 (West 2001); Utah Code Ann. § 78B-9-302 (West 2008); Vt. Stat. Ann. tit. 13, § 5561(a)(1) (2007); Va. Code Ann. § 19.2-327.2 (2001); Wash. Rev. Code § 10.73.170(3) (2000); W. Va. Code § 15-2B-14(b)(1) (2004); Wis. Stat. § 974.07(7)(a)(1) (2001); Wyo. Stat. Ann. § 7-12-303(c)(ix) (2008).

31 This concern has been raised twice in the past three years with the repeal of the death penalty in New Mexico and severe limitation of the death penalty in Maryland. Statement of Governor Bill Richardson, Governor Bill Richardson Signs Repeal of the Death Penalty (2009), http://www.deathpenaltyinfo.org/ documents/Richardsonstatement.pdf; Maryland Commission on Capital Punishment, Final Report 18-19 (2008), available at http://www.goccp.maryland.gov/capital-punishment/documents/death -penalty-commission-final-report.pdf. It also appears that protecting the innocent from execution was a motivating factor in some popular historical movements to abolish capital punishment in the states, including Michigan's abolition of capital punishment in 1846, Rhode Island's abolition of the death penalty in 1852, and Maine's abolition of the death penalty in 1876. See Hugo Adam Bedau & Michael L. Radelet, Miscarriages of Justice in Potentially Capital Cases, 40 Stan. L. Rev. 21, 76 (1987)

The states, then, are showing an increased concern for protecting legally convicted individuals whom are shown to be factually innocent subsequent to a trial. [32] This consensus is shown mostly through enacting statutes that allow convicts to seek evidence of their innocence after a valid adjudication of guilt and occasionally through the adoption of over-inclusive solutions to avoid executing the innocent. Accordingly, the Court concludes that objective indicia of societal standards indicates a consensus that the execution of innocent convicts should be prohibited, whether that innocence is proved before or after trial. Indeed, the national consensus among the states appears nearly unanimous on this score.

32 While these enactments show near unanimous consensus among the states, Mr. Davis goes further by offering other evidence that the Court finds too general to be helpful in its inquiry. For example, while it is true that the overall number of death sentences in America is declining (see Doc. 80 at 10-11), there is no way to know whether this decline is caused by accuracy concerns, decreased societal support for the death penalty, newfound prosecutorial restraint in seeking imposition of the death penalty, or some other unknown reason.

ii. Precedent and Understanding

While national consensus is important, the task of interpreting the Constitution, including the Eighth Amendment, remains in the hands of federal courts. Graham, 130 S. Ct. at 2026. "The judicial exercise of independent judgment requires consideration of the culpability of the offenders at issue in light of their crimes and characteristics, along with the severity of the punishment in question." Id. This inquiry also considers whether the practice at issue serves "legitimate penological goals." Id.; Roper, 543 U.S. at 571-72. And, a court must consider prior precedent and understanding of the Eighth Amendment. Kennedy, 128 S. Ct. at 2658.

a. Punishment, Innocence, and the Requirement that the Convict Kill

The Court begins with prior precedent regarding innocence and punishment. If there is a principle more firmly embedded in the fabric of the American legal system than that which proscribes punishment of the innocent, it is unknown to this Court. It is well established that the punishment of the innocent or those otherwise without culpability is at odds with the constitution, including the Eighth Amendment. [33] E.g., Herrera, 506 U.S. at 419 (O'Connor, J., concurring) ("I cannot disagree with the fundamental legal principle that executing the innocent is inconsistent with the Constitution."); U.S. Coin & Currency, 401 U.S. at 726 (Brennan, J., concurring) ("[T]he government has no legitimate interest in punishing those innocent of wrongdoing . . . ."); Robinson, 370 U.S. at 667 ("Even one day in prison would be a cruel and unusual punishment for the 'crime' of having a common cold."); Thompson v. City of Louisville, 362 U.S. 199, 206, 80 S. Ct. 624, 4 L. Ed. 2d 654 (1960) ("[I]t is a violation of due process to convict and punish a man without evidence of his guilt."); Mooney v. Holohan, 294 U.S. 103, 113, 55 S. Ct. 340, 79 L. Ed. 791 (1935) (holding that where defendant asserted his innocence and a wrongful conviction due to perjured testimony and improperly suppressed evidence, habeas courts must hear the claim); Calder, 3 U.S. at 388 ('The Legislature may . . . declare new crimes . . . but they cannot change innocence into guilt; or punish innocence as a crime . . . .").

33 The Court does not understand the dicta in Herrera to dispute this foundational legal principle. Rather, the dicta in Herrera questions whether the right of the innocent not to be punished can be asserted in the post-trial context, specifically in the context of federal habeas. See Herrera, 506 U.S. at 400-02. While not all constitutional violations pertaining to criminal rights may be asserted post-trial, see Stone v. Powell, 428 U.S. 465, 486, 96 S. Ct. 3037, 49 L. Ed. 2d 1067 (1976), it appears that the cruel and unusual punishment clause maintains its vitality in the habeas context, see Ford v. Wainwright, 477 U.S. 399, 411-12, 106 S. Ct. 2595, 91 L. Ed. 2d 335 (1986). Moreover, to the extent that the objection regarding the reach of habeas is historical, it bears noting that much of the modern reach of habeas corpus is beyond historical conceptions of habeas corpus, see Harlan Grant Cohen, "**Undead**" Wartime Cases: Stare Decisis and the Lessons of History, 84 Tul. L. Rev. 957 (2010), and cursory reviews of habeas corpus history generally referenced by courts do not even begin to do justice to the complicated question of what historical figures would have understood habeas to reach, see Paul D. Halliday & G. Edward White, The Suspension Clause: English Text, Imperial Contexts, and American Implications, 94 Va. L.R. 575 (2008).

Further, "[t]he Court has recognized that defendants who do not kill, intend to kill, or foresee that life will be taken are categorically less deserving of the most serious forms of punishment than are murderers." Graham, 130 S. Ct. at 2027. Indeed,

> if a person sentenced to death in fact killed, attempted to kill, or intended to kill, the Eighth Amendment itself is not violated by his or her execution regardless of who makes the determination of the requisite culpability; by the same token, if a person sentenced to death lacks the requisite culpability; the Eighth Amendment violation can be adequately remedied by any court that has the power to find the facts and vacate the sentence.

Cabana v. Bullock, 474 U.S. 376, 386, 106 S. Ct. 689, 88 L. Ed. 2d 704 (1986), abrogated on other grounds by Pope v. Illinois, 481 U.S. 497, 503 n.7, 107 S. Ct. 1918, 95 L. Ed. 2d 439 (1987). That is, to justify the imposition of the death penalty, the condemned must have killed. While these precedents refer to a crime of conviction rather than an individualized assessment of guilt, the motivating concern would remain the same: each defendant sentenced to death must have engaged in conduct giving rise to the requisite culpability. It is unclear why a patently erroneous, but fair, criminal adjudication would change the transcendental fact that one who has not actually murdered cannot be executed.

b. Legitimate Penological Goals

"[C]apital punishment is excessive when . . . it does not fulfill the two distinct social purposes served by the death penalty: retribution and deterrence of capital crimes." Kennedy, 128 S. Ct. at 2661. The Court considers whether executing innocent convicts furthers these goals. [34]

> 34 While this analysis may appear axiomatic, the Court nonetheless considers whether any penological goal is served in executing those who can demonstrate their innocence, as per the analysis required under Graham.

Punishment deters crime by affecting the relevant cost--benefit analysis of the potential criminal. Roper, 543 U.S. at 561-62; Thompson v. Oklahoma, 487 U.S. 815, 837, 108 S. Ct. 2687, 101 L. Ed. 2d 702 (1988) (plurality opinion). Because deterrence functions by altering the incentive structure surrounding the potential criminal's cost--benefit analysis, "'capital punishment can serve as a deterrent only when murder is the result of premeditation and deliberation.'" Enmund v. Florida, 458 U.S. 782, 799, 102 S. Ct. 3368, 73 L. Ed. 2d 1140 (1982) (quoting Fisher v. United States, 328 U.S. 463, 484, 66 S. Ct. 1318, 90 L. Ed. 1382 (1946) (Frankfurter, J., dissenting)). For this reason, the court has found deterrence wanting where the individual in question was not capable of a sufficient cost?benefit analysis due to a lack of mental sophistication or lack of an opportunity to engage in the requisite calculus. Roper, 543 U.S. at 571-72; Atkins, 536 U.S. at 319-20; Enmund, 458 U.S. at 799-800 ("[T]here is no basis in experience for the notion that death so frequently occurs in the course of a felony for which killing is not an essential ingredient that the death penalty should be considered as a justifiable deterrent to the felony itself."). Because the innocent convict never murders, he never engages in the requisite cost benefit analysis and therefore lacks the opportunity to be deterred. Stated differently, deterrence is not served in the case of the innocent convict because there is no conduct to deter. Accordingly, deterrence does not justify executing the "actually" innocent.

Retribution is also not furthered by executing the innocent.
Retribution can be understood as either an attempt to express the
community's moral outrage or to restore balance for the wrong to the
victim. [35] Roper, 543 U.S. at 571. "The heart of the retribution
rationale is that a criminal sentence must be directly related to the
personal culpability of the criminal offender." Tison v. Arizona, 481
U.S. 137, 149, 107 S. Ct. 1676, 95 L. Ed. 2d 127 (1987). Individuals
may lack the requisite culpability for retribution through capital
punishment where diminished mental function erodes culpability,
Roper, 543 U.S. at 572, or where their actions are not sufficiently evil,
Enmund, 458 U.S. at 801. As the Supreme Court explained when
considering the death penalty for felony murder:

> For purposes of imposing the death penalty, Enmund's criminal
> culpability must be limited to his participation in the robbery, and
> his punishment must be tailored to his personal responsibility and
> moral guilt. Putting Enmund to death to avenge two killings that he
> did not commit and had no intention of committing or causing
> does not measurably contribute to the retributive end of ensuring
> that the criminal gets his just deserts. This is the judgment of most
> of the legislatures that have recently addressed the matter, and we
> have no reason to disagree with that judgment for purposes of
> construing and applying the Eighth Amendment.

Id. at 801. If a person who commits a robbery that results in felony
murder lacks the requisite culpability for retribution through capital
punishment, one who commits no crime surely lacks the culpability
to justify capital punishment on the basis of retribution. Accordingly,
neither retribution nor deterrence is served by the execution of the
innocent.

35 While retribution and revenge overlap, they are not the same.
Retribution aims to restore a harmonious balance to society; revenge sates
individual desires. Retribution restores balance by providing a wrongdoer
with his just deserts. Graham, 130 S. Ct. at 2028, Enmund, 458 U.S. at 801.
However, balance is restored only with accuracy; a mislaid blow, no matter
how swift, only increases the moral imbalance by imposing additional
unjustified suffering. Revenge, meanwhile, requires only that another suffer
as much as the victim. It desires swiftness, but requires minimal accuracy.
Revenge may be derived from either the deserving party or a simple
scapegoat. When retribution is taken against the correct party, both revenge
and retribution may be had, but neither should be mistaken for the other.

iii. Conclusion

The consensus among the states appears to be that a truly persuasive demonstration of innocence subsequent to trial renders punishment unconstitutional. Prior precedent and understanding of the Eighth Amendment accords with this consensus. Moreover, executions of the "actually" innocent do not serve any legitimate penological purpose. Accordingly, the execution of those who can make a truly persuasive demonstration of innocence fails each step of the Graham analysis. It can be said, then, that executing the "actually" innocent violates the cruel and unusual punishment clause of the Eighth Amendment of the United States Constitution. [36]

---

[36] It bears noting that this constitutional right will have little effect on the finality of state judgments. First, the right will not lengthen the present process because, presumably, it is subject to all the normal rules regarding when constitutional violations may be raised in habeas petitions. Second, the present system already allows habeas petitioners to assert their innocence subsequent to a trial, it simply requires the claim of innocence be coupled with another constitutional violation or a showing of due diligence. See 28 U.S.C. § 2244(b) (2) (B) (ii); House, 547 U.S. 518, 126 S. Ct. 2064, 165 L. Ed. 2d 1; Schlup, 513 U.S. 298, 115 S. Ct. 851, 130 L. Ed. 2d 808. Because trials are not a perfect science, a defendant with a strong case of innocence will always find a "constitutional violation" that he can attach to his innocence claim, allowing him to challenge his conviction. See, e.g., Goldman v. Winn, 565 F. Supp. 2d 200 (D. Mass. 2008); Wilson v. Vaughn, 304 F. Supp. 2d 652 (S.D. Pa. 2004), rev'd, 533 F.3d 208 (3d Cir. 2008) (illustrating that an innocent defendant will find marginal constitutional violations to attach to a persuasive claim of innocence). One would not expect any real change in the number or frequency of habeas petitions because all claims of innocence are likely already being made under present law. Third, once one acknowledges that innocent mistakes are made and discovered-- as one must in light of DNA exonerations over the past twenty years--it becomes apparent that the present system does more harm to societal respect for the criminal justice system and its judgments than a system that allows for the assertion of innocent, but clear, mistake. As a practical matter, by forcing mistakenly convicted individuals to tether those claims to constitutional mistake, the system suffers twice--once for its mistake and again for the "error" that was manufactured to allow the claim of innocence to be heard. Finally, even if this right does implicate a state's interest in finality of judgment, it is difficult to imagine that a state's finality interest can actually override an innocent individual's interest in not being punished. Cf. Patterson, 432 U.S. at 208 ("'[I]t is far worse to convict an innocent man than to let a guilty man go free.' " (quoting Winship, 397 U.S.

at 372)); Winship, 397 U.S. at 364 ("It is critical that the moral force of the criminal law not be diluted by a standard of proof that leaves people in doubt whether innocent men are being condemned.").

II. BURDEN OF PROOF

Having recognized the claim, the Court must determine the burden of proof to apply. In Herrera, the Supreme Court explained:

> [B]ecause of the very disruptive effect that entertaining claims of actual innocence would have on the need for finality in capital cases, and the enormous burden that having to retry cases based on often stale evidence would place on the States, the threshold showing for such an assumed right would necessarily be extraordinarily high.

506 U.S. at 417 (emphasis added). This language was later elaborated on in House when the Supreme Court explained that "[t]he sequence of the Court's decisions in Herrera and Schlup--first leaving unresolved the status of freestanding claims and then establishing the gateway standard--implies at the least that Herrera requires more convincing proof of innocence than Schlup." House, 547 U.S. at 555. The Supreme Court has also stated:

> The meaning of actual innocence as formulated by Sawyer, and Carrier does not merely require a showing that a reasonable doubt exists in the light of the new evidence, but rather that no reasonable juror would have found the defendant guilty. It is not the district court's independent judgment as to whether reasonable doubt exists that the standard addresses; rather the standard requires the district court to make a probabilistic determination about what reasonable, properly instructed jurors would do. Thus, a petitioner does not meet the threshold requirement unless he persuades the district court that, in light of the new evidence, no juror, acting reasonably, would have voted to find him guilty beyond a reasonable doubt.

Schlup, 513 U.S. at 329 (emphasis added). Accordingly, it is clear that the standard must be (1) extraordinarily high, (2) more demanding than Schlup, and (3) crafted from the perspective of a reasonable juror.

Mr. Davis contends that the proper burden of proof is to require a showing of "a clear probability that any reasonable juror would have reasonable doubt about his guilt." (Doc. 27 at 30 (emphasis omitted).)

Arguing before this Court, Mr. Davis clarified "clear probability" to mean a sixty percent chance. (Evidentiary Hearing Transcript at 513.) Based on Justice White's lone concurrence in Herrera and the dissent in House, the State argues that the standard should be that "no rational trier of fact could find proof of guilt beyond a reasonable doubt." [37] (Doc. 21 at 51-52 (quotations and alterations in original omitted).)

[37] This is essentially the same burden of proof applicable to a claim under Jackson v. Virginia, 443 U.S. 307, 318-19, 99 S. Ct. 2781, 61 L. Ed. 2d 560 (1979) ("[T]he relevant question is whether, after viewing the evidence in the light most favorable to the prosecution, any rational trier of fact could have found the essential elements of the crime beyond a reasonable doubt."), which sets forth the burden for showing that the evidence at trial was insufficient to establish guilt beyond a reasonable doubt.

Schlup offers a guiding principle for crafting the appropriate burden of proof: "'a standard of proof represents an attempt to instruct the factfinder concerning the degree of confidence our society thinks he should have in the correctness of factual conclusions for a particular type of adjudication.'" Schlup, 513 U.S. at 325 (quoting Winship, 397 U.S. at 369 (Harlan, J., concurring)). This suggests that the burden should be directly related to how much confidence can be placed in a jury verdict in a given situation. Conceptually, there are three general reasons why a jury might reach an erroneous verdict: (1) a constitutional error led a jury to consider something inappropriate or caused patently important evidence to be withheld, (2) a jury heard a set of facts that was complete at the time of trial but later found to be incomplete based on evidence that surfaced subsequent to the trial, and (3) a jury made an innocent mistake based upon the evidence before it. Said differently, the totality of the evidence heard by the jury vis a vis the understanding of that evidence at the time of habeas can be described three ways: (1) corrupted, (2) incomplete, or (3) complete.

The highest degree of confidence can be placed in a jury verdict when the jury heard the complete body of relevant evidence. This scenario has already given rise to a standard of review on habeas. When a petitioner challenges the sufficiency of the evidence at his trial, Jackson v. Virginia asks whether, "after viewing the evidence in the light most favorable to the prosecution, any rational trier of fact could have found the essential elements of the crime beyond a reasonable doubt." 443 U.S. 307, 318-19, 99 S. Ct. 2781, 61 L. Ed. 2d 560 (1979). Because there should be more confidence in a jury verdict rendered after a jury has heard a complete body of evidence, the Court concludes that this standard--the one proffered by the State--is too high.

The lowest degree of confidence in a jury verdict would presumably occur when the jury hears a corrupted body of evidence. Because the procedural protections in place to protect the innocent from conviction have been breached, confidence in the result of the trial is generally undermined. Accordingly, the Supreme Court has adopted a relatively low burden of proof in these cases, requiring a petitioner to show that "it is more likely than not that no reasonable juror would have convicted him in the light of the new evidence." Schlup, 513 U.S. at 327. As the Supreme Court has already explained, this burden of proof is too low for this case. [38] House, 547 U.S. at 555.

> 38 While Mr. Davis asserts that Schlup equates to a fifty-one percent chance, and his standard requires a sixty percent likelihood, the Court does not see any meaningful difference between those two standards. Even if this nine percent difference is meaningful, proof to a sixty percent certainty is not an "extraordinarily high" burden of proof. For example, if one were to receive sixty percent of his paycheck each month, he would not say that he was receiving an extraordinarily high portion of his paycheck. Accordingly, the Court rejects Mr. Davis's proposed standard as inconsistent with existing law. See Herrera, 506 U.S. at 417.

This case, which argues that the evidence heard at trial was incomplete [39] in some key manner, falls in the middle. It requires a burden higher than House, but lower than Jackson. In Schlup, the Supreme Court discussed three standards: the "more likely than not" [40] standard adopted by Schlup, the "no rational trier of fact" standard from Jackson, and the "clear and convincing" [41] standard in Sawyer. Schlup, 513 U.S. at 327-30. The Supreme Court has already explained that the showing of "more likely than not" imposes a lower burden of proof than the "clear and convincing" standard required under Sawyer. Schlup, 513 U.S. at 327. And, in the same opinion, it implied that the Sawyer standard was not quite as high as that of Jackson, which required a "binary response" as to whether "the trier of fact has power as a matter of law or it does not." Schlup, 513 U.S. at 330. While Sawyer is a factually distinct case, [42] it represents the only standard for considering actual innocence endorsed by the Supreme Court that falls in between Schlup and Jackson and appears to meet the "extraordinarily high" requirement of Herrera. Accordingly, the Court will borrow the "clear and convincing" language of Sawyer for this context. Mr. Davis must show by clear and convincing evidence that no reasonable juror would have convicted him in the light of the new evidence. [43]

39 The Court finds it fair to characterize recantation evidence or new scientific evidence as evidence that bears on the completeness of the body of evidence at trial. While the new evidence may change the manner in which the prior evidence is interpreted and the ultimate outcome of the case, it does not nullify the existence of the prior evidence.

40 This standard was originally announced in Murray v. Carrier, 477 U.S. 478, 496, 106 S. Ct. 2639, 91 L. Ed. 2d 397 (1986), and adopted as the appropriate standard for gateway claims of actual innocence in Schlup, 513 U.S. at 327-32.

41 Sawyer v. Whitley, 505 U.S. 333, 112 S. Ct. 2514, 120 L. Ed. 2d 269 (1992) set the standard of proof for showing "actual innocence" in the context of an erroneous jury verdict with respect to the sentencing phase of a capital trial. The Sawyer standard requires a petitioner to show "by clear and convincing evidence that but for constitutional error, no reasonable juror would find him eligible for the death penalty under [State] law." 505 U.S. at 348.

42 Sawyer applies in the context where one is "actually innocent of the death penalty." Schlup, 513 U.S. at 323 (internal quotations omitted). The Court has not borrowed this standard because it considers the question in this case analogous to the question of whether Mr. Davis is innocent of the death penalty. Rather, the Court has borrowed it because, based upon other Supreme Court case law, it is the only language that appears to accord with the other requirements for crafting a burden of proof in this case.

43 The Court believes this standard to be appropriate because it comports with the high level of respect society has for jury verdicts rendered subsequent to an uncorrupted process, while acknowledging that even the best efforts of society may occasionally yield results that later prove clearly incorrect.

III. APPLICATION OF FACTS TO LAW

The Court now considers whether Mr. Davis has shown, by clear and convincing evidence, that no reasonable juror would have convicted him in light of the evidence he has presented since trial. [44] Mr. Davis's post-trial evidence can be categorized by purpose: evidence that diminishes the State's initial showing of guilt and evidence that tends to prove innocence. The Court first considers each piece of evidence individually and then considers it holistically.

[44] In the case currently before this Court, Mr. Davis's guilt was proven at trial beyond a reasonable doubt, but not to a mathematical certainty. However, Mr. Davis does not challenge his conviction based on residual doubt. Nor can he, as such a challenge appears foreclosed by Supreme Court precedent. Cf. Oregon v. Guzek, 546 U.S. 517, 126 S. Ct. 1226, 163 L. Ed. 2d 1112 (2006) (doubting that there is a right to even introduce mitigation evidence regarding residual doubt much less a mandate that elimination of all residual doubt is required prior to the imposition of the death penalty). If state prosecutors in Georgia are comfortable seeking the death penalty in cases of heinous crimes where their proof creates less than an absolute certainty of guilt, and the people of Georgia, through their validly enacted laws allow such a system knowing that it may occasionally result in the erroneous imposition of punishment, Guzek suggests that the Constitution will not interfere. Regardless, this question is not before the Court and will not be considered further. The Court considers only whether Mr. Davis has satisfied the requirements for establishing a freestanding claim of actual innocence as defined above.

A. AEDPA and Factual Deference

Even in the context of an original habeas petition, the Anti-Terrorism and Effective Death Penalty Act ("AEDPA") requires deference to prior state court factual determinations. [45] 28 U.S.C. § 2254(d)(2), (e)(1); Felker v. Turpin, 518 U.S. 651, 662, 116 S. Ct. 2333, 135 L. Ed. 2d 827 (1996) ("Our authority to grant habeas relief to state prisoners is limited by § 2254 . . . ."). 28 U.S.C. § 2254(d) (2) [46] requires federal courts to defer to state court adjudications unless the state adjudication was based on an unreasonable determination of the facts. 28 U.S.C. § 2254(e) (1) [47] requires federal courts to defer to state court factual determinations unless they are disproven by clear and convincing evidence. [48] These two sections provide independent

standards of deference that courts must be careful not to merge. [49]
Miller-El v. Cockrell, 537 U.S. 322, 341-42, 123 S. Ct. 1029, 154 L.
Ed. 2d 931 (2003).

45 The State contends that language in the transfer order requires 28 U.S.C.
§ 2244(b) to be applied. (Doc. 21 at 37, 62-63.) The court disagrees. The
transfer order required this Court to determine "whether evidence that
could not have been obtained at the time of trial clearly establishes
petitioner's innocence." Davis, 130 S. Ct. at 1 (emphasis added). Section
2244(b) (2) (B) bars a Court from considering a claim unless its factual
predicate could not be discovered through the exercise of "due diligence"
and there is a showing of innocence. Section 2244(b) (2) (B) 's due diligence
requirement addresses the availability of a claim at all stages of litigation,
including prior collateral review, not simply its availability at trial. See In re
Magwood, 113 F.3d 1544, 1548 (11th Cir. 1997) Accordingly, the language
requiring this Court to consider the availability of evidence only post-trial
does not track § 2244 (b). And, as this Court has already explained, the
Supreme Court's order actually implies that § 2244(b) is inapplicable. (Doc.
11 at 3 n.3.)

There are at least two reasons why these bars may not be applicable. First,
applying these bars in the Supreme Court's original jurisdiction creates an
oddity that allows the decision of a district court to bind the Supreme Court
or limit its jurisdiction based on implied repeal of jurisdiction under
AEDPA. Cf. McCleskey v. Zant, 499 U.S. 467, 479-81, 111 S. Ct. 1454, 113
L. Ed. 2d 517 (1991) (discussing the history of § 2244(b) and res judiciata);
Rodriguez v. United States, 480 U.S. 522, 524, 107 S. Ct. 1391, 94 L. Ed. 2d
533 (1987) (implied repeals of jurisdiction are disfavored). Second, §
2244(b) likely binds only lower courts. The Supreme Court has already
suggested that § 2244(b) does not bind it but only "informs" its jurisdiction.
Felker v. Turpin, 518 U.S. 651, 662-63, 116 S. Ct. 2333, 135 L. Ed. 2d 827
(1996) This reading accords with both the structure of the bill, see 28
U.S.C. § 2244 (b) (specifically referencing circuit and district courts in § (b)
(3), (4) respectively, and requiring each type of court to apply different
burdens of proof to § (b) (1), (2), a structure that avoids the creation of
duplicative text that would otherwise be required to reprint § (b) (1), (2)
under § (b) (3), (4)), and AEDPA's legislative history, see 141 Cong. Rec.
S7596-02 (daily ed. May 26, 1995) (statement of Senator Orrin Hatch)
("[W]e restrict the filing of repetitive petitions by requiring that any second
petition be approved for filing in the district court by the court of appeals.
A repetitive petition would only be permitted in two circumstances: One, if
it raises the claim based on a new rule of constitutional law that is
retroactively applicable; or, two, if it is based on newly discovered evidence
that could not have been discovered through due diligence in time to
present the claim in the first petition and that, it proven, would show by a

clear and convincing evidence that the defendant was innocent." (emphasis added)).

46 28 U.S.C. § 2254(d) (2) provides:

> An application for a writ of habeas corpus on behalf of a person in custody pursuant to the judgment of a State court shall not be granted with respect to any claim that was adjudicated on the merits in State court proceedings unless the adjudication of the claim resulted in a decision that was based on an unreasonable determination of the facts in light of the evidence presented in the State court proceeding.

47 28 U.S.C. § 2254(e) (1) provides:

> In a proceeding instituted by an application for a writ of habeas corpus by a person in custody pursuant to the judgment of a State court, a determination of a factual issue made by a State court shall be presumed to be correct. The applicant shall have the burden of rebutting the presumption of correctness by clear and convincing evidence.

48 It bears noting that § 2254 (e) (1) deference is often inapplicable in this case. First, the State concedes this deference is inapplicable to witnesses who testified at the federal hearing, even if these witnesses' affidavits were considered by the state court. (Doc. 79 at 25-26.) Second, the order of the Supreme Court of Georgia mostly rejected the affidavits as insufficiently material to prove the ultimate fact in issue--Mr. Davis's innocence. Davis, 283 Ga. at 441-48, 660 S.E.2d at 358-63. Such determinations are relevant to § 2254(d) (2) deference rather than § 2254 (e) (1).

49 Courts distinguish these sections as follows:

> § 2254(d) (2) Is reasonableness standard would apply to the final decision reached by the state court on a determinative factual question, [and] § 2254(e) (1) 's presumption of correctness . . . to the individual factfindings, which might underlie the state court's final decision or which might be determinative of new legal issues considered by the habeas court.

Teti v. Bender, 507 F.3d 50, 58 (1st Cir. 2007). The Court will follow this distinction while adjudicating Mr. Davis's claim.

The application of 28 U.S.C. § 2254(d) (2) and (e) (1) is especially convoluted in this case because this Court held an evidentiary hearing while the state court did not. The Eleventh Circuit has explained the problem created by AEDPA deference under these circumstances:

> The argument as to why § 2254(d) might not apply in certain instances in which a federal evidentiary hearing is premised in sound practicality. If the federal evidentiary hearing uncovers new, relevant evidence that impacts upon a petitioner's claim(s) and was not before the state court, it is problematic to ascertain how a federal court would defer to the state court's determination. That is, the new, relevant evidence was never before the state court so it never considered the impact of the evidence when denying relief, and there is arguably nothing to defer to.

> In contrast, the argument that a federal evidentiary hearing does not alter the federal standard of review is as follows. AEDPA places a highly deferential standard of review in habeas cases and provides that habeas relief "shall not be granted with respect to any claim that was adjudicated on the merits in State court proceedings" unless certain conditions are met. 28 U.S.C. § 2254(d). The words "shall" and "any" are powerful words and render AEDPA applicable to all claims raised in a habeas petition regardless of whether a federal evidentiary hearing is held. After all, ADPA itself dictates under what circumstances a federal evidentiary hearing can be held. See 28 U.S.C. § 2254(e). A petitioner's habeas claim, even if subject to a proper federal evidentiary hearing, is still "any" claim for the purposes of § 2254(d) 1 highly deferential standard of review, and the new evidence in the federal proceeding is considered in determining whether the state court reached an unreasonable determination.

LeCroy v. Sec'y, Fl. Dept. Corr., 421 F.3d 1237, 1263 n.30 (11th Cir. 2005). The Supreme Court has not resolved this issue, and the circuit courts are split. Some hold AEDPA deference inapplicable under these circumstances. Bryan v. Mullin, 335 F.3d 1207, 1216 (10th Cir. 2003) (en banc); Nunes v. Mueller, 350 F.3d 1045, 1055 (9th Cir. 2003). One finds both sections applicable. Morrow v. Dretke, 367 F.3d 309, 315 (5th Cir. 2004). The majority of circuits adopt a middle ground that deference is applicable, but operates with decreased force. Teti, 507 F.3d at 58 ("'[T] he extent to which a state court provides a full and fair hearing is no longer a threshold requirement before deference applies; but it might be a consideration while applying deference under § 2254(d) (2) and § 2254 (e) (1).'" (quoting Lambert V. Blackwell, 387 F.3d 210, 235 (3d Cir. 2004))); Lambert, 387 F.3d at 235 (same); see Brown v. Smith, 551 F.3d 424, 429 (6th Cir. 2008) (where federal habeas evidentiary hearing uncovers "substantial" new evidence, AEDPA deference does not apply); Matheney v. Anderson, 377 F.3d 740, 747 (7th Cir. 2004) ('"The evidence obtained in such a hearing is quite likely to bear on the reasonableness of the state courts' adjudication . . . but we do not see why it should alter the standard of federal review.'" (quoting Pecoraro v. Walls, 286 F.3d 439, 443 (7th Cir. 2002) (alterations in original))). This Court concurs with the middle approach and applies it here. The Court now considers Mr. Davis's showing. [50]

50 The Court notes that while AEDPA deference is applicable, it has not affected any of this Court's determinations. In all cases where this deference was applicable, this Court found itself in accord with the Supreme Court of Georgia's determinations.

B. Evidence Diminishing the State's Showing at Trial (Recantation Evidence)[51]

51 To the extent that it is relevant, the evidence regarding the bullets and shell casings both diminishes the State's showing at trial and tends to show innocence. As the primary focus is on Mr. Davis's ability to prove his innocence, the Court has discussed this evidence in the section regarding innocence. See Analysis Part III.C.iv.

The Court begins by considering the recantation evidence. Courts look upon recantation evidence with suspicion. E.g., United States v. Baker, 479 F.3d 574, 578 (8th Cir. 2007); United States v. Santiago, 837 F.2d 1545, 1550 (11th Cir. 1988); United States v. Hedman, 655 F.2d 813, 818 (7th Cir. 1981). As the Eighth Circuit Court of Appeals has explained:

It is easy to understand why this should be so. The trial is the main event in the criminal process. The witnesses are there, they are sworn, they are subject to cross-examination, and the jury determines whether to believe them. The stability and finality of verdicts would be greatly disturbed if courts were too ready to entertain testimony from witnesses who have changed their minds, or who claim to have lied at the trial.

United States v. Grey Bear, 116 F.3d 349, 350 (8th Cir. 1997)

Additionally, it bears noting that even with regard to credible recantations, not all recantations are of equal value. A witness may recant only a small, insignificant portion of his prior testimony, making the recantation irrelevant. In its closing argument at trial, the State explained that the evidence of the MacPhail murder [52] was (1) eyewitness testimony regarding who was wearing the white and yellow shirts, and the actions taken by the individual in each shirt; [53] (2) personal identifications of Mr. Davis as the shooter; and (3) secondhand confessions by Mr. Davis. (See Trial Transcript at 1496-1502.) Accordingly, to actually diminish the State's case in a meaningful manner, a recantation would have to somehow attack one of these three types of evidence. With this background, the Court considers the recantation evidence.

[52] The State also referenced the evidence regarding bullets and shell casings. (Trial Transcript at 1502.) However, this evidence was offered to show that the same person who was responsible for the murder of Officer MacPhail was also responsible for the Cloverdale shooting, it was not offered as evidence to show that any specific individual committed either crime. (Id. at 1502-03.)

[53] The Court includes under this heading testimony that the same person-- the one in the white shirt--both assaulted Larry Young and shot Officer MacPhail. (Trial Transcript at 1497.)

i. Antoine Williams

Antoine Williams was the night porter at the Burger King on the night of the shooting. At trial, his testimony was used to establish that the person in the white shirt both struck Larry Young with the pistol and shot Officer MacPhail, and to directly identify Mr. Davis as the person in the white shirt. (Trial Transcript at 958-64, 969-70, 1497, 1499-1500.) Mr. Davis contends that Mr. Williams has since recanted his direct identification. (Doc. 2 at 6-7.)

The earliest statements from Antoine Williams are two statements given to the police in the days following the murder. In his first statement, he explains that the same person struck Larry Young and shot Officer MacPhail, and that this person was wearing a white shirt.

(Pet. Ex. 32-00 at 1-2.) In his second statement, Antoine Williams identified Mr. Davis as the shooter from a photo array with a sixty percent certainty. (Pet. Ex. 32-PP at 1-2.) He also stated that he could distinguish yellow and white on the night in question, despite watching the events through the tinted windows of his car. (Id. at 1-2.)

At trial, Mr. Williams identified Mr. Davis as the shooter and testified that the same person who struck Larry Young shot Officer MacPhail. (Trial Transcript at 958-64.) However, he initially backed off his earlier statement about his ability to distinguish the yellow and white shirts. [54] (Id.) Mr. Williams next statement, the recantation affidavit, stated that he was unsure of his direct identification of Mr. Davis as the shooter. [55] (Doc. 3, Ex. 4 at 3.)

[54] Despite initially recanting his statement regarding the shirt colors, Mr. Williams ultimately reaffirmed his statement to the police, explaining that his memory would have been better closer to the events in question. (See Trial Transcript at 958-60.)

[55] In his affidavit and at the evidentiary hearing, Mr. Williams also explained that he signed his police statements without reviewing them because he cannot read. (Doc. 3, Ex. 4 at 3; Evidentiary Hearing Transcript at 12-13.) However, this fact is a red herring. While Mr. Williams may have been unable to read his police statements, he does not contest the accuracy of their contents. (Evidentiary Hearing Transcript at 10-26.)

At the evidentiary hearing, Mr. Williams testified that he was not sure who shot the police officer and that he felt pressure to identify Mr. Davis as the shooter at trial. (Evidentiary Hearing Transcript at 12-15.) However, Mr. Williams never testified that his earlier statement or testimony were false, only that he could not remember what he said. [56] (Id. at 15-21.) He also contradicted his testimony regarding feeling pressured at trial during cross-examination:

Q: But it's your testimony the police never pressured you to say anything in those two statements from August 19th or August--

A: --Ma'am, nobody never pressured me, ma'am. just.

Q: And nobody suggested for you to say anything specific?

A: No, ma'am, never.

(Id. at 24.)

56 For example, with respect to his initial identification of Mr. Davis, Mr. Williams testified: 'SQ: Do you remember telling [Detective Ramsey] you were 60 percent sure that Troy Davis was the person that shot Officer MacPhail? A: I maybe did, ma'am. I can't remember. Being honest, I can't." (Evidentiary Hearing Transcript at 21.) Saying that one cannot remember his prior testimony is different from admitting that it is false.

Mr. Williams's testimony does not diminish the State's case. First, it is not proper to consider Mr. Williams's testimony a recantation--he never indicated that his earlier statements were false, only that he can no longer remember what he said. And, to the extent that his present testimony is inconsistent with what he had previously said, he indicated that his memory would have been better at the time of the crime. (Id. at 18.) Second, Mr. Williams testified that his prior testimony was never coerced by state officials. 57 (Id. at 18-19, 24.) This testimony accords with the record; Mr. Williams's statements were far from ideal and if the State was to coerce testimony, it surely would have coerced testimony more favorable than that actually provided by Mr. Williams. (See Pet. Ex. 32-PP at 1 (direct identification was only sixty percent certain) Trial Transcript at 958-60, 972 (unable to distinguish between yellow and white shirt).) Accordingly, Mr. Williams's testimony established only that his statements were never coerced and that he can no longer remember his previous statements--not that his prior testimony was false or, more importantly, that Mr. Davis was not the shooter. 58

57 Although Mr. Williams's own testimony undermines allegations of coercion, there was also credible testimony by the officers and prosecutors that Mr. Williams was not coerced. (Evidentiary Hearing Transcript at 306, 347, 442.)

58 Mr. Davis will surely object to this finding, claiming that Mr. Williams unequivocally identified Mr. Davis at trial as the shooter and has now "recanted" that identification. However, such a claim would be an exaggeration both as to the recantation and trial testimony. At trial, Mr. Williams's identification was not unequivocal, he testified on cross-examination that his initial identification was to a certainty of only sixty percent (Trial Transcript at 969-70) and never stated that his certainty had increased by the time of trial. Before this Court, Mr. Williams again expressed uncertainty as to the shooter's identity, but he never testified that Mr. Davis was, in fact, not the shooter. (See Evidentiary Hearing Transcript at 10-26.) This is a far cry from Mr. Williams testifying that he lied under oath when identifying Mr. Davis at trial or that, despite his prior statements,

he is now sure that Mr. Davis was, in fact, not the shooter. Moreover, Mr. Williams testified that his memory would have been better closer to the events in question, implicitly deferring to his prior statements. (See id. at 18.)

ii. Kevin McQueen

Kevin McQueen was the "jailhouse snitch." At trial, his testimony was used to relate Mr. Davis's confession to the MacPhail murder. (Trial Transcript at 1230-32, 1501.) Mr. Davis contends that Mr. McQueen admits his prior testimony was a "complete fabrication." (Doc. 2 at 7.)

At trial, Mr. McQueen claimed that Mr. Davis confessed the following events to him. Mr. Davis began his night by shooting at the group from Yamacraw--the Cloverdale shooting. (Trial Transcript at 1230.) Mr. Davis then went to his girlfriend's house for a time, and later to the Burger King to eat breakfast. (Id. at 1231.) While at Burger King, Mr. Davis ran into someone who "owed [him] money to buy dope." (Id.) There was a fight regarding the drug money, and when Officer MacPhail came over, Mr. Davis shot him. (Id. at 1231-32.)

At the hearing before this Court, Mr. McQueen testified that there was 'no truth" to his trial testimony. (Evidentiary Hearing Transcript at 28.) He claimed that he fabricated the testimony to get revenge on Mr. Davis for an altercation in the jail and because he received benefits from the State. (Id. at 29, 32.) Mr. McQueen put the same recantation into an affidavit on December 5, 1996, but stated his only reason for testifying falsely was the altercation between he and Mr. Davis. (Doc. 3, Ex. 6 at 1-2.)

Other than claiming that Mr. Davis was guilty of both the MacPhail murder and Cloverdale shooting, Mr. McQueen's trial testimony totally contradicts the events of the night as described by numerous other State witnesses. Supra Background Part III.N. Indeed, while other witnesses described a fight over alcohol, Mr. McQueen described a fight over drugs; and while other witnesses claimed Mr. Davis went to shoot pool immediately prior to the murder, Mr. McQueen claimed Mr. Davis went to get breakfast. Id. These inconsistencies make it clear that Mr. McQueen's trial testimony was false, a fact confirmed by Mr. McQueen's recantation. [59] (Evidentiary

Hearing Transcript at 31.) Given that Mr. McQueen's trial testimony was so clearly fabricated, and was actually contrary to the State's theory of the case, it is unclear why the State persists in trying to support its veracity. (Id. at 33-39.) Regardless, the recantation is credible, with the exception of the allegation of prosecutorial inducements, but only minimally reduces the State's showing at trial given the obviously false nature of the trial testimony." [60]

59 While the Court credits Mr. McQueen's recantation, it does not credit the portion of his testimony claiming that he received inducements to testify at trial. As Mr. Lock credibility testified, Mr. McQueen received no favorable treatment for his testimony. (Evidentiary Hearing Transcript at 453-54 ("Q: So my question to you, Mr. Lock, is: to your knowledge as the chief assistant district attorney at this time did Mr. McQueen get any benefit for the information that he was giving . . . regarding Mr. Davis? A: No, and I'm relatively certain that any assistant district attorney that contemplated doing that would have come to me about doing it.").)

60 That is to say, if a witness testified credibly at trial and then recanted, that recantation would obviously be much more damaging to the State's case than a recantation by a witness who only confirmed what should have been apparent to all at the time of trial--that the testimony was fabricated.

iii. Jeffery Sapp

Jeffery Sapp was a long-time friend of Mr. Davis. At trial, Mr. Sapp's testimony was used to relate Mr. Davis's confession to the MacPhail shooting. [61] (Trial Transcript at 1251-52, 1501.) Mr. Davis contends that Mr. Sapp has "recanted his testimony in full" and that his false trial testimony was "the result of police pressure." (Doc. 2 at 7-8.)

61 Monty Holmes provided similar statements to the police regarding a confession by Mr. Davis. Supra Background Part I.T. Monty Holmes, who did not testify at trial, has since recanted his police statement, claiming police coercion. (Doc. 3, Ex. 33 at 2.) Because Mr. Holmes's testimony did not form a portion of the evidence presented to the jury, his recantation does not diminish the proof at trial. Moreover, the State provided credible, live testimony from Officers Ramsey and Oglesby that Mr. Holmes was not coerced by police. (Evidentiary Hearing Transcript at 247, 317.)

Jeffery Sapp testified twice in this case, first at Recorder's Court and then at trial. Both times he testified that Mr. Davis confessed to shooting Officer MacPhail, but that Mr. Davis claimed the shooting was in self-defense. (Recorder's Court Transcript at 166-67; Trial Transcript at 1251-52.) Under direct-examination at trial, Mr. Sapp further testified that he had made up a portion of Mr. Davis's confession. (Trial Transcript at 1253.) In his recantation affidavit, Mr. Sapp claimed that he fabricated the entire confession due to police harassment. (Doc. 3, Ex. 7 at 1-2.) At the hearing before this Court, Mr. Sapp again testified that he falsified Mr. Davis's entire confession due to police pressure. (Evidentiary Hearing Transcript at 51-57.) In addition to this testimony, Mr. Sapp attempted to lie about other facts regarding this case to exculpate Mr. Davis. For example, he attempted to hide his knowledge of Mr. Davis's street name: Rough as Hell ("RAH") [62] (Id. at 61.)

> 62 Sapp testified as follows:
>
>> Q: And what does Rah stand for?
>>
>> A: Raheem.
>>
>> Q: Does it also stand for 'Rough as Hell?"
>>
>> A: No, ma'am. It's like a Muslim name that the older guys gave us to quit eating pork.
>
> (Evidentiary Hearing Transcript at 61.) This testimony cannot be characterized as anything other than a direct lie by Mr. Sapp, who long ago testified to his knowledge of what RAH stood for. (Recorder's Court Transcript at 162.)

Jeffery Sapp's recantation is valueless because it is not credible. First, as noted above, his false exculpatory testimony at the hearing indicates that he was not a credible witness. Second, the truth of his trial testimony is corroborated by other statements given to police. (Id. at 351.) Third, his claims of state coercion are impossible to square with various aspects of his allegedly false testimony, such as claiming that Mr. Davis acted in self-defense. [63] (Trial Transcript at 1253.) Indeed, if the State wanted to coerce false testimony, they would not include within it an affirmative defense. Also, Mr. Sapp felt comfortable enough at trial to claim that a portion of his police statement was false, dealing with some details of Mr. Davis's confession, but still testified that Mr. Davis confessed to the MacPhail shooting. [64] (Id. at 1251-55.) Fourth, his claims of state coercion are refuted by credible, contrary testimony from both prosecutors and Officer Ramsey. (Evidentiary Hearing Transcript at 240, 442, 465.) In sum, neither Mr. Sapp's recantation nor his claims of police coercion are credible. Accordingly, his recantation does not diminish the State's case.

63 Ironically, at the hearing there was credible testimony from Officer Ramsey that Mr. Davis's mother threatened Mr. Sapp should he testify at trial. (Evidentiary Hearing Transcript at 350-51.)

64 Even if Mr. Sapp's claims of fabricating a confession were credible, they are not new evidence that was unavailable prior to trial. At trial he testified:

> Q: Do you recall making a statement to the police about this matter?
>
> A: Yeah.
>
> Q: Do you recall making the statement on August 21 in the middle of the afternoon?
>
> A: No, they came to my house that morning, about two o'clock in the morning.
>
> Q: Two o'clock in the morning?
>
> A: Yeah, beating on my door, woke me up, so you know, I just said a lot of stuff that I ain't even meant. A lot of stuff he didn't even tell me, I just made up.
>
> ...
>
> Q: Do you remember what you said in that statement?
>
> A: No, I can't remember what I said.
>
> ...
>
> A: He shot the officer and got a good look at him, and it was self-defense. And all the rest, I just said. He never did tell me any of that.

(Trial Transcript at 1253.) His present recantation is a second attempt at recantation in which he goes further than he did at trial; it is new only in its breadth and rationale, not in its existence. Moreover, it is unclear why, if Mr. Sapp was being coerced to testify, he felt comfortable testifying that his previous inculpatory testimony was largely false.

iv. Darrell Collins

Darrell Collins was the third individual involved in the altercation
with Larry Young. At trial, he testified that Mr. Davis was wearing
the white shirt and assaulted Larry Young. [65] (Trial Transcript at
1124, 1128, 1158, 1497.) According to Mr. Davis, Darrell Collins has
since recanted the latter portion of that testimony, which was
originally secured through police coercion. (Doc. 2 at 6.)

[65] Mr. Collins also told the police that Mr. Davis was responsible for the
Cloverdale shooting, but recanted this testimony at trial, (Trial Transcript at
1120.) He also testified at trial that he included this in his police statement
due to police coercion. (Id. at 1137.)

In statements that Mr. Collins gave to the police in the days following
the shootings, he stated that Mr. Davis was responsible for the
Cloverdale shooting, struck Larry Young on the head, and wore a
white shirt on the night of the incidents. (Pet. Ex. 32-C at 1-2, Pet.
Ex. 32-D at 2.) At the trial, Mr. Collins reaffirmed that Mr. Davis was
wearing the white shirt and assaulted Mr. Young. (Trial Transcript at
1124, 1128, 1158.) However, Mr. Collins testified that he lied about
Mr. Davis's involvement in the Cloverdale shooting due to police
intimidation. (Id. at 1120.)

In his recantation affidavit, Mr. Collins claimed a second lie--that he
never saw Mr. Davis strike Larry Young. (Doc. 3, Ex. 3 at 2-3.) He
averred that he was comfortable revealing the first lie at trial but not
the second because he felt the police cared more about whether Mr.
Davis assaulted Mr. Young than Mr. Davis's responsibility for the
Cloverdale shooting. (Id.) At the hearing, Mr. Collins again claimed
that he lied about both the assault on Larry Young and the
Cloverdale incident due to police coercion. (Evidentiary Hearing
Transcript at 83, 91, 94.) Specifically, he claims that he simply
parroted what the police told him to say. (Id. at 88-91, 96, 106-07,
118.) However, he did not recant his earlier testimony that Mr. Davis
was wearing the white shirt on the night of the shootings. [66] (Id. at
115, 129.)

[66] At the hearing, Mr. Collins did not recant his testimony regarding the
white shirt. Instead, he testified that he presently had no memory of what
color shirt Mr. Davis was wearing that night, but would assume that

whatever he told the police about the color of Mr. Davis's shirt would have been a lie because all inculpatory testimony he provided is presumptively false in his mind. (Evidentiary Hearing Transcript at 129.) Of course, that statement is very different from stating that, as a matter of his own knowledge, he is sure that he was lying when he placed Mr. Davis in the white shirt.

Mr. Collins testimony is neither credible nor a full recantation. First, regardless of the recantation, Mr. Collins's previous testimony, that has never been unequivocally recanted, still provides significant evidence of Mr. Davis's guilt by placing him in the white shirt. Second, if Mr. Collins's claim that he simply parroted false statements fed to him by police is truthful, query why Mr. Collins never directly identified Mr. Davis as Officer MacPhail's murderer. Surely, this would have been the best available false testimony, and given Mr. Collins's proximity to the murder it would have been as reasonable as any other false testimony. Third, there was credible testimony from Officer Sweeney and Mr. Lock that Mr. Collins's testimony was not coerced. [67] (Id. at 322-23, 442.) Fourth, Mr. Collins generally lacked credibility, testifying to an implausible version of events: that he was less than ten feet [68] from Larry Young when the assault occurred and did not turn away from the confrontation until Officer MacPhail arrived, but saw nothing. (Id. at 83-84, 109-10.) Given the close proximity, it would be safe to assume that surely Mr. Collins saw either Mr. Coles or Mr. Davis strike Mr. Young--not that Mr. Coles simply saw nothing. Because Mr. Collins continues to provide evidence of Mr. Davis's guilt and his recantation is not credible, his testimony does not diminish the State's case.

67 Further, even if Mr. Collins's allegations regarding coercion and false testimony are true, they are not new. Mr. Collins testified at trial that he was coerced and that his statements regarding Mr. Davis's involvement in the Cloverdale shooting were fabricated. (Trial Transcript at 1143.) Moreover, his explanation as to why he revealed only the lie regarding the Cloverdale shooting at trial is not believable. (See Doc. 3, Ex. 3 at 2-3 (explaining that Mr. Collins believed the police cared more about his false testimony regarding Mr. Young than the Cloverdale incident).) Indeed, it would be puzzling to think that the police would not find Mr. Collins's accusations of harassment in the context of the Cloverdale shooting offensive but would be bothered by the exact same allegations with respect to the assault on Larry Young.

68 Mr. Collins testified that he was as close to the assault as he was to the court reporter while he was on the witness stand-- a distance of approximately five feet. (Evidentiary Hearing Transcript at 112.)

v. Harriett Murra

Harriett Murray was Larry Young's girlfriend. At trial, her testimony was used to place Mr. Davis in the white shirt and to directly identify him as the gunman in the MacPhail shooting. (Trial Transcript at 846-51, 856, 1497-98.) Mr. Davis contends that Ms. Murray's "recantation" affidavit is important because it described Mr. Coles and not Mr. Davis as the shooter. (Doc. 2 at 7.) Ms. Murray is deceased and did not testify at the evidentiary hearing.

The first recorded statements by Ms. Murray are two police statements; one on August 19, 1989 and one on August 24, 1989. In the former, she described Officer MacPhail's shooter as wearing a white shirt. (Pet. Ex. 32-U at 2.) In the latter, Ms. Murray identified Troy Davis as the shooter by first identifying Mr. Davis as one of the three men at the shooting, and then using a process of elimination-- she eliminated Mr. Coles as the shooter because she recognized him as the person in the yellow shirt and Mr. Collins because he was too short to be the person in the white shirt. (Pet. Ex. 32-V at 2.)

During her Recorder's Court and trial testimony, Ms. Murray testified that the shooter was wearing a white shirt and was the same person who assaulted Mr. Young. (Recorder's Court Transcript at 56-58, 60-63; Trial Transcript at 846-51.) At trial, Ms. Murray also directly identified Mr. Davis as the gunman. (Id. at 865.) Ms. Murray was also thoroughly cross-examined at trial as to discrepancies between her various statements regarding the assault on Larry Young, and her difficulty in indentifying Mr. Davis as Officer MacPhail's murderer. (Id. at 871-79, 888-89.)

Ms. Murray's "recantation" is an unnotarized affidavit, begrudgingly obtained. (Evidentiary Hearing Transcript at 41 ("Q: Mr. Hanusz, can you explain why the affidavit was not notarized. A: The affidavit was not notarized because neither Mr. Mack nor myself are South Carolina notaries, and Ms. Murray would not allow us time to get a notary or accompany us to a notary to have it sworn.").) It does not contain any direct recantation, any admission that Ms. Murray lied under oath, or even a statement that Ms. Murray was aware that her affidavit varied from her trial testimony. [69] (Doc. 3, Ex. 8 at 1.) The only "recantation" in the affidavit is an indirect one--Ms. Murray states that she saw the "man who was arguing with Larry, chasing him from the Time-Saver, and who slapped Larry shoot the police officer." (Id. (emphasis added).) Mr. Davis finds this change important because Ms. Murray indicated that Mr. Coles was arguing with Mr. Young, despite testifying that Mr. Davis slapped Larry Young and shot Officer MacPhail. On this basis, Mr. Davis reasons that Ms. Murray has now identified Mr. Coles as the shooter instead of Mr. Davis. (Doc. 2 at 7.)

[69] The affidavit does not allege police coercion. (Doc. 3, Ex. 8.) However, it bears noting that there was credible testimony at the hearing that Ms. Murray was not coerced. (Evidentiary Hearing Transcript at 288-89.)

This affidavit is not helpful to Mr. Davis's showing because it seems unlikely that it was intended to recant or alter Ms. Murray's testimony regarding who shot Officer MacPhail. It would have been a simple matter for Ms. Murray to directly state that her identification at trial of Mr. Davis as the murderer was mistaken, but she chose not to do so. To the contrary, her affidavit, at first blush, actually appears to affirm her trial testimony; only a close examination reveals the minor inconsistency--that the same person who shot Officer MacPhail and assaulted Larry Young, also argued with Larry Young. (See Doc. 3, Ex. 8.) Given that Ms. Murray spent a minimal amount of time reviewing the affidavit, even refusing to wait to have it notarized, it seems likely that she was unaware of this inconsistency. (See Evidentiary Hearing Transcript at 41.) This reading is confirmed by her behavior regarding the securing of the affidavit. Surely if Ms. Murray believed her testimony placed an innocent man on death row, she would have found time to wait for a notary public to validate her Statement.

More importantly, it is not obvious that the implication of this 'recantation" even exculpates Mr. Davis. Ms. Murray's affidavit simply states that the same individual who assaulted Larry Young and shot Officer MacPhail, also argued with Larry Young. (Doc. 3, Ex. 8 at 11.) Nowhere does it provide any identifying information as to who took all three actions. That is, there is no way to know whether

Ms. Murray believed that Mr. Coles or Mr. Davis took all three actions. Moreover, the affidavit states that the individual argued with Larry Young, it does not attribute any specific threats to him. (Id.) It could easily be that Ms. Murray considered all three of the individuals to have been "arguing" with Larry Young, an interpretation that does not require any implied recantation of Ms. Murray's prior testimony. Accordingly, the Court finds this affidavit valueless to Mr. Davis's showing. [70]

> [70] Even it this Court adopted Mr. Davis's reading of this affidavit, it would be valueless because it contains no new evidence. As Mr. Davis notes, the only way to understand this affidavit as a recantation is by reference to inconsistencies between her initial police statements and later testimony. (Doe. 2 at 7.) These same inconsistencies were known to Mr. Davis at trial and were put before the jury. (Id. at 871-79, 888-89.)

vi. Dorothy Ferrell[71]

> [71] At the hearing, the admission of Ms. Ferrell's affidavit was discussed, but never decided due to an intervening discussion. (Evidentiary Hearing Transcript at 458-73.) However, Ms. Ferrell's affidavit is already in the record in this case because it was presented with Mr. Davis's first federal habeas petition. (See Doc. 3 at 2.) Therefore, resubmitting it at the hearing was unnecessary to require its consideration by this Court.

Dorothy Ferrell was a guest at the Thunderbird Motel, located across Oglethorpe Avenue from the Burger King parking lot. At trial, Ms. Ferrell's testimony was used to show that the shooter was wearing a white shirt and to directly identify Mr. Davis as the gunman. (Trial Transcript at 1015, 1021, 1497, 1499.) Mr. Davis contends that Ms. Ferrell has clearly disavowed her prior statement, stating that she lied at his trial based on promises of favorable treatment by the District Attorney. (Doc. 2 at 5-6.) Mr. Davis intentionally declined to allow Ms. Ferrell to testify, preventing her testimony from being challenged on cross-examination and denying this Court the opportunity to personally assess her credibility. (Evidentiary Hearing Transcript at 272-73.)

Ms. Ferrell gave two statements to the police: one on August 19, 1989 and one on August 24, 1989. In the former, she described the shooter as wearing a white shirt. (Pet. Ex. 32-Y at 2.) In the latter, she again related that the shooter was wearing a white shirt. (Pet. Ex. 32-Z at 4.) She also identified Mr. Davis from a photo line-up and discussed a prior identification of Mr. Davis based on a picture she saw in a police cruiser; however, she admitted to seeing a picture of Mr. Davis on the news between the two identifications. (Id. at 2-4.) Both at the probable cause hearing and at trial, Ms. Ferrell testified that that shooter was wearing a white shirt and directly identified Mr. Davis as the shooter. (Recorder's Court Transcript at 137-40; Trial Transcript at 1015, 1021.) At trial, a number of inconsistencies between her trial testimony and prior testimony were pointed out for the jury during cross-examination. (Id. at 1043-52.)

In her recantation affidavit, Ms. Ferrell claims that she never saw who shot the police officer and that her testimony was coerced. (Doc. 3, Ex. 1.) Mr. Davis has also submitted a letter from Ms. Ferrell to District Attorney Spencer Lawton, asking for special treatment for her trial testimony. [72] (Doc. 3, Ex. 2.) Ms. Ferrell did not testify at the evidentiary hearing. [73] Unlike Ms. Murray, Ms. Ferrell was available to testify and, in fact, was sitting just outside the courtroom waiting to be called to testify. (Evidentiary Hearing Transcript at 272-73.) Despite her ready availability, Mr. Davis made the tactical decision not to call her to the witness stand. [74] (Id.) This decision is especially curious because, based upon the contents of her affidavit and her lack of any obvious connections to Mr. Davis, it would appear she should have been his star witness.

72 At the evidentiary hearing, Ms. Ferrell did not testify at all, and Mr. Lawton was never questioned regarding inducements to Dorothy Ferrell. (Evidentiary Hearing Transcript at 456-65.) Even if the letter was sent, there is no evidence that Mr. Lawton offered any inducement to Ms. Ferrell in exchange for her testimony.

73 Given that Mr. Davis specifically requested this hearing, claiming that a determination based on affidavits was insufficient (Doc. 2 at 28), his decision to rely on an affidavit where live testimony was readily available strongly suggests his belief that this recantation would not have held up under cross-examination.

74 Mr. Davis explained the decision not to call Ms. Ferrell as based upon "the circumstances under which she's been avoiding the Petitioner made us reluctant to call her, even though she was perfectly willing to meet with the state yesterday." (Evidentiary Hearing Transcript at 273.)

Ms. Ferrell's affidavit is a clear recantation, but Mr. Davis's intentional decision to keep Ms. Ferrell from testifying destroys nearly its entire value. In determining actual innocence, affidavits are disfavored because the affiants' statements are obtained without the benefit of cross-examination and an opportunity to make credibility determinations." Herrera, 506 U.S. at 417. Surely, this general antipathy towards affidavit testimony counts double where the affiant is available, and the affidavit is submitted in lieu of live testimony to prevent cross-examination and credibility determinations. [75] Moreover, much of Ms. Ferrell's affidavit testimony was directly contradicted by credible, live testimony at the hearing. Officer Ramsey testified that he never coerced her testimony in any way or suggested what the contents of her testimony should be, and that Ms. Ferrell actually approached a different officer without solicitation and identified Mr. Davis as the shooter. (Evidentiary Hearing Transcript at 342-44.) And, Mr. Lock credibly testified that he never attempted to coerce a witness to stick to a prior statement. (Evidentiary Hearing Transcript at 442.) Given the suspicious manner in which this recantation was presented and the credible live testimony contradicting it, the recantation holds very little weight.

[75] This Court made very clear to Mr. Davis that presenting the affidavit instead of live testimony would severely diminish the value of its contents because he was intentionally preventing the State from cross-examining the witness. (Evidentiary Hearing Transcript at 272-73.) Mr. Davis was apparently so concerned as to what Ms. Ferrell would say on the stand that he explained, "[w]e understand that her testimony is not going to be afforded as much weight. We're okay with that." (Id. at 273.)

vii. Larry Young

Larry Young was the individual assaulted in the Burger King parking lot. At trial, his testimony was used to establish that his assailant was definitely not the person in the yellow shirt, that the person in the yellow shirt was Mr. Coles, and that the person in the white shirt struck him. (Trial Transcript at 801-02, 805-06, 811-13, 832-33, 1497.) Mr. Davis contends that Mr. Young has recanted his trial testimony. (Doc. 2 at 6.)

Mr. Young gave a statement to the police on August 19, 1989. He stated that he was not sure, but that he believed his assailant was the man in the white shirt. (Pet. Ex. 32-N at 3.) He also gave a detailed description of the man in the yellow shirt. (Id. at 6.) At the probable cause hearing, Mr. Young testified that the person in the yellow shirt was Mr. Coles, and that he was assaulted by someone other than Mr. Coles, likely the person in the white shirt. (Recorder's Court Transcript at 12-14, 18-21, 43.) At trial, Mr. Young testified that he was arguing with the person in the yellow shirt, that the person in the yellow shirt was not Mr. Davis, and that he was not sure who struck him but did not believe it was the person in the yellow shirt. [76] (Id. at 801-02, 805-06, 811-13, 832-33.) In his recantation affidavit, he claims that the police refused to allow him medical treatment and that his testimony was coerced. (Doc. 3, Ex. 5.) Like Mr. Collins, Mr. Young claims he testified by simply stating what the police wanted him to say. (Id.) Mr. Young was included on Mr. Davis's witness list and was expected to testify at the evidentiary hearing. (Doc. 45 at 1.) However, Mr. Young was never called to the stand.

[76] While Mr. Young's testimony indicated that he did not know exactly who struck him, in closing argument the prosecutor did treat Mr. Young's testimony as claiming that the individual in the white shirt assaulted him. (Trial Transcript at 1497.) Accordingly, the Court will treat Mr. Young's testimony as if it was used to help establish that the white shirt assaulted him.

Like the affidavit of Ms. Ferrell, the value of Mr. Young's affidavit is minimal. First, affidavits are disfavored in this context because they do not allow for cross-examination and credibility determinations. Herrera, 506 U.S. at 417. Just as with Ms. Ferrell, Mr. Davis chose to present less reliable affidavit evidence of Mr. Young's testimony to avoid cross-examination. Second, Officer Whitcomb testified credibly that he neither coerced Mr. Young's testimony nor suggested to him what to say. (Evidentiary Hearing Transcript at 253-55.) Mr. Young was not present to contradict this testimony, and his affidavit is insufficient for the task. [77] Accordingly, this affidavit, like Ms. Ferrell's, carries some, but not much weight.

[77] Moreover, as with many other witnesses, if the State was prepared to coerce false testimony, they could have coerced much more inculpatory information. Mr. Young was at the scene of the murder and was the victim of the assault. Surely the State would have had Mr. Young directly identify Mr. Davis at trial if they were looking to coerce false testimony.

viii. Summary

Not all recantations are created equal; a witness may recant only a portion of their testimony or the witness may recant in a manner that is not credible. To hear Mr. Davis tell it, this case involves credible, consistent recantations by seven of nine state witnesses. (Doc. 2 at 5-11.) However, this vastly overstates his evidence. Two of the recanting witnesses neither directly state that they lied at trial nor claim that their previous testimony was coerced. Supra Analysis Parts III.B.i (Antoine Williams), III.B.v (Harriet Murray). Two other recantations were impossible to believe, with a host of intrinsic reasons why their author's recantation could not be trusted, and the recantations were contradicted by credible, live testimony. Id. Parts III.B.iii (Jeffrey Sapp), III.B.iv (Darrell Collins). Two more recantations were intentionally and suspiciously offered in affidavit form rather than as live testimony, blocking any meaningful cross-examination by the state or credibility determination by this Court. Id. Parts III.B.vi (Dorothy Farrell), III.B.vii (Larry Young). Moreover, these affidavit recantations were contradicted by credible, live testimony. While these latter two recantations are not totally valueless, their import is greatly diminished by the suspicious way in which they were offered and the live, contrary testimony. Finally, Kevin McQueen's recantation is credible, but his testimony at trial was patently false, as evidenced by its several inconsistencies with the State's version of the events on the night in question. Id. Part III.B.ii (Kevin McQueen). Accordingly, it is hard to believe Mr. McQueen's testimony at trial was important to the conviction, rendering his recantation of limited value. Ultimately, four of Mr. Davis's recantations do not diminish the State's case because a reasonable juror would disregard the recantation, not the earlier testimony; and the three others only minimally diminish the State's case.

C. Other Evidence

Mr. Davis also offers evidence to directly prove his innocence, as opposed to simply diminishing the State's case. This evidence includes: (1) hearsay confessions by Mr. Coles, (2) statements regarding Mr. Coles conduct subsequent to the murder, (3) alternative eyewitness accounts, and (4) new evidence regarding the physical evidence in this case.

i. Hearsay Confessions

Mr. Davis has proffered several hearsay confessions by Mr. Coles regarding the murder of Officer MacPhail. At the hearing, both Mr. Hargrove [78] and Mr. Gordon [79] testified that Mr. Coles confessed Officer MacPhail's murder to them. (Evidentiary Hearing Transcript at 156-173, 192-94.) The record also contains affidavits from Shirley Riley [80] and Darold Taylor [81] relating hearsay confessions. (Doc. 3, Exs. 17, 18.) Mr. Davis contends that these confessions are "powerful" evidence of his innocence. [82] (Doc. 84 at 17.) While the confessions are not meaningless, they lack the power imparted to them by Mr. Davis.

78 Mr. Hargove testified that Mr. Coles confessed the murder to him while at a house party. (Evidentiary Hearing Transcript at 157, 162-63.)

79 Mr. Gordon contends that Mr. Coles stated that "I shouldn't' a did that shit," but Mr. Gordon can only speculate as to the meaning of these words. (Evidentiary Hearing Transcript at 193-94.) It is not clear that "that shit" refers to murdering Officer MacPhail, it could just as easily refer to hassling Larry Young and starting the events of that evening in motion. However, for the purposes of this petition, the Court will assume that Mr. Coles was referring to Officer MacPhail's murder.

80 Ms. Riley averred that Mr. Coles confessed the murder to her, but that she suspected the confession was a lie to impress her. (Doc. 3, Ex. 17 at 1.)

81 Mr. Taylor stated that Mr. Coles once confessed the murder to him, but told Mr. Taylor to "stay out his business" when pressed on the issue. (Doc. 3, Ex. 18 at 5-6.)

82 Mr. Davis attempted to offer an additional hearsay confession through Ms. Qulana Glover. The Court declined to admit this confession for reasons stated at the hearing and in its order on the motion for reconsideration. (Evidentiary Hearing Transcript at 480-83; Doc. 91.) However, the Court notes that it is aware of the contents of Ms. Glover's testimony. (Evidentiary Hearing Transcript at 483.) That testimony would have been cumulative and would have suffered from the same defects discussed in this section. Accordingly, had the Court considered the testimony, it would have had no effect on the outcome of this case.

Confessions composed of hearsay are "particularly suspect" because the reliability of the underlying confession will often be impossible to ascertain. See Herrera, 506 U.S. at 417. When other petitioners have attempted to use hearsay confessions as part of a Herrera showing, the showing was found wanting even when the confessions were offered in conjunction with other evidence of innocence. See, e.g., House, 547 U.S. at 555 ("We conclude here, much as in Herrera, that whatever burden a hypothetical freestanding innocence claim would require, this petitioner has not satisfied it."); Herrera, 506 U.S. at 417; Cooper v. Brown, 510 F.3d 870, 885 (9th Cir. 2007). The previous failures of such confessions to satisfy Herrera lead to the conclusion that while hearsay confessions may tip the balance in an otherwise close case, they will rarely, if ever, form the crux of a showing of actual innocence. [83]

> [83] This conclusion rests on sound considerations. As the Supreme Court of Georgia noted, if such proof could form the crux of a showing of innocence, it would be easy for " 'a person [to] subvert the ends of justice by [falsely] admitting the crime to others and then absenting himself.' " Davis, 283 Ga. at 444, 660 S.E.2d at 360 (quoting Timberlake v. State, 246 Ga. 488, 492, 271 S.E.2d 792, 796 (1980)) (alteration in original) Likewise, for any minimally connected convict, rounding up several persons who will concoct false confessions should not be difficult. This is likely why such proof has never been sufficient under Herrera. Cf. House, 547 U.S. at 540; Herrera, 506 U.S. at 417.

This case illustrates exactly why this type of evidence is only marginally probative. Even if this Court found the witnesses relating the confessions credible, that would not prove that Mr. Coles was being truthful when confessing to these witnesses. [84] Here, assuming Mr. Coles actually made the confessions, there is an obvious explanation for why he would have confessed falsely--he believed that his reputation as a dangerous individual would be enhanced if he took credit for murdering Officer MacPhail. [85] (See Doc. 3, Ex. 17 at 1.) Mr. Davis had the burden of proving the confessions were truthful and not made for the above reason. [86] Of course, the easiest way to meet that burden would have been to put Mr. Coles on the stand and show him not to be credible on this subject. [87] Additionally, if Mr. Davis had other highly probative evidence of his innocence or Mr. Coles's guilt--for example, if Mr. Coles firearm was found and determined to be the murder weapon--that too would render these confessions more meaningful. However, there is no truly persuasive evidence substantiating the hearsay confessions, so they are only of minimal value to this Court. [88]

84 One writer has explained the hearsay problem as follows:

> In the hearsay situation, two "witnesses" are involved. The first complies with all three of the ideal conditions[--oath, personal presence at trial, and cross-examination--]for the giving of testimony but merely reports what the second "witness" said. The second "witness" is the out-of-court declarant whose statement was not given in compliance with the ideal conditions but contains the critical information.

2 Kenneth S. Broun, McCormick on Evidence § 245 (6th ed. 2009). Because the important witness does not testify under ideal conditions, it becomes very difficult to gauge the accuracy and sincerity of the "second witnesses" testimony. See id.

85 Indeed, Ms. Riley suspected that Mr. Coles was falsely confessing for this very reason. (Doc. 3, Ex. 17 at 1.)

86 Mr. Davis attempts to turn his high burden into a prima facie one. He contends that once a hearsay confession is offered, regardless of its reliability, the Court must assume the truth of the matter asserted and the State has a duty to disprove it. (See Doc. 84 at 12.) This is incorrect, the State has no such burden. Of course, if Mr. Davis did offer truly persuasive evidence of the matter asserted in the hearsay confession or of his innocence, the State may have a need to call Mr. Coles to rebut Mr. Davis's case. That is likely why the alternative suspect was called in House, where the petitioner presented the hearsay confessions and disproved two highly probative pieces of DNA evidence--blood on House's jeans and semen on the victim's nightgown--used to secure his conviction. 547 U.S. at 540-48.

87 As Mr. Davis explained, Mr. Coles will likely deny his involvement in the crime and proffer some explanation for the confessions, or outright deny that he made them. (Evidentiary Hearing Transcript at 158-59.) However, the Court is not required to accept such testimony at face-value. In the end, Mr. Davis appeared to forget that the witness stand is the crucible of credibility; and his reluctance to put Mr. Coles to the test robbed the Court of its ability to accurately assess Mr. Coles's claim that he did not shoot Officer MacPhail.

88 Further, it bears noting that one of the persons relating the confession-- Mr. Gordon--was not a credible witness. See infra Analysis Part III.C.iii.

His credibility is discussed fully in the section regarding alternate eyewitness accounts of the murder, which is the true import of his testimony.

ii. Mr. Coles's Conduct Immediately After the Shooting

Mr. Davis has presented evidence regarding Mr. Coles's "suspicious" conduct immediately subsequent to the shooting. At the hearing, April Hutchinson testified that, immediately after the murder, Mr. Coles asked her to walk with him so that it would "seem like he didn't do anything." [89] (Evidentiary Hearing Transcript at 140.) The record also reflects affidavit evidence from Tonya Johnson, reflecting that Mr. Coles and his friend "Terry" disposed of firearms subsequent to the murder, and Anita Saddler, stating that Mr. Coles was carrying a firearm on the night of the MacPhail shooting. [90] (Doc. 3, Exs. 22, 25.)

89 Ms. Hutchinson also offered general testimony that Mr. Coles was a person of whom the community was afraid. (Evidentiary Hearing Transcript at 140-41.) This evidence is not probative of Mr. Coles's guilt-- simply because Mr. Coles was feared does not mean that he was responsible for murdering Officer MacPhail.

90 Ms. Saddler also averred that Mr. Coles was acting nervous and jittery, and appeared to have some knowledge regarding the MacPhail murder. (Doc. 3, Ex. 25 at 4.) Again, this does not show Mr. Coles's guilt. Given his proximity to the murder, it is not surprising that he appeared both nervous and knowledgeable in the wake of the shooting. Antoine Williams was also knowledgeable and nervous after witnessing the murder, but his nervousness is not meaningful proof that he murdered Officer MacPhail. (See Evidentiary Hearing Transcript at 20.)

Ms. Hutchinson's testimony does little to prove Mr. Coles's guilt. She testified that Mr. Coles wanted to walk with her so that it would "seem like he didn't do anything." (Evidentiary Hearing Transcript at 140.) However, there is no way to know what Mr. Coles meant by "do anything," rendering this testimony meaningless. When considering this statement, it must be remembered that Mr. Coles instigated the altercation with Larry Young, which lead directly to the assault of one person and the murder of another. It would not be surprising if, at the time, Mr. Coles believed he was responsible for something illegal, even if he was not responsible for shooting Officer MacPhail.

The testimony regarding the guns is not irrelevant, but it is not highly probative either. Apparently, a disturbing number of people were armed on the night Officer MacPhail was murdered. At some point that evening Mr. Coles, Mr. Davis, "Terry," Mark Wilds, and Lamar Brown all carried a firearm. (Trial Transcript at 912-13; Doc. 3 Ex. 22; Evidentiary Hearing Transcript at 181.) Presumably, these individuals were not licensed to carry firearms, so they were engaging in illegal activity simply by virtue of possessing the weapons and would have had reason to hide their weapons. Indeed, "Terry" was also hiding his firearm, but no one contends that he shot Officer MacPhail. (Doc. 3, Ex. 22..) At best, then, the fact that Mr. Coles possessed a firearm simply shows only that he had the means to shoot Officer MacPhail, not that he was actually the gunman. [91]

[91] Also of import is the fact that this is not new evidence. Less than a week after the MacPhail shooting occurred, Mr. Coles admitted that he possessed a firearm the night of the murder. (Pet. Ex. 24-A.)

iii. Alternate Eyewitness Accounts

Mr. Davis has presented several alternative eyewitness accounts regarding the events that occurred in the early hours of August 19, 1989. Two witnesses now directly state that they witnessed Mr. Coles murder Officer MacPhail. They are, Benjamin Gordon, [92] who testified at the hearing, and Joseph Washington, who testified at trial and provided his story through an affidavit. (Evidentiary Hearing Transcript at 184-85; Doc. 3, Ex. 27 at 1-2.) Three other witnesses cannot identify the murderer, but provide other potentially relevant details through affidavits. Gary Hargrove saw the body of the officer near Mr. Coles after the shooting. (Doc. 3, Ex. 15 at 1.) Daniel Kinsman avers that the shooter was left-handed and the gun was shiny. (Doc. 3, Ex. 28 at 2.) Peggie Grant claims to have seen Red Coles wearing a white shirt later that night. (Doc. 3, Ex 26 at 1.)

[92] Mr. Gordon also recanted some of his prior statements regarding who was responsible for the Cloverdale shooting. (Evidentiary Hearing Transcript at 178-79.) Several other affiants also provided testimony exculpating Mr. Davis from the Cloverdale shooting. (See Doc. 3, Exs. 30,

31, 32.) The Court does not discuss this testimony because the conviction for the Cloverdale shooting is not specifically challenged in this petition and is largely irrelevant to the murder conviction. (Doc. 2 at 2 (Since Mr. Davis' trial, evidence has surfaced that shows not only that Troy Davis is innocent, but that Sylvester 'Redd' Coles murdered Officer MacPhail.").) As is explained below, Mr. Davis's conviction for the Cloverdale shooting followed from his conviction for the MacPhail murder, not vice-versa. Infra Analysis Part III.C.iv.

The Court begins with the eyewitness account from Mr. Gordon, whose testimony is not credible. At the evidentiary hearing, over twenty years after the murder, Mr. Gordon testified for the first time that he saw Mr. Coles shoot Officer MacPhail. (Evidentiary Hearing Transcript at 184-85.) This testimony marks the third version of Mr. Gordon's post-trial statement, which adds new exculpatory details each time. (See Doc. 3, Exs. 13, 14.) Mr. Gordon contends that his new eyewitness account was not provided earlier because he was fearful of Mr. Coles. [93] (Evidentiary Hearing Transcript at 191-92.) However, this explanation is belied by Mr. Gordon's previous conduct--this is not the first time he accused Mr. Coles of the murder despite previously stating that he did not see who shot Officer MacPhail. Specifically, in 2008, Mr. Gordon signed an affidavit relating a confession by Mr. Coles to the murder and stating that "I could not tell who done the shooting, but I distinctly recall seeing the person fire the second shot." (Doc. 3, Ex. 13.) It is difficult to understand why fear prevented Mr. Gordon from previously relating that he saw Mr. Coles shoot Officer MacPhail if, at that time, he felt comfortable relating Mr. Coles's confession to the murder. The only explanation for Mr. Gordon's ever-evolving testimony is that it changes to reflect whatever details he believes are necessary to secure Mr. Davis's release. Therefore, his testimony is not credible.

93 He also testified that he was told to "stick" to his statement at trial. (Evidentiary Hearing Transcript at 203-04.) Given that Mr. Gordon was generally not credible and Mr. Lock testified credibly and contrarily, the Court credits Mr. Lock's testimony on this point. (Evidentiary Hearing Transcript at 442.)

Joseph Washington also claims, through an affidavit, to have witnessed Mr. Coles shoot Officer MacPhail, but his testimony is not credible. [94] (Doc. 3, Ex. 27 at 1-2.) At trial, Mr. Washington was badly impeached when cross-examination revealed inconsistent or missing details in his testimony, and he claimed the impossibility of having been two places at the same time. Supra note 9. Additionally, this testimony is suspect because it is presented in affidavit form, insulating Mr. Washington from being impeached again during a new cross-examination. Herrera, 506 U.S. at 417. The fact that Mr. Washington was badly impeached during his initial testimony, coupled with the presentation of this testimony in affidavit form, leads the Court to find it not credible.

> 94 It is also important to note that Mr. Washington's eyewitness testimony is not new with the exception of the fact that he now avers that Mr. Coles was wearing a white shirt. (Doc. 3, Ex. 27.) Mr. Washington testified at trial that he witnessed Mr. Coles shoot Officer MacPhail. (Trial Transcript at 1341-47.)

The affidavits of Gary Hargrove and Daniel Kinsman provide indirect eyewitness testimony that does not further Mr. Davis's showing of innocence. 95 Mr. Kinsman stated that the barrel of the gun was "shiny" and that the shooter used his left hand. (Doc. 3, Ex. 28 at 2.) However, there is no evidence that either Mr. Coles or Mr. Davis are left handed. And, regardless of whether the barrel of the weapon was black or chrome, it could still have been "shiny." Therefore, this evidence neither exculpates Mr. Davis nor inculpates Mr. Coles. Gary Hargrove averred that he did not see the shooting, but that he saw the Officer's body near Mr. Coles immediately after the shooting, that Mr. Coles was stopped and facing the Officer when the shooting occurred, and that the person running away was Mr. Davis. This affidavit is not clear evidence of innocence and could be read as further evidence of Mr. Davis's guilt, Indeed, according to trial testimony, it was the individual who was running from the Officer that shot him. (See Trial Transcript at 848-51, 910-11.) Accordingly, these affidavits do not further Mr. Davis's showing.

> 95 The Court reiterates that affidavit testimony is disfavored because it is obtained without the benefit of cross-examination and an opportunity to make credibility determinations. Herrera, 506 U.S. at 417.

Finally, Mr. Davis presented the affidavit of Peggie Grant, Ms. Hutchinson's mother. This affidavit places Mr. Coles in the white shirt soon after the murder occurred. (Doc. 3, Ex. 26.) Because this evidence was presented in affidavit form, it is disfavored and its value diminished. Herrera, 506 U.S. at 417. Moreover, this evidence is refuted by ample record evidence that either places Mr. Coles in the yellow shirt or Mr. Davis in white shirt. (See Trial Transcript at 805-06, 914, 959-60, 979-82, 1015-21, 1128, 1162-63, 1216-17.) [96] However, despite the fact that the contents of this affidavit are widely refuted, it does provide a small amount of additional value to Mr. Davis's showing by placing Mr. Coles in a white shirt.

> [96] One of the witnesses who testified on this subject was Eric Ellison. Given Mr. Davis's general allegations of coercion, it bears noting that there was credible testimony at the hearing indicating that Mr. Ellison was not coerced. (Evidentiary Hearing Transcript at 258-59.)

iv. The Shell Casing

The final piece of evidence presented at this hearing was the new Georgia Bureau of Investigation ("GBI") Report regarding the munitions from the Cloverdale shooting and MacPhail murder. [97] (Pet. Exs. 31, 31-A.) The new report indicates that it is unclear whether the bullets found at the Cloverdale and MacPhail shooting were fired from the same firearm, despite noting "some agreement of individual characteristics." [98] (Pet. Ex. 31.) The shell casing tests were inconsistent, finding that some of the casings from the various shootings were fired in the same gun while others were not. (Id.)

> [97] The State introduced evidence regarding Mr. Davis's "bloody" shorts. (See Resp. Ex. 67.) However, even the State conceded that this evidence lacked any probative value of guilt, submitting it only to show what the Board of Pardons and Paroles had before it. (Evidentiary Hearing Transcript at 468-69.) Indeed, there was insufficient DNA to determine who the blood belonged to, so the shorts in no way linked Mr. Davis to the murder of Officer MacPhail. The blood could have belonged to Mr. Davis, Mr. Larry Young, Officer MacPhail, or even have gotten onto the shorts entirely apart from the events of that night. Moreover, it is not even clear that the substance was blood. (See Pet. Ex. 46.)

> [98] The Court is able to determine the origin of the bullets and shell casings by correlating the evidence inventory sheets in the police report to the GEI Report. (See Reep. Ex. 30 at 295-302.)

In Mr. Davis's filings, the import of this evidence has become a moving target. Initially, he made little mention of it. (See Doc. 2 at 3.) Later, he used this evidence as proof of Mr. Coles's guilt and erroneous factfinding by the Georgia Supreme Court. (Doc. 27 at 4, 45.) Presently, he contends the shell casings were deposited by third parties, destroying the link between the two shootings. (Doc. 80 at 18.)

At trial, the munitions evidence was largely used to establish Mr. Davis's guilt for the Cloverdale shooting by bootstrapping it to his guilt for the MacPhail murder. During closing argument, the State explained the munitions evidence as follows:

> And then there are the silent witnesses in this case. Just as Davis, wearing a white shirt, pistol-whipped Larry and murdered Officer McPhail, so also did Troy Anthony Davis, using the same gun, shoot Micheal Cooper and murder Officer McPhail.
>
> You will recall the testimony of Roger Parian, director of the Crime Lab, when he was discussing the bullets. He was talking about the bullets from the parking lot of the Burger King and from the body of Officer McPhail, and he was talking then about comparing that with the bullet from -- that was recovered from Micheal Cooper's head when he'd been shot in the face.
>
> And what Roger Parian told you is that they were possibly shot from the same weapon. There were enough similarities in the bullets to say that the bullet that was shot in Cloverdale into Micheal Cooper was shot -- was possibly shot from the same gun that shot into the body of Officer McPhail in the parking lot of the Burger King.
>
> But he was even more certain about the shell casings. He was quite more certain about that, and he said in fact that the one that was recovered from the Trust Company Bank right across from the Burger King parking lot was fired from the same weapon that fired four other shell casings that were recovered in Cloverdale right down the street from the pool party, Cloverdale and Audabon.

(Trial Transcript at 1502-03 (emphasis added).) Reading this argument, two facts are immediately apparent: (1) there was never a definitive contention at trial that the bullets matched and (2) the link between the shootings was used to prove that Mr. Davis not only shot Officer MacPhail but also Michael Cooper. This latter point is confirmed by the balance of the State's closing argument, which is dedicated almost entirely to eyewitness accounts regarding the MacPhail murder. (Id. at 1496-1502.)

There are two reasons why this report has limited value to showing Mr. Davis's innocence with respect to the MacPhail murder. [99] First, the munitions evidence only showed that the shootings were linked; it remained for the State to prove Mr. Davis's guilt as to one shooting before this evidence became relevant. Importantly, the shooting the State proved independent of the munitions was the MacPhail murder. (See Trial Transcript at 1496-1503.) Accordingly, disproving the munitions evidence is not relevant to Mr. Davis's guilt of the MacPhail murder, even if it is cogent to the Cloverdale shooting. Second, it is not clear that the GBI report varies from the trial testimony. At trial, the testimony indicated a possibility that the bullets matched, a possibility that is also reflected in the GBI report. (Compare Trial Transcript at 1292, with Pet. Ex. 31.) Likewise, the GBI report does reflect that some of the shell casings matched, and it appears that the shell casings discussed at trial are listed as matching in the GBI report. (Compare Trial Transcript at 1294, with Pet. Ex. 31 ("Microscopic examination and comparison reveals the cartridge cases, Items 4C, 4F, 5C and 5F, were fired in the same firearm.").) Accordingly, whatever value this may have with respect to the Cloverdale shooting, it has minimal, if any, value to proving Mr. Davis innocent of the MacPhail murder.

99 The Court does not express an opinion on the relevance of this report to Mr. Davis's guilt regarding the Cloverdale shooting, as that issue is not before this Court. See supra note 92.

v. Summary

Mr. Davis vastly overstates the value of his evidence of innocence. First, some of the evidence is not credible and would be disregarded by a reasonable juror. Specifically, the eyewitness identifications of Mr. Coles as the shooter by Mr. Gordon and Mr. Washington are not credible. Supra Analysis Part III.C.iii. Likewise, regardless of the credibility of the witnesses offering the hearsay confessions, it is difficult to credit the truth of the underlying statement, which is totally uncorroborated. [100] Id. Part III.C.i. Indeed, one witness recounting such a confession doubted its truth. id.

100 As was explained, there is a strong explanation for why Mr. Coles may
have confessed falsely, and Mr. Davis has done nothing to disprove this,
despite having the burden to do so placed squarely on his shoulders. See
supra Analysis Part III.C.i.

Second, other proffered evidence was not exculpatory with respect to
the MacPhail murder. Specifically, to the extent that the munitions
evidence has actually changed since trial, it is relevant to the
Cloverdale shooting, not the MacPhail murder. Id. Part III.C.iv.
Likewise, the eyewitness accounts of Gary Hargrove and Daniel
Kinsman are inapposite. Id. Part III.C.iii.

Third, still other evidence that Mr. Davis brought forward is too
general to provide anything more than smoke and mirrors. That is,
that Mr. Coles was generally feared; possessed a gun, as did an
alarming number of people that night; and acted nervous after the
murder, as did several other witnesses does very little to actually
suggest that Mr. Coles murdered Officer MacPhail. Id. Part III.C.ii.
These facts could be true about any number of persons, regardless of
whether they were murderers.

Fourth, Ms. Grant's affidavit testimony regarding Mr. Coles wearing a
white shirt is likely to be discounted in light of an overwhelming
body of contrary evidence. Id. Part III.C.iii. Finally, much of this
evidence was proffered in affidavit form, the value of which is
seriously diminished. Herrera, 506 U.S. at 417.

D. Balancing of All of the Evidence[101]

101 28 U.S.C. § 2254(d) (2) deference applies to the final factual
determination in this case. However, this deference has not played a
determinative role, as this Court concurs with the State Court's conclusion.

The burden was on Mr. Davis to prove, by clear and convincing
evidence, that no reasonable juror would have convicted him in light
of the new evidence. In making this determination, the Court looks at
all the evidence to make " probabilistic determination about what
reasonable, properly instructed jurors would do.' " House, 547 U.S. at
537-38 (quoting Schlup, 513 U.S. at 329)

The Court begins with the evidence that proved Mr. Davis's guilt. As was explained above, the State provided three types of evidence: (1) eyewitness testimony regarding who was wearing the white and yellow shirts, and what actions the individual in each shirt took; (2) personal identifications of Mr. Davis as the shooter; and (3) secondhand confessions by Mr. Davis. (See Trial Transcript 1496-1502.) The State offered significant testimony on these points. The following witnesses identified Mr. Davis as the person in the white shirt: Harriett Murray (id. at 846, 850, 862-65), Antoine Williams (id. at 959-64), Steven Sanders (id. at 979-83), Dorothy Ferrell (id. at 1020-21), Darrell Collins (id. at 1128), and Eric Ellison (id. at 1216-17). Mr. Coles was placed in the yellow shirt by Larry Young (isd. at 805-06) and Valerie Coles Gordon (id. at 1162-63). Four witnesses [102] stated that the person in the white shirt murdered Officer MacPhail (id. at 850, 959-60, 979, 1015), and four [103] directly identified Mr. Davis as Officer MacPhail's murderer (Id. at 862-65, 963-64, 982-83, 1021). In addition, Harriett Murray (Id. at 847-50), Antoine Williams (Id. at 960-64), and Steven Sanders (Id. at 979-82) indicated that the individual in the white shirt both assaulted Larry Young and murdered Officer MacPhail. Finally, Kevin McQueen (Id. at 1231-32) and Jeffery Sapp (Id. at 1251-52) related secondhand confessions from Mr. Davis.

102 These witnesses were Harriett Murray (Trial Transcript at 850), Antoine Williams (Id. at 959-60), Steven Sanders (id. at 979), and Dorothy Ferrell (id. at 1015)

103 These witnesses were Harriett Murray (id. at 862-65), Antoine Williams (id. at 963-64), Steven Sanders (id. at 982-83), and Dorothy Ferrell (id. at 1021)

Mr. Davis's proof to the contrary at trial included the testimony of Joseph Washington, who identified Mr. Coles as the individual who shot Officer MacPhail. (Id. at 1342-43.) Tayna Johnson testified that she observed Mr. Coles at the Cloverdale party on August 18, 1989 wearing a white shirt. (Id. at 1362-63.) She also testified that she observed Mr. Coles acting nervous after the MacPhail shooting. (Id. at 1361.) Jeffery Sams testified that he saw Mr. Coles, not Mr. Davis, with a firearm the night of the MacPhail shooting. (Id. at 1377-81.) Mr. Davis's mother, Virginia Davis, testified that Mr. Davis left the house for the Cloverdale party wearing a multi-color shirt and the Mr. Davis could not have spoken to Mr. Sapp the afternoon of August 19, 1989. (Id. at 1389, 1411-12.) Finally, Mr. Davis took the stand in his own defense. He denied shooting at Mr. Ellison's car during the Cloverdale party (Id. at 1417-18), assaulting Mr. Young (id. at 1423), and shooting Officer MacPhail (id. at 1424). Mr. Davis testified that he did not see who shot Officer MacPhail (id. at 1424), but stated that it was Mr. Coles who slapped Mr. Young (id. at 1423). Also, Mr. Davis denied speaking to Mr. Sapp on August 19, 1989. (Id. at 1431.)

Mr. Davis's new evidence does not change the balance of proof from trial. Of his seven "recantations," only one is a meaningful, credible recantation. Supra Analysis Part III.B. The value of that recantation is diminished because it only confirms that which was obvious at trial-- that its author was testifying falsely. Id. Part III.B.ii (Kevin McQueen). Four of the remaining six recantations are either not credible or not true recantations and would be disregarded. Id. Parts III.B.i (Antoine Williams), III.B.iii (Jeffrey Sapp), III.B.iv (Darrell Collins), III.B.v (Harriet Murray). The remaining two recantations were presented under the most suspicious of circumstances, with Mr. Davis intentionally preventing the validity of the recantation from being challenged in open court through cross-examination. Id. Parts III.B.vi (Dorothy Ferrell), III.B.vii (Larry Young). Worse, these witnesses were readily available--one was actually waiting in the courthouse--and Mr. Davis chose not to present their recantations as live testimony.

Mr. Davis's additional, non-recantation evidence also does not change the balance of proof from trial. At the outset, the Court notes that much of this evidence was presented in affidavit form. Affidavit evidence is viewed with great suspicion'[104] and has diminished value. Herrera, 506 U.S. at 417. Moreover, this evidence, whether presented as live testimony or in affidavit form, suffers other serious defects. The two witness identifications of Mr. Coles as the shooter were not credible, and Peggie Grant's affidavit testimony placing Mr. Coles in a white shirt is widely refuted in the record. Id. Part III.C.iii. The hearsay confessions carry little weight because the underlying confessions are uncorroborated and there is good reason to believe that they were false. [105] Id. Part III.C.i. Further diminishing the value of this evidence is the fact that Mr. Davis had the means to test the validity of the underlying confessions by calling and impeaching Mr. Coles, but chose not to do so. [106] Other evidence in this category simply lacks probative value; the munitions evidence and the accounts from April Hutchinson, Tonya Johnson, Anita Saddler, Gary Hargrove, and Daniel Kinsman are either totally inapposite or are of the most minimal probative value. See id. Parts III.C.ii, III.C.iii, III.C.iv. As a body, this evidence does not change the balance of proof that was presented at Mr. Davis's trial.

104 This suspicion occurs because Mr. Davis has prevented the reliability of this evidence from being tested in open court through cross-examination and credibility determinations. Herrera, 506 U.S. at 417.

105 There is a strong explanation for why Mr. Coles may have confessed falsely, and Mr. Davis has done nothing to disprove this despite having the burden to do so squarely on his shoulders. See supra Analysis Part III.C.i. Indeed, one witness recounting such a confession doubted that Mr. Coles was being truthful when confessing. Id.

Ultimately, while Mr. Davis's new evidence casts some additional, minimal doubt on his conviction, it is largely smoke and mirrors. The vast majority of the evidence at trial remains intact, and the new evidence is largely not credible or lacking in probative value. After careful consideration, the Court finds that Mr. Davis has failed to make a showing of actual innocence that would entitle him to habeas relief in federal court. [107] Accordingly, the Petition for a Writ of Habeas Corpus is DENIED. [108]

106 Mr. Davis has made clear that he knew both Mr. Coles's work and home address. (Doc. 84, Ex. 1.) Had Mr. Davis at any time sought the help of this Court to subpoena Mr. Coles prior to the conclusion of the hearing, the Court would have ordered the United States Marshall Service to serve Mr. Coles. Mr. Davis never made such a request, instead choosing to attempt self-service at the eleventh hour. His half-hearted efforts belie his true intentions: to be able to say that he "attempted" to provide Mr. Coles testimony when, in fact, he never intended to do so.

107 The Court further notes that whether it adopted the lower burden proposed by Mr. Davis, or even the lowest imaginable burden from Schlup, Mr. Davis's showing would have satisfied neither.

108 After careful consideration and an in-depth review of twenty years of evidence, the Court is left with the firm conviction that while the State's case may not be ironclad, most reasonable jurors would again vote to convict Mr. Davis of Officer MacPhail's murder. A federal court simply cannot interpose itself and set aside the jury verdict in this case absent a truly persuasive showing of innocence. To act contrarily would wreck complete havoc on the criminal justice system. See Herrera, 506 U.S. at 417.

CONCLUSION

Before the Court is Petitioner Troy Anthony Davis's Petition for a Writ of Habeas Corpus. (Doc. 2.) Pursuant to the order of the Supreme Court, this Court has held a hearing and now determines this petition. Davis, 130 S. Ct. at 1. For the above stated reasons, this Court concludes that executing an innocent person would violate the Eighth Amendment of the United States Constitution. However, Mr. Davis is not innocent: the evidence produced at the hearing on the merits of Mr. Davis's claim of actual innocence and a complete review of the record in this case does not require the reversal of the jury's judgment that Troy Anthony Davis murdered City of Savannah Police Officer Mark Allen MacPhail on August 19, 1989. Accordingly, the petition is DENIED. The Clerk of Court is DIRECTED to file a copy of this order on the docket and forward this order to the Supreme Court of the United States.

SO ORDERED this 24th day of August 2010.

/s/ William T. Moore, Jr.

WILLIAM T. MOORE, JR.

UNITED STATES OF AMERICA,
Plaintiff - Appellee,
v.
KENNETH DEAN STURM,
Defendant - Appellant.

UNITED STATES OF AMERICA,
Plaintiff - Appellee,
v.
CHRISTOPHER ADAM DAYTON,
Defendant - Appellant.

No. 09-1386, No. 09-5022

UNITED STATES COURT OF APPEALS FOR THE TENTH CIRCUIT

2011 U.S. App. LEXIS 7042

April 4, 2011, Filed

Before BRISCOE, Chief Judge, and KELLY, LUCERO, MURPHY, HARTZ, O'BRIEN, TYMKOVICH, GORSUCH, HOLMES, and MATHESON, Circuit Judges.

ORDER GRANTING REHEARING EN BANC

Today, the court issued Order & Judgments in numbers 09-1386, United States v. Sturm, and 09-5022, United States v. Dayton. Those decisions were issued simultaneously. The appeals present a common and important issue, and the court has determined that for purposes of consistency the matters should be reheard by the entire *en banc* court. Accordingly, we *sua sponte* order *en banc* rehearing in both these appeals, and vacate both decisions. The parties are directed to brief the following issue:

> Whether the jurisdictional element of 18 U.S.C. §§ 2252 and 2252A requires proof that the particular image of child pornography that is the identified object of the defendant's statutorily proscribed possession, receipt, or distribution traveled in interstate or foreign commerce, or whether it is sufficient to establish the jurisdictional

element to show that the original or some other iteration of that image traveled in interstate or foreign commerce at some point prior to the defendant's alleged commission of the charged crime? In other words, does the term "visual depiction," as employed in 18 U.S.C. §§ 2252 and 2252A, refer specifically to the particular image possessed, received, or distributed by the defendant, or does it instead refer to the substance of an image of child pornography and thereby encompass not only the particular image possessed, received, or distributed by the defendant, but also any prior generations of that image, including the original?

Each separate party may file a brief on the issue identified above, but we urge counsel on the same sides to coordinate their arguments to reduce repetition. The supplemental briefs should be filed electronically in the respective appeals. That is, the parties should file their briefs in their original case numbers only. They need not file in both case numbers. The supplemental briefs shall be no longer than 20 pages in a 13 point font and the optional reply briefs shall be no longer than 10 pages in a 13 point font.

The appellants shall file their supplemental briefs on or before May 25, 2011. The appellees shall file their response briefs within 30 days of those submissions. The appellants may file optional reply briefs within 14 days of service of the government's briefs.

ORDER AND JUDGMENT*

> * This order and judgment is not binding precedent except under the doctrines of law of the case, res judicata and collateral estoppel. It may be cited, however, for its persuasive value consistent with Federal Rule of Appellate Procedure 32.1 and Tenth Circuit Rule 32.1.

Defendant-Appellant Christopher Adam Dayton brings a sufficiency-of-the-evidence challenge to his convictions for distributing and possessing child pornography, in violation of 18 U.S.C. § 2252(a)(2) and (a)(4)(B). Mr. Dayton does not dispute that he distributed and possessed child pornography. Rather, Mr. Dayton argues that, because the government did not offer evidence that the images and videos charged in the indictment had traveled in interstate or foreign commerce, the government failed to offer sufficient proof of the requisite jurisdictional nexus of a movement across state lines under *United States v. Schaefer*, 501 F.3d 1197 (10th Cir. 2007). Generally, in

Schaefer, we held that "the government was required to prove that any Internet transmissions containing child pornography that moved to or from [the defendant's] computer crossed state lines" and noted that "the government offered no proof that *the particular images* on the CDs in question moved across state lines." *Id.* at 1202, 1206 (emphasis added).

Thus, Mr. Dayton contends that evidence showing original photographs or videos that contain the charged images were produced outside of the state of Oklahoma is not sufficient under *Schaefer*; instead, the government must prove that the *particular* images stored on and downloaded from his computer moved in interstate or foreign commerce. Mr. Dayton urges us to reverse and enter a judgment of acquittal on both counts. In the alternative, he argues that the district court improperly instructed the jury on the element of distribution.

Exercising jurisdiction under 28 U.S.C. § 1291, we REVERSE Mr. Dayton's convictions and REMAND the case to the district court with instructions to VACATE its judgment and enter a judgment of acquittal.

I. Background

On March 30, 2007, in Tulsa, Oklahoma, FBI Special Agent Cecchini, who is assigned to the FBI's Innocent Images National Initiative, accessed the peer-to-peer ("P2P") program LimeWire through the Internet as part of an undercover investigation into child pornography. LimeWire is a free-access file-sharing program that allows users to make files available to all other LimeWire users by placing them in a shared file folder. Any LimeWire user may access that folder to download files. [1] LimeWire provides users with a search function, involving the use of keywords, that allows them to search for particular types of files. When a LimeWire user locates a file he wishes to download, LimeWire automatically will find all of the users who possess that file in their shared folders and will download parts of the file from all of them, thereby increasing the download speed. The FBI has a specialized version of LimeWire that circumvents the usual downloading process and allows agents to download the file from only one person "so that [it] can definitively say that this one

person, this one [Internet Protocol ("IP")] address offered that file."
R., Vol. II, Pt. 1, Tr. at 110. [2]

1 Other LimeWire users may not add to another user's shared folder; they may only access that folder for downloads. This means that if a file is in a LimeWire user's shared folder, then that user put it there.

2 Agent Cecchini testified that an IP address is assigned by an Internet service provider and is unique to a computer such that no two computers share the same IP address.

Using LimeWire, Agent Cecchini ran a keyword search for "8 yo girl," a term associated with child pornography that refers to an eight-year-old child. The search revealed a file matching that description belonging to an IP address in Tulsa, Oklahoma. That IP address had been assigned by Internet service provider Cox Communications, and the shared folder contained 323 shared files. From the shared folder associated with the Tulsa IP address, Agent Cecchini downloaded three complete and one partial video files that appeared to contain child pornography. With that information, agents issued a subpoena to Cox Communications, which provided them with subscriber information for that IP address. Agents thereafter located the physical address of the residence associated with the IP address and obtained a search warrant.

On the morning of April 18, 2007, eleven FBI agents and other personnel executed the search warrant at Mr. Dayton's residence, which he shared with other family members. Mr. Dayton acknowledged that the Cox account and IP address were his and admitted that "he'd been downloading child pornography and using LimeWire for about three months." *Id.* at 135. Mr. Dayton also wrote a statement, in which he confessed that "about 3-4 months ago I started to use [L]ime[W]ire and axedentle [sic] saw child porn and started to download it. I hated myself for it and deleted it[,] but I download[ed] it agen [sic] and I'm sory [sic]. And [I] burned it to 3 cds." R., Vol. I, Pt. 1, at 90 (Attach. to Mot. Suppress, filed Mar. 21, 2008). Agents seized a computer and two hard drives from the Dayton home, along with 169 CDs and DVDs. A forensic examiner for the FBI later discovered pictures and video files constituting child pornography on the hard drives and CDs.

On May 9, 2007, Mr. Dayton was charged in a two-count indictment with knowingly distributing or attempting to distribute visual depictions of minors engaged in sexually explicit conduct, in violation of 18 U.S.C. § 2252(a)(2), and knowingly possessing or attempting to possess visual depictions of minors engaged in sexually explicit conduct, in violation of 18 U.S.C. § 2252(a)(4)(B). On March 21, 2008, Mr. Dayton moved to dismiss the indictment for failure to establish the interstate commerce nexus of either charge.

Mr. Dayton argued that Cox Communications was solely an intrastate Internet provider. Although he acknowledged that it was possible that the government could have additional evidence of the interstate nexus in its possession--which it had not shared with him but which it planned to offer at trial--he contended that if the government intended to rely only upon the evidence concerning Cox Communications, that evidence was insufficient to prove an interstate nexus under *Shaefer*. Mr. Dayton also moved to suppress his statements to police, arguing that they were obtained in violation of the Fifth and Sixth Amendments. The district court took both motions under advisement until the close of the government's case, and the case proceeded to a three-day jury trial.

At trial, Agent Cecchini testified about the investigation that led to Mr. Dayton's indictment. The jury also was shown the four videos that Agent Cecchini downloaded from Mr. Dayton's computer through LimeWire. While those videos played, Agent Cecchini described the sexual acts depicted. He testified that the videos appeared to depict adults involved in various sexual acts with minor children. Another witness, Dr. Deborah Lowen, a Tulsa area pediatrician specializing in the area of child-abuse pediatrics, testified that the children depicted ranged in age from approximately five to fourteen years of age.

The following evidence, which is relevant to the question of whether the images moved across state lines, was adduced at trial. Agent Cecchini testified that he had seen one of the videos "many times" and that the minor female (referred to as "Vicky") in the video was from Richland, Washington. R., Vol. II, Pt. 1, Tr. at 123. He also testified that he had seen all of the videos before, and that he previously had received these images from foreign countries. However, Agent Cecchini testified that he did not know if Mr.

Dayton had distributed any of the videos to anyone else and did not know where Mr. Dayton had gotten the images. Agent Cecchini also stated that agents knew that the Cox Communications IP address was located in Tulsa, Oklahoma, but he did not know where Cox Communications's server was located. Agent Cecchini acknowledged that in transferring files from Mr. Dayton's computer to the FBI's office in Tulsa, the images did not at that time move in interstate commerce.

Another witness for the government, FBI Special Agent Trifiletti, a specialist in victim identification, testified that he had identified the minors in three of the images recovered from Mr. Dayton as girls from Paraguay who were ten and twelve years old. Agent Trifiletti testified that the images were manufactured in Paraguay and that the FBI knew the identity of the man who had taken the pictures and disseminated them for profit. He stated that, in order for the Paraguayan images to be found on a computer in Oklahoma, they necessarily had to travel in interstate and foreign commerce. He explained:

> I can see no way for it [to get from Paraguay to the United States] other than to have been sent by Internet, mail, airplane. Maybe an analogy is appropriate; if we had a photograph taken of this courtroom today and it wound up in New York a number of years later, how did it leave Oklahoma? It's true of these photos as well. At some point, these photographs left Paraguay to be in the United States.

R., Vol. II, Pt. 2, Tr. at 235. He also testified that "I don't know how they got to the United States, other than that they left Paraguay in digital form." *Id.* at 239.

After the close of the government's case, Mr. Dayton moved for a judgment of acquittal under Federal Rule of Criminal Procedure 29, based on his contention that the evidence was insufficient to establish the interstate nexus. The court denied the motion, finding that "there are specific exhibits which have traveled in interstate commerce, or foreign commerce in this particular case." *Id.* at 253. But the court took under advisement the question of exactly which images would be submitted to the jury.

The parties revisited this issue at the initial jury instruction conference, where the judge ruled on which images would be submitted to the jury. The district court granted Mr. Dayton's Rule 29 motion as to "a great number of the images" based on the court's conclusion that, under its reading of *Schaefer*, the government had failed to offer sufficient evidence to prove the interstate commerce nexus. *Id.* at 311. However, the court denied the motion as to seven images, concluding that the nexus had been proven as to them. Those seven images included the three pictures from Paraguay and the four videos downloaded by Agent Cecchini.

Because Agent Trifiletti had testified as to the identity of the three Paraguayan children, and knew that they had never left Paraguay, the district court judge concluded that, "I don't think there's any question" that those three images traveled in interstate commerce. *Id.* at 313. The court further held that the evidence was sufficient to prove interstate travel as to the four videos. It based that conclusion in part on Agent Cecchini's testimony "that he had downloaded these files . . . from every state but two. And so he had definitely seen th[o]se files on the Internet and from other investigations in other areas." *Id.* at 311, 313-14.

For three out of the four videos, the court not only considered that testimony but also relied on what it considered to be proof that the videos were made outside of the United States. As to the first video, the district court considered the words "cambodian [sic]" and "sex tourist" in the title to be proof that the video was made outside the country; the court also found that the video "ha[d] all the makings and markings of something that was produced in Southeast Asia" because it featured a child who was "obviously Southeast Asian," "an older woman . . . who's obviously Southeast Asian," and "an overweight white person who could be a tourist." *Id.* at 313. As to the second video, which was referred to during the trial as the "baby-sitter abuse tape," the court relied on the fact that the child was speaking a foreign language that sounded like German or Russian. *Id.* at 314. The court found that the third video, the "Vicky" video, had been identified by Agent Cecchini as involving a girl from Richland, Washington, and that the same video had been involved in a case in Virginia. *Id.*

The district court held that the remaining images should not be submitted to the jury because "Cox is located in Oklahoma City, so the government cannot prove interstate travel that way." *Id.* at 315. Moreover, "[t]he government hasn't presented evidence that any of the files allegedly distributed by defendant moved in interstate or foreign commerce at the time defendant distributed them since [Agent] Cecchini downloaded them from a location in Oklahoma. In fact, they went from Tulsa, Oklahoma to Tulsa, Oklahoma." *Id.* at 316. Moreover, although the court believed that the government could prove the interstate nexus by showing that the image moved in interstate commerce at some point in time, the court interpreted *Schaefer* as requiring a connection between an image to a *specific* out-of-state location or source of origin, and the court found that such a connection had not been established for the remaining images. Under *Schaefer*, the court rejected as insufficient Agent Cecchini's testimony that he had seen the images before on the Internet because that testimony did not link any particular image to a particular out-of-state location.

In denying in part Mr. Dayton's Rule 29 motion, the district court declined to adopt Mr. Dayton's reading of *Schaefer*. The court acknowledged that, under Mr. Dayton's interpretation of *Schaefer*, he would have to be found not guilty of the charges against him because there was no proof that the images traveled in interstate or foreign commerce at the time that the defendant received them from LimeWire and because the distribution from Mr. Dayton to Agent Cecchini occurred wholly within Tulsa, Oklahoma. More specifically, the court refused to read *Schaefer* as "requir[ing] proof that the visual depiction possessed or distributed, moved directly to defendant's computer from an out-of-state location, or moved to an out-of-state location directly from defendant's computer." *Id.* at 317. The district court believed that such a broad interpretation of *Schaefer* would prevent the federal government from prosecuting child pornography cases.

At the preliminary jury instruction conference, Mr. Dayton also objected to the proposed instruction on the definition of "distribute," which would instruct the jury that a person distributes child pornography when he places it in a shared folder, thereby making it available to others to search out and download in a P2P network.

The district court overruled his objection pursuant to *United States v. Shaffer*, 472 F.3d 1219, 1223-25 (10th Cir. 2007).

At the close of the defendant's case, Mr. Dayton renewed his Rule 29 motion. The district court again denied the motion as to those seven images. Those images were submitted to the jury for deliberation, and the jury convicted Mr. Dayton on both counts--possession and distribution--as to all seven images. Thereafter, the court denied Mr. Dayton's motion to suppress, which the court previously had held in abeyance.

At Mr. Dayton's sentencing hearing, the court found that Mr. Dayton had an "extraordinary physical impairment" under the U.S. Sentencing Guidelines Manual ("U.S.S.G.") because he has severe Crohn's disease. [3] The court found that home detention would not be appropriate after Mr. Dayton had been convicted. Recognizing that there was a mandatory statutory minimum of sixty months' imprisonment, the court decided to grant a downward variance of ten levels, reducing the total offense level from thirty-six to twenty-six. [4] An offense level of twenty-six, with a criminal history category of I, corresponded to an advisory Guidelines range of sixty-three to seventy-eight months' imprisonment. [5] The district court noted that, in granting the downward variance, it had not only reviewed Mr. Dayton's extensive medical records, but had considered the sentencing factors enumerated in 18 U.S.C. § 3553(a), including Mr. Dayton's lack of any prior criminal history. The court sentenced Mr. Dayton to sixty-three months' imprisonment, to be followed by ten years of supervised release. The court allowed Mr. Dayton to remain free on bond pending placement in an appropriate facility that could meet his medical needs. This appeal timely followed.

3 Section 5H1.4 provides in relevant part that:

> [p]hysical condition or appearance, including physique, is not ordinarily relevant in determining whether a departure may be warranted. However, an extraordinary physical impairment may be a reason to depart downward; *e.g.*, in the case of a seriously infirm defendant, home detention may be as efficient as, and less costly than, imprisonment.

U.S.S.G. § 5H1.4 (2009) (amended 2010).

4 Although § 5H1.4 speaks in terms of a downward *departure*, the defendant filed a motion for a downward *variance*, so the district court chose to vary downward rather than depart downward. The court noted the inconsistency of that action with § 5H1.4's reference to a departure, but stated that "whether it's deemed a variance or a departure, it's appropriate." R., Vol. III, at 123 (Sentencing Hr'g, dated Jan. 12, 2009). *See generally United States v. Atencio*, 476 F.3d 1099, 1101 n.1 (10th Cir. 2007) ("We now clarify that when a court reaches a sentence above or below the recommended Guidelines range through application of Chapters Four or Five of the Sentencing Guidelines, the resulting increase or decrease is referred to as a 'departure.' When a court enhances or detracts from the recommended range through application of [18 U.S.C.] § 3553(a) factors, however, the increase or decrease is called a 'variance.'"), *overruled in part on other grounds by Irizarry v. United States*, 553 U.S. 708, 713 n.1, 128 S. Ct. 2198, 171 L. Ed. 2d 28 (2008).

5 This was a significant reduction in the applicable advisory Guidelines range for Mr. Dayton. Without that downward variance, the advisory Guidelines range for an offense level of thirty-six, and a criminal history category of I, was 188 to 235 months' imprisonment.

II. Discussion

On appeal, Mr. Dayton argues that the government offered insufficient evidence of an interstate nexus to support his convictions for possession and distribution of child pornography under 18 U.S.C. § 2252(a)(2) and (a)(4)(B). He contends that, under *Schaefer*, the government cannot satisfy the statutory interstate commerce requirement by demonstrating that copies of the images--*viz.*, copies of the particular images that are the subject of the instant criminal charges--at some prior point in time had traveled in interstate commerce. Mr. Dayton also argues, in the alternative, that the district court improperly instructed the jury on the element of distribution. In his view, *Shaffer*'s holding that a person distributes child pornography by making it available to others on a P2P network is potentially irreconcilable with *Schaefer*'s admonition that more than the mere use of the Internet is required to prove an interstate nexus. He seeks "guidance and [a] ruling on what a proper instruction would be given the[se] holdings." Aplt. Br. at 63.

The government responds that it proved that the videos, which Mr. Dayton indisputably distributed, had been transported in foreign or interstate commerce because

> [a]n FBI agent identified the victim featured in one of the videos as "Vicky" from Richland, Washington, and testified that the video had been made in Washington. Another of the videos contained ample circumstantial evidence to allow a reasonable jury to conclude that it was produced in Southeast Asia, and thus to infer that it must have been transported in interstate commerce prior to its distribution by Dayton.

Aplee. Br. at 14. [6] As to the possession count, the government contends that proof that Mr. Dayton "possessed digital images that originated in Paraguay was sufficient to establish that the images must have been transported in foreign commerce to be found in Oklahoma." *Id.* at 13. [7]

6 The government limits its argument before us concerning the distribution count: it only seeks to establish that the videos concerning "Vicky" and the purported Southeast Asian minor satisfy the statute's jurisdictional nexus. The government emphasizes that it "presented evidence that would have allowed a reasonable jury . . . to conclude that *two* of the videos Dayton distributed were created outside Oklahoma." Aplee. Br. at 26 (emphasis added); *see id.* at 23 ("[T]he government presented sufficient evidence to allow a reasonable jury to find that *at least two* of the videos were produced outside of the state of Oklahoma." (emphasis added)). Notably, although the government mentions the district court's consideration of the video of a minor who allegedly was speaking a foreign language that sounded like German or Russian (i.e., the video described as the "baby-sitter abuse tape"), it does not attempt to defend the district court's decision to send that video to the jury. *See id.* at 23 n.2.

7 In its jurisdictional argument concerning the possession count, the government exclusively focuses on the three images that allegedly originated in Paraguay.

The government maintains that *Schaefer*'s focus on whether a "particular image" has traveled in interstate commerce is impractical in the digital age. It urges us to limit *Schaefer* to its facts and to "hold that proof that *an image* originated outside the state in which it was found is sufficient to establish that it was transported in interstate or foreign commerce." *Id.* at 15 (emphasis added). More specifically, the government argues that "[t]his Court should hold that evidence establishing that *an image* traveled in interstate commerce *at some point in time* is sufficient to establish the jurisdictional element of § 2252." *Id.* at 37 (emphasis added). In other words, the government contends that the jurisdictional inquiry should not be focused upon whether the *particular* images depicting child pornography--*viz.*, the particular images obtained on digital files in connection with the investigation and criminally charged in this case--traveled interstate (i.e., crossed state lines), but instead on whether the originals of those images, or even any copies of them that depict the same child pornography, traveled interstate. As to Mr. Dayton's argument regarding the jury instruction on distribution, the government maintains that the district court did not abuse its discretion in giving that instruction because *Schaefer* "addressed only the sufficiency of evidence to meet the interstate commerce element of the distribution statute, and did not affect the continuing validity of *Shaffer's* definition of distribution." *Id.* at 15.

A. Standard of Review

"Whether the government presented sufficient evidence to support a conviction is a legal question that we review de novo." *United States v. Hasan*, 609 F.3d 1121, 1132-33 (10th Cir. 2010) (quoting *United States v. Parker*, 551 F.3d 1167, 1172 (10th Cir. 2008)) (internal quotation marks omitted); *see also United States v. Cesareo-Ayala*, 576 F.3d 1120, 1125-26 (10th Cir. 2009) (reviewing de novo defendant's challenge to denial of motion for acquittal on sufficiency-of-the-evidence grounds). Under the Due Process Clause, the evidence is sufficient to support a conviction if, "after viewing the evidence in the light most favorable to the prosecution, *any* rational trier of fact could have found the essential elements of the crime beyond a reasonable doubt." *Jackson v. Virginia*, 443 U.S. 307, 319, 99 S. Ct. 2781, 61 L. Ed. 2d 560 (1979). In reviewing a sufficiency-of-the-evidence challenge, we "view the evidence in the light most favorable to the government in order to determine whether all of the evidence . . . together with the reasonable inferences to be drawn therefrom, convinces us that a rational factfinder could reasonably have found the appellant guilty of the crime charged beyond a reasonable doubt." *United States v. Burkley*, 513 F.3d 1183, 1188 (10th Cir. 2008) (alteration omitted) (quoting *United States v. Chavez-Palacios*, 30 F.3d 1290, 1293-94 (10th Cir. 1994)) (internal quotation marks omitted).

B. Mr. Dayton's Sufficiency-of-the-Evidence Challenge

We will begin with the issue that we find to be dispositive--whether there was insufficient evidence that the images Mr. Dayton distributed and possessed had traveled in interstate or foreign commerce. Because this issue dictates our resolution of this appeal, we need not address Mr. Dayton's remaining claim.

Mr. Dayton was convicted of distributing and possessing child pornography in violation of 18 U.S.C. § 2252(a)(2) and (a)(4)(B). At the time of Mr. Dayton's conviction, the statute (which has since been amended) [8] provided in relevant part that a person shall be guilty of distributing child pornography if he

> knowingly receives, or distributes, any visual depiction that has been mailed, or has been shipped or transported in interstate or foreign commerce, or which contains materials which have been mailed or so shipped or transported, by any means including by computer, or knowingly reproduces any visual depiction for distribution in interstate or foreign commerce or through the mails, if--
>
> > (A) the producing of such visual depiction involves the use of a minor engaging in sexually explicit conduct; and
> >
> > (B) such visual depiction is of such conduct . . . .

18 U.S.C. § 2252(a)(2) (2006) (amended 2008). It also provided in relevant part that a person is guilty of possessing child pornography if he

> knowingly possesses 1 or more books, magazines, periodicals, films, video tapes, or other matter which contain any visual depiction that has been mailed, or has been shipped or transported in interstate or foreign commerce, or which was produced using materials which have been mailed or so shipped or transported, by any means including by computer, if--
>
> > (i) the producing of such visual depiction involves the use of a minor engaging in sexually explicit conduct; and
> >
> > (ii) such visual depiction is of such conduct . . . .

Id. § 2252(a)(4)(B) (2006) (amended 2008).

8 The amendment has the effect--as apparently intended by Congress--of broadening the jurisdictional scope of the child pornography statute. *See United States v. Lewis*, 554 F.3d 208, 216 (1st Cir.) ("[W]e should note that Congress recently amended the child pornography statutes, including the one before us, to expand the jurisdictional coverage. It did so by replacing all instances of 'in interstate' with 'in or affecting interstate' commerce. The legislative history indicates that Congress was unhappy with circuit court decisions narrowly construing the prior statute . . . ." (citation omitted)(quoting Effective Child Pornography Prosecution Act of 2007, Pub. L. No. 110-358, § 103)), *cert. denied*, 129 S. Ct. 2753, 174 L. Ed. 2d 261 (2009); *see also United States v. Wright*, 625 F.3d. 583, 599 (9th Cir. 2010) ("In 2008, Congress passed the 2007 Act," which was "[b]ased in part on a finding in the 2007 Act that '[t]he transmission of child pornography using the Internet *constitutes* transportation in interstate commerce' . . . ." (alteration in original) (emphasis added) (quoting Pub. L. No. 110-358, § 102(7))).

The distribution and possession sections contain coterminous jurisdictional requirements, namely, that the images "ha[ve] been mailed, or ha[ve] been shipped or transported in interstate or foreign commerce." We must determine whether there was sufficient evidence to satisfy those jurisdictional requirements in this case. [9]

9 As is evident from the plain language of the statute, there is another way to satisfy the requisite jurisdictional nexus of § 2252(a)(4)(B)--that is, by proving that the images were "produced using materials which have been mailed or so shipped or transported [in interstate or foreign commerce], by any means including by computer." On appeal, the government argues that it also satisfied the jurisdictional requirement for Mr. Dayton's possession charge through testimony at trial that the computer hard drives upon which the images were discovered were manufactured in Thailand. Specifically, Agent Cecchini testified that the two hard drives used by Mr. Dayton were labeled with the phrase "Product of Thailand" or "Made in Thailand." R., Vol. II, Pt. 1, Tr. at 167-68. Thus, the government argues that "because the images were found on a hard drive that was manufactured in Thailand, they were produced using materials that were shipped or transported in foreign commerce." Aplee. Br. at 13-14 (internal quotation marks omitted). *See generally United States v. Schene*, 543 F.3d 627, 639 (10th Cir. 2008) (holding, under plain-error review, where the hard drive was manufactured in Singapore that "[i]t is obvious that the government's evidence was sufficient . . . to show that each 'image of child pornography' had been copied or downloaded to [the defendant's] hard drive in one capacity or another, and was therefore 'produced using materials that have been mailed, or shipped

or transported in interstate or foreign commerce.'" (quoting 18 U.S.C. § 2252A(a)(5)(B)).

However, this argument is wholly without merit and may be disposed of in short order. The government failed to charge the materials prong of the statute in the Indictment and, therefore, the jury's verdict could not properly rest on this basis. *See United States v. Rahseparian*, 231 F.3d 1257, 1264-66 (10th Cir. 2000) (explaining that the indictment clearly did not charge the defendant with a particular part of the statute and stating that "it is a fundamental precept of federal constitutional law that a court cannot permit a defendant to be tried on charges that are not made in the indictment" (alteration omitted) (quoting *Hunter v. New Mexico*, 916 F.2d 595, 598 (10th Cir. 1990) (per curiam)) (internal quotation marks omitted)); *cf. United States v. Bishop*, 469 F.3d 896, 902 (10th Cir. 2006) ("If an indictment charges particulars, the jury instructions and evidence introduced at trial must comport with those particulars."), *abrogated in part on other grounds by Gall v. United States*, 552 U.S. 38, 128 S. Ct. 586, 169 L. Ed. 2d 445 (2007); *United States v. Gonzalez Edeza*, 359 F.3d 1246, 1250 n.1 (10th Cir. 2004) (explaining that the rule against constructive amendment of the indictment "protects *both* a defendant's right to be subjected only to charges set by a grand jury and his interests in having sufficient notice"); *United States v. Hien Van Tieu*, 279 F.3d 917, 921 (10th Cir. 2002) (same).

The Indictment charged only that Mr. Dayton had possessed images that themselves had been transported in interstate or foreign commerce and contained no reference to the materials prong of § 2252(a)(4)(B). Count Two of the Indictment charged that Mr. Dayton

> knowingly possessed and attempted to possess visual
> depictions of minors engaging in sexually explicit conduct,
> as that term is defined in Title 18, United States Code,
> Section 2256(2)(A)(i-v), to-wit: video files and graphic image
> files . . . , each of which files had been transported in
> interstate or foreign commerce by computer, the producing
> of each of which files involved the use of minors engaging
> in sexually explicit conduct, and each of which files were of
> such sexually explicit conduct, in violation of Title 18,
> United States Code, Section 2252(a)(4)(B).

R., Vol. I, Pt. 1, at 24 (Indictment, filed May 9, 2007). Because Mr. Dayton was not charged with the possession of images that had been "produced using materials which have been mailed or so shipped or transported, by any means including by computer," that conduct simply could not have properly formed the basis for his conviction. Therefore, the government's reliance on that method of proving the requisite jurisdictional nexus must fail.

Moreover, although the government preserved this argument before the district court by objecting to the court's decision not to instruct the jury on the hard drives' Thai origins, we note that the government preserved that objection only when urged to do so by the district court, which was seeking guidance in interpreting Tenth Circuit precedent on this issue. The government admitted that its case really turned on whether the images traveled at some point in interstate or foreign commerce and not on the alleged foreign origin of the hard drives.

In this endeavor, we are guided by two of our prior cases -- *United States v. Wilson* and *United States v. Schaefer.* [10] As we will explain, those cases instruct us to focus upon whether the *particular images* distributed or possessed by the defendant themselves moved in interstate commerce. *Wilson* involved a sufficiency-of-the-evidence challenge to a conviction under § 2252(a)(4)(B). 182 F.3d 737, 739-40 (10th Cir. 1999). That case implicated the "materials" prong discussed above. *See supra* note 9. The *Wilson* court held that the evidence was insufficient to demonstrate the jurisdictional nexus for which Mr. Wilson had been indicted--that is, "that the visual depictions contained on the [computer] diskettes were produced using materials that traveled in interstate or foreign commerce." *Id.* at 741 (footnote omitted). In reaching that conclusion, we rejected a law enforcement agent's testimony "that some of the images at issue *originated* from German magazines" as insufficient to satisfy the jurisdictional nexus requirement. *Id.* at 744 (emphasis added). We reasoned that the agent

> offered no explanation, however, as to how *those particular images* found their way to the diskettes in defendant's possession. Nor did the prosecution otherwise attempt to outline the possible methods by which defendant could have obtained the files through interstate commerce (e.g., obtaining copies of the German magazines and scanning the images into his computer; downloading copies of the images from an out-of-state computer via the Internet or a BBS, etc.).

Id. (emphasis added). The *Wilson* court offered the following example to illustrate its point:

> Imagine a person possesses a magazine and makes a color photocopy (copy # 1) of one of the images contained therein. Further imagine such person uses copy # 1 to make a second color photocopy (copy # 2). Although the magazine would be a "material" used to produce copy # 1, it would not be a "material" used to produce copy # 2. Thus, the fact that some of the images possessed by defendant originated *at some point* in German magazines does not demonstrate, without more, that the German

> magazines were actually "materials" used to produce *the images possessed by defendant.*

Id. at 744 n.5 (emphasis added). *Wilson* clearly rejected the idea that testimony regarding the foreign (or out-of-state) origins of the original image was sufficient to establish the jurisdictional nexus as to the particular copy of that image that was the subject of the prosecution.

> 10 In an attempt to resolve the question that Mr. Dayton presents in this appeal, the Dissent ventures into the realm of statutory analysis and explores legislative and congressional findings. This endeavor, however, is misguided. The Dissent contends that "the critical task in resolving Dayton's jurisdictional challenge is determining precisely what was intended by the statutory phrase 'visual depiction.'" Dissent at 3. The Dissent then seeks to accomplish this task by, first, looking to the plain language of the statute's definition of "visual depiction" and, then, to the legislative history and congressional findings purportedly relevant to the meaning of this term. As the Dissent sees it, this inquiry is analytically necessary. Under the circumstances surrounding this case, we disagree. Whether the Dissent is willing to accept it or not, we do not write on a blank slate in addressing the jurisdictional issue that Mr. Dayton raises in this appeal. As we note in text, our analysis is guided by our prior decisions in *Wilson* and *Schaefer.*

In *Schaefer*, we applied *Wilson* to facts like those present here. In that case, Mr. Schaefer brought a sufficiency-of-the-evidence challenge to his convictions for receiving child pornography and possessing child pornography. 501 F.3d at 1198. There, we held that the jurisdictional nexus requires movement across state lines and that it is not enough to assume that an Internet connection necessarily establishes interstate travel. *Id.* at 1200-01. [11] We reasoned that, although "in many, if not most, situations the use of the Internet will involve the movement of communications or materials between states[,] . . . this fact does not suspend the need for evidence of this interstate movement." *Id.* at 1201. We held that "[a]fter establishing a computer or Internet connection as the method of transport, the government must still prove that the Internet transmission also moved *the images* across state lines." *Id.* (emphasis added). *Schaefer* followed *Wilson*'s holding that the government must demonstrate interstate travel for the *particular* images at issue in the criminal prosecution. [12] We stated that even if we assume *arguendo* that the images appearing in the foreign-language movie clips and the image of the young girl originated outside of the State of Kansas (like the images from the German magazine in *Wilson*), the government offered no proof that the particular images on the CDs in question moved across state lines. In particular, the government offered no proof that Mr. Schaefer accessed the images through an *interstate* Internet connection and either downloaded them directly to the CDs or downloaded them to his computer and later transferred them to the CDs.

Id. at 1206; *see also id.* at 1206 n.11 ("Indeed, the government offered no solid proof linking Mr. Schaefer's use of the Internet--whether involving an interstate connection or not--to the pornographic images on the CDs. For example, the government made no effort to show that the *specific images* stored on Mr. Schaefer's computer also appeared on the CDs." (emphasis added)). This hypothetical in *Schaefer* rejects the notion, advocated by the government in this case, that the foreign or out-of-state origin of an image is sufficient to demonstrate an interstate nexus. [13]

11 The Ninth Circuit recently interpreted essentially identical language in a pre-2008-amendment child pornography statute in the same way. *See Wright*, 625 F.3d at 594 ("[S]ection 2252A(a)(1)'s jurisdictional element is focused not on the *means* the defendant uses to mail, transport, or ship child pornography, and *its* connection to interstate commerce. Rather, it requires that the defendant mail, transport, or ship child pornography interstate."); *see also id.* at 597-98 ("Whether the defendant transported child pornography by mail, by sea, or by computer, the government must still prove it crossed state lines.").

12 The Dissent's contention that *Schaefer*'s panel "simply assumed, without directly deciding, that the phrase ['visual image'] referred to specific images possessed by defendant," Dissent at 14, is fatuous at best. As our analysis makes patent, *Schaefer* squarely held (relying upon *Wilson*) that the focus of the jurisdictional inquiry is on the *particular* image of child pornography possessed or received by the defendant.

13 The Dissent notes that the government's understanding of the statute's jurisdictional requirement--which the Dissent embraces--is "analogous to the manner in which we interpret federal firearms offenses." Dissent at 8 n.5. True enough. But the jurisdictional principles governing firearms statutes do not indicate that we should adopt a different approach here.

Indeed, those principles establish the same analytic baseline--*viz.*, whether there is sufficient proof that the *particular* item at issue has crossed state lines. In the case of a firearm, if the government establishes that the particular firearm has crossed state lines at some point prior to the prosecution, it has carried its jurisdictional burden. That fact frequently can be established by mere visual inspection of the firearm itself--with the operative inquiry in that instance being whether this *kind of* firearm is made in the state where it is found; if not, a rational jury could find that it crossed state lines to reach that state. *See, e.g., United States v. Snow*, 82 F.3d 935, 941 (10th Cir. 1996) (noting that the "unrefuted and unchallenged evidence" by a law enforcement agent on direct examination "established there are only two gun manufacturers in Wyoming, neither of which manufacture the type of weapon [the defendant] was charged with stealing and possessing[,]" and that this evidence along with other evidence related to the origin the type of gun was sufficient proof "to establish that at some point the gun had to have crossed state or national lines in order to have been available for sale in Wyoming"); *cf. United States v. Overstreet*, 40 F.3d 1090, 1095 (10th Cir. 1994) (holding that the district court did not abuse its discretion in admitting testimony of a law enforcement agent who "had no knowledge or opinion about the firearm identified in the indictment" but stated that "there are not, and have never been, any manufacturers of revolvers in Oklahoma . . . [and] any revolver used during a carjacking in Oklahoma necessarily travelled in interstate commerce"). Alas, in the digital context, things are not that simple. By merely examining an image of child pornography, we cannot establish whether that *particular* image, as opposed to a prior iteration of that image, has crossed state lines. More is needed. Therefore, our interpretation of the jurisdictional requirement in the firearms context does not detract from the conclusion that we reach here. In both contexts, the objective of the jurisdictional inquiry is to determine whether the *particular* item at issue has crossed state lines; the evidentiary burden to establish that fact is simply lighter in most instances in the firearms context.

It is patent that our reasoning based upon *Wilson* was an essential foundation of our jurisdictional holding in *Schaefer*; consequently, it is binding upon us here. *See Bates v. Dep't of Corr. of Kan.*, 81 F.3d 1008, 1011 (10th Cir. 1996) ("[A] panel of this Court is bound by a holding of a prior panel of this Court but is not bound by a prior panel's *dicta.*"); *see also* Michael Abramowicz & Maxwell Stearns, *Defining Dicta*, 57 Stan. L. Rev. 953, 1065 (2005) ("A holding consists of those propositions along the chosen decisional path or paths of reasoning that (1) are actually decided, (2) are based upon the facts of the case, and (3) *lead to the judgment.* If not a holding, a proposition stated in a case counts as dicta." (emphasis added)).

Therefore, under *Wilson* and *Schaefer* we must determine whether there was sufficient evidence to establish that the particular images stored on Mr. Dayton's hard drives and CDs and accessed by Agent Cecchini through LimeWire themselves traveled across state lines. We do not look to previous copies of those images or even the originals of those images, but rather focus our jurisdictional inquiry only on the particular images distributed and possessed by Mr. Dayton. [14]

14 The Dissent contends that our reading of *Wilson* and *Schaefer* results in the absurd situation wherein successful child pornography prosecutions are only possible where the defendant "physically transport[s] the hard drive or CDs containing [the illicit images] across state lines." Dissent at 10. This argument is specious at best, and is belied by our own case law. For instance, we recently acknowledged, in *United States v. Dobbs*, the possibility that a computer user who knowingly accesses images of child pornography online *may* be found guilty of receipt under 18 U.S.C. § 2252(a)(2), so long as in doing so he had "the ability to exercise control over them by, for example, clicking on or enlarging them." 629 F.3d 1199, 1204 (10th Cir. 2011). In such instances, as the Dissent there recognized, the files created as a result of the defendant's online activity (i.e., the files in the computer's cache) are not the basis for conviction, per se; rather, they are only circumstantial "proof" of the crime. *Id.* at 1213 (Briscoe, C.J., dissenting) ("[T]he existence of copies of the images in the cache of his computer was, like fingerprints left at the scene of the crime, merely evidence of his actual criminal activity."). Had it been shown in *Dobbs* that the defendant knowingly viewed these images when on his screen and had the ability to manipulate them, our decision would have turned on whether the government also could show that those images arrived on his screen by virtue of an "Internet transmission [that] moved the images across state lines," *Schaefer*, 501 F.3d at 1201, regardless of whether a distinct file was created on the defendant's computer. Recognizing this, we believe that nothing in our precedent, or our decision here today, compels--or, for that matter, supports--the Dissent's peculiar conclusion that, going forward, only the transportation of physical media containing digital images across state lines will allow for a successful child pornography prosecution.

The government urges us *not* to follow *Schaefer*. It argues that a subsequent panel of this court limited *Schaefer* to its facts. *See United States v. Vigil*, 523 F.3d 1258, 1266 (10th Cir. 2008). We are not persuaded by the government's argument. In *Vigil*, a panel concluded with respect to a prosecution under the Hobbs Act, 18 U.S.C. §

1951(a), that "[a] rational jury could certainly conclude that Mr. Vigil's acts either actually or potentially affected interstate commerce." *Id.* at 1267. In reaching that conclusion, the *Vigil* court rejected the defendant's reliance on *Schaefer*, finding that "*Schaefer* is distinguishable." *Id.* at 1266. The *Vigil* court distinguished *Schaefer* first by saying, "the court concluded in *Schaefer* that Congress did not intend to exercise its full Commerce Clause power in enforcing the child pornography statute." *Id.* In contrast, the *Vigil* court reasoned that the Hobbs Act *did* involve Congress's full exercise of Commerce Clause power, saying that "[t]he words of the Hobbs Act suggest that Congress intends to use all of its authority under the [C]ommerce [C]lause." *Id.*

The *Vigil* court next compared and contrasted the absence of any evidence regarding interstate commerce in *Schaefer* with the sufficient evidence of interstate commerce before it. *Id.* The court explained that the government's only evidence in *Schaefer* regarding the jurisdictional nexus was that the defendant in that case used the Internet, which did not automatically mean that there was a movement across state lines. *Id.* Based on that limited quantum of proof, the *Vigil* court stated that "*Schaefer* is limited to its facts--the government's say so was not enough to prove that the Internet operates in interstate commerce, no matter how obvious." *Id.* (citing *Schaefer*, 501 F.3d at 1207-08 (Tymkovich, J., concurring)). In contrast, the government in *Vigil* had presented evidence that the defendant's actions had "either actually or potentially affected interstate commerce." *Id.* at 1267.

Viewed in the context of its analysis, we do not read *Vigil*'s description of *Schaefer* as being "limited to its facts" as enervating in any material way the precedential force of *Schaefer*'s child pornography, jurisdictional holding. To some extent, all judicial decisions are limited to their facts. *See Robinson v. Diamond Hous. Corp.*, 463 F.2d 853, 862, 150 U.S. App. D.C. 17 (D.C. Cir. 1972) ("Every case is 'limited to its facts,' if by that phrase one means that the court based its judgment on the facts presented to it. But most cases are also decided with reference to some more general normative principle which extends beyond the specific circumstances of the case before the court. Indeed, it is the existence of such broader norms which distinguishes a decision which is principled and rational from one which is *ad hoc* and arbitrary.").

As a function of common-law decisionmaking, all cases must be viewed as products of their factual context; it is from that context that decisions derive precedential force. *See Allegheny Gen. Hosp. v. NLRB*, 608 F.2d 965, 969-70 (3d Cir. 1979) ("The essence of the common law doctrine of precedent or [s]tare decisis is that the rule of the case creates a binding legal precept. . . . A judicial precedent attaches a specific legal consequence to a detailed set of facts in an adjudged case or judicial decision, which is then considered as furnishing the rule for the determination of a subsequent case involving identical or similar material facts and arising in the same court or a lower court in the judicial hierarchy."), *abrogated on other grounds by St. Margaret Mem'l Hosp. v. NLRB*, 991 F.2d 1146 (3d Cir. 1993); *see also* Jeff Todd, *Undead* Precedent: The Curse of a Holding *"Limited To Its Facts"*, 40 Tex. Tech L. Rev. 67, 75 (2007) ("To some extent, the process of applying prior cases to current litigation already involves limiting the precedential case to its facts. The holding of a particular case may control the result in future cases, but only those in which the facts are similar to the precedent case in all relevant respects." (footnote omitted) (internal quotation marks omitted)); Abramowicz & Maxwell, *supra*, at 1065 (noting that a "holding consists of," *inter alia*, "those propositions along the chosen decisional path or paths of reasoning that (1) are actually decided, [and] (2) are *based upon the facts of the case . . . .*" (emphasis added)).

This is particularly true in the federal system because federal courts are constitutionally forbidden from issuing advisory opinions and are restricted to adjudicating concrete cases or controversies. U.S. Const. art. III, § 2, cl. 1; *see United Pub. Workers of Am. (C.I.O.) v. Mitchell*, 330 U.S. 75, 89, 67 S. Ct. 556, 91 L. Ed. 754 (1947) ("As is well known the federal courts established pursuant to Article III of the Constitution do not render advisory opinions.").

The phrase "limited to its facts" has often been used imprecisely, and courts have not reached a uniform view as to its meaning. *See* Todd, *supra*, at 68 ("Numerous appellate courts, both federal and state, have limited--or 'restricted' or 'confined'--a holding to its facts, and *many more rely upon cases with such holdings.* Although thousands of decisions have been limited in this manner, the meaning of this curse remains cloaked in shadow and mist. The courts declare this limitation but do not describe precisely what it means." (emphasis added) (footnotes omitted)). [15] We heretofore have not clarified what we meant in *Vigil* when we referred to *Schaefer* as being "limited to its facts." As an initial matter, it goes without saying that the *Vigil* court was not empowered to overrule--even tacitly or indirectly--our holding in *Schaefer. See, e.g., Thompson v. Weyerhaeuser Co.*, 582 F.3d 1125, 1130 (10th Cir. 2009) ("Absent an intervening Supreme Court or en banc decision justifying such action, we lack the power to overrule our own precedent."). Furthermore, the context in which the "limited to its facts" statement was made clearly reveals that the *Vigil* court was merely comparing the absolute lack of evidence in *Schaefer* of an interstate nexus--where the only evidence of such a nexus was "the government's say so," *Vigil*, 523 F.3d at 1266--and the more substantial (and ultimately sufficient) evidence of that nexus in *Vigil, see id.* at 1266-67. *Vigil*'s use of *Schaefer* as an "analog[y]," *id.* at 1266, surely cannot mean that we must await the unlikely occurrence of a factually identical case before we can apply *Schaefer*'s jurisdictional holding and reasoning. *See* Comment, *Bush v. Gore and the Uses of "Limiting"*, 116 Yale L. J. 1159, 1162 (2007) ("The use of 'limited by' serves as a caveat and not as an absolute bar to future application of the case. That a case is 'limited by its facts' does not mean that its application is limited only to those facts." (footnote omitted)); *cf. also Hudson v. Palmer*, 468 U.S. 517, 533, 104 S. Ct. 3194, 82 L. Ed. 2d 393 (1984) ("While *Parrat [v. Taylor*, 451 U.S. 527, 101 S. Ct. 1908, 68 L. Ed. 2d 420 (1981),] is necessarily limited by its facts to negligent deprivations of property, it is evident . . . that its reasoning applies as well to intentional deprivations of property.").

---

15 Many courts have recognized the continued vitality of cases long-since "limited to [their] facts." *See, e.g., Holmes v. United States*, 876 F.2d 1545, 1548 (11th Cir. 1989) (noting that, while the earlier case of *Trujillo v. United States*, 377 F.2d 266 (5th Cir. 1967), had been "limited to its facts," "[n]either the former Fifth Circuit nor the Eleventh Circuit has reversed the holding in *Trujillo* [and] [t]hus, the ruling remains binding precedent on this court"); *Davis v. Page*, 618 F.2d 374, 383 n.9 (5th Cir. 1980) (supporting its decision regarding the rights of indigent parents to counsel in Florida child dependency proceedings by reference to the Supreme Court's holding in *Boddie v. Connecticut*, 401 U.S. 371, 91 S. Ct. 780, 28 L. Ed. 2d 113 (1971), which the court recognized "ha[d] been strictly limited to its facts"); *Bacon v. Hennepin Cnty. Med. Ctr.*, No. 06-CV-2359, 2007 U.S. Dist. LEXIS 91103, 2007 WL 4373104, at *9 (D. Minn. Dec. 11, 2007) (noting that there was nothing inherently "unique" about the facts of a decision that had been

"limited to its facts," and then applying that decision over a more recent, conflicting appellate ruling based on the principle that the earliest opinion--absent a subsequent en banc or Supreme Court ruling--is binding in the case of an intra-circuit split); *see also Stewart v. Blackwell*, 444 F.3d 843, 859-60, 868 (6th Cir. 2006) (relying extensively on *Bush v. Gore*, 531 U.S. 98, 121 S. Ct. 525, 148 L. Ed. 2d 388 (2000), in determining that Ohio had violated the Equal Protection Clause by failing to utilize uniform voting technologies across the state, despite the Supreme Court stating that its holding in *Bush* was "limited to the present circumstances"), *superseded by* 477 F.3d 691 (6th Cir. 2007), *vacating as moot* 356 F. Supp. 2d 791 (N.D. Ohio 2004); *Focus Inv. Assocs., Inc. v. Am. Title Ins. Co.*, 992 F.2d 1231, 1242-43 (1st Cir. 1993) (relying in large part on the logic of *Phalen Park State Bank v. Reeves*, 312 Minn. 194, 251 N.W.2d 135, 141 (Minn. 1977), a decision which the authoring court had itself "limited to the unique facts and circumstances presented in this case," en route to finding that the appellant had standing to raise a usury defense).

To be sure, other courts have a different view. For example, some courts have treated the decision to limit a case to its facts as akin to an implicit overruling. *See, e.g., Schumacher v. United States*, 931 F.2d 650, 654 (10th Cir. 1991) (dismissing the persuasive value of the logic of *McNamara v. Comm'r of Internal Revenue*, 827 F.2d 168 (7th Cir. 1987), a case that had subsequently been "limited to its facts"); *Ingalls Shipbuilding Div., Litton Sys., Inc. v. White*, 681 F.2d 275, 288 n.13 (5th Cir. 1982) ("[S]ince the disposition of *Joyner* is expressly limited to its facts, we do not regard th[is] circumscribed decision[] as creating a precedential rule that controls our conclusion in this case." (internal citation omitted)), *overruled on other grounds by Newpark Shipbuilding & Repair, Inc. v. Roundtree*, 723 F.2d 399 (5th Cir. 1984); *Bacon*, 2007 U.S. Dist. LEXIS 91103, 2007 WL 4373104, at *9 ("To assert that an opinion of an appellate court has been 'limited to its facts' is usually a polite way of saying 'implicitly overruled.'").

This lack of uniformity in how courts have interpreted the phrase "limited to its facts" counsels that it is wise to focus on the specific context in which the language is used. As noted *infra*, based upon a careful examination of the *Vigil* case--the context at issue here--it is apparent that this phrase, as applied to *Schaefer*, does not weaken in any material way the precedential force of *Schaefer*'s jurisdictional holding and its supporting rationale.

In any event, the facts to which *Vigil* purportedly limited *Schaefer* formed the bedrock for a legal holding regarding the jurisdictional scope of precisely the same child pornography provisions that are at issue here. Nothing in *Vigil* reasonably could be read to cast doubt on the merits of this jurisdictional holding or *Schaefer*'s interpretation of *Wilson*'s focus on the particular images at issue in a criminal prosecution. We underscore that *Vigil* involved a jurisdictional challenge under the Hobbs Act and not the child pornography statute at issue here. 523 F.3d at 1266. It only commented on *Schaefer* in deflecting the defendant's argument by "analog[y]" that "his actions did not affect interstate commerce." *Id.* Because our court in *Vigil* was not construing the language of the child pornography statutes, and, more specifically, not attempting to discern the scope of their jurisdictional provisions, we cannot conclude that *Vigil* calls into question the soundness of our jurisdictional holding in *Schaefer* and its underlying rationale. [16]

16 We are likewise not given pause by our *unpublished*--and therefore non-precedential--decision in *United States v. Swenson*, which held that there was no plain error in the defendant's conviction for images produced in South America because "[a] reasonable jury could (even if it need not) conclude from this evidence that, for the image to wend its way from South America to Wyoming, it had traveled in interstate or foreign commerce." 335 F. App'x 751, 753 (10th Cir. 2009). *Swenson* ignored *Wilson* and *Schaefer*'s distinction between an original and a copy and the resultant possibility that a defendant could have obtained the *particular* images from *within the state's borders* as contemplated by *Wilson*. Nor are we swayed by the more recent *unpublished* decision in *United States v. Espinoza*, which relied on *Swenson* in what the court deemed a "factually similar case." No. 09-8102, 403 Fed. Appx. 315, 2010 U.S. App. LEXIS 24125, 2010 WL 4739519, at *3 (10th Cir. Nov. 23, 2010). *Espinoza* adopted *Swenson*'s reasoning whole cloth, and in doing so replicated its error.

Accordingly, we review the evidence of the jurisdictional nexus adduced at Mr. Dayton's trial as that evidence relates to the particular images distributed and possessed by Mr. Dayton. First, as to the distribution charge, the government clearly did not prove travel in interstate or foreign commerce in showing that Agent Cecchini (in Tulsa) accessed those images from Mr. Dayton (also in Tulsa) through LimeWire. Although the government knew that Mr. Dayton's ISP was Cox Communications, no evidence was introduced regarding the location of Cox's servers. *Cf. United States v. Sturm*, 560 F. Supp. 2d 1029, 1032-33 (D. Colo. 2008) (denying a motion to dismiss for lack of a jurisdictional nexus because there was evidence that the Colorado-based defendant used AOL to obtain child pornography, that AOL's computer servers were located in Virginia, and any images on the defendant's hard drive must have been routed through AOL's servers in Virginia). On appeal, the government contends that testimony regarding the origins of the original video images is sufficient to establish the interstate nexus. We disagree. It is not enough to say that the (regrettably) well-known victim in the "Vicky" series was from Washington State and that Agent Cecchini had not only seen that video image before in other investigations, but that he had received it from other countries. No evidence was introduced concerning whether the particular video image of "Vicky" *distributed by Mr. Dayton* had traveled in interstate or foreign commerce. Furthermore, we also find insufficient the evidence that one video image *may* have been originally filmed in Southeast Asia [17] and that Agent Cecchini testified he had seen all of these video images during prior investigations. As in *Schaefer*, "the government offered no proof that the particular [video images] in question moved across state lines." 501 F.3d at 1206. Similarly, the evidence proffered as to the possession charge related only to the origins of the original pictures--*viz.*, Agent Trifiletti's testimony that the victims depicted in those pictures lived in Paraguay and had never left that country. There was no evidence as to how Mr. Dayton obtained the particular pictures he possessed.

[17] The district court's conclusion as to the Southeast Asian origination of the video was based only on the perceived race of the people depicted in the video and the video's titular reference to "cambodian" and "sex tourist."

Consequently, we must conclude that the government's jurisdictional proof regarding both the distribution and possession counts was insufficient to support Mr. Dayton's convictions under 18 U.S.C. § 2252(a)(2) and (a)(4)(B). [18]

[18] The Dissent sounds an alarmist call for an en banc proceeding, suggesting that *Schaefer*'s jurisdictional holding is "improperly hampering the prosecution of child pornography cases in this circuit." Dissent at 15 n.9. Putting aside the fact that our task as judges is not to interpret statutes in a manner that best facilitates government prosecutions, but rather in a manner that effectuates Congress's will, we underscore that the impact of *Schaefer*'s holding is necessarily very limited. Congress amended the statute in 2008, effectively broadening the jurisdictional language that was at issue in *Schaefer*. See *supra* note 8. Therefore, *Schaefer* only affects the presumably

small number of pending cases that were prosecuted under the pre-amendment statute, and insofar as *Schaefer*'s holding could be viewed as having legally improper effects--a perspective that we reject--those effects will be short-lived. It ineluctably follows that expending the tremendous judicial resources associated with an en banc proceeding with the aim of correcting those short-lived effects would be a dubious undertaking indeed.

III. Conclusion

For the reasons discussed above, we conclude that the government presented insufficient proof to establish the requisite jurisdictional nexus under 18 U.S.C. § 2252(a)(2) and (a)(4)(B). Accordingly, we REVERSE Mr. Dayton's convictions and REMAND the case to the district court with instructions to VACATE its judgment and enter a judgment of acquittal.

ENTERED FOR THE COURT

Jerome A. Holmes

Circuit Judge

DISSENT

BRISCOE, Chief Judge, dissenting:

I respectfully dissent. In my view, the majority adopts an unnecessarily restrictive interpretation of the statutory phrase "visual depiction," as employed in 18 U.S.C. §§ 2252(a)(2) and (a)(4)(B), and in turn imposes an unduly burdensome level of proof on prosecutors seeking convictions under these child pornography statutes. Properly interpreted, the phrase "visual depiction" refers to the substance of an image of child pornography, and thus encompasses not only the particular digital copy of that image received, possessed, or distributed by the defendant, but also any prior generations of that image (digital or otherwise). Applying that definition in this case, I conclude the evidence presented by the government at trial was sufficient to allow the jury to find that the images at issue were transported in interstate commerce. I also conclude there is no merit to Dayton's challenge to the district court's instruction defining the term "distribute." Thus, I would affirm Dayton's convictions and resulting sentence.

I. Sufficiency of evidence - interstate commerce

Dayton contends that the evidence presented by the government at trial was insufficient to prove the requisite interstate nexus under the two statutes he was convicted of violating. In reviewing this contention, "we ask whether, viewing the evidence in the light most favorable to the government as the prevailing party, any rational trier of fact could have found the essential [jurisdictional] element[] of the crime beyond a reasonable doubt." United States v. Hutchinson, 573 F.3d 1011, 1033 (10th Cir. 2009).

Dayton's convictions for distributing and possessing child pornography arose under 18 U.S.C. §§ 2252(a)(2) and (a)(4)(B), which, at the time of his indictment, provided:

> (a) Any person who--
>
> * * *
>
> (2) knowingly receives, or distributes, any visual depiction that has been mailed, or has been shipped or transported in interstate or foreign commerce, or which contains materials which have been mailed or so shipped or transported, by any means including by computer, or knowingly reproduces any visual depiction for distribution in interstate or foreign commerce by any means including by computer or through the mails, if--
>
>> (A) the producing of such visual depiction involves the use of a minor engaging in sexually explicit conduct; and
>>
>> (B) such visual depiction is of such conduct; [or]
>
> * * *
>
> (4) * * *
>> (B) knowingly possesses 1 or more books, magazines, periodicals, films, video tapes, or other matter which contain any visual depiction that has been mailed, or has been shipped or transported in interstate or foreign commerce, or which was produced using materials which have been mailed or

so shipped or transported, by any means including
by computer, if--

> (I) the producing of such visual
> depiction involves the use of a minor
> engaging in sexually explicit conduct;
> and

> (ii) such visual depiction is of such
> conduct . . .

shall be punished as provided in subsection (b) of this section.

18 U.S.C. §§ 2252(a)(2) and (a)(4)(B) (2006). As Dayton correctly
notes, both of these statutory subsections require, as a jurisdictional
element, proof that the "visual depictions" at issue were "mailed . . .
or . . . shipped or transported in interstate or foreign commerce . . . ."
[1] Id.

---

1 The jurisdictional element of 18 U.S.C. § 2252(a)(4)(B) can be satisfied in
an alternative manner, i.e., by proof that the visual depictions at issue were
produced with materials that were mailed, shipped, or transported in
interstate or foreign commerce. As the majority correctly notes, however,
the indictment in this case did not rely on this alternative manner of
proving the jurisdictional element.

As I see it, the critical task in resolving Dayton's jurisdictional
challenge is determining precisely what was intended by the statutory
phrase "visual depiction." [2] In the majority's view, a "visual
depiction," in the context of a case like this involving digital images
of child pornography, refers narrowly to a specific graphics file (such
as the files found on Dayton's hard drive and CDs). Thus, under the
majority's view, identical digital copies of the same image constitute
separate "visual depictions" for purposes of the statute, and each
such "visual depiction" must have traveled in interstate or foreign
commerce in order to satisfy the jurisdictional element. In other
words, it matters not that the original version, or an earlier generation
copy, of the substantive image has traveled in interstate commerce;
instead, the precise copy possessed by the defendant must have
traveled in interstate commerce. [3] In contrast, the government

effectively suggests that the phrase "visual depiction" refers to the substance of the digital image, and not necessarily to a specific graphics file. In other words, the government suggests, identical copies of the same image constitute the same "visual depiction" for purposes of the statute. Consequently, under the government's view, it is enough to satisfy the jurisdictional element if the original version or prior generation copies of the image at issue have previously traveled in interstate or foreign commerce. See United States v. Vosburgh, 602 F.3d 512, 534 n.22 (3d Cir. 2010) (suggesting, without deciding, that different digital copies of the same image "might be considered the same 'visual depictions,' since they are, for all intents and purposes, the same pictures").

2 Although the majority concedes that our task is to "interpret statutes . . . in a manner that effectuates Congress's will," Maj. Op. at 35 n.18, it suggests that the inquiry is foreclosed, and Dayton's jurisdictional challenge controlled entirely, by "our prior decisions in Wilson and Schaefer." Id. at 20 n.10. I disagree. As discussed in greater detail below, neither Wilson nor Schaefer addressed the meaning of the statutory phrase "visual depiction." Thus, neither is controlling.

3 How this could ever be proven, we are left by the majority only to guess. Indeed, the only conceivable way that the precise copy possessed by the defendant could satisfy the jurisdictional nexus would be if it was physically transported (as it resides on some form of media) across state lines.

To resolve which of these interpretations is correct, I begin, as I must, with the language of the statute. See Engine Mfrs. Ass'n v. South Coast Air Quality Mgmt. Dist., 541 U.S. 246, 252, 124 S. Ct. 1756, 158 L. Ed. 2d 529 (2004) ("Statutory construction must begin with the language employed by Congress and the assumption that the ordinary meaning of that language accurately expresses the legislative purpose.") (internal quotation marks omitted). The statutory definition of the phrase "visual depiction," as of the time of Dayton's conduct and indictment, was non-exclusive, stating simply that "'visual depiction' includes undeveloped film and videotape, and data stored on computer disk or by electronic means which is capable of conversion into a visual image." 18 U.S.C. § 2256(5) (2007). [4] Although this definition makes reference to digital images (i.e., "data .

.. which is capable of conversion into a visual image"), it does nothing to resolve the question at issue.

4 The statutory definition of "visual depiction" applicable to Dayton's case originated in 1996, as part of the Child Pornography Prevention Act of 1996. In late 2008, after Dayton was indicted, Congress amended this statutory definition to read:

"visual depiction" includes undeveloped film and videotape, data stored on computer disk or by electronic means which is capable of conversion into a visual image, and data which is capable of conversion into a visual image that has been transmitted by any means, whether or not stored in permanent format . . . .

18 U.S.C. § 2256(5) (2010).

I therefore turn to the ordinary meaning of the phrase. See Hardt v. Reliance Standard Life Ins. Co., 130 S. Ct. 2149, 2156, 176 L. Ed. 2d 998 (2010) (noting that courts must assume the ordinary meaning of statutory language expresses the legislative purpose). The term "visual" is commonly defined as "[c]arried out or performed by means of vision," and "an object of vision or sight; capable of being seen; perceptible, visible." Oxford English Dictionary (2d ed. 1989; online version Nov. 2010). In turn, the term "depiction" is defined as "[t]he action of depicting; painted representation, picture; graphic description," and the term "depict" is defined as "[t]o portray, delineate, figure anyhow," and "[t]o represent, as a painting or picture does." Id. Together, then, these terms refer to a portrayal or representation that is capable of being seen, i.e., a visually observable image. Unfortunately, however, this again fails to resolve the question at issue.

I thus turn, for further assistance, to legislative history and express Congressional findings. In 1996, Congress amended the statutory definition of "visual depiction" in order to expressly "include stored computer data." S. Rep. No. 104-358, at 10 (1996). In doing so, Congress found that "where children are used in its production, child pornography permanently records the victim's abuse, and its continuing existence causes the child victims of sexual abuse continuing harm by haunting those children in future years . . . ." Congressional Findings, 110 Stat. 3009-26, notes following 18 U.S.C. § 2251 (quoting Pub. L. 104-208) (emphasis added). In 2003, Congress, in an effort to bolster child pornography laws, passed the Prosecutorial Remedies and Other Tools to end the Exploitation of Children Today Act (PROTECT Act). At that time, Congress expressly found that "[t]he vast majority of child pornography prosecutions today involve images contained on hard drives, computer disks, and/or related media." Congressional Findings, 117 Stat. 676, notes following 18 U.S.C. § 2251 (quoting Pub. L. 108-21). More importantly, Congress found that "[c]hild pornography circulating on the Internet has, by definition, been digitally uploaded or scanned into computers and has been transferred over the Internet, often in different file formats, from trafficker to trafficker," and that, consequently, "[a]n image seized from a collector of child pornography is rarely a first-generation product . . . ." Id. (emphasis added).

In my view, the legislative history and Congressional findings firmly support the government's assertion that the original version of an image of child pornography, as well as all subsequent generations of that same image, constitute the same "visual depiction" for purposes of prosecution under §§ 2252(a)(2) and (a)(4)(B). As outlined above, Congress was well aware that images of child pornography, following their initial production (by whatever method), are repeatedly copied, typically digitally, by child pornography traffickers and collectors, and that, as a result, images seized from collectors nowadays are "rarely . . . first-generation product[s] . . . ." Id. In other words, Congress was well aware that it is routine for a single image of child pornography to be repeatedly digitally copied and distributed over the Internet to traffickers and collectors throughout the world. And the difficulty of eradicating all such images is undoubtedly why Congress recognized that an image of child pornography, once produced for the first time, will continue to "haunt" a victim "in future years." Congressional Findings, 110 Stat. 3009-26, notes following 18 U.S.C. § 2251 (quoting Pub. L. 104-208). In turn, that is why Congress expressly found that "[t]he Government . . . has a compelling interest in ensuring that the criminal prohibitions against child pornography remain enforceable and effective." Congressional Findings, 117 Stat. 676, notes following 18 U.S.C. § 2251 (quoting Pub. L. 108-21). In sum, the legislative history and Congressional findings weigh heavily, if not decisively, in favor of the more expansive interpretation of the phrase "visual depiction" urged by the government.

If that were not enough, I further conclude, as a matter of common sense, that the government's interpretation of the phrase "visual depiction" is superior to that of the majority. By treating all copies of the same substantive image as a single "visual depiction," the government's proposed interpretation properly allows courts and jurors to take into account the relevant history of the substantive image, i.e., where it originated and where it traveled prior to the defendant receiving and possessing it. [5] In other words, the government's proposed interpretation allows courts and jurors to consider when the substantive image first entered the "stream of interstate [or foreign] commerce," United States v. Yellow Cab Co., 332 U.S. 218, 228-29, 67 S. Ct. 1560, 91 L. Ed. 2010 (1947), overruled on other grounds by Copperweld Corp. v. Independence Tube Corp., 467 U.S. 752, 104 S. Ct. 2731, 81 L. Ed. 2d 628 (1984), and it acknowledges the reality, as Congress has found, that images of child pornography typically remain forever in that stream. In contrast, the majority's position renders irrelevant the prior history of the image; it thus matters not where or how the image itself originated, or how many hundreds or thousands of times the image has been digitally copied and distributed to traffickers and collectors around the world. Instead, the majority's position focuses narrowly, and unreasonably in my view, on the history of the particular digital copy possessed by the defendant. And given what we have learned in this case and others about the creation of digital copies, the unfortunate reality is that the majority's position will effectively stymie the intent of Congress by preventing the prosecution of many child pornography collectors. In this case, for example, it is beyond dispute that "new [digital] copies [of the images at issue] . . . were created in the process of" Dayton both downloading the image files from other LimeWire users' shared folders onto his own hard drive, and in turn saving some of those files onto CDs. [6] United States v. Guagliardo, 278 F.3d 868, 871 n.3 (9th Cir. 2002). In other words, those copies were created at the moment they were recorded on the hard drive and CDs. Consequently, it would have been impossible for those image files to have traveled in interstate commerce during the creation process, thus meaning that they could only be actionable under the majority's interpretation of § 2252(a)(4)(B) if Dayton (or someone else) physically transported the hard drive or CDs containing them across state lines. [7] Given the force with which Congress has spoken on the issue of child pornography, that is surely not the result it intended.

5 In this regard, the government's interpretation is analogous to the manner in which we interpret federal firearms offenses. It is well established in federal firearms cases that once a firearm has been shipped or transported in interstate or foreign commerce, the jurisdictional element of the statute is satisfied, and there is no necessity of proving that the firearm was so transported or shipped immediately prior to arriving in the defendant's possession, or that the defendant himself transported or shipped the firearm in interstate commerce. E.g., Barrett v. United States, 423 U.S. 212, 224, 96 S. Ct. 498, 46 L. Ed. 2d 450 (1976) ("conclud[ing] that [18 U.S.C.] § 922(h) covers the intrastate receipt . . . of a firearm that previously had moved in interstate commerce.").

6 Federal Bureau of Investigation (FBI) Agent Joseph Cecchini testified at trial that at the time the search warrant for Dayton's home was executed, he and another officer interviewed Dayton. According to Cecchini, Dayton admitted he was the subscriber to the Internet account at issue and understood the Internet was "a worldwide entity and information travels worldwide." ROA, Vol. 2, Part 1 at 134. In turn, Cecchini testified, Dayton readily admitted that he used the Internet "for downloading files, movies, pictures, that kind of stuff," id., and had "been downloading child pornography and using LimeWire for about three months prior to us being there." Id. at 135. When asked by Cecchini what he did with the images of child pornography after he downloaded them from the Internet, Dayton "said that he had them for a while. He said some of them, he deleted. He said some of them, he kept and some of them he put onto a DVD or DVDs." Id. at 136.

7 The majority asserts this conclusion "is specious at best, and is belied by our own case law." Maj. Op. at 25 n.14. But the only decision the majority cites in support is its own recent majority opinion in United States v. Dobbs, 629 F.3d 1199, 2011 WL 14459 (10th Cir. 2011). Dobbs, according to the majority, "acknowledged . . . the possibility that a computer user who knowingly accesses images of child pornography online may be found guilty of receipt under 18 U.S.C. § 2252(a)(2), so long as in doing so he had 'the ability to exercise control over them by, for example, clicking on or enlarging them.'" Maj. Op. at 26 n.14 (quoting Dobbs, 629 F.3d 1199, 2011 WL 14459 at *4). The problem, however, is that the majority decision in Dobbs never delved into the issues we now face, i.e., what is a "visual depiction," and how, precisely, can a visual depiction be shipped or

transported in interstate commerce. Instead, the majority decision in Dobbs focused exclusively on whether the defendant in that case "knowingly received" the images of child pornography that were found in the cache of his computer. 629 F.3d 1199, 2011 WL 14459 at *4. Thus, the majority decision in Dobbs tells us nothing about how the jurisdictional element in this or similar cases can be satisfied.

To be sure, the majority in this case now suggests that, "[h]ad it been shown in Dobbs that the defendant knowingly viewed the[] [charged] images on his screen and had the ability to manipulate them, [its] decision would have turned on whether the government also could show that those images arrived on his screen by virtue of an Internet transmission [that] moved the images across state lines, regardless of whether a distinct file was created on the defendant's computer." Maj. Op. at 26 n.14 (internal quotation marks and citation omitted). But the majority fails to explain how, precisely, that could be so under its interpretation of the phrase "visual depiction." If, as the majority concludes, a "visual depiction" refers narrowly to a specific copy of an image found in the defendant's possession, the defendant's online activity in Dobbs simply could not have, for the reasons discussed above, satisfied the jurisdictional element.

Only my dissenting opinion in Dobbs directly addressed the question of how the jurisdictional element in a receipt case under 18 U.S.C. § 2252(a)(2) can be proven. And, consistent with my position here, I effectively concluded in Dobbs that the original version of an image of child pornography, as well as all subsequent generations of that same image, constitute the same "visual depiction" for purposes of prosecution under § 2252(a)(2). Consequently, I concluded that the government's proof that the images ultimately found in the cache of the defendant's computer were created out-of-state was sufficient to satisfy § 2252(a)(2)'s jurisdictional nexus. 629 F.3d 1199, 2011 WL 14459 at *18 ("I conclude that because a reasonable jury could find that the two images at issue traveled in interstate commerce at some point before arriving on Dobbs's computer, there was sufficient evidence to support the jurisdictional element.").

The majority is mistaken in suggesting that its interpretation is mandated by our prior decision in United States v. Wilson, 182 F.3d 737 (10th Cir. 1999). Wilson, which I authored, involved a different charge, and in turn a different jurisdictional element, than either of the counts at issue here. Specifically, the defendant in Wilson was convicted of "a single count of possessing three or more matters (i.e., . . . ten computer diskettes) containing visual depictions . . . of minors engaging in sexually explicit conduct which were produced using materials that had been mailed, shipped, or transported in interstate or foreign commerce, in violation of 18 U.S.C. § 2252(a)(4)(B)

(1996)." 182 F.3d at 739-40. On appeal, the defendant argued that "the evidence presented at trial was insufficient to establish the jurisdictional element of the charged crime, i.e., that the visual depictions were produced using materials that had been mailed, shipped, or transported in interstate or foreign commerce." Id. at 740. In addressing this issue, we noted that "the prosecution's strategy at trial for proving the jurisdictional element was extremely vague" and "ever-shifting . . . ." Id. at 742. We ultimately addressed and rejected each of those vague theories. We also noted, in passing, that one of the case agents testified at trial "that some of the images at issue originated from German magazines." Id. at 744. In addition to noting that the prosecution failed to rely on this evidence at trial to prove the jurisdictional element, we emphasized that the agent "offered no explanation . . . as to how those particular images found their way to the diskettes in defendant's possession," "[n]or did the prosecution otherwise attempt to outline the possible methods by which defendant could have obtained the files through interstate commerce . . . ." Id. at 744. Thus, we "reject[ed] the possibility that [the agent's] testimony regarding the origination of the images, standing alone, was sufficient to satisfy the jurisdictional element" for a charge brought pursuant to 18 U.S.C. § 2252(a)(4)(B), which required proof that the materials used to produce the pornographic depictions were transported in interstate or foreign commerce. Id.

The majority in this case seizes on the following footnote in Wilson:

> We offer the following example to demonstrate why [the defendant]'s testimony could not, by itself, satisfy the jurisdictional element. Imagine a person possesses a magazine and makes a color photocopy (copy # 1) of one of the images contained therein. Further imagine such person uses copy # 1 to make a second color photocopy (copy # 2). Although the magazine would be a "material" used to produce copy # 1, it would not be a "material" used to produce copy # 2. Thus, the fact that some of the images possessed by defendant originated at some point in German magazines does not demonstrate, without more, that the German magazines were actually "materials" used to produce the images possessed by defendant.

Id. at 744 n.5. Contrary to the conclusion drawn by the majority, this footnote says nothing about the meaning of the statutory phrase "visual depiction." Indeed, the interpretive question we now face regarding the meaning of that statutory phrase was neither argued nor considered in Wilson. Thus, the above-quoted footnote from Wilson must be read in proper context: it opined only that the German magazines cited by the case agent failed to qualify as "materials" used to produce the specific images possessed by the defendant -- which, again, was our focus in this prosecution for violation of 18 U.S.C. § 2252(a)(4)(B). It did not, as suggested by the majority, mandate a particular interpretation of the statutory phrase "visual depiction" or require any type of proof of "interstate travel for the *particular* images at issue in the criminal prosecution." Maj. Op. at 22 (emphasis in original).

As for the other decision relied on by the majority, United States v. Schaefer, 501 F.3d 1197 (10th Cir. 2007), there is no indication that the parties or the panel therein considered the proper interpretation of the statutory phrase "visual depiction." Indeed, the opinion does not even quote the statutory definition of the phrase, let alone attempt to decipher its meaning. Instead, it appears that the panel in Schaefer simply assumed, without directly deciding, that the phrase referred to the specific images possessed by the defendant. Having said that, however, the decision arguably supports, at least to a limited degree, the government's proposed interpretation in this case. In particular, the Schaefer decision at one point states that, "on the[] facts [before it], the government was required to prove that any Internet transmissions containing child pornography that moved to or from [the defendant's] computer crossed state lines." 501 F.3d at 1202. Such proof, however, would not establish that the specific images possessed by the defendant (some of which were contained in "unallocated clusters" and in the "internet cache" on his hard drive, and some of which were contained on a CD) traveled in interstate commerce. Rather, such proof would establish that identical, prior generation copies of the same image traveled by way of the Internet to the defendant's computer, where the copies at issue were then created (in the case of the images on his hard drive, by way of the computer's internal operations, and in the case of the images on the CD, by subsequent action of the defendant in copying the images to the CD). [8] In the end, because Schaefer did not expressly consider the proper interpretation of the phrase "visual depiction," and because any conclusions that can be drawn therefrom regarding that issue are inconsistent, I submit the best course (as other panels have done since its issuance) is to construe it as narrowly limited to its unique facts. [9] See United States v. Vigil, 523 F.3d 1258, 1266 (10th Cir. 2008) ("Schaefer is limited to its facts--the government's say so was not enough to prove that the Internet operates in interstate commerce, no matter how obvious.").

8 In short, Schaefer is internally inconsistent: on the one hand, it states that the specific images possessed by the defendant must have traveled in interstate commerce; on the other hand, it suggests that the interstate nexus could be satisfied by proof that identical, prior-generation copies of the images at issue traveled across state lines to the defendant's computer. Unfortunately, neither Schaefer nor the majority opinion in this case acknowledge this inconsistency.

Moreover, although the majority suggests that the Ninth Circuit agreed with Schaefer when it "recently interpreted essentially identical [jurisdictional] language in a pre-2008-amendment child pornography statute," Maj. Op. at 22 n.11, that is only half-right. To be sure, the Ninth Circuit in United States v. Wright, 625 F.3d 583 (9th Cir. 2010), agreed with Schaefer that a defendant's mere use of an "interstate facility" is insufficient to satisfy jurisdictional language that refers to child pornography or visual depictions being mailed, or transported or shipped in interstate or foreign commerce. Id. at 594. But that is the end of the similarities between the two cases. The remainder of Wright's jurisdictional discussion focused on the unique language of the statutory provision the defendant in that case was charged with violating, i.e., the pre-2008 version of 18 U.S.C. § 2252A(a)(1). Unlike the receipt, possession, and distribution provisions of § 2252 and § 2252A, which prior to 2008 required proof that the visual depictions or child pornography at issue "ha[d] been mailed, or ha[d] been shipped or transported in interstate commerce," 18 U.S.C. § 2252(a)(2), the pre-2008 version of § 2252A(a)(1) required proof that the defendant himself "knowingly mail[ed], or transport[ed] or ship[ped] in interstate or foreign commerce . . . any child pornography." Thus, in short, Wright said nothing about the proper interpretation of the statutory phrase "visual depiction," or about the jurisdictional elements of §§ 2252(a)(2) and (a)(4)(B).

9 Having said that, I submit that the instant case is a suitable candidate for reconsidering, en banc, the jurisdictional holdings contained in Schaefer (the government in Schaefer sought only panel, but not en banc, rehearing). As exemplified by this case and Dobbs, the jurisdictional holdings in Schaefer are, in my view, improperly hampering the prosecution of child pornography cases in this circuit. For example, the government in this case and Dobbs was needlessly prevented, based upon the holdings in Schaefer, from relying on numerous additional images of child pornography possessed by the defendants. In Dobbs, the government's computer

forensic specialist testified that the defendant received approximately 159 images of child pornography. The government's trial evidence in turn focused on seventeen of those images. Ultimately, however, the trial court in Dobbs ruled, based upon Schaefer, that there was sufficient evidence of interstate transport with respect to only two of the images. Although this ruling did not result in the dismissal of either of the two counts alleged against the defendant, it significantly narrowed the scope of each of those counts.

Although the majority suggests there is no need for any en banc proceedings because "Congress amended [18 U.S.C. § 2252] in 2008, effectively broadening [its] jurisdictional language," Maj. Op. at 35-36 n.18, the fact remains that the statute, as currently written, continues to utilize the phrase "visual depiction." Thus, Schaefer and the instant case will, until revisited and reversed by the entire court, continue to impact future child pornography prosecutions in this circuit.

Concluding, then, that the government's proposed interpretation of the statutory phrase "visual depiction" is the proper one, I turn to the evidence presented by the government in this case to determine whether it was sufficient to satisfy the requisite jurisdictional elements. With respect to the distribution charge, the government presented evidence testimony from FBI Agent Joseph Cecchini that one of the video images that formed the basis of the charge was made in Richland, Washington. In my view, this evidence was clearly sufficient to establish the requisite interstate nexus. That is, taking this evidence in the light most favorable to the government, with all reasonable inferences therefrom, a jury could conclude that an image created in the state of Washington necessarily crossed state lines before ultimately arriving on a computer in Oklahoma. [10] See United States v. Schene, 543 F.3d 627, 639 (10th Cir. 2008) (holding that there was sufficient evidence to prove that a hard drive found in Oklahoma was a "material" that had traveled in interstate or foreign commerce upon proof that the hard drive was manufactured in Singapore). The same is true for the possession charge. As to that count, the government presented testimony from FBI agent Christopher Trifiletti that the images found on the CD in Dayton's possession were originally produced in Paraguay. Thus, I reject Dayton's assertion that the government's jurisdictional proof was insufficient to support his convictions.

10 Although the government presented evidence of three other video images in support of the distribution charge, it is unnecessary for me to determine whether the government's evidence sufficiently established that those images also traveled in interstate or foreign commerce. See Griffin v. United States, 502 U.S. 46, 56-57, 112 S. Ct. 466, 116 L. Ed. 2d 371 (1991) (holding that when an indictment charges "several acts in the conjunctive, . . . the verdict stands if the evidence is sufficient with respect to any one of the acts charged") (internal quotation marks omitted).

II. Jury instruction - distribution

Dayton also argues that the district court erred in instructing the jury on the element of distribution. "When reviewing claims of error in regard to jury instructions, we review the instructions as a whole de novo to ensure that the applicable law was correctly stated . . . ." United States v. Allen, 603 F.3d 1202, 1213 (10th Cir. 2010).

The district court defined the term "distribute" for the jury as follows:

> In this case, to distribute means to deliver, transfer, disperse, or dispense to another person. You are instructed that if a person knowingly makes images available on a peer-to-peer file sharing network, such as Limewire, this is considered "distribution" of the images. In other words, the Government may meet its burden of proof on this element by showing that Defendant knowingly allowed others access to his Limewire shared folder.

ROA, Vol. 1, Part 2, at 240. In doing so, the district court relied on our decision in United States v. Shaffer, 472 F.3d 1219 (10th Cir. 2007).

In Shaffer, the defendant was charged with distributing child pornography in violation of 18 U.S.C. § 2252A(a)(2) by "download[ing] images and videos from a peer-to-peer computer network and stor[ing] them in a shared folder on his computer accessible by other users of the network." 472 F.3d at 1220-21. We rejected the defendant's argument that to "distribute" requires a defendant to "actively transfer possession to another." Id. at 1223. We held instead that the defendant "distributed" child pornography by allowing others access to download the child pornography files in his peer-to-peer program's shared folder. Id. ("We have little difficulty in concluding that Mr. Shaffer distributed child pornography .... [H]e freely allowed [others] access to his computerized stash of images and videos and openly invited them to take, or download, those items.").

Although Dayton contends the district court erred by instructing the jury according to Shaffer, and a correct instruction would have relied instead on Schaefer, I disagree. Schaefer, as already discussed, focused exclusively on the jurisdictional nexus (the interstate commerce element) for charges of receiving and possessing child pornography. See Schaefer, 501 F.3d at 1198. Nothing therein addressed distribution of child pornography in general, or the definition of "distribution" in particular.

Dayton's argument that the jury instruction "permitted a less stringent evidentiary foundation to prove the interstate commerce nexus," Aplt. Br. at 62, is wholly without merit. Distribution and jurisdiction are independent elements: the government was required to prove that Dayton knowingly distributed the visual depictions and that those visual depictions had previously traveled in interstate or foreign commerce. [11] Notably, the district court in this case separately and clearly instructed the jury on both of those elements.

11 Dayton appears to suggest that the government was required to prove that he distributed the files in interstate or foreign commerce. However, that is not what the statute requires. Section 2252(a)(2) prohibits "knowingly ... distributing ... any visual depiction that has been mailed, or has been shipped or transported in interstate or foreign commerce ...." (emphasis added). Thus, it is not necessary that Dayton's distribution was itself in interstate or foreign commerce.

I would affirm Dayton's convictions and sentence.

ELIZABETH PEARSON, ET AL., Plaintiffs,
v.
FAIRLAKES VILLAGE CONDO.
ASSOC., ET AL., Defendants

&

Third-party Plaintiffs,
v.
DCI PUERTO RICO, INC., ET AL.,
Third-party Defendants

&

Third-party Plaintiff,
v.
NATIONAL INS. CO.,
Third-party Defendant.

CIV. NO.: 10-1296(SCC)
UNITED STATES DISTRICT COURT FOR
THE DISTRICT OF PUERTO RICO

2012 U.S. Dist. LEXIS 35306

March 13, 2012, Decided
March 13, 2012, Filed

U.S. MAGISTRATE JUDGE SILVIA CARREÑO-COLL,

OPINION AND ORDER

On June 5, 2011, Third-party Defendant DCI Puerto Rico, Inc. ("DCI"), filed a third-party complaint against National Insurance Co. ("National"). Docket No. 81. Referring us to liquidation proceedings underway in Puerto Rico court, National now moves for dismissal or a stay of the third-party suit against it. Docket No. 100. We deny both motions.

According to National, DCI's suit should be terminated on the basis of a liquidation order issued by the Puerto Rico Court of First Instance, San Juan Division. *See* Docket No. 100, at 2. [1] Alone, the liquidation order has no effect on the proceedings in this court. This is because of the bedrock principle that state courts are without power to enjoin the proceedings of federal courts. [2] *Fragoso v. Lopez,* 991 F.2d 878, 881 (1st Cir. 1993) (quoting *Gen. Atomic Co. v. Felter,* 434 U.S. 12, 17, 98 S. Ct. 76, 54 L. Ed. 2d 199 (1977) (per curiam)). Federal courts have a "virtually unflagging obligation . . . to exercise the jurisdiction given to them." *Colo. River Water Conservation Dist. v. United States,* 424 U.S. 800, 817, 96 S. Ct. 1236, 47 L. Ed. 2d 483 (1976). To warrant dismissal or a stay, then, National must show that abstention is appropriate here despite the valid exercise of jurisdiction. To this end, it cites a number of cases applying *Burford* abstention, which is the doctrine most relevant to cases of this sort. *See Burford v. Sun Oil Co.,* 319 U.S. 315, 63 S. Ct. 1098, 87 L. Ed. 1424 (1943). As interpreted by the First Circuit, *Burford* abstention permits "federal courts 'sitting in equity' to refrain from interfering with 'proceedings or orders of state administrative agencies' when 'timely and adequate state court review is available.'" *Fragoso,* 991 F.2d at 882 (quoting *New Orleans Pub. Serv., Inc. v. City Council of New Orleans* ("*NOPSI*"), 491 U.S. 350, 360-64, 109 S. Ct. 2506, 105 L. Ed. 2d 298 (1989)).

1 At the time National filed its motion to dismiss, it included only a Spanish-language copy of the liquidation order. Docket No. 100-1. It stated, however, that an English translation would be forthcoming. Docket No. 100, at 2 n.1. We subsequently set a deadline to submit the translation, Docket No. 108, but National refused to comply. Docket No. 122. Pursuant to Local Rule 5(g), then, we cannot consider the liquidation order's substance, though we acknowledge the proceedings' existence, confirmed as it is by the notice of liquidation filed at Docket No. 111-1.

2 Likewise, Puerto Rico statutes purporting to stay or dismiss actions such as this do not apply in federal court. *See Fragoso v. Lopez,* 991 F.2d 878, 881-82 (1st Cir. 1993) (characterizing Puerto Rico's liquidation stay and dismissal statutes as procedural for the purposes of the *Erie* doctrine).

In *Fragoso,* appellee insurance company, during the pendency of the appeal, filed a motion to dismiss or stay the proceedings based on state court liquidation order. *See id.* at 880. The First Circuit held that *Burford* abstention was inapplicable under the circumstances and denied the motions. *Id.* 885-86. Several factors were at play in the First Circuit's decision.

The Circuit offered three reasons why *Burford* might not be applicable to the case at all--each of which reasons is also relevant here. [3] First, it held that *Burford* only applied to federal courts sitting in equity, but the suit in *Fragoso* was in tort. *Id.* at 882 (citing *NOPSI*, 491 U.S. at 361). Likewise, the suit here is grounded in contract, not equity. *Id.* [4] Second, the Circuit noted that *Burford* abstention was meant to "shield[ ] 'state administrative agencies' from federal court interference." *Id.* at 883 (quoting *NOPSI*, 491 U.S. at 361). But the Circuit doubted whether Puerto Rico's insurance liquidation scheme "creates a state administrative agency, as opposed to a judicial structure, to which deference under *Burford* might be paid." *Id.* (footnote omitted). *But see Sevigny v. Employers Ins. of Wasau*, 411 F.3d 24, 28 (1st Cir. 2005) (noting that in some circumstances, "a state court might itself be analogized to an agency for purposes of *Burford*"). The same concern is applicable here. Third, the *Fragoso* court noted that "*Burford* abstention is implicated when the federal courts are asked to interfere with state processes by *reviewing* the proceedings or orders of state administrative agencies." *Fragoso*, 991 F.2d at 883 (citing *NOPSI*, 491 U.S. at 361). But in *Fragoso*--as here-- there was no question of "review [of] the actions or decisions of any state body." *Id.*

[3] The extent to which the First Circuit's consideration of these factors was dispositive is unclear. After strongly suggesting that *Burford* abstention was per se irrelevant to the situation, it went on to perform an abstention analysis of the case's facts "for argument's sake." *Fragoso*, 991 F.2d at 883. As in *Fragoso*, we think the threshold factors make *Burford* inapplicable here, but we perform the complete abstention analysis out of an abundance of caution.

[4] In *Quackenbush v. Allstate Ins. Co.*, 517 U.S. 706, 116 S. Ct. 1712, 135 L. Ed. 2d 1 (1996), the Supreme Court clarified *Fragoso*'s statements with regard to equity. The Court noted that while *Burford* abstention "derives from the discretion historically enjoyed by courts of equity," *id.* at 728, a per se rule limiting abstention to suits in equity was inappropriate. *Id.* at 730. Instead, the relevant question was whether the federal court was being "asked to provide some form of discretionary relief." *Id.* Thus, *Burford* abstention might be appropriate where, e.g., a federal court stayed itself "pending the resolution by the state courts of a disputed question of state law." *Id.* at 730-31. National points to no such concerns here, however.

The First Circuit went on to apply the *Burford* doctrine to the case then at bar. *Id.* First, it held that the case "frame[d] no 'difficult question[ ] of state law' bearing on significant public policy issues such as would prompt abstention." *Id.* (quoting *NOPSI*, 491 U.S. at 361). In *Fragoso*, there was an uncomplicated statute of limitations issue, *id.*; here, DCI simply seeks indemnification under an insurance contract. "Thus, the first avenue to *Burford* abstention is dead." *Id.* The court then considered whether "federal review [would] disrupt 'state efforts to establish a coherent policy with respect to a matter of substantial public concern.'" *Id.* at 883-84 (quoting *NOPSI*, 491 U.S. at 361). It held that federal review would not: "we do not believe, in general, that federal court decisionmaking of the kind that exists alongside state insurance liquidation proceedings so significantly disrupts state regulatory frameworks to call for abstention." *Id.* at 884. Cases of this sort, it held, "will have at most an indirect effect on the liquidator's claims process by potentially giving rise to an additional claim against the insurance company." *Id.* (holding that such a case "will neither discombobulate local proceedings nor frustrate the Commonwealth's regulatory system").

Two of the factors considered in *Fragoso* do support National's position, but in light of the totality of the circumstances, they do not overcome the strong presumption against abstention. First, in *Fragoso*, the district court had reached a final judgment before the liquidation order was issued. *See id.* at 885 ("A case such as Fragoso's, where trial is complete and solely legal questions suitable for federal appellate resolution are pending on appeal, is a very weak candidate for abstention."). Here, of course, final judgment has not been entered, but the case *is* ready for trial, and we think that principles of judicial economy therefore militate against abstention. *See id.* (noting that "abstention serves the interests not only of federalism, but of comity and judicial efficiency" (internal quotations omitted)). Moreover, courts in this district have repeatedly cited *Fragoso* in denying motions to dismiss or stay in light of state liquidation proceedings, notwithstanding *Fragoso*'s language about finality. *See,e.g., Phico Ins. Co. v. Pavia Health Inc.*, 413 F. Supp. 2d 76, 80-81 (D.P.R. 2006); *Velez-Oliveras v. Asociacion Hosp. del Maestro, Inc.*, 198 F. Supp. 2d 70, 72-73 (D.P.R. 2002); *Cruz-Fernandez v. Univ. Health Servs.*, Civ. No. 00-2513(HL) (D.P.R. Feb. 13, 2002) (order denying motion for reconsideration). Second, *Fragoso* did not involve a coverage issue. *See id.* This case does, but National has not argued that it is anything but an uncomplex question of indemnification. It has not suggested, for instance, that there might arise an issue of differing contractual interpretations in the federal and state fora. To the contrary, the third-party complaint suggests that the insurance contract in this case is exclusive between DCI and National. *See* Docket No. 81. [5]

> 5 National's coverage analysis is moreover grounded in questionable precedent, relying, as it does, principally on *Gonzalez v. Media Elements, Inc.*, 946 F.2d 157 (1st Cir. 1991). That case was "limit[ed] . . . to its own facts" by *Fragoso*, 991 F.2d at 885, which is to say it was implicitly overruled. *See* Jeff Todd, **Undead** *Precedent: The Curse of a Holding "Limited to its Facts,"* 40 TEX. TECH. L. REV. 67, 74 (2007).

Taking all of these factors into account, we conclude that *Burford* abstention is inappropriate here. Abstention "is an extraordinary and narrow exception to [our] duty . . . to adjudicate [the] controversy properly before" us. *Allegheny Cnty. v. Frank Mashuda Co.*, 360 U.S. 185, 188, 79 S. Ct. 1060, 3 L. Ed. 2d 1163 (1959). Our adjudication of this controversy might inconvenience the state liquidation proceedings, but a minor disruption of a state's regulatory system does not license abstention: if it did, abstention would be proper "in any instance where a matter was within an administrative body's jurisdiction." *Fragoso*, 991 F.2d at 887 (internal quotations omitted) ("[T]he mere existence of state procedures, or even the existence of a complex state apparatus designed to handle a specific class of problems. does not necessarily justify abstention."). National's motion is accordingly DENIED. [6]

> 6 The First Circuit has also explicitly rejected another line of cases that National relies upon, in particular *Lac D'Amiante Du Quebec v. Am. Home Assurance Co.*, 864 F.2d 1033 (3d Cir. 1988). *See Fragoso*, 991 F.2d at 884 & n.9 ("We believe, therefore, that the circuit court cases favoring abstention in insurer insolvency matters are suspect in light of *NOPSI*."). *Lac D'Amiante*, it should be noted, formed the basis for the First Circuit's decision in *Media Elements*, which it went on to reject in *Fragoso*. *Id.* at 884 n.9.

* * *

We turn now to a related issue: the conduct of National's counsel, James McCartney. Apparently deciding himself and his client no longer party to this case--without any court order to that effect--he failed to attend the pretrial conference set for January 11, 2012. *See* Docket No. 104. McCartney was asked repeatedly to explain his failure, Docket Nos. 104, 119, and his unwillingness to do so caused the Court to enter an order to show cause why sanctions should not be imposed. *See* Docket No. 121. Additionally, McCartney failed, on behalf of National, to submit a certified translation of the liquidation order as had been ordered. *See* Docket No. 108.

On February 14, 2012, McCartney responded to our show cause order. Docket No. 122. Summarizing the liquidation order, which he once again failed to translate, he stated that he had not attended the conference because he had been forbidden to do so by the Puerto Rico Court of First Instance. Indeed, McCartney professed to find himself "between Scylla and Charybdis"--at risk of being sanctioned for not abiding by our orders, but also at risk of contempt charges in state court for following the same. We find such concerns to be unwarranted: as we have said, the liquidation order is inapplicable to the federal proceedings. Consequently, National and its counsel do not violate the stay by proceeding here. *Cf. Donovan v. Dallas*, 377 U.S. 408, 414, 84 S. Ct. 1579, 12 L. Ed. 2d 409 (1964). [7]

> [7] In *Donovan*, a Texas state court held a number of people in contempt for violating an injunction from initiating or prosecuting federal suits related to the subject matter of the state suit. The Supreme Court held that the injunction was invalid; accordingly, it vacated the contempt convictions. *Donovan v. Dallas*, 377 U.S. 408, 414, 84 S. Ct. 1579, 12 L. Ed. 2d 409 (1964); *see also Merrill Lynch, Pierce, Fenner & Smith v. Doe*, 868 F. Supp. 532 (S.D.N.Y. 1994) (enjoining state-court contempt proceedings against a party for violating a state-court injunction against prosecuting a federal suit); *Univ. Marine Ins. Co., Ltd. v. Beacon Ins. Co.*, 592 F. Supp. 945 (W.D.N.C. 1984) (same).

The bottom line is this: no sanctions will be imposed, but National remains a party to this case. As such, and because trial is imminent, its counsel may not at this time withdraw without substitute counsel entering an appearance. McCartney's motion to withdraw is therefore DENIED. [8]

> [8] Though National remains in the case, it need not at this point file a translation of the liquidation order because of the denial today of its motions to dismiss and stay the proceedings.

ROBERT C. KAUFHOLD, et al., Plaintiffs,
v.
GERALD CAIAFA, et al., Defendants.

Civ. No. 2:11-cv-01460 (WJM)

UNITED STATES DISTRICT COURT FOR THE DISTRICT OF NEW JERSEY

872 F. Supp. 2d 374
2012 U.S. Dist. LEXIS 75215

May 31, 2012, Decided
May 31, 2012, Filed

UNITED STATES DISTRICT JUDGE WILLIAM J. MARTINI

OPINION

Plaintiffs Robert C. Kaufhold and Joseph Aurthur McGuckin were the guitarist and drummer of the iconic punk rock band, the Misfits. Plaintiffs filed this action against the band's bassist, Gerald Caiafa, and his music label, Cyclopian Music, Inc. ("Cyclopian") (collectively "Defendants"), alleging that Defendants improperly asserted exclusive ownership rights over the Misfits trademarks. This matter comes before the Court on Defendants' motion to dismiss under Federal Rule of Civil Procedure 12(b)(6) for failure to state a claim upon which relief may be granted. There was no oral argument. Fed. R. Civ. P. 78(b). For the reasons set forth below, Defendants' motion to dismiss is DENIED.

I. BACKGROUND

The following facts are drawn from the Amended Complaint.

The Misfits was a punk rock band formed in 1977. The band is known for pioneering and defining the musical genre of "horror punk," combining the themes, imagery, and narrative of horror fiction with punk rock music. During all relevant times, the Misfits had four members: a guitarist, a drummer, a bass player, and a vocalist. Plaintiff Kaufhold was the Misfits' guitarist from approximately November 1978 to approximately October 1980, and performed under the name Bobby Steele. Plaintiff McGuckin was the Misfits' drummer and performed under the name Arthur Googy from approximately April 1979 to approximately April 1982. McGuckin was the longest serving drummer in the band. Defendant Caiafa joined the band in 1977 as a replacement for the original bass player Diane DiPiazza, and performed under the name Jerry Only. Glenn Anzalone p/k/a Glenn Danzig ("Danzig"), the band's vocalist, is not a party to this action.

The band's primary recording period was from 1978 to 1982 (Plaintiffs refer to this as the band's "classic period"). Am. Compl. ¶ 18, ECF No. 7. During this period, the band performed under the name the "Misfits" and used certain logos and stylized versions of that name (the "Misfits Marks"), which distinctively identified their services to the public. Although the Misfits disbanded in 1983, classic-period Misfits recordings continue to be sold today. For the past 15 years, Plaintiffs have received, and continue to receive, royalties for their work on the Misfits recordings.

For 12 years after the breakup of the Misfits, between 1983 and 1995, there was no group that toured or recorded as the Misfits. The Amended Complaint alleges that, during these 12 years, Defendant Caiafa publicly rejected his association with the Misfits and the Misfits Marks. The Amended Complaint further alleges that, from 1983 through 1995, Plaintiff Kaufhold was the only member of the band to use the Misfits Marks. Kaufhold alleges that he used the Misfits Marks from 1983 to the present on flyers, posters, and advertisements. From 1988 through 1992, Kaufhold sold the Misfits Live '79 record (which prominently features the Misfits trademark) at shows for his band the **Undead**. Kaufhold continues to sell the Misfits Live '79 album to this day from his website. Immediately after his departure from the Misfits, and continuing through today, Kaufhold played and recorded Misfits songs in concert, and even recorded a 12 song album of Misfits songs entitled "12 Hits From Hell." Kaufhold also sold Misfits branded t-shirts from the time he exited the band.

In 1994, a settlement agreement was executed between Defendant Caiafa and other former members of the Misfits ("1994 Settlement").

Plaintiffs were not parties to the 1994 Settlement. However, after the settlement was reached, Caiafa allegedly informed Plaintiffs that the parties to the settlement had agreed that each of the former members of the band (including Plaintiffs) co-owned the Misfits Marks, and no member would apply for exclusive rights to use the Misfits Marks. In 1995, a second settlement agreement was executed ("1995 Settlement"), wherein the parties agreed to allow Caiafa to apply for the exclusive right to use the Misfits Marks. Plaintiffs were not parties to the 1995 Settlement, and Caiafa did not tell Plaintiffs about the 1995 Settlement.

In 1996, the Misfits Box Set was released, containing nearly all of the band's classic-period material recorded from 1977 to 1983. The release of the box set in 1996 made the Misfits' complete early catalog widely available for the first time. Also around 1996, Caiafa recruited new band members and began to tour as the Misfits (referred to here as the "new Misfits"). [1] The new Misfits did a 25th Anniversary Tour and a 30th Anniversary Tour. The new Misfits also released albums in 1997, 1999, and 2003. None of these albums cracked the Billboard Record charts top 100. Defendants Caiafa and Cyclopian sold and continue to sell merchandise with the Misfits Marks.

1 From 2001 through 2005 Caiafa took over lead vocal duties in addition to playing bass guitar, and recruited veteran musicians Dez Cadena, former guitarist of Black Flag, and Marky Ramone, former drummer of the Ramones.

Beginning in approximately October 2000, without the knowledge of the Plaintiffs, Caiafa and Cyclopian filed five applications with the U.S. Patent and Trademark Office ("PTO") to register the Misfits Marks, three of which have matured into trademark registrations. In applying for registration, Caiafa represented that Cyclopian was the owner of the Marks, and that, to the best of his knowledge and belief, no other person had the right to use the Marks in commerce. The Amended Complaint alleges that, at the time he made those representations, Caiafa knew that Kaufhold had senior rights to the Marks and made those representations with the intent to deceive the PTO.

Plaintiffs assert that they were completely unaware of the trademark applications as well as the exploitation of the Misfits Marks by Defendants. It was not until August of 2009 that Plaintiff McGuckin saw a billboard in New York City for Van's sneakers with the Misfits Marks that he had any indication that the Misfits Marks were being exploited other than in the continued record sales. McGuckin proceeded to research the improper use of the Misfits Marks, notifying Kaufhold of the extent of their use sometime in the early part of 2010. On June 11, 2010, Plaintiffs filed an action against Defendants in the Southern District of New York. *See Kaufhold, et al. v. Cyclopian Music, Inc. et al.*, No. 1:10-cv-04588, 2010 U.S. Dist. LEXIS 132252, 2010 WL 5094630, at *2 (S.D.N.Y. Dec. 14, 2010). In an Opinion and Order dated December 14, 2010, the Honorable Denise Cote granted Defendants' motion to dismiss that action, finding that the Southern District lacked personal jurisdiction over Defendants. 2010 U.S. Dist. LEXIS 132252, [WL] at *5.

On March 15, 2011, Plaintiffs filed a complaint in this Court. On June 22, 2011, Plaintiffs filed the Amended Complaint at issue here. In the Amended Complaint, Plaintiffs assert three causes of action: (1) trademark infringement under 15 U.S.C. § 1125(a); (2) cancellation of Defendants' trademark registrations based on fraudulent procurement; and (3) declaratory judgments that Plaintiffs co-own the Misfits Marks and that Defendants' trademark applications are based on Caiafa's fraudulent claims to the PTO. Defendants now move to dismiss the Amended Complaint in its entirety.

II. LEGAL STANDARD

Federal Rule of Civil Procedure 12(b)(6) provides for the dismissal of a complaint, in whole or in part, if the plaintiff fails to state a claim upon which relief can be granted. The moving party bears the burden of showing that no claim has been stated. *Hedges v. United States*, 404 F.3d 744, 750 (3d Cir. 2005). In deciding a motion to dismiss under Rule 12(b)(6), a court must take all allegations in the complaint as true and view them in the light most favorable to the plaintiff. *See Warth v. Seldin*, 422 U.S. 490, 501, 95 S. Ct. 2197, 45 L. Ed. 2d 343 (1975); *Trump Hotels & Casino Resorts, Inc. v. Mirage Resorts Inc.*, 140 F.3d 478, 483 (3d Cir. 1998).

Although a complaint need not contain detailed factual allegations, "a plaintiffs obligation to provide the 'grounds' of his 'entitlement to relief requires more than labels and conclusions, and a formulaic recitation of the elements of a cause of action will not do." *Bell Atl. Corp. v. Twombly*, 550 U.S. 544, 555, 127 S. Ct. 1955, 167 L. Ed. 2d 929 (2007). Thus, the factual allegations must be sufficient to raise a plaintiffs right to relief above a speculative level, such that it is "plausible on its face." *See id.* at 570; *see also Umland v. PLANCO Fin. Servs., Inc.*, 542 F.3d 59, 64 (3d Cir. 2008). A claim has "facial plausibility when the plaintiff pleads factual content that allows the court to draw the reasonable inference that the defendant is liable for the misconduct alleged." *Ashcroft v. Iqbal*, 556 U.S. 662, 129 S.Ct. 1937, 1949, 173 L. Ed. 2d 868 (2009) (citing *Twombly*, 550 U.S. at 556). While "[t]he plausibility standard is not akin to a 'probability requirement' . . . it asks for more than a sheer possibility." *Iqbal*, 129 S.Ct. at 1949 (2009).

III. DISCUSSION

Defendants move to dismiss the Amended Complaint on two grounds: (1) the doctrine of laches, and (2) failure to state a claim under the Lanham Act. Each issue will be addressed in turn.

a. THE DOCTRINE OF LACHES

Defendants assert that Counts I and III of the Amended Complaint are barred by the doctrine of laches. [2] Because the laches defense depends on disputed factual issues, the motion to dismiss based on the laches defense is denied as premature.

---

2 Defendants initially argued that all of Plaintiffs' claims were time-barred under the doctrine of laches. Defs.' Br. at 9. However, Defendants appear to acknowledge in their reply brief that the remedy of laches does not apply to Count II (Cancellation of U.S. Trademark Registrations). *See* Defs.' Reply Br. at 6 n.2. Indeed, it is well-settled in the Third Circuit and elsewhere that the defense of laches is not available for a claim for cancellation based on fraudulent procurement. *Marshak v. Treadwell*, 240 F.3d 184, 192-94 (3d. Cir. 2001) (according to the Supreme Court, the PTO, and the plain language of the statute, a fraudulent procurement claim may be asserted at any time); *see also* 15 U.S.C. § 1064(3).

Because the Lanham Act does not include a specific statute of limitations, the Third Circuit has found that laches applies to bar stale claims. *Santana Products, Inc. v. Bobrick Washroom Equip., Inc.*, 401 F.3d 123, 138 (3d Cir. 2005). Under Third Circuit law, the doctrine of laches bars a Lanham Act claim when there is "(1) inexcusable delay in bringing suit, and (2) prejudice to the defendant as a result of the delay." *Id.* "Inexcusable delay" for purposes of laches is measured by looking to "the most analogous" state statute of limitations. *Santana*, 401 F.3d at 135. Claims under the Lanham Act are properly analogized to New Jersey's six year fraud statute. *See Zinn v. Seruga*, No. 05-372, 2009 U.S. Dist. LEXIS 89915, 2009 WL 3128353, at *24 (D.N.J. Sep. 28, 2009); N.J.S.A. § 2A:14-1. It is the law in this Circuit that, "[o]nce the statute of limitations has expired, the defendant 'enjoys the benefit of a presumption of inexcusable delay and prejudice.'" *Santana*, 401 F.3d at 138-39 (quoting *EEOC v. The Great Atlantic & Pacific Tea Co.*, 735 F.2d 69, 80 (3d Cir. 1984)). When this presumption applies, the burden shifts to the plaintiff to prove that its delay in bringing the claim was excusable, and that the delay did not prejudice the defendant. *See Santana*, 401 F.3d at 138-39.

Plaintiffs do not dispute that Defendants are entitled to the presumption of delay and prejudice in this case. Instead, Plaintiffs argue that "Defendants are barred from asserting the equitable claim of latches [sic] based on their own inequitable conduct." Pls.' Opp. Br. at 12. Plaintiffs are correct that, "[w]here there is evidence of other factors which would make it inequitable to recognize the defense despite undue delay and prejudice, the defense may be denied." *See A.C. Aukerman Co. v. R.L. Chaides Construction Co.*, 960 F.2d 1020, 1032 (Fed. Cir. 1992).

Plaintiffs argue that it would be inequitable to recognize the defense of laches in this case for two reasons. First, Plaintiffs argue that the defense is barred by the doctrine of unclean hands because Defendants' own actions caused the delay. *See Intertech Licensing Corp. v. Brown & Sharpe Mfg. Co., Inc.*, 708 F. Supp. 1423, 1429 (D. Del. 1989) (A plaintiff may overcome a presumption of laches when "the one asserting the defense of laches was responsible for the plaintiff's delay"). Specifically, Plaintiffs allege that Caiafa told them that no member of the band would apply for exclusive rights to use the Misfits Marks after the 1994 Settlement, and then misleadingly failed to tell them, only one year later, when the other former band members agreed to let Caiafa apply for exclusive rights to use the Marks. Second, Plaintiffs argue that Defendants' submission of a fraudulent PTO application operates to bar the defense of laches. *See Merisant Co. v. McNeil Nutritionals, LLC*, 515 F.Supp.2d 509, 523 (E.D. Pa. 2007).

Ruling on Defendants' laches defense at this stage would be premature. "[W]hen the defense of laches is clear on the face of the complaint, and where it is clear that the plaintiff can prove no set of facts to avoid the insuperable bar, a court may consider the defense on a motion to dismiss." *Solow Bldg. Co., LLC v. Nine West Group, Inc.*, No. 00-7685, 2001 U.S. Dist. LEXIS 8848, 2001 WL 736794, *3 (S.D.N.Y. June 29, 2001). However, when the defense of laches depends on disputed facts, it is inappropriate to make a determination on a motion to dismiss. *See Compagnie Des Bauxites de Guinee v. L'Union Atlantique S.A. D'Assurances*, 723 F.2d 357, 363 (3d Cir. 1983) (dismissal on the basis of laches was inappropriate when the defense depended on "disputed issues of fact."); *Fannie v. Chamberlain Mfg. Corp., Derry Div.*, 445 F. Supp. 65, 75 (W.D. Pa. 1977) (denying laches defense in a motion to dismiss as "premature" because there were open "questions of fact").

With respect to the laches defense in this case, the only issue in dispute is whether there was inequitable conduct on the part of Defendants. The facts underlying inequitable conduct are heavily disputed. For example, the parties dispute whether Caiafa's failure to inform Plaintiffs of the 1995 Settlement constituted bad faith, whether Kaufhold was using the Marks continuously after leaving the band, whether Defendants were aware of Kaufhold's use of the Marks, whether Defendants acted with intent to deceive the PTO when they applied for the Marks, etc. Moreover, these disputed facts go to the heart of the merits of the case. As such, dismissal on the basis of laches at this stage of the litigation would be inappropriate.

Accordingly, the motion to dismiss Counts I and III based on the defense of laches is denied as premature. Defendants may re-raise the defense at a later stage of litigation.

b. FAILURE TO STATE A CLAIM UNDER THE LANHAM ACT

Defendants argue that all of Plaintiffs' Lanham Act claims fail as a matter of law because Plaintiffs have not alleged continuous use in commerce of the Misfits Marks. The Court disagrees.

Defendants are correct that each Count in the Amended Complaint requires Plaintiffs to allege use of the Marks in commerce. Counts I and III require a showing that Plaintiffs own the Marks. *See A & H Sportswear, Inc. v. Victoria's Secret Stores, Inc.*, 237 F.3d 198, 210 (3d Cir. 2000) (to state a claim for trademark infringement under 15 U.S.C. § 1125(a), a plaintiff must establish, among other things, that he owns the mark); Am. Compl. ¶ 98 ("Plaintiffs seek a declaratory judgment that they are, at the very least, co-owners of the *Misfits* Marks"). To establish ownership, a plaintiff must plead (among other things) that he has used the mark continuously in commerce. *Ford Motor Co. v. Summit Motor Prods., Inc.*, 930 F.2d 277, 292 (3d Cir. 1991) ("[T]he first party to adopt a trademark can assert ownership rights, provided it continuously uses it in commerce"). Similarly, Count II, cancellation on the basis of fraudulent procurement, requires Plaintiffs to show (among other things) that they have an actual commercial interest in the Marks. *See Kelly v. Duprees MJA, LLC*, No. 08-6046, 2012 U.S. Dist. LEXIS 40597, 2012 WL 1019473, at *4 (D.N.J. Mar. 23, 2012) ("To have the requisite standing [to bring a cancellation claim], a party must demonstrate a real and rational basis for his belief that he would be damaged by the registration sought to be cancelled, stemming from an actual commercial or pecuniary interest in his own mark"); *Int'l Order of Job's Daughters v. Lindeburg & Co.*, 727 F.2d 1087, 1091 (Fed.Cir. 1984).

The Amended Complaint contains numerous factual allegations that support Plaintiffs' claim of continuous commercial use of the Marks. The Amended Complaint alleges that classic-period Misfits recordings featuring Plaintiffs have been sold throughout the relevant time period (from 1978 to the present). Am. Compl. ¶¶ 25-27, 32-33, 57. The Amended Complaint further alleges that Plaintiffs have been receiving, and continue to receive, royalties for their work on these recordings. Am. Compl. ¶¶ 25, 56. It is well-settled in this Circuit that receiving royalties for previously recorded material constitutes commercial use of a trademark. *See Marshak v. Treadwell*, 240 F.3d 184, 200 (3d Cir. 2001) ("[T]he commercial exploitation of classic . . . recordings in this country constitutes use"); *Kelly v. Estate of Arnone ex rel. Ahern*, No. 08-6046, 2009 U.S. Dist. LEXIS 66945, 2009 WL

2392108, at *6 (D.N.J. Aug. 3, 2009) (holding that a band member "continue[d] to receive royalties and, therefore, ha[d] an ongoing commercial interest in the mark," especially because "albums featuring [the band member] continue[d] to be marketed online and in stores"); *see also Kingsmen v. K-Tel Int'l, Ltd.*, 557 F. Supp. 178, 183 (S.D.N.Y. 1983) ("[T]he fact that these individuals continue to receive royalties for [their] recordings" establishes commercial use of the mark "[e]ven though plaintiffs disbanded their group in 1967").

Moreover, the Amended Complaint contains a litany of allegations regarding Kaufhold's commercial use of the Marks. For example, the Amended Complaint alleges that: (1) Kaufhold used the Misfits Marks on flyers, posters, and advertisements from 1983 to the present (Am. Compl. ¶ 31); (2) Kaufhold sold the Misfits Live '79 album featuring Misfits Marks from 1988 through 1992 (Am. Compl. ¶ 32); (3) Kaufhold continues to sell the Misfits Live '79 album from his website (Am. Compl. ¶ 33); (4) Kaufhold has played and recorded Misfits songs in concert since his departure from the band (Am. Compl. ¶ 34); (5) Kaufhold recorded a 12 song album of Misfits songs titled "12 Hits From Hell" (Am. Compl. ¶ 34); and (6) Kaufhold sold Misfits branded t-shirts from the time he exited the band (Am. Compl. ¶ 37).

Based on these factual allegations, the Court finds that Plaintiffs have sufficiently alleged continuous use in commerce of the Misfits Marks. Accordingly, the motion to dismiss Plaintiffs' Lanham Act claims is denied.

IV. CONCLUSION

For the reasons stated above, Defendants' motion to dismiss is DENIED. An appropriate order follows.

/s/ William J. Martini

WILLIAM J. MARTINI, U.S.D.J.

Date: May 31, 2012

CHRISTOPHER M. BAIR, Plaintiff,
v.
**THE ATTORNEY GENERAL,
THE PRESIDENT OF THE UNITED STATES,
THE HONORABLE JUDGE PRESIDING AT
THE UNITED STATES COURT OF
FEDERAL CLAIMS, Defendants.**

No. 14-460C

UNITED STATES COURT OF
FEDERAL CLAIMS

116 Fed. Cl. 699
2014 U.S. Claims LEXIS 537

June 13, 2014, Decided
June 13, 2014, Filed

JUDGE MARIAN BLANK HORN

ORDER

On May 27, 2014, pro se plaintiff Christopher M. Bair, who, at times, refers to himself as "Pro epio 'Airenost,'"[1] filed a number of documents, which the Clerk's Office should not have accepted as a "complaint," but assigned a case number. Given that plaintiff only submitted a random assortment of documents, which in no way resembles a complaint, and in which he never mentions the jurisdiction of this court, the Clerk's Office should have returned Mr. Bair's submission, together with his filing fee, instead of opening a case file and assigning a case number.

> 1 Plaintiffs documents are difficult to follow. Original words, capitalizations, grammar, and spelling are quoted as they appear in the documents filed by plaintiff.

The documents in plaintiff's initial filing are comprised of a series of letters addressed to Attorney General Eric Holder, The President of the United States, Barack Obama, and to the "Honorable Judge Presiding" at the United States Court of Federal Claims, together

with assorted United States District Court forms.[2] The letters
submitted include:

> 1. An April 10, 2014 letter addressed to "the Public Office of the
> Attorney General, and to the President of the United States."
> 2. An April 28, 2014 letter addressed to "the Public Office of the
> Attorney General."
> 3. A May 21, 2014 letter addressed to "the Honorable Judge
> Presiding" at the United States Court of Federal Claims.
> 4. A second May 21, 2014 letter addressed to "the Honorable Judge
> Presiding" at the United States Court of Federal Claims.
> 5. A May 23, 2014 letter addressed to "the Honorable Judge
> Presiding" at the United States Court of Federal Claims.
> 6. A second May 23, 2014 letter addressed to "The Honorable
> Judge Presiding" at the United States Court of Federal Claims.

Plaintiff alleges that, under the leadership of President Barack
Obama, the United States government committed various acts
against him and others entitling plaintiff to $2.5 billion in damages.

> 2 In this court, however, the only proper defendant is the United States,
> which plaintiff did not name as defendant. Rule 10(a) of the Rules of the
> United States Court of Federal Claims (RCFC) (2013) states that "[t]he title
> of the complaint must name all the parties . . . , with the United States
> designated as the party defendant." RCFC 10(a); see also 28 U.S.C §
> 1491(a)(1) (2012). The United States Supreme Court has indicated that for
> suits filed in the United States Court of Federal Claims and its predecessors,
> "[i]f the relief sought is against others than the United States the suit as to
> them must be ignored as beyond the jurisdiction of the court." United
> States v. Sherwood, 312 U.S. 584, 588, 61 S. Ct. 767, 85 L. Ed. 1058 (1941)
> (citation omitted). Stated differently, "the only proper defendant for any
> matter before this court is the United States, not its officers, nor any other
> individual." Stephenson v. United States, 58 Fed. Cl. 186, 190 (2003)
> (emphasis in original); see also United States v. Sherwood, 312 U.S. at 588;
> Brown v. United States, 105 F.3d 621, 623 (Fed. Cir.), reh'g denied (Fed.
> Cir. 1997); Hover v. United States, 113 Fed. Cl. 295, 296 (2013) ("As an
> initial matter, it is well settled that the United States is the only proper
> defendant in the United States Court of Federal Claims."); Warren v.
> United States, 106 Fed. Cl. 507, 510-11 (2012) ("It is well settled that the
> United States is the only proper defendant in the Court of Federal
> Claims."); May v. United States, 80 Fed. Cl. 442, 444 ("Jurisdiction, then, is
> limited to suits against the United States."), aff'd, 293 F. App'x 775 (Fed.
> Cir.), reh'g and reh'g en banc denied (Fed. Cir. 2008).

The court also notes that plaintiff has filed similar complaints with
the United States District Court for the Northern District of Ohio
and the United States Court of Appeals for the Sixth Circuit, all of

which were dismissed either for failure to state a claim or for failure to pay the requisite filing fee. See Bair v. Clinton et al., No. 13-3498 (6th Cir. June 21, 2013) (dismissing the case for failure to pay the docketing fee); Bair v. Clinton et al., No. 5:13-cv-00593-JRA, 2013 U.S. Dist. LEXIS 43453 (N.D. Ohio Mar. 27, 2013) (Dismissing the case because "the complaint does not state any conceivable, viable cause of action against the defendants."); Bair v. Armhurst, No. 3:12-cv-02933-JJH (N.D. Ohio Mar. 20, 2013) ("Even liberally construed, the Complaint in the instant case fails to sufficiently state any federal claims . . . ."); Bair v. Hemelgarn et al., No. 5:12-cv-02922-JRA, 2013 U.S. Dist. LEXIS 16681 (N.D. Ohio Feb. 7, 2013) (Holding that plaintiff's complaint "does not contain allegations which are intelligible to this court. The complaint is therefore appropriately subject to summary dismissal." (citation omitted)); Bair v. Parishi et al., No. 5:12-cv-02940-SL (N.D. Ohio Dec. 5, 2012) (dismissing plaintiffs complaint for failure to pay the filing fee).

In the first letter from plaintiff addressed to the President, dated April 10, 2014, plaintiff requests "immediate monetary relief through settlement by Federal Law," but does not cite to any cognizable federal statute. In the letter, plaintiff claims that defendant "put members of my family and others in a specific Mansion in *Sunnydale*, SC. Know to the Superior Justice Committee as 'The Executive Manor of Infernal Hell Hodge.'" (emphasis in original). Plaintiff further claims that in "The Executive Manor" is a "false floor sudden trap door" that "drops its victims thirty feet down into a infected maze of necrotic type high speed contagious disease and **undead** creatures including demon dogs." As a result, plaintiff claims, "[m]y family and others like it have been rearranged, separated, demolished, and forced into despair."

In the April 10, 2014 letter, plaintiff also claims that he had "been desolately abused and forced into cardiac arrest many times by your colleges," and that he had been the target of "hundreds devised plots of 'hire to kill' by means of reference type literature . . . " Plaintiff further claims that "[t]here has been many assaults and many crimes made against me inside the banking system as well." These and other alleged assaults, including an invasion of plaintiff's privacy, were alleged to have been committed using "satellites with radiance type sophisticated weaponry."

Plaintiff also alleges that President Obama had "even used my name improperly. By referring to me, in times of dire importance by the name Chris Bliss, Chris Bliso, Chris Bease, or Beasty." Plaintiff claims that he had "also been totally demised; barbarously, fiendishly, and deliberately completely neglected and lied to" about "The Executive Manor." Plaintiff further alleges in his April 10, 2014 letter that the President and his administration had "also made crimes against me by keeping the knowledge of these crimes a secret from the Public and I." In his April 10, 2014 letter, plaintiff requests the President pay him $2.5 billion "in the respect of your total involvement in this ominous quandary," but in a subsequent paragraph, immediately offers a settlement of $60,000,000.00.

Also included as part of plaintiffs initial filing is an April 28, 2014 letter plaintiff addressed to the United States Office of the Attorney General, although plaintiff addressed the letter "To the Public Office of the Attorney General." In the April 28, 2014 letter, plaintiff revokes "the offer of settlement" and informs the Attorney General that "I shall continue to seek Lawful Justice for his own Presidential and criminal actions." Plaintiff also claims the

> President's own self-involvement in the death of a child that was frozen solid inside the false mansion. Where in which an impostor who poses as my Father has froze the child with an Arcille type nitrogestic-rayl freeze blaster. And then the President stood idle-by when someone shattered the unfortunate child to pieces.

Plaintiff then calls for the President's "resignation from all duties." Plaintiff concludes the April 28, 2014 letter by invoking "my right to the Act of Dyslexia of 1984. Of that, the Opportunity Knowledge Acts: Four, Six, and Thirteen."

Moreover, as part of plaintiff's initial filing, he submits four letters addressed to the United States Court of Federal Claims, two dated May 21, 2014 and two dated May 23, 2014, one of which requests "your Honor give matter of this atrocity the full brightness of your shining light." In one May 21, 2014 letter, plaintiff claims that "[t]his travesty has grown to an unfathomable proportion. To the extent of almost complete annihilation of my whole blood-line." In addition to the cardiac arrests plaintiff references in his April 10, 2014 letter to President Obama, plaintiff claims that the President "left me barictea, barzaude, and even procuplia." Plaintiff further claims that "Barack Obama has committed a number of brutal acts against myself and even most possibly against a young boy . . . . " Plaintiff claims that the child's blood "was completely collected by members of the United States Secret Service and including White House agents of the Federal Bureau of Investigation."

In addition, included with plaintiff's letter filings are incomplete and unsigned "UNITED STATES DISTRICT COURT" documents with the following headings: "SUBPOENA TO APPEAR AND TESTIFY AT A HEARING OR TRIAL IN A CIVIL ACTION," "SUMMONS IN A CIVIL ACTION," "ANTICIPATORY SEARCH AND SEIZURE WARRANT," and "SEARCH AND SEIZURE WARRANT ON ORAL TESTIMONY." (emphasis and capitalization in original). Also included in plaintiff's initial filing are two copies of a document titled: "To be added to submitted for with Claim to case," listing items of which it appears plaintiff would like the court to take note. Some of these items include: "Request of Federal Special Victims Legal Guarantee: Federalolice," "A statement to for a Requim for Personance," and "The Official terms of Derituviea." Additionally, although plaintiff appears to have paid the court's filing fee, he submitted an unsworn affidavit stating his "Total annual yearly income: $17,160.000." Plaintiff also asserted that he owns $83,385.00 worth of various stock and property, and "25,056,089.000" Mexican pesos worth of stock in an American-Mexican company.

On June 9, 2014, the court received two additional letters from plaintiff. One letter, dated June 6, 2014, was addressed to the undersigned, while the other letter, dated June 7, 2014, was addressed to the Clerk of the Court. Neither document was signed, in violation of RCFC 11(a). Moreover, neither letter contained proof of service on the defendants, in violation of RCFC 5.3. The letters were filed, with the court's leave, only to complete the record. Both the letters contain many incomprehensible words, as well as spelling and grammatical errors, including the misspelling of the Clerk of the Court's name. Neither letter states a specific claim or provides any support for plaintiffs previous filings. For example, in the June 6, 2014 letter addressed to the undersigned, plaintiff writes:

> These squars I choose in Ebresquose. I do in retrospect of the rilesicls anoutenti by the Reiso-suitor known as 'Larken'. To be in as the forthwith typesos: (D), (G), (I), (Z). This is so to be with a Declaration of Answaraklia. A rightouse and deliberate honor that is begiven to people in assistance to the transacclumation of adversary.

In the June 7, 2014 letter addressed to the Clerk of the Court, plaintiff writes: "It is by me at this time that I make malstueva adovickiea to the Declaration of utrichi to that of the third type, without mastuvince allowed. With beareance to the light of the Court's berklintiea."

On June 11, 2014, the court received two more letters from the plaintiff, both dated June 9, 2014, and both, once again, replete with spelling and grammatical errors, including the misspelling of the undersigned's name and the Clerk of the Court's name. In one letter, addressed to the undersigned, plaintiff states: "I have chosen the Court of Federal Claims in respect due to me where upon my stiroea to be in doubts of such accordance." In the other June 9, 2014 letter, this one addressed to the "Clerk of Courts," plaintiff appears to be seeking a correction to a letter he previously submitted to the court, asking the Clerk of the Court to amend the spelling of "umritchi" to "umritichi." Neither letter was submitted in accordance with the Rules of the Court of Federal Claims. These letters were also filed, with the court's leave, only to complete the record.

When determining whether a complaint filed by a pro se plaintiff is sufficient to invoke review by a court, pro se plaintiffs are entitled to liberal construction of their pleadings. See Haines v. Kerner, 404 U.S. 519, 520-21, 92 S. Ct. 594, 30 L. Ed. 2d 652 (requiring that allegations contained in a pro se complaint be held to "less stringent standards than formal pleadings drafted by lawyers"), reh'g denied, 405 U.S. 948, 92 S. Ct. 963, 30 L. Ed. 2d 819 (1972); see also Erickson v. Pardus, 551 U.S. 89, 94, 127 S. Ct. 2197, 167 L. Ed. 2d 1081 (2007); Hughes v. Rowe, 449 U.S. 5, 9-10, 101 S. Ct. 173, 66 L. Ed. 2d 163 (1980); Estelle v. Gamble, 429 U.S. 97, 106, 97 S. Ct. 285, 50 L. Ed. 2d 251 (1976), reh'g denied, 429 U.S. 1066, 97 S. Ct. 798, 50 L. Ed. 2d 785 (1977); Matthews v. United States, No. 2013-5109, 750 F.3d 1320, 2014 U.S. App. LEXIS 8384, 2014 WL 1758664, at *1 (Fed. Cir. May 5, 2014); Diamond v. United States, 115 Fed. Cl. 516, 524 (2014). "However, '"[t]here is no duty on the part of the trial court to create a claim which [the plaintiff] has not spelled out in his [or her] pleading.'"'" Lengen v. United States, 100 Fed. Cl. 317, 328 (2011) (alterations in original) (quoting Scogin v. United States, 33 Fed. Cl. 285, 293 (1995) (quoting Clark v. Nat'l Travelers Life Ins. Co., 518 F.2d 1167, 1169 (6th Cir. 1975))); see also Bussie v. United States, 96 Fed. Cl. 89, 94, aff'd, 443 F. App'x 542 (Fed. Cir. 2011); Minehan v. United States, 75 Fed. Cl. 249, 253 (2007). "While a pro se plaintiff is held to a less stringent standard than that of a plaintiff represented by an attorney, the pro se plaintiff, nevertheless, bears the burden of establishing the Court's jurisdiction by a preponderance of the evidence." Riles v. United States, 93 Fed. Cl. 163, 165 (2010) (citing Hughes v. Rowe, 449 U.S. at 9 and Taylor v. United States, 303 F.3d 1357, 1359 (Fed. Cir.) ("Plaintiff bears the burden of showing jurisdiction by a preponderance of the evidence."), reh'g and reh'g en banc denied (Fed. Cir. 2002)); see also Harris v. United States, 113 Fed. Cl. 290, 292 (2013) ("Although plaintiffs pleadings are held to a less stringent standard, such leniency 'with respect to mere formalities does not relieve the burden to meet jurisdictional requirements.'" (quoting Minehan v. United States, 75 Fed. Cl. at 253)).

None of the documents filed by plaintiff are in the form of a proper complaint or are even vaguely in compliance with the court's rules, and should not have been filed as a complaint by the Clerk's Office in the first place. Nevertheless, because these filings were accepted by the Clerk's Office as a complaint, the court addresses the allegations. The court also recognizes that pro se plaintiffs should be afforded liberal construction of their pleadings. See Haines v. Kerner, 404 U.S. at 520-21. Even given this more liberal approach, plaintiffs letters and other submissions are totally deficient as filings in this court. Moreover, plaintiff's filings fail to establish any cause of action in this court.

It is well established that "'subject-matter jurisdiction, because it involves a court's power to hear a case, can never be forfeited or waived.'" Arbaugh v. Y & H Corp., 546 U.S. 500, 514, 126 S. Ct. 1235, 163 L. Ed. 2d 1097 (2006) (quoting United States v. Cotton, 535 U.S. 625, 630, 122 S. Ct. 1781, 152 L. Ed. 2d 860 (2002)). "[F]ederal courts have an independent obligation to ensure that they do not exceed the scope of their jurisdiction, and therefore they must raise and decide jurisdictional questions that the parties either overlook or elect not to press." Henderson ex rel. Henderson v.

Shinseki, 131 S. Ct. 1197, 1202, 179 L. Ed. 2d 159 (2011); see also
Hertz Corp. v. Friend, 559 U.S. 77, 94, 130 S. Ct. 1181, 175 L. Ed. 2d
1029 (2010) ("Courts have an independent obligation to determine
whether subject-matter jurisdiction exists, even when no party
challenges it." (citing Arbaugh v. Y & H Corp., 546 U.S. at 514));
Special Devices, Inc. v. OEA, Inc., 269 F.3d 1340, 1342 (Fed. Cir.
2001) ("[A] court has a duty to inquire into its jurisdiction to hear and
decide a case." (citing Johannsen v. Pay Less Drug Stores N.W., Inc.,
918 F.2d 160, 161 (Fed. Cir. 1990))); View Eng'g, Inc. v. Robotic
Vision Sys., Inc., 115 F.3d 962, 963 (Fed. Cir. 1997) ("[C]ourts must
always look to their jurisdiction, whether the parties raise the issue or
not."). "The objection that a federal court lacks subject-matter
jurisdiction . . . may be raised by a party, or by a court on its own
initiative, at any stage in the litigation, even after trial and the entry of
judgment." Arbaugh v. Y & H Corp., 546 U.S. at 506; see also Cent.
Pines Land Co., L.L.C. v. United States, 697 F.3d 1360, 1364 n.1
(Fed. Cir. 2012) ("An objection to a court's subject matter jurisdiction
can be raised by any party or the court at any stage of litigation,
including after trial and the entry of judgment." (citing Arbaugh v. Y
& H Corp., 546 U.S. at 506)); Rick's Mushroom Serv., Inc. v. United
States, 521 F.3d 1338, 1346 (Fed. Cir. 2008) ("[A]ny party may
challenge, or the court may raise sua sponte, subject matter
jurisdiction at any time." (citing Arbaugh v. Y & H Corp., 546 U.S. at
506; Folden v. United States, 379 F.3d 1344, 1354 (Fed. Cir.), reh'g
and reh'g en banc denied (Fed. Cir. 2004), cert. denied, 545 U.S.
1127, 125 S. Ct. 2935, 162 L. Ed. 2d 865 (2005); and Fanning, Phillips
& Molnar v. West, 160 F.3d 717, 720 (Fed. Cir. 1998))); Pikulin v.
United States, 97 Fed. Cl. 71, 76, appeal dismissed, 425 F. App'x 902
(Fed. Cir. 2011). In fact, "[s]ubject matter jurisdiction is an inquiry
that this court must raise *sua sponte*, even where . . . neither party has
raised this issue." Metabolite Labs., Inc. v. Lab. Corp. of Am.
Holdings, 370 F.3d 1354, 1369 (Fed. Cir.) (citing Textile Prods., Inc.
v. Mead Corp., 134 F.3d 1481, 1485 (Fed. Cir.), reh'g denied and en
banc suggestion declined (Fed. Cir.), cert. denied, 525 U.S. 826, 119
S. Ct. 73, 142 L. Ed. 2d 58 (1998)), reh'g and reh'g en banc denied
(Fed. Cir. 2004), cert. granted in part sub. nom Lab. Corp. of Am.
Holdings v. Metabolite Labs., Inc., 546 U.S. 975, 126 S. Ct. 543, 163
L. Ed. 2d 458 (2005), cert. dismissed as improvidently granted, 548
U.S. 124, 126 S. Ct. 2921, 165 L. Ed. 2d 399 (2006).

Pursuant to the RCFC and the Federal Rules of Civil Procedure, a plaintiff need only state in the complaint "a short and plain statement of the grounds for the court's jurisdiction," and "a short and plain statement of the claim showing that the pleader is entitled to relief." RCFC 8(a)(1), (2) (2013); Fed. R. Civ. P. 8(a)(1), (2) (2014); see also Ashcroft v. Iqbal, 556 U.S. 662, 677-78, 129 S. Ct. 1937, 173 L. Ed. 2d 868 (2009) (citing Bell Atl. Corp. v. Twombly, 550 U.S. 544, 555-57, 570, 127 S. Ct. 1955, 167 L. Ed. 2d 929 (2007)). "Determination of jurisdiction starts with the complaint, which must be well-pleaded in that it must state the necessary elements of the plaintiffs claim, independent of any defense that may be interposed." Holley v. United States, 124 F.3d 1462, 1465 (Fed. Cir.) (citing Franchise Tax Bd. v. Constr. Laborers Vacation Trust, 463 U.S. 1, 103 S. Ct. 2841, 77 L. Ed. 2d 420 (1983)), reh'g denied (Fed. Cir. 1997); see also Klamath Tribe Claims Comm. v. United States, 97 Fed. Cl. 203, 208 (2011); Gonzalez-McCaulley Inv. Grp., Inc. v. United States, 93 Fed. Cl. 710, 713 (2010). "Conclusory allegations of law and unwarranted inferences of fact do not suffice to support a claim." Bradley v. Chiron Corp., 136 F.3d 1317, 1322 (Fed. Cir. 1998); see also McZeal v. Sprint Nextel Corp., 501 F.3d 1354, 1363 n.9 (Fed. Cir. 2007) (Dyk, J., concurring in part, dissenting in part) (quoting C. Wright and A. Miller, Federal Practice and Procedure § 1286 (3d ed. 2004)). "A plaintiffs factual allegations must 'raise a right to relief above the speculative level' and cross 'the line from conceivable to plausible.'" Three S Consulting v. United States, 104 Fed. Cl. 510, 523 (2012) (quoting Bell Atl. Corp. v. Twombly, 550 U.S. at 555), aff'd, No. 2012-5104, 562 Fed. Appx. 964, 2014 U.S. App. LEXIS 7026, 2014 WL 1394969 (Fed. Cir. Apr. 11, 2014). As stated in Ashcroft v. Iqbal, "[a] pleading that offers 'labels and conclusions' or 'a formulaic recitation of the elements of a cause of action will not do.' 550 U.S. at 555. Nor does a complaint suffice if it tenders 'naked assertion[s]' devoid of 'further factual enhancement.'" Ashcroft v. Iqbal, 556 U.S. at 678 (quoting Bell Atl. Corp. v. Twombly, 550 U.S. at 555).

When deciding a case based on a lack of subject matter jurisdiction or for failure to state a claim, this court must assume that all undisputed facts alleged in the complaint are true and must draw all reasonable inferences in the non-movant's favor. See Erickson v. Pardus, 551 U.S. 89, 94, 127 S. Ct. 2197, 167 L. Ed. 2d 1081 (2007) ("In addition, when ruling on a defendant's motion to dismiss, a judge must accept

as true all of the factual allegations contained in the complaint."
(citing Bell Atl. Corp. v. Twombly, 550 U.S. at 555-56 (citing
Swierkiewicz v. Sorema N. A., 534 U.S. 506, 508 n.1, 122 S. Ct. 992,
152 L. Ed. 2d 1 (2002)))); Scheuer v. Rhodes, 416 U.S. 232, 236, 94 S.
Ct. 1683, 40 L. Ed. 2d 90 (1974) ("Moreover, it is well established
that, in passing on a motion to dismiss, whether on the ground of
lack of jurisdiction over the subject matter or for failure to state a
cause of action, the allegations of the complaint should be construed
favorably to the pleader."), abrogated on other grounds by Harlow v.
Fitzgerald, 457 U.S. 800, 102 S. Ct. 2727, 73 L. Ed. 2d 396 (1982),
recognized by Davis v. Scherer, 468 U.S. 183, 190, 104 S. Ct. 3012, 82
L. Ed. 2d 139 (1984); United Pac. Ins. Co. v. United States, 464 F.3d
1325, 1327-28 (Fed. Cir. 2006); Samish Indian Nation v. United
States, 419 F.3d 1355, 1364 (Fed. Cir. 2005); Boise Cascade Corp. v.
United States, 296 F.3d 1339, 1343 (Fed. Cir.), reh'g and reh'g en
banc denied (Fed. Cir. 2002), cert. denied, 538 U.S. 906, 123 S. Ct.
1484, 155 L. Ed. 2d 226 (2003).

The Tucker Act grants jurisdiction to this court as follows:

> The United States Court of Federal Claims shall have jurisdiction to
> render judgment upon any claim against the United States founded
> either upon the Constitution, or any Act of Congress or any
> regulation of an executive department, or upon any express or
> implied contract with the United States, or for liquidated or
> unliquidated damages in cases not sounding in tort.

28 U.S.C. § 1491(a)(1). As interpreted by the United States Supreme
Court, the Tucker Act waives sovereign immunity to allow
jurisdiction over claims against the United States (1) founded on an
express or implied contract with the United States, (2) seeking a
refund from a prior payment made to the government, or (3) based
on federal constitutional, statutory, or regulatory law mandating
compensation by the federal government for damages sustained. See
United States v. Navajo Nation, 556 U.S. 287, 289-90, 129 S. Ct.
1547, 173 L. Ed. 2d 429 (2009); United States v. Mitchell, 463 U.S.
206, 216, 103 S. Ct. 2961, 77 L. Ed. 2d 580 (1983); see also Greenlee
Cnty., Ariz. v. United States, 487 F.3d 871, 875 (Fed. Cir.), reh'g and
reh'g en banc denied (Fed. Cir. 2007), cert. denied, 552 U.S. 1142,
128 S. Ct. 1082, 169 L. Ed. 2d 810 (2008); Palmer v. United States,
168 F.3d 1310, 1314 (Fed. Cir. 1999).

"Not every claim invoking the Constitution, a federal statute, or a regulation is cognizable under the Tucker Act. The claim must be one for money damages against the United States . . . ." United States v. Mitchell, 463 U.S. at 216; see also United States v. White Mountain Apache Tribe, 537 U.S. 465, 472, 123 S. Ct. 1126, 155 L. Ed. 2d 40 (2003); Smith v. United States, 709 F. 3d 1114, 1116 (Fed. Cir.), cert. denied, 134 S. Ct. 259, 187 L. Ed. 2d 262 (2013); RadioShack Corp. v. United States, 566 F.3d 1358, 1360 (Fed. Cir. 2009); Rick's Mushroom Serv., Inc. v. United States, 521 F.3d at 1343 ("[P]laintiff must . . . identify a substantive source of law that creates the right to recovery of money damages against the United States."). In Ontario Power Generation, Inc. v. United States, the United States Court of Appeals for the Federal Circuit identified three types of monetary claims for which jurisdiction is lodged in the United States Court of Federal Claims. The court wrote:

> The underlying monetary claims are of three types. . . . First, claims alleging the existence of a contract between the plaintiff and the government fall within the Tucker Act's waiver . . . . Second, the Tucker Act's waiver encompasses claims where "the plaintiff has paid money over to the Government, directly or in effect, and seeks return of all or part of that sum." Eastport S.S. [Corp. v. United States, 372 F.2d [1002,] 1007-08, 178 Ct. Cl. 599, 605-06,] [(1967)] (describing illegal exaction claims as claims "in which 'the Government has the citizen's money in its pocket'" (quoting Clapp v. United States, 117 F. Supp. 576, 580, 127 Ct. Cl. 505 (1954)) . . . . Third, the Court of Federal Claims has jurisdiction over those claims where "money has not been paid but the plaintiff asserts that he is nevertheless entitled to a payment from the treasury." Eastport S.S., 372 F.2d at 1007. Claims in this third category, where no payment has been made to the government, either directly or in effect, require that the "particular provision of law relied upon grants the claimant, expressly or by implication, a right to be paid a certain sum." Id.; see also Testan [v. United States], 424 U.S. [392,] 401-02, 96 S. Ct. 948, 47 L. Ed. 2d 114 [1976] ("Where the United States is the defendant and the plaintiff is not suing for money improperly exacted or retained, the basis of the federal claim-whether it be the Constitution, a statute, or a regulation-does not create a cause of action for money damages unless, as the Court of Claims has stated, that basis 'in itself . . . can fairly be interpreted as mandating compensation by the Federal Government for the damage sustained.'" (quoting Eastport S.S., 372 F.2d at 1009)). This category is commonly referred to as claims brought under a "money-mandating" statute.

Ontario Power Generation, Inc. v. United States, 369 F.3d 1298,
1301 (Fed. Cir. 2004); see also Twp. of Saddle Brook v. United States,
104 Fed. Cl. 101, 106 (2012).

To prove that a statute or regulation is money-mandating, a plaintiff
must demonstrate that an independent source of substantive law
relied upon "'can fairly be interpreted as mandating compensation by
the Federal Government.'" United States v. Navajo Nation, 556 U.S.
at 290 (quoting United States v. Testan, 424 U.S. at 400); see also
United States v. White Mountain Apache Tribe, 537 U.S. at 472;
United States v. Mitchell, 463 U.S. at 217; Blueport Co., LLC v.
United States, 533 F.3d 1374, 1383 (Fed. Cir. 2008), cert. denied, 555
U.S. 1153, 129 S. Ct. 1038, 173 L. Ed. 2d 468 (2009). The source of
law granting monetary relief must be distinct from the Tucker Act
itself. See United States v. Navajo Nation, 556 U.S. at 290 (The
Tucker Act does not create "substantive rights; [it is simply a]
jurisdictional provision[] that operate[s] to waive sovereign immunity
for claims premised on other sources of law (e.g., statutes or
contracts)."). "'If the statute is not money-mandating, the Court of
Federal Claims lacks jurisdiction, and the dismissal should be for lack
of subject matter jurisdiction.'" Jan's Helicopter Serv., Inc. v. Fed.
Aviation Admin., 525 F.3d 1299, 1308 (Fed. Cir. 2008) (quoting
Greenlee Cnty., Ariz. v. United States, 487 F.3d at 876); Fisher v.
United States, 402 F.3d 1167, 1173 (Fed. Cir. 2005) (The absence of a
money-mandating source is "fatal to the court's jurisdiction under the
Tucker Act."); Peoples v. United States, 87 Fed. Cl. 553, 565-66
(2009).

After reviewing all the disparate documents plaintiff submitted, the
court cannot determine a cogent claim in plaintiffs filings over which
this court has jurisdiction. Plaintiff does not cite to any identifiable
United States statute for the $2.5 billion in damages he seeks.
Likewise, plaintiff does not allege any express or implied contract
with the United States, nor does he seek a refund from prior payment
made to the government. See United States v. Navajo Nation, 556
U.S. at 289-90 (holding that the Tucker Act waives sovereign
immunity to allow jurisdiction over claims against the United States
(1) founded on an express or implied contract with the United States,
(2) seeking a refund from a prior payment made to the government,
or (3) based on federal constitutional, statutory, or regulatory law

mandating compensation by the federal government for damages sustained). Although the court has reviewed the pro se plaintiffs submission liberally, """[t]here is no duty on the part of the trial court to create a claim which [the plaintiff] has not spelled out in his [or her] pleading.""" Lengen v. United States, 100 Fed. Cl. at 328 (alterations in original) (quoting Scogin v. United States, 33 Fed. Cl. at 293 (quoting Clark v. Nat'l Travelers Life Ins. Co., 518 F.2d at 1169.

Furthermore, even if Mr. Bair had a fact based claim for alleged wrongdoing by a federal official, he would be raising a tort claim, and his suit would not fall within the jurisdiction of this court. The Tucker Act expressly excludes tort claims, including those committed by federal officials, from the jurisdiction of the United States Court of Federal Claims. See 28 U.S.C. § 1491(a)(1); see also Keene Corp. v. United States, 508 U.S. 200, 214, 113 S. Ct. 2035, 124 L. Ed. 2d 118 (1993); Rick's Mushroom Serv., Inc. v. United States, 521 F.3d at 1343; Alves v. United States, 133 F.3d 1454, 1459 (Fed. Cir. 1998); Brown v. United States, 105 F.3d 621, 623 (Fed. Cir.), reh'g denied (Fed. Cir. 1997); Golden Pac. Bancorp v. United States, 15 F.3d 1066, 1070 n.8 (Fed. Cir.), reh'g denied, en banc suggestion declined (Fed. Cir.), cert. denied, 513 U.S. 961, 115 S. Ct. 420, 130 L. Ed. 2d 335 (1994); Sellers v. United States, 110 Fed. Cl. 62, 66 (2013); Kalick v. United States, 109 Fed. Cl. 551, 558, aff'd, 541 F. App'x 1000 (Fed. Cir. 2013); Hampel v. United States, 97 Fed. Cl. 235, 238, aff'd, 429 F. App'x 995 (Fed. Cir. 2011), cert. dismissed, 132 S. Ct. 1105, 181 L. Ed. 2d 973 (2012); Woodson v. United States, 89 Fed. Cl. 640, 650 (2009); McCullough v. United States, 76 Fed. Cl. 1, 3 (2006), appeal dismissed, 236 F. App'x 615 (Fed. Cir.), reh'g denied (Fed. Cir.), cert. denied, 552 U.S. 1050, 128 S. Ct. 675, 169 L. Ed. 2d 529 (2007); Agee v. United States, 72 Fed. Cl. 284, 290 (2006); Zhengxing v. United States, 71 Fed. Cl. 732, 739, aff'd, 204 F. App'x 885 (Fed. Cir.), reh'g denied (Fed. Cir. 2006).

CONCLUSION

Plaintiff's filings do not rise to the level of a complaint which should have been filed in this court. In addition, none of Mr. Bair's allegations are within the jurisdiction of this court. Plaintiff's "complaint" is DISMISSED. The Clerk of the Court shall enter JUDGMENT consistent with this Order.

UNDEAD IN THE FEDERAL COURTS

This book is part of a series is entitled Law of the Horse.
The series is collections of character creatures in
the opinions of U.S. Courts.

<u>available:</u>

Werewolf in the Federal Courts
Red Herring in the Supreme Court
Mad Scientist in the Federal Courts
Cocker Spaniel in the Federal Courts
Dachshund in the Federal Courts
Zombie in the Federal Courts
Valentine's Day in the Federal Courts
Creativity in the Supreme Court

more coming soon...

Other artwork by Joshua Warren can be found at:
www.warrbo.com